I0831589

The Travel Diary of

PETER TOLSTOI

Portrait of Peter Andreevich Tolstoi by I. G. Tannauer, 1719.

The Travel Diary of

PETER TOLSTOI

A Muscovite in Early Modern Europe

Translated by

Max J. Okenfuss

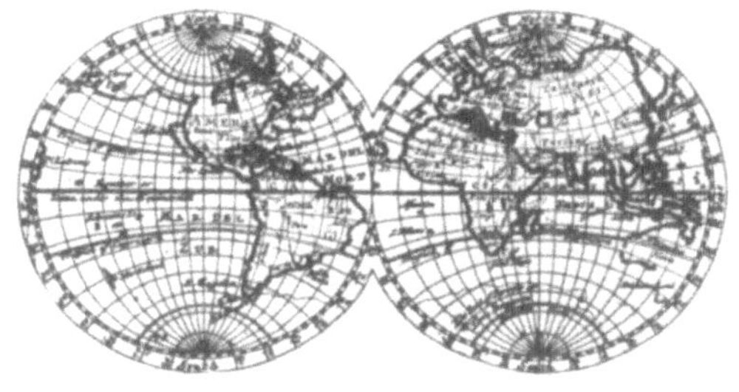

Northern Illinois University Press · DeKalb · 1987

Maps used throughout are from *Geography Rectified; or A Description of the World, in All Its Kingdoms, Provinces, Countries, . . .* 2nd. ed., enl., by Robert Morden (London, 1688). Reproduced courtesy of Special Collections, Washington University Libraries, St. Louis, Mo.

Library of Congress Cataloging-in-Publication Data

Tolstoĭ, Petr Andreevich, graf, 1645–1729.
[Putevoĭ dnevnik P. A. Tolstogo. English]
The travel diary of Peter Tolstoi : a Muscovite in Early-modern Europe / translated by Max J. Okenfuss.
p. cm.
Translation of: Putevoĭ dnevnik P. A. Tolstogo.
Bibliography: p.
Includes index.
ISBN 0-87580-130-7 : $35.00
1. Tolstoĭ, Petr Andreevich, graf, 1645–1729—Journeys. 2. Statesmen—Soviet Union—Biography. 3. Europe—Description and travel—17th–18th centuries. I. Title.
DK130.T64A3 1987
914'.04252—dc19 87-17616
[B] CIP

Published by the Northern Illinois University Press, DeKalb, Illinois 60115

Design by Anne Schedler

For Bruce

Contents

List of Illustrations

Translator's Introduction

In 1697 Tsar Peter sent a Russian nobleman, one Peter Andreevich Tolstoi, to Venice to study naval science. During a two-year stay he traveled widely in southern Europe and recorded his observations in a diary. It is an authentic and candid account of early-modern culture through the eyes of a Muscovite traveler, for whom the accomplishments and routines of Western civilization were always new and exciting, often unbelievable, and sometimes incomprehensible.

Scholars have given us some excellent studies of early-modern Europe. There are enduring old encyclopedic surveys[1] and vivid interpretations. Notable among the latter was Paul Hazard's *La Crise de la Conscience Européenne*,[2] which argued that the era of Tolstoi's life and travels was the crucible for the emergence of modern culture: "Never was there a greater contrast, never a more sudden transition than this"—such was Hazard's dramatic judgment in the opening lines of that classic. More recently the entire early-modern period has been wholly reexamined in the *Monde Braudelian* and in the spirit of "the *Annales* school," and the result is a new understanding of the impact of demographic pressures, of technology, and of material culture in the making of the modern world. Other recent historians have focused on ritualized behavior and on the behavior of the crown in early-modern Europe, and they have taught us not only about a world we have lost, but of the subtle ways in which the medieval world survived into the recent past.[3]

If the scholarly literature, old and new, on early-modern culture is rich, why should one read Peter Tolstoi? First, he was there and he experienced first-hand what

[1] See, for example, Smith, *A History of Modern Culture*, vol. I, *Origins of Modern Culture 1543–1687;* vol. II, *The Enlightenment 1687–1776.*

[2] Translated as *The European Mind, 1680–1715.*

[3] I am thinking of Braudel, *Capitalism and Material Life 1400–1800* (orig. French ed., 1967; English ed., New York, 1973; revised ed., *The Structures of Everyday Life*, 1981); also, works such as Burke, *Popular Culture*, and Davis, *Society and Culture*.

the modern historian can only imagine. As a Muscovite, he absorbed and recorded the fundamental and unspoken values of the cultures he visited. His account has an immediacy that no third-person history can capture. This means, among other things, that unlike the modern secular historian, Tolstoi speaks the language of religion intimately. To Tolstoi, Christianity was not merely the most important aspect of his earthly life, it was life itself, and in reading his Diary one is drawn into an age of belief in which miracles happen and prayers can calm an ill wind. Reading Tolstoi, one can feel the full force of that Christianity which was still synonymous with civilization in the West as well as in his native Russia. In short, to read Tolstoi is to inject oneself directly into the vibrant life of that bygone age.

This is not to say that Tolstoi is a sure guide to all of early-modern culture. His account deals primarily with southern Europe. I take seriously Paul Hazard's casual old suggestion that there were once two rather distinct Europes, one northern and one southern, which had endured as definable cultural spheres for millennia, and which were being replaced in Tolstoi's own lifetime by the West-to-East cultural slope of modern history.[4] The fullest introduction to Tolstoi's southern realm is Fernand Braudel's *Mediterranean and the Mediterranean World in the Age of Philip II*,[5] and unfortunately no comparable study exists for the world of the North and Baltic sea basins in the early modern period. This southern bias is one limitation on the value of Tolstoi's book as a guide to European culture. Furthermore, Tolstoi tells us most about Venice in the age of her decline, and his account would be different had he lived elsewhere for a comparable length of time. Tolstoi visited a Venice that was different than other Italian cities of the late seventeenth century, a Venice that prided itself on its antiquity and its faithfulness to tradition, and that very stasis is what Tolstoi describes so well.[6]

Tolstoi's Diary is also limited by a relative paucity of comments on international politics. He had occasion to inquire into the nature of the Polish elective monarchy, into the genealogy of the Hapsburgs, and into the political structure of Venice and Spanish Naples; but the format of a travel diary is not the place to find extended political commentary. His questions about European society are serious and interesting, and his inquiry into the life style and values of European nobilities are especially valuable, but only by chance does the Diary reflect the dominant political motivation of his age, Louis XIV's dreams of French hegemony over Europe. Tolstoi wrote with circumspection because his effects were searched at numerous borders, and because everywhere there was some suspicion that Peter the Great's unprecedented first generation of "students" abroad might in fact be spies.[7] In general, however, his frontier crossings were less traumatic than those of many travelers.

[4] I refer to casual comments in his delightful, important, but sorely neglected *Books, Children and Men*.

[5] Original edition, 1949; English version, 2 vols., New York, 1972–73.

[6] I learned much from Molmenti, *Venice*, 6 vols.; the last two volumes on the period of Tolstoi's Diary are subtitled *The Decadence*.

[7] Meehan-Waters, *Autocracy and Aristocracy*, p. 40.

Tolstoi is not an informed or accurate reporter of the past or present intellectual accomplishments of Western civilization. Although he was a contemporary of Newton, his Diary does not reflect the Newtonian revolution. A cataloguer of Roman and paleo-Christian relics, Tolstoi lacked the classical education of West Europeans on the Grand Tour,[8] and he was unable to provide the classical allusions that were the common currency of that enlightened age. Compared to most contemporary English voyagers, for example, Tolstoi seems often naive and credulous.

Indeed, I once thought that Tolstoi's tone of awe and bewilderment were the reason to read the Diary. Since I first read the Diary over twenty years ago—and I can thank my thesis advisor, Professor Richard Pipes, for encouraging me to read widely in Russian sources—my understanding of it has changed. The *Annales* school of historians has in general made me more respectful of sources as eloquent in their own right. But more specifically, two of my senior colleagues unknowingly alerted me to other reasons to read Tolstoi, and to publish a translation of the Diary. Professor Dietrich Gerhand, now deceased, whose classes I inherited, alerted me to the persistence of Old Europe and made me more sensitive to long-term changelessness in any culture.[9] And it is the changelessness in European culture that Tolstoi captured so well, better than more knowledgeable and sophisticated European diarists: he remarks about things they found utterly unremarkable. Just what sorts of things became clearer to me when Professor Edward Weltin, my colleague emeritus in Ancient History at Washington University, pointed out to me that some bizzare and unmodern principle of selection determined just what Tolstoi was and was not shown in Rome during one torrid week in August 1698. I now believe that when one understands why Tolstoi wrote numerous pages about the Mamartine Prison and Tre Fontana in Rome, and why he scribbled only a few insignificant lines about the Capitol, one has grasped the value and uniqueness of Tolstoi's Diary.

As a diarist, Tolstoi was more concerned with the enduring values of Christianity than with the latest novelties or innovations in politics, art, or philosophy. He had not had a classical education, did not carry a guidebook, and did not write as one in a conscious continuum of travelers, as did early-modern visitors to Russia and as did Englishmen who were already in seventeenth-century Italy. One reads him most profitably when one realizes that he knew little of the intellectual accomplishments of European high culture of his own age. Paul Hazard, in his *Crisis of the European Conscience,* catalogued ably the intellectual ferment of Tolstoi's lifetime: the dethroning of the classical mind; the replacement of classical stasis by the dynamics of travel, change, and the exotic; the rise of Pyrrhonism, of heterodoxy, of the cult of reason; the denial of miracles; the new scientific explanation of comets; the new Biblical criticism, Locke's Empiricism, and Toland's Deism; the replacement of medieval corporatism by the politics of natural law, and the replacement of traditional

[8] See, for example, Mead, *Grand Tour;* Frantz, *English Traveller;* or Sells, *The Paradise of Travellers.*

[9] I refer especially to his final book, *Old Europe, A Study in Continuity 1000–1800.*

Christian morality by a social morality anticipating the philosophes—these were the historic intellectual achievements of Tolstoi's own era, but one searches in vain to find their clear echo in the Diary. One reads the Diary precisely because much of what was novel and modern in 1697–98 is almost totally missing. Perhaps only because the study of fortifications was part of his official curriculum do we learn where Europeans were building them "in the new manner," "with belvederes," but intellectual novelty is less obvious in the Diary. Tolstoi reminds us how long it took new ideas to penetrate ordinary society, even noble society, while he also reminds us of that which was truly enduring and visible at the moment he traveled.

Tolstoi's observations are fresh and vivid because his Muscovite value system informs him that a smoky, dim, old icon of the Mother of God attributed to St. Luke the Evangelist was more important than a shining Madonna by Raphael; that an antique, battered statue of Nero the Persecutor was more significant than Michelangelo's David; and that a simple, clean hospital with a medicinal herb garden, built for the purposes of Christian charity, was more impressive than the most elaborately decorated and guilded of new baroque churches. Tolstoi knew that great art belonged in a church because it honored the living omnipotent God greatly, not because it established the artistic reputation of the artist for future generations of art historians. An icon-worshipping Muscovite, fully Christian but barely European, Tolstoi knew that churches were constructed by the best architects and decorated by the best artists because their employ told God how much sinful mortals honored His House of Worship. For Tolstoi, and indeed for the believing Poles, Austrians, Italians, and Maltese who guided him, a church was to be visited to revere the sacred relics it preserved. For Tolstoi, the Sistine Chapel might be an over-painted empty hall—it may not have been shown to him—of utter insignificance when compared to the dark, tiny, underground chapel in the old Mamartine Prison where Sts. Peter and Paul had actually and physically suffered for Christ's sake, or a simple chapel that housed a barb from Christ's Crown of Thorns. To recapture these old truths is the reason to read Tolstoi, and they set his observations apart from those of more "sophisticated" travelers.

Tolstoi

Who was this Tolstoi? Prior to his two-year voyage to Europe in 1697–99, he was an obscure, uncultured, religiously motivated, Old Muscovite servitor of the upper service class, destined for a career like his father's.[10] He was a direct ancestor of Fedor

[10]The standard biography has been Pavlov-Sil'vanskii, "Graf Petr Andreevich Tolstoi," pp. 1–41. This essay was expanded from his article in the *Russkii biograficheskii slovar'*. Most recent is the study by Pavlenko, *Ptentsy gnezda Petrova*, pp. 110–232, which deals primarily with his later diplomatic career. In English, references to Tolstoi have been scattered, fragmentary, and unsubstantial until the appearance of the history of the Tolstoi family, Tolstoy, *The Tolstoys;* it is very good on the Tolstois in seventeenth-century Muscovy, but devotes only a few paragraphs to the Diary.

Petrovich, the artist of the Napoleonic age; the poet Aleksei Konstantinovich; the minister of education Dmitrii Andreevich; and of course the novelist, five generations removed, and other Tolstois in between, some of whom come to life as characters in *War and Peace*.

The Tolstois had long been in Russian service. Originally a "West Russian" family, Lithuanians with roots in Chernigov, they appear in Muscovy during the reign of the state builder, Ivan III, in the second half of the fifteenth century. Under Tsar Aleksei Mikhailovich Romanov in the seventeenth century, Peter Andreevich's grandfather, Vasilii Ivanovich, attained the rank of *okol'nichii*, with similar duties but a lower rank than the *boiar*, shortly before his death in 1649. His son, Andrei Vasil'evich, was named *dumnyi dvorianin* under Aleksei and *okol'nichii* in the reign of Sophia, dying in that rank about 1698. Both served at court in Moscow and as military governors, *voevody*, in the provinces. Peter Andreevich seemed destined for a similar career until his life was forever changed in 1697, when the future Peter the Great gathered up his court chamberlains, the *stol'niki* (the gentlemen of the table) and the *spal'niki* (those of the bedroom), and sent them to Europe to study.

The Tolstois—grandfather, father, and son—arose to prominence because of a marriage. When at midcentury Olearius listed the upper officialdom of Muscovy, no Tolstois appeared among the *boiare*, the *okol'nichie*, or the *dumnye dvoriane*, the members of the Boyar Duma or state council. Suddenly they appeared, because his father married a Miloslavskii, the family of Tsar Aleksei's first wife. Their new in-laws were among the select. Il'ia Danilovich Miloslavskii headed the *Inozemskoi Prikaz*, which administered foreign military officers, and the *Aptekarskii Prikaz*, which was in charge of the court physicians, pharmacists, barbers, and distillers; Ivan Andreevich Miloslavskii headed the *Iamskoi Prikaz*, which controlled the courier system. With these new relations, the Tolstoi family suddenly prospered.[11]

In 1676, at age thirty-one, our Peter Tolstoi had received the rank of *stol'nik*, literally one of those who served the Tsar at table (contemporary English documents translate the term as "cup bearer"). In the dynastic struggles of 1682, however, he erred: he was one of the chief conspirators behind the *strel'tsy* uprising, engineered by the regent Sophia and the Miloslavskiis, the family of Tsar Aleksei's first wife, against young Peter (b. 1672), and the family of his second wife, the Naryshkins. The reason for his rebellion was simple: his mother was a Miloslavskii, and clan loyalty dictated his politics. Only through the graces of Fedor Apraksin, his relative and a youthful and thereafter life-long companion of the future Peter the Great, was he able to survive the disgrace of the Miloslavskiis. In 1693, appropriate to his rank, he reemerged as the *voevoda* of Velikii Ustiug, administering the area linking the Western trade of the port of Archangel to the heartland of Muscovy, where he

[11]On the court and the tsar's advisors at midcentury, see Olearius, *Travels of Olearius*, pp. 218–26, and especially Crummey, *Aristocrats and Servitors*. Andrei Vasil'evich, Peter's father, was the only Tolstoi to attain the elite position of membership in the Boyar Duma, or royal council.

would meet the twenty-year-old Peter. He would participate in the second Azov campaign (1696) before being named, at age fifty-two—the oldest of the group—one of the courtiers Peter sent to Venice or to Holland for military studies.

In 1697, therefore, Peter Tolstoi was just another Muscovite servitor like his father and grandfather, one step removed from the inner councils of power in Muscovy. For his age, he was a bit less exalted than his father, almost certainly because of his youthful political miscalculation that was based on family ties. Indeed this was later the subject of jokes at Peter the Great's court, as the tsar reminded Tolstoi that his was a too-clever head that could easily have been removed. The story appears frequently in several versions, and Peter's words are legend: "*Golova, golova, kaby ty ne tak umna byla, davno byla otrubit' tebia velel* (Oh head, oh head, were you not so wise, I would have ordered you chopped off long ago)." In 1699 he returned from Europe, in the words of his biographer, "a poor mariner, but a man fully prepared to take part in the general transformation of Russia." He had been more interested in traveling than in applying himself seriously to the intricacies of ships' construction, and Peter apparently learned this quickly.

Tolstoi's subsequent career is irrelevant to the Diary, but the story can be told in brief. Two years in Europe transformed him from Muscovite provincialism to European cosmopolitanism. He was never to utilize the limited naval skills he acquired in Venetian ships and schools, the skills he nonetheless tried so hard to document in the Diary. Returning to Russia, he received no appointment for three years, until 1701, when he was named Russia's first permanent ambassador to Constantinople. He held the post until 1714, but it was not pleasant duty, since the Turks—Mustafa II and then the new Sultan Ahmed III—were never reconciled to a Russian naval presence in the Sea of Azov, nor to the niceties of post–Westphalian European diplomacy. Twice after 1710, when the fleeing Charles XII and French diplomacy reinstigated war between Russia and the Ottoman Empire, Tolstoi alone (and later with his replacement, Peter Shafirov) was taken hostage and consigned to the rats in the Tower of the Seven Bastions. Perhaps his greatest achievement in Constantinople was, through lies and huge bribes, to prevent a Swedish-Tatar alliance in early 1709, which, if concluded, would have adversely affected the outcome of the glorious battle of Poltava. Named a senator upon return to Russia in 1714, he was an old man when, in 1716–17 he accompanied Peter the Great to Warsaw, Amsterdam, and Paris, and conducted negotiations with George I in The Hague. Perhaps his most unsavory task, and the one for which his family was cursed "unto the 25th generation,"[12] came in 1717, when he was ordered to Vienna to a lodge in the Tyrol, and eventually to the Castel Sant' Elmo in Naples, to entice and persuade the errant heir Aleksei Petrovich—with lies, deceit, and false promises—to return to Russia and to his angry father. As the head of Peter the Great's Secret Chancellery and as chief interrogator, he conducted the investigation of Aleksei's treason and was nominally

[12] Tolstoy, *The Tolstoys*, p. 80.

in charge of the bloodbath that followed. For his services he was rewarded with a promotion in the Table of Ranks with the Order of St. Andrew the First-Called, and with peasant villages.

When Peter the Great instituted his regular system of government, based on Swedish models, Tolstoi became the first president of the College of Commerce (1717–22) and one of Peter's closest advisors. In 1719 in Berlin he argued against a treaty between Hanover and England (the roots of the British-French-Prussian Alliance of 1725), and in 1722, at age seventy-seven, he accompanied Peter to Astrakhan. During these years he was one of Peter's companions in revelry, despite the facts that his legs were too aged to dance and that he drank unwillingly. He planned the coronation of Catherine I in 1724, and she promptly named him Count Tolstoi, a title that passed through generations, even to the novelist. On that day, as grand marshal, he preceded Peter in solemn procession, carrying a staff topped by a massive gold eagle and an emerald "as big as a hen's egg."

After the death of Peter the Great, as long-time confidant, president of the College of Commerce, and trusted friend of Catherine I, Tolstoi briefly became one of the bosses, the *verkhovniki;* these were the elite who were, to various degrees, under a variety of weak, disinterested, inept, and/or incapacitated monarchs, appointed to guide the destinies of the Russian state until the ascension of Catherine II almost forty years later. Tolstoi and the parvenu Menshikov brought Catherine I to power, and he was widely recognized as her most trusted ally. The French ambassador noted his daily contact with her, and described him as able and experienced, "the wisest head in Russia." In February 1726 he became officially a *verkhovnik,* a member of the governing Supreme Privy Council.

Tolstoi's ascendency was short-lived. Formerly a leading proponent of the Petrine reforms, known as "one of the ablest, most thoughtful and strong-willed of the Tsar's collaborators,"[13] he now denounced their cost in human terms. In November 1726 he outlined the impoverished plight of the Russian peasantry, who were equally fearful of the soldiers and the tax collectors—ready to flee to the forests at their sight—and unable to meet their tax obligations without selling off their livestock and homes. It was almost his final act: in the spring of 1727 he again, as in 1682, had to take a dynastic stand. He opposed the proposed marriage between Grand Prince Peter Alekseevich and Menshikov's daughter, and for that opposition he paid dearly. He was arrested and ended his public career with a final, six-week, humiliating journey in the summer of 1727. This time he traveled with a guard of five officers and ninety soldiers, who conducted him to the far north, to Archangel and the old Solovetskii monastery. He died ingloriously a year and a half later, on January 30, 1729, in his eighty-fourth year, a full thirty years after his return from the West. There had been one final grief: his beloved son Ivan Petrovich, whom Peter had made governor of Azov (1708), was incarcerated with him and preceded

[13] Wittram, *Peter I. Czar und Kaiser,* II, 378–79.

him in death by several months. On his final journey northward he passed through Velikii Ustiug, which he had once administered, and where he had first met Peter thirty-five years earlier.

I find two lessons in Tolstoi's life. One is the exhilarating saga of his personal transformation. Objectively, his service career was not much different than that of his forebears. But the journey of 1697–99 changed him. Once an obscure courtier, he became the leading diplomat of the Petrine age, achieving a title, status, and honor that he was able to bequeath to his heirs. Elsewhere I have argued that he was personally transformed in Europe. He was able to retain his old Muscovite, Orthodox religiosity while adopting from Europe a new sense of a noble's social obligations, an appreciation of Christian charity, a new attitude toward wealth and time and their uses, and a new habit of logical thinking. In learning that these attitudes were not incompatible with his faith, Tolstoi was transformed, and when others of his class learned these lessons, Russia's eighteenth-century nobility would be born. In short, I see Tolstoi as the devout but enlightened prototype for the Shcherbatovs, Bolotovs, Novikovs, and Radishchevs who would later appear in Russia's social history.[14]

The second lesson is melancholy. The name Tolstoi would probably never be known to us but for Peter Andreevich. He passed on the title of Count to his heirs. His life should have ended early, in the Romanov's dynastic turmoils of the 1680s, a half-century before his death. Fortunate to survive the *strel'tsy* uprising and its repression, fortunate not to be considered too old for study abroad in his fifties and to survive the unpleasantness of Turkish captivity, fortunate to survive the clash of dynastic wills between Peter and his son in 1717, Tolstoi would die humiliated and disgraced because he opposed the marriage of a Romanov to the daughter of one common-born. Peter the Great raised Tolstoi from the ceremonial anonymity of the Muscovite court and made him a European among Russians; Menshikov, whom Peter had likewise raised from the obscure ranks of street vendors, would cast him down again.

Finally, it should not surprise us that Peter Tolstoi began his second and more cosmopolitan career over the age of fifty, or that he remained active in governmental service into his eighties. His grandson, Andrei Ivanovich, the great-grandfather of the novelist, lived to age eighty-two; his son, Fedor Andreevich, a famous collector of manuscripts that eventually went to the Leningrad Public Library, lived from 1758 to 1849; the artist Fedor Petrovich was born in 1783 and died in 1873. Lev Nikolaevich, the best known, lived from 1828 to 1910. The Tolstois were a long-lived family.

[14] See my essay, "The Cultural Transformation of Peter Tolstoi," pp. 228–37. See also my "Peter Tolstoi in Rome," pp. 35–41; and "On Crime and Punishment," pp. 23–7.

Reading the Diary

Many of the important lessons of Tolstoi's Diary—the leisurely pace of daily life before the industrial revolution, the supremacy of ritualistic behavior over caprice, the acceptance of hierarchy as the natural order of society, the universality of religion, the responsibilities of rank—are best absorbed by reading the Diary itself. The reader may, however, need to know in advance a little more about the purposes of Tolstoi's Diary, the Russia he left, and the Europe he visited.

Tolstoi was not primarily a writer. His sole literary exercise seems to have been an unpublished translation of Ovid's *Metamorphosis* from the Italian, which is probably lost. A limited correspondence survives, as does some diplomatic reporting.[15] The Diary was apparently a private document, not intended for publication. It contains no explicit statement of purpose. It opens with a transcription of the official documents that instructed Tolstoi to study abroad, and it concludes with a prayer of thanksgiving for a safe return. It is not addressed to his sons and was not explicitly intended for their education or edification. From the text itself two purposes—or better, two overriding concerns—can be deduced. First and foremost, Tolstoi was concerned with documenting fully the things he did to fulfill the tsar's instructions. From the opening page to the day of his departure from Venice almost two years later, Tolstoi solicited and transcribed into the Diary the certificates and testimonials that stated that he had seriously and consistently applied himself to naval studies, and especially that he did everything possible to take part personally in naval warfare; presumably he carefully transported the originals home as well. Still, we do not know why he alone of all the courtiers wrote so detailed an account of his voyage. Was it because he was older and more experienced than the other *stol'niki?* Did he fear more than others Peter's wrath because of his youthful indiscretion in 1682? Did he suspect, even before his departure, that he would be an unsuccessful student of shipbuilding and navigation, and therefore decided to keep a diary to prove that he had indeed tried to learn? We do not know. No other Petrine pupil kept such a detailed log; it is unique among the few autobiographical writings of the age; but then, Tolstoi's relations with Tsar Peter had been unique. It has been suggested that he was sent abroad because the Tsar feared leaving a former conspirator in Russia during his own Grand Tour, which began the same year.

From the pages of the Diary itself, one can glean another preoccupation of Tolstoi. Devout Muscovite that he was, he had more questions about religion than about anything else. Indeed, to repeat, for him life and religion were inseparable. There are many aspects of this general concern, among them Christian charity, the

[15] Pavlov-Sil'vanskii provided the bibliography, which is still useful; see "Tolstoi," pp. 39–41. Some diplomatic correspondence has since appeared in the series *Letters and Papers of Peter the Great* (in Russian). Pavlenko cites no new sources for the period of the Diary in his recent biographical sketch, but does provide a guide to archival sources for his later diplomatic career; see *Ptentsy*, pp. 319–22.

reality of miracles, the direct intervention of God in human affairs, the intercession of the saints, and the power of the clergy to influence morality. But behind every page of the Diary looms one great question: Was Tolstoi's native Russian-Greek Orthodox Christianity the "One True Faith"? Tolstoi explores this question in a variety of ways: He wants to know what happened when Orthodox churches and their icons were taken over by the Catholics in warfare. He wants to know precisely the extent to which Uniate, Armenian, and Catholic Masses differ from Orthodox Liturgy. He seeks the significance of variations in sacred vestments. He wants to know whether Greeks or Romans built the holiest churches in Christendom, and who held them now. I suspect—though the issue is never directly raised nor resolved in the Diary itself—that Peter Tolstoi returned to Russia a believing Eastern Orthodox Christian who regarded Catholics as heretics, primarily because the genuine miracle-working icons in modern Roman churches were "of ancient Greek painting," whereas the wondrous artwork of recent centuries had no such miraculous effect. Orthodoxy was the True Faith because the relics of antiquity, those of the common church before 1054, worked miracles consistently, while the ones more recently canonized by the Roman Church did not. If this supposition is true, it would go a long way in explaining Tolstoi's relative indifference to the art of the Renaissance, which he saw daily in Europe, and his fascination with relics and holy sites that antedated the schism of the churches in 1054.

This supposition, that Tolstoi was attempting to demonstrate the legitimacy of the primitive and of the present Orthodox Church as well as the heresy of the Catholics and those tainted by Catholicism, helps to explain that which he does and does not describe, as, for example, when he was in Rome. It also explains the sharp contrast between his Italy and that of John Evelyn, an earlier traveler whose comments are used to annotate portions of this edition of Tolstoi's Diary.

This is not the place to write a history of the divided Eastern and Western Churches or to explore the full ramifications of the *filioque* clause casually inserted into the Nicene creed by Westerners about the time of Charlemagne. It is enough to know that since 1054 the two Churches were divided by serious theological issues and that the East consistently advocated conciliarism, the notion that the councils of the five patriarchs, the five senior bishops, were higher than popes in Church governance. In the fifteenth century an attempt at reconciliation had been made at the Council of Ferrara-Florence in 1439–45, in return for a promise of help against the Turks. The patriarch of Constantinople, the Byzantine emperor John VIII Paleologus, and other Eastern dignitaries had signed a decree of Union, conceding the issue of the procession of the Holy Spirit and recognizing papal primacy. For the Latin Church henceforth, the schism had been resolved, and it mattered not that the signatures were later repudiated or that Muscovites promptly incarcerated the Russian metropolitan, who had been made a cardinal in the West and brought home word of the Union.

For seventeenth-century Russians the issue remained unresolved and volatile. Within a century of Ferrara-Florence, the Russian Church had convinced itself that

Byzantium had fallen to the Turks in 1453 because of the sinful Union a few years earlier, and over time it even convinced itself that it alone was the One True Church, the Third Rome, and the Second Jerusalem. Had the Russians enjoyed the luxury of cultural isolation, they might have sustained this belief into modern times. But increasing involvement in the affairs of Europe dictated otherwise. Between roughly 1550 and 1650, the Russian Church was challenged constantly by new ideas because of many events: increasing traffic with Western Europe; the importation, in the age of religious wars, of military advisors and then whole armies of mercenaries from the West; invasion and occupation by Catholic Poles and Lutheran Swedes in the Time of Troubles; the coming of the Reformation and the Counter-Reformation to Eastern Europe; the Union in 1595 between the Orthodox Church of Poland-Lithuania and Rome; the trickle and then the flow of nominally Orthodox intellectuals from the Ukraine, many of them Jesuit-educated. It was only a matter of time before the Church's foundations and practices were questioned.

Peter Tolstoi was born in 1645, the same year that Tsar Aleskei addressed to the patriarch of Constantinople, through his patriarch, Nikon, a series of questions concerning the Russian service books and Liturgy, and thus began the Church reforms. He was twenty-one years old when a Russian Church council condemned the opponents of the Nikonian reforms; the Eastern patriarchs added an anathema the next year. He surely knew that for many, perhaps a majority, of Russians, Nikon was the Anti-Christ who "abolished the ancient faith of the fathers and established the impious heterodoxy of Rome." He was twenty-four when thousands of Russians neglected their fields, abandoned their huts, assembled in prayer, and lay down in their hewn coffins to await the final trumpet call of the Archangel. Between these events in the 1660s and his departure for Europe in 1697, perhaps as many as twenty thousand Russians chose suicide rather than accept the "new" religion of Nikon. Countless others fled to the wastelands of the north, since Tsarevna Sophia's decree of 1684 threatened every Old Ritualist with death at the stake. Before he departed for Western Europe, Tolstoi had lived through a half-century of religious turmoil that had thrown into question every aspect of the Russian faith, the form of the Liturgy, the validity of all traditional Russian practices even to the making of the Sign of the Cross, the nature of liturgical singing and the use of music in the service, the proper form of icons, the ecclesiastical dress of the clergy, even the form of the church building itself. All of these questions and more are reflected in the pages of his Diary.

A few words can be said about the Russia Tolstoi left behind. Historians no longer regard seventeenth-century Muscovy as a blank slate awaiting the reforms of Peter the Great.[16] Seventeenth-century Muscovy was not closed or obscurantist, however accurate those terms might be for some of the clergy or for the mass of the peas-

[16]The seventeenth century in Russian history is still a fertile ground for research, but among recent titles that suggest its vitality—especially the revolutions of the reign of Tsar Aleksei, Peter the Great's father—the following can be mentioned: for social history, Crum-

antry. Although Western visitors to Moscow could still perpetuate the "rude and barbarous" imagery of the sixteenth century, vibrant signs of change could be seen everywhere, long before Peter the Great began his active reformist reign in the late 1690s. Russia had been an active trading partner with Western Europe, first with the English and increasingly with the Dutch, for well over a century. Much of that trade, entering at Archangel, passed through Velikii Ustiug, which Tolstoi governed in the early 1690s. The last great surge of Islam, characterized by the siege of Vienna on July 14, 1683 (mentioned in the Diary), had resulted in concerted efforts throughout Western Christendom to involve the Russians in normal diplomacy and warfare, and especially to gain their support for a new and final crusade against the Infidel. Tsar Peter's step-sister Sophia, who ruled the Russian state in the 1680s, had been particularly receptive to those overtures. News from European states was by mid-century systematically collected by the Russian Foreign Office (*Posol'skii Prikaz*), digested, and regularly presented to the court of Peter's father, Aleksei. That same office, and others in the Muscovite government, regularly employed Western specialists and technicians, from artists and linguists to armorers, to ply their crafts and to instruct young Russians in them. A Dutchman, Vinius, had helped to further unite the realm by improving a postal service long admired by visitors. At least in the capital, Western books appeared, from Vesalius on human anatomy to the magnificent Blaeu Atlas, which recorded European knowledge of the entire globe since the Renaissance Age of Discovery. In both civil and religious architecture, one can also find examples of clear Western influence long before the 1690s. In addition, the Russian military was being revamped along Western lines, using foreign officers and regiments who could conduct warfare against European armies and fortified places, and abandoning the steppe warfare of armed horsemen that had accounted for the very rise of Moscow. Perhaps most important, Muscovy had, with that new military force, acquired the Ukraine and the city of Kiev from Poland-Lithuania in Tolstoi's lifetime. Moscow thus began to attract a host of Western-educated intellectuals, many of them with heterodox religious views, and all of them steeped in languages and learning alien to the Muscovites. Within a generation these West Russians would contribute to the Church schism, and, to the horror of conservative Orthodox churchmen, begin to open classical grammar schools and academies in Russia. Seventeenth-century Russia was therefore a dynamic society, and although not all in that society were equally affected, the course of the future Petrine reforms could already be predicted. Indeed, the sending of the *stol'niki* to Europe was but an extension, with typical Petrine flamboyance and enthusiasm, of the *prikaz* training of Peter's father's times.

Tolstoi visited a Europe very different from the Europe of recent history, a Eu-

---

mey, *Aristocrats;* Hellie, *Enserfment and Military Change in Muscovy,* and his *Slavery in Russia, 1450–1725,* both revisionist and very important; for economic change, see Fuhrmann, *Origins of Capitalism in Russia;* a brief survey of innovation in the arts is Hughes, "The 17th-Century 'Renaissance' in Russia"; and on the "Westernization" of court life, see Longworth, *Alexis: Tsar of All the Russias.*

rope that stood on the threshold of a great political transformation. The titles of modern histories indicate the importance of the moment. For example, a volume in William L. Langer's *Rise of Modern Europe* series emphasizes the appearance of "great powers." Its theme is the new dominance of the modern nation-states—England, Russia, Austria, and Prussia—and the collapse of the old powers—Holland, Spain, Venice, Poland, and the Ottoman Empire. The same theme is more sharply focused in a volume of *The New Cambridge Modern History,* which addresses specifically Britain and Russia as new powers.[17] From the advantageous perspective of the twentieth or even from the mid-eighteenth century, such future-looking interpretive titles are of course justified. From the viewpoint of January 1697, they are unwarranted, and this is precisely why Peter sent his first naval scholars to "decadent" Holland and Venice.

This point must be made emphatically. John Wolf's text opens, appropriately, with a map of Europe circa 1700. If one looks at the city of Milan and its hinterland, one finds the legend, "To Austria, 1714"; if one looks at the southern half of the Italian boot, one reads "To Austria, 1714"; at Sicily, "To Savoy, 1714; to Austria, 1720"; at Sardinia, "To Austria, 1714; to Savoy, 1720." In these instances, one can learn nowhere from whom these territories were taken; it is impossible to know that in the 1690s these were in fact parts of the vast kingdom of Spain in the Old World; knowing that Spain's possessions would be dismembered in a generation, that Spain would be so impoverished that she could scarcely afford the funeral of Charles II in 1700, we forget that in early 1697 none of this was obvious or inevitable to ordinary Europeans. In the early eighteenth century Peter the Great modeled his new government on the centralized institutions not of England or France, but of Sweden, unaware of his own future role in bringing the glorious Vasa realm to its modern obscurity. He sent navigators to Venice, Queen of the Adriatic, unaware that she was rapidly losing her great-power status. To read Tolstoi profitably one should transport oneself back to early 1697, when Spain, Holland, Sweden, and Venice were still great powers, regarded as such by contemporaries, Russian and European alike. Diplomats long knew that Spain was ripe for partition, that Louis XIV's reforms had regenerated France since the Fronde, and many recognized the rising power of England; but little of this was yet visible in far-off Muscovy.

In the year when Tsar Peter sent students abroad, the most important international event was the Treaty of Ryswick, signed on September 30, 1697, among France, England, Spain, and Holland. At that date, although the Dutch and the Spanish had been less than spectacularly successful on the battlefield, there was little diplomatic evidence that the overall balance of power had yet changed dramatically, that the Great Powers were ascendent. Most of the French conquests of Spanish territory were restored to Spain; likewise, Dutch losses were restored, so there was little tangible evidence that her fortunes were in serious decline. Farther east, a delicate balance existed between the Austrians and the Ottomans. The Ottomans were still re-

[17] Wolf, *Emergence of the Great Powers 1685–1715;* Bromley, *Rise of Great Britain and Russia.*

garded as a major military and economic power, and all Mediterranean and central European diplomacy was directed to containing their threat. The Empire seemed marginally secure, but only after Peter dispatched the *stol'niki* was that security confirmed. Having defeated the Turkish invasion of Vienna in 1683, the imperial generals Charles of Lorraine and Louis of Baden drove the Turks beyond the Danube, but not until the autumn of 1697 did the news come of a crushing defeat for the Ottomans by Eugene of Savoy at Zenta. The war would not formally end until the Treaty of Karlowitz (1699), and only then was it really clear that the Empire had won almost all of Hungary and Transylvania, and that the Turk no longer could realistically aspire to further territorial gains on the European continent. There was of yet no serious challenge to Austrian domination in the Germanies from an ascendent Prussia: soon, in 1701, Frederick III, Elector of Brandenburg, would assume the ominous title "König in Preussen," but that too was in the unknown future.

In northern Italy the post-Renaissance kingdom of Savoy seemed safe and steady in the hands of Victor Amadeus II (1675–1730). In the south, the vast dominion of Naples remained safely under the rule of Spanish viceroys, as did Milan in the north, and that suzerainty was so longstanding as to appear permanent and natural. Venice, of chief concern here, had suffered a major loss—Crete—in 1669 but had reemerged under Francesco Morosini to regain Morea (Greece) and most of the Dalmatian coast, where Tolstoi and other Russians would study under their Slavic-Venetian masters, harassed only occasionally by a Turkish corsair. In 1697, therefore, there were no signs that the old powers were in decay in the international arena, or that the new national monarchies would soon sweep them aside.

There is a cultural, intellectual, and technical dimension to this problem of perception. With the gift of hindsight, we know that in the 1690s the cutting edge of modern philosophy, psychology, and education was embodied in John Locke, and modern physics and mathematics in Newton. We conveniently forget that Locke's influence and reputation were negligible until Coste's French translations made him available on the continent, and that Newton's principle of universal gravitation was rejected by many as an unproven occult doctrine, inferior in explanatory power to the older Cartesian-Wolffian world view. Knowing what Britain became and what Britain produced in the eighteenth century, we can forget that in the 1690s she could have had a reputation for religious intolerance, civil war, and regicide. No one in Russia knew in January 1697 that Britain would soon be the world's leading naval power, that Britain would alone open the industrial age, that Newton would be deified, that Locke would be translated into every European language, or that Voltaire would attribute English genius to English liberty in 1733. In an earlier essay on Peter Tolstoi, I wrote that he had been "sent to the wrong place at the wrong time," suggesting that Venice was already a decadent Catholic Renaissance city-state sustained by the small trade of penal galleys on inland seas, when compared to the vibrant economies of northern national monarchies with their fleets of large ocean-going sailing ships.[18] That observation remains true, but to understand Tolstoi we

[18] "Cultural Transformation," p. 228.

must remember that neither he nor his Venetian friends yet fully realized that their naval technology was outdated, that their form of government and even their political boundaries were about to be destroyed, that the one contemporary intellectual mentioned by name in the Diary would soon be forgotten except by Italian antiquarians. In short, few knew that Venice was no longer the center of the universe, or that the Mediterranean was no longer the basin of world civilization. In the 1680s Captain-General (later Doge) Francesco Morosini had conquered all and more than Venice had previously lost to the Turks in the Ionian Sea and Morea. Venice was enjoying a period of economic growth and even opulence, and to all who inquired, Venice appeared not decadent but indeed at the very pinnacle of her power and prosperity.

Even in the 1690s Venice was not outwardly in decline. She could afford to modernize her fleet, to build heavier and more heavily armed ships, and to pioneer new and effective naval tactics in which mobile, oar-powered galleys successfully cooperated with sailed gunships in combat. She was the world center for theater, for opera, and for comedy. It was the great age for the building and the reconstruction of country villas for the nobility, the period when their country houses graced the banks of the Brenta from Venice to Padua. This evidenced her strength and wealth, not her decadence. New churches continued to be built, and their richness and gilding, and their employment of architects and artisans like Longhena, gave no evidence of impending collapse. Old festivals and ceremonies continued to be observed—if anything, more lavishly and expensively than before. Although it had been almost thirty years since Colbert craftily had lured some of her glassmakers from Murano to France, there was as yet no serious challenge to Venice's preeminence in glassmaking, or in the textile industry, including luxury lace making.

Great changes—political, demographic, industrial, and cultural—were on the near horizon, and soon they would totally restructure Old Europe. But in the 1690s, based on all the evidence available in Europe and in Moscow, Peter the Great made a wise, informed, and reasoned decision when he sent his naval scholars, including Peter Tolstoi, to Venice, Queen of the Adriatic. Tolstoi visited Europe on the eve of its modern transformation. Politically, that revolution occurred at the end of the War of Spanish Succession, with the Treaty of Utrecht in 1714, which announced the arrival of the new powers; culturally, it meant the beginning of the British and French Enlightenments, with the age of Pope, Montesquieu, and the young Voltaire. But this was not Tolstoi's world. He visited Old Europe before anyone knew with certainty that it was about to expire.

The Text and the Translation

Tolstoi's Diary consists of 161 handwritten half-sheets, physically located a century ago in the library of Kazan' University in Russia. Portions had twice been transcribed and printed unsatisfactorily, and twice the manuscript had been described when, in 1888, Count Dmitri Tolstoi, the former Minister of Education (1866–80), undertook the task of publishing it accurately and in its entirety.[19] Rightfully dissatisfied with the extant excerpts, he promised a true copy, which was published in seven installments in *Russkii arkhiv* in 1888;[20] it ran to almost three hundred printed pages, and it is the basis for the present translation. The Diary itself shows no significant evidence of subsequent editing. It is what it purports to be—a diary, a journal kept daily, with some missing dates, and some apologies for incomplete descriptions "due to a lack of time"; Tolstoi never completed these sections. Several times he misspells or misinterprets a word; when he later uses the correct form, he does not go back and correct the earlier passage. There is every reason to believe we have the Diary as he wrote it while he was in Europe.

Based on the published Diary, this translation aims at completeness, accuracy, and readability. The whole Diary is presented here, together with the annotations that I thought would be useful to the general educated reader. An earlier draft included a larger bibliography and far more footnotes. In the end I have included only those references that seem most useful. In particular, I have omitted the Russian bibliography: Russian specialists will not need it, and it will be of no use to anyone who elects to read an English translation.

As to the question of accuracy, I have tried to follow Tolstoi faithfully in style and content. For example, when he chooses to use Arabic numerals instead of spelled-out numbers, I follow his usage. When he is needlessly repetitive—"and I dined in the town of X, and stayed the night in that town of X, and left that town of X in the morning, and from that town of X went 2 miles"—I usually attempt to reproduce the singsong cadence of his own language. Likewise, I have often tried to reproduce his convoluted sentence structure, and even to retain sentence length and word order wherever possible, short of outright barbarity. Tolstoi writes in a unique "Russian," a transitional language no longer Old Church Slavonic but still far from modern Russian. It is fair to say that there is neither a grammar nor a dictionary for his style of Russian. I have used the standard Russian dictionaries, old, new, etymological and bilingual, but I have recorded the investigative process in the footnotes only when serious doubts remained. I have used Tolstoi's Russian and the local form for place names when they first appear, but thereafter I use only the local spelling. Tolstoi introduces scores of foreign words, mostly Polish and Italian, into the Diary;[21] when they first appear, to satisfy the curiosity of the Russianist, I give both

[19] On the career of Dmitrii Tolstoi, see Sinel, *The Classroom and the Chancellery*.

[20] The Diary appeared as P. Tolstoi, "Putevoi Dnevnik P. A. Tolstago," *Russkii arkhiv*, 1888, XXVI, T. I, pp. 161–204, 321–68, 505–52; T. II, pp. 5–62, 113–56, 225–64, 369–400. These divisions have been retained in the translation, and the page numbers of the Russian text are included for the convenience of those who wish to refer to the original.

[21] Tolstoi's neologisms are the only aspect of the Diary to have been studied in the Soviet Union. Val'kova, *Leksika "Puteshestviia" P. A. Tolstogo;* Drobinina, "Iz istorii ogogashcheniia russkoi leksiki," pp. 128–46; and her "K voprosu o proiskhozhdenii sovremennoi muzykal'noi i teatral'noi terminologii," pp. 123–40. The most recent bibliography of both Western and Soviet scholarship on linguistic borrowing in the Petrine era is in Otten, *Der*

the transliterated Russian and the foreign forms, and thereafter employ the foreign only, as it became part of Tolstoi's personal lexicon. Page references to the printed Russian text are provided within slash marks for the convenience of specialists who might wish to refer to the original. Words and place names that remained uncertain, conjectural, or only probable are indicated with a telling (?). In short, I have tried to be scrupulously faithful to the original in style and content.

Throughout I have tried to make the English text readable, for there is no other reason to do a translation. Tolstoi's Russian utilizes many passive voice constructions that are awkward to the English ear, but I retain many of them where readability does not greatly suffer. All abbreviations in the text itself (Ger., Pol., etc.) are Tolstoi's. A scholarly recording of neologisms, variant spellings, and uncertainties necessarily disturbs the flow of the text, but I can only hope that the translation reads as well as the original. In the interests of accuracy I have retained in the text the hundreds of phrases placed in apposition, "forestiere, that is, foreigners," although they too may aggravate the reader. I have removed scores of commas, divided long sentences, and inserted paragraph breaks more consistent with English usage.

Tolstoi was much impressed by the art and architecture of Renaissance and Baroque Europe, which he saw daily in Venice, Padua, Milan, Florence, Rome, and elsewhere. He had difficulty describing what he saw. His biographer, Pavlov-Silvanskii, noted that Tolstoi, a seventeenth-century Muscovite, standing before the magnificence of the Cathedral of Milan or a painting by Raphael, "could not find words in his language to express his impressions." There is an element of truth in this. Standing before some of the greatest art and architecture of the Renaissance, Tolstoi could only write "it is of marvelous workmanship," or, most typically, "it is fine," *izriadnaia*. This word calls for special comment. It is perhaps the most used, even over-used, adjective in Tolstoi's language of artistic appreciation. Often it appears half a dozen times or more in a single passage, and it is used hundreds of times throughout the Diary. Its Russian etymology is simple enough; it literally means *out of the ordinary*. That is unfortunately too awkward a phrase to be used scores of times adjectivally in the translation. Its closest synonym in English, however, the Latin-rooted *extraordinary*, has connotations of superiority that the Russian lacks. *Unusual* is accurate, but smacks too much of the peculiar, the odd, or the rare to be accurate. *Splendid* has the right feel, the right level of appreciation, but it lacks any etymological affiliation, and its connotations of brilliance and luster are inappropriate. In the end I have uncomfortably, inconsistently, and variously rendered *izriadnyi* as fine, really fine, quite fine, or very fine, depending on context, as barely adequate compromises. Likewise, I have rendered the adverbial form, *izriadno*, as finely built, finely adorned, etc. The point is not that Tolstoi was unappreciative of what he saw, but that he had some difficulty expressing his impressions. Although in the process of recording his travels he used *izriadnyi* rather abundantly, he also at-

---

Reisebericht eines anonymen Russen über seine Reise nach Westeuropa im Zeitraum 1697/1699, pp. 73–76.

tempted to borrow words from West European languages to embellish his vocabulary of artistic sensibility. I can only hope that the translation conveys both Tolstoi's dilemma and his partial resolution of it.

Finally, I can record my numerous debts. Above I noted the assistance and wisdom of my thesis director, Richard Pipes, and of my senior colleagues at Washington University, Professors Dietrich Gerhard and Edward Weltin, and I repeat my thanks here. I owe a special thanks to Professor Peter Riesenberg, whose knowledge of Italy, past and present, was always available to me; likewise, Renata Rotkowicz, formerly of the Olin Library, guided me through Poland—historical, geographical, and linguistic. The entire manuscript was read by my former student and now colleague, Harold Ellis; we have had the ideal student-teacher relationship, in that I have always learned as much from him as I taught. My old mentor and close friend, Roderick E. McGrew, has been a source of inspiration and encouragement throughout, and only he knows how much I depend on him in all matters of importance. Others also helped, including unknown Austrian farmers, tour guides, friendly Italians who listened patiently to my fractured questions, the staffs of the Greek College in Venice and of the Athanasian College in Rome, an American Catholic priest who guards the Mamartine prison in Rome, and the students of Padua University, who left me unmolested in spite of Tolstoi's dire prediction.

All at Northern Illinois University Press—Mary Lincoln, Susan Bean, Steve Franklin, as well as my editor, Alice Calaprice, and my readers, anonymous and not-so-anonymous—have been patient and helpful with a difficult manuscript. To work with them is to respect the work they do. I acknowledge too technical assistance from Ida Holland of Special Collections, Olin Library, and Jeannine Quinn, Slide Curator, Department of Art and Archeology, Washington University. I received financial support for parts of this project from the Gladys Krieble Delmas Foundation and from the Graduate School, Washington University. I owe a special thanks to my wife, Beth. Her contribution was far greater than the note taking she undertook as together we retraced Tolstoi's footsteps in Europe. Without her support and encouragement, the project would not have been completed. Two students at Washington University, Constance E. Brown and Andrew Scott Naylor, labored on the index. Users of the translation will appreciate their efforts.

Weights and Measures

On his outward journey Tolstoi recorded distances between cities and attempted to calculate the total distance to Venice. The Russian measure was the verst (Russian *versta*), which is nearly identical with a kilometer (.663 miles, 1.067 kilometers). The verst consisted of 500 sazhens, each of 7 feet. Of smaller measures of distance, Tolstoi mentions the arshin (3 arshins make a sazhen; each is 28 inches), and the vershok (16 vershoks make an arshin; each is 1.75 inches).

In the Diary, Tolstoi mentions two measures of capacity: the *vedro* (pail, 3.25 gallons or 12.3 liters), and the *bochka* (barrel, consisting of 40 vedros, 121 gallons). He uses two measures of weight: the *funt,* which approximates our pound (.0–3 pounds, 14.4 ounces) and the *pud,* which is 40 funts (36.113 U.S. pounds). In the interest of accuracy of translation, Tolstoi's terminology of measurement is retained throughout.

No attempt has been made to translate Tolstoi's monetary units into standard or modern forms. The reader should know that the standard unit in Muscovy was the ruble, which consisted of 100 kopecks; the *chervonets* (plural, *chervontsy*), often translated as the ducat, equaled about 3 rubles. The *efimok* (plural, *efimki*) was roughly equivalent to the Thaler (Joachimsthaler) and to the ruble. There were 200 Muscovite *denga* (plural, *dengi*) in a ruble, and an *altyn* equaled 6 Muscovite *dengi,* or 3 kopecks.

For further details, consult Sergei G. Pushkarev, *Dictionary of Russian Historical Terms from the Eleventh Century to 1917* (New Haven, 1970).

The Travel Diary of
PETER TOLSTOI

I

January 11, 1697–May 18, 1697

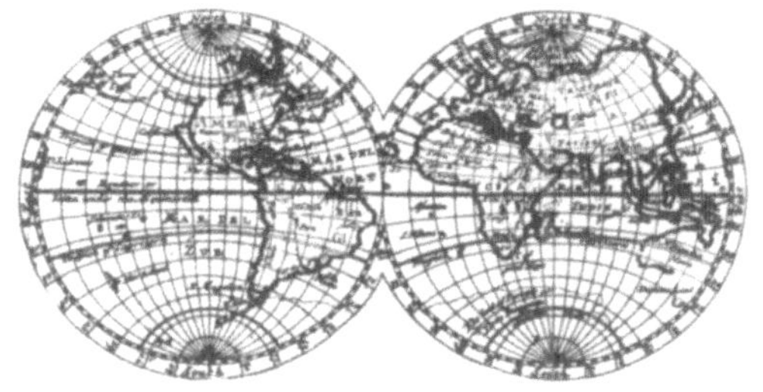

Moscow · Warsaw · Olomouc
The Empire

7205 [1697],[1] ***January 11.*** By command of the Great Sovereign, orders were given to the chamberlains Prince Iurii Iur'evich Trubetskoi; Princes Petr and Fedor Alekseevich and Dmitrii Mikhailovich Golitsyn; Prince Boris Ivanovich Kurakin; Vasilii and Volodimir Petrovich Sheremetev; Mikhail Afanas'evich Matiushkin; Prince Ivan Danilovich Gagin; Prince Iakov Ivanovich Lobanov-Rostovskii; Mikhail Fedorovich Rtishchev; Avram Fedorovich Lopukhin; Princes Iurii, Mikhail, and Andrei Iakovlevich Khilkov; Ivan, Matvei, and Iurii Alekseevich Raevskii; Prince Grigorii Fedorovich and Prince Vladimir Mikhailovich Dolgorukii; Aleksandr and Sergei Ivanovich and Aleksei Matveevich Miloslavskii; Prince Ivan Nikitinich Urusov; Petr Andreevich Tolstoi; Nikita Ivanovich and Fedor Emel'ianov Buturlin; Vasilii Semenovich Tolochanev; Vasilii Mikhailovich Glebov; Iurii Fedorovich Ladyzhen-

[1] 7205 = 1697. Until 1700 Russia used its own creation-based calendar, with September 1 celebrated as New Year's Day. Then Peter, having judged first-hand and correctly that the progressive states of Europe were the northern Protestant powers, adopted their calendar for Russia. Unfortunately, he thus adopted the Julian calendar, which European countries one by one would abandon during the eighteenth century, often with popular protest and distress. In the eighteenth century the old Julian calendar had fallen eleven days behind the Gregorian, which more closely approximated the actual solar year. Anywhere the change was made, a subject who went to bed on the eve of the conversion awoke to discover that eleven calendar days had passed when he arose the next morning. In addition, some Protestants regarded the new calendar as a deceitful papist fraud.

On the other hand, in the seventeenth century it did not surprise Europeans that Russians should count years from the Biblical creation. No less a mind than Isaac Newton took the problem seriously; see Manuel, *Isaac Newton.* In the middle of the century the sophisticated visitor Olearius could only quibble with the Russians' count of 5,508 years from the Creation to the birth of Christ, since he knew "in accord with the true Bible story of the creation of the world" that the figure should be 5,603; see Olearius, *Travels of Olearius in Seventeenth-Century Russia,* p. 67 (hereafter referred to as Olearius). Olearius will be cited frequently concerning mores in seventeenth-century Russia.

skii; Mikhail Il'inich Chirikov; Andrei, Ivan, and Mikhail Petrovich Izmailov, who were ordered to go to the European Christian states on the matter of military sciences; each was given a document as to which science he was to study.

Accordingly, by command of the Great Sovereign, the above-mentioned chamberlain Petr Tolstoi was given a document, and in it was written:

Document Pertaining to Study.

1. To know maps or *karty,* compasses, and other naval indicators.
2. To operate a ship both as in combat and as on a simple voyage, to know all the pertinent tackle and instruments, sails, ropes, and the oars on penal[2] and other ships, etc.
3. As far as possible to try to be at sea in time of combat; and if that does not happen, to try diligently to get into combat; and both those who do and those who do not see combat are to get from the naval masters testimonial letters, handwritten and printed, that they did their duty in this matter.[3]
4. If one wants to receive great favor upon his return, let him learn the studies ordered above and know how to handle the ships on which they have had experience.
5. When they return to Moscow, each must bring back two learned masters of naval affairs at their own expense, and when the masters arrive, those expenses will be repaid. Beyond this, each will take along one soldier for study. And anyone who does not want to take along a soldier may take along an acquaintance or one's own slave to study, but the soldier will go at treasury expense. And if someone takes along a person, in addition to a soldier, for each so taken the treasury will pay one hundred rubles. And the soldier or slave whom one wishes to take along is to be reported to the commissar-general immediately.[4]
6. To leave Moscow in wintertime, so that no one remains there after the last of February.
7. Passports and travel documents will be issued by the Diplomatic Office, and that Office is ordered to act promptly.

[2]The reference to penal ships indicates galleys, on which convict labor was used.

[3]Anxious to demonstrate that he had fulfilled his charge to the letter, Tolstoi below carefully narrates all his naval training, and he solicited, for inclusion in the journal, testimonials from his teachers and captains, which indicated that he had indeed tried to engage in naval combat. In Tolstoi's meticulous concern for amassing this evidence, one may also see the extraordinary effort he took to remove the lingering cloud of suspicion generated by the Miloslavskii affair in his youth.

[4]"Thirteen master ship carpenters from the Venetian Arsenal were sent to help Russia build a galley fleet." Lane, *Venice,* p. 410. Tolstoi's personal role in their recruitment is unclear. They helped to build the fleet in the south at Voronezh that was used to acquire Azov from the Turks. Tolstoi took along a soldier, Ivan Staburin, who is named twice in the Diary. See below, October 31, 1697, and June 23, 1698.

And in ***7205 [1697] on January 30*** a travel certificate was sent to the court of Petr Andreev Tolstoi, and in it is written:

We, by grace of God, the most glorious and powerful Great Sovereign, Tsar and Grand Prince Petr Alekseevich of all Great, Little and White Russia Autocrat, of Moscow, Kiev, Vladimir, Novgorod, Tsar of Kazan', Astrakhan', and Siberia, Sovereign of Pskov and Grand Prince of Smolensk, Tver, Iugra, Perm', Viatka, Bulgaria, and others, Sovereign and Grand Prince of the Nizhnii Novgorod lands, of Chernigov, Riazan', Rostov, Iaroslavl', Beloozero, Udoria, Obdoria, and Kondinskaia land, and Ruler of all northern lands and Sovereign of Iberiia, Tsar of Kartalin and Georgia, Prince of the Cherkass and Gora, of Kabardin lands, and by the rights of his father and grandfathers, Heir and Sovereign and Possessor of the eastern, western and northern patrimonies.[5] Our Tsarist Majesty to the most glorious and powerful great lord, the Imperial Roman majesty and royal /169/ majesty, our most beloved brother and friend, health and prosperity, unceasing and everlasting increase, also to all in general and in particular, to the most holy electors and other princes of the most illustrious Rzeczpospolita and to both peoples of the Polish Crown and of the great Lithuanian principality[6] and to other councils, their rulers spiritual and worldly, to archbishops, bishops, princes, generals, military commanders, margraves, counts, castellers and hetmans of troops, colonels and other leaders, barons, elders, mayors, nobles, vassals, presidents, commandants, captains, appointees, vice-domos, governors, *Rotmeisters,* cornets, marshals and leaders of cities, towns, villages, and other places and societies, *Burgomeisters,* and at sea admirals and vice-admirals and other such commanding and free naval procurers; and to guardians of bridges and waterways and to others who will demand the present certificate, whatever their status, rank, level, competence, or estate, we declare good will and every blessing. Our Tsarist Majesty orders our born-gentryman Petr Andreev sent to the European Christian states, principalities, and free cities on the business of military sciences; and when he arrives in any state, principality, or free city, to the most glorious, powerful and great lords, to the Imperial Roman majesty and royal majesties, to our beloved

[5]This is the official title of the Tsar of Muscovy in the late seventeenth century. See Szeftel, "The Title of the Muscovite Monarch," pp. 59–81, for variations and development. In the age of kings, it was the essential precondition for diplomacy that titles be used fully and accurately. See, for example, the imperial and tsarist titles that precede the text of the anti-Turkish pact of 1698 in Korb, *Diary of an Austrian Secretary of Legation,* I, 1–2 (hereafter referred to as Korb, I or II). Korb traveled from Vienna to Moscow and back just at the moment of Tolstoi's travels, and his diary elucidates many of Tolstoi's comments. "They refuse any letter addressed to his Tsarist Majesty if the slightest detail of his title is omitted"; Olearius, p. 137.

[6]The reference is to the Polish-Lithuanian state, joined in a single nation in the Union of Lublin, July 1, 1569. The two nations were to have a common sovereign and parliament, although Lithuania was to retain a separate administration and army. In 1573 Henry of Valois was elected king on the condition that he recognize the right of the nobility to elect kings, the origin of the elective monarchy for which the state became famous, or infamous.

brothers and friends, also to all in general and in particular, to the glorious electors and other princes of the most illustrious Polish and Lithuanian Rzeczpospolita, and to other such councils and their rulers clerical and secular, to princes and generals and admirals and to all mentioned above, whatever their status, rank, level, competence, or estate, to grant him for our Tsarist Majesty and all who are with him, for his effects and things that he has with him, by land and by sea to let him pass anywhere without detention and to dwell where he happens to be freely, without danger. And to the above-mentioned gentryman Petr, when he departs and when he returns to our state, grant that no obstacle, animosity, or annoyance be placed in his way. And further let him be granted assistance, freedom, and a warm welcome everywhere. And our Tsarist Majesty will bestow good will and favor to those in our state and in yours who will do this. Our Tsarist Majesty has given him this testimonial document for his safe passage and life.

Written at court, in the great Tsarist city of Moscow, in the year 7205 from the creation of the world, on the 30th day of January. In the 15th year of our reign.

The authentic certificate of the Great Sovereign is impressed with red /170/ wax. On the above-mentioned certificate is written "Petr Tolstoi, gentryman," but his court rank is omitted so that in foreign regions no one would know the rank or sort of person sent to these states for the above-mentioned sciences.

The Great Sovereign gave the above-mentioned chamberlain two certificates for the prince of Venice in Italy concerning his reception; and in them was written:

We by the grace of God, (etc.)

To the most glorious and nobled prince and lord Silvester Valerio, by the grace of God archduke of the Venetian possessions and to the whole Venetian senate, His Majesty's warmest salutations. By order of our Great Sovereign, His Tsarist Majesty, we are sending to you in Venice gentrymen of His Tsarist Majesty, who willingly and discreetly are directed to Europe to observe the new military arts and activities. And for this we, Great Sovereign, graciously wish that you accept our gentrymen into your possessions graciously, and also into your cities, wherever they may be, to allow them to stay and to show them good will and to be of assistance, attending to their needs; and when they have fulfilled their purpose and want to return to our state, to allow their return without restraint. And our Great Sovereign will allow your gracious people into our state in the same manner.

One of the above certificates of the Great Sovereign to the prince of Venice was given to the chamberlain Prince Petr Alekseevich Golitsyn, and another to Volodimir Petrovich Sheremetev. And because the Great Sovereign ordered me, Petr Andreevich Tolstoi, to leave Moscow for Italy, I departed in the year ***[7]205 on the 26th of February*** and stayed in the Dorogomilov suburb.[7]

[7] Having delayed his departure a month until the last moment, Tolstoi departed by sleigh and sledge in the dead of winter, with a retinue that would accompany him for the first part of his journey. Some sense of travel in this age and part of the world can be found in the descrip-

February 28, leaving the Dorogomilov suburb, I spent the night in the village of Odintsovo, 15 versts from Moscow.[8]

March 1. I arrived for dinner in the hamlet of Viaz'ma, 15 versts from the village of Odintsovo. This day I spent the night at the monastery of the Virgin in the hamlet of Kubinskoe (Kubinka), 20 versts from Viaz'ma.

March 2. I arrived to dine on the estate of *okol'nichi*[9] Fedor Tikhonovich Zykov in the village of Kapovo, 15 versts from Kubinskoe. This day I arrived to spend the night in Mozhaisk, 25 versts from Kapovo. In Mozhaisk I stayed in the postriders' settlement. Mozhaisk is a town of stone, on a hill, in which there is a church of Nicholas the Wonder Worker at the gates. In this church there is a carved image in wood of St. Nicholas, which truly never fails to work miracles for those who come to it.[10] The Moskva river flows a half verst from Mozhaisk beneath the Luzhetskii monastery./171/

March 3. Leaving Mozhaisk, I dined on the estate of the Kolotskii monastery in the village of Ostrozhek, 30 versts from Mozhaisk. The same day I stayed at the estate of Sergei Avramov Lopukhin, in the hamlet of Tsarevo-Zaimishche,[11] 40 versts from the village of Ostrozhek.

---

tion of the suite of the Austrian ambassador, which departed Vienna on January 10, 1699, about the time of Tolstoi's return. There were eight carriages and fifty horses: in addition to fine coaches for the officials, there was a *batterie de cuisine* and a "baggage fourgon,—an enormous machine, the chief impediment on the road," as well as two vehicles for carrying wine and other burdens. Korb, I, 8–9.

[8] A verst (Rus. *versta*) is almost precisely a kilometer (1.0668 km), or two-thirds of a mile (.663 mi). Tolstoi thus traveled about ten miles his first day, about twenty the next; on his best days he seems to have been capable of fifty miles. Until the nineteenth century, human history moved at the speed of a horse.

[9] As noted in the introduction above, this is a Russian civil rank roughly equivalent in duties to a boyar; literally, those close to the tsar. See Crummey, *Aristocrats*.

[10] 10. The Cathedral of St. Nicholas dates from the sixteenth century; St. Nicholas has a special significance for Tolstoi. Where Korb, passing through Mozhaisk, noted simply that "St. Nicolas is revered as patron there" (II, 41), Tolstoi emphasizes the miraculous powers of the shrine.

[11] "We dined near the village of Wasseiniz Czariwa, which Wickart [*Muscovite Itinerary*] calls Sumieschne Tsariwa, others pronounce Segmestia Tsariovoa." Korb, II, 42.

March 4. I dined in the hamlet of Tsarevo-Zaimishche. This day I stayed at the estate of the Ivanovskii monastery, which is in Viaz'ma, in the hamlet of Fedorovskoe, 28 versts from Tsarevo-Zaimishche.

March 5. I arrived to dine in Viaz'ma 12 versts from Fedorovskoe. I stayed close by Viaz'ma at the home of a townsman. Viaz'ma has two wooden forts, and the larger has five stone towers. There are two stone churches in the city, and the monastery of John the Baptist is beyond the city; the walls of this monastery are wooden, but the church is of stone. Beneath the city of Viaz'ma flows the river Viaz'ma. This day I arrived for the night in the hamlet of Semlevo, 20 versts from Viaz'ma. Knights live in this hamlet.

March 6. I dined in the village of Semlevo. This night I stayed at the Boldin monastery, 40 versts from Semlevo. In the Boldin monastery the cathedral is of stone, and another church has a stone refectory but is of wooden construction. I heard vespers this day at the monastery. The cathedral in this monastery is named for the Holy Trinity and in the chapel are hidden the relics of the Reverend Gerasim.[12]

March 7. I dined in the town of Dorogobuzh, 10 versts from Boldin monastery. The town of Dorogobuzh is all of wood, and sits on a hill above the Dnepr river, and there is another town lower down, and both towns are of logs.[13] In Dorogobuzh I stayed in a large suburb in a townsman's home, near the markets. In Dorogobuzh I heard the Liturgy in the cathedral this day. The cathedral in the lower town is wooden, built in the form of a cross, and named for the Nativity of Christ. This day I stayed on the estate of the Biziukov monastery, in the hamlet of Usviat'e, 8 versts from Dorogobuzh.

March 8. I dined in the postriders' settlement in Smolensk district, which is called Pnëvo, 42 versts from Usviat'e. From the aforementioned settlement of Pnëvo it is not quite 3 versts to the ice crossing over the river Dnepr in the forest. At this place the river Dnepr is not very wide. From the postriders' settlement of Pnëvo

[12] "The Basilean Monastery called Bogdin," Korb, II, 44. Gerasim of Boldin (d. 1554) was the founder of four monasteries in the region of Smolensk, on the model of the more worldly rules of Joseph of Volokolamsk; while still in the tradition of asceticism of other Russian monasteries, they placed more emphasis on wealth, estate management, and charitable activities. See Smolitsch, *Russisches Mönchtum,* pp. 252–53, and more generally on the movement, see Fedotov, *The Russian Religious Mind,* pp. 302–15.

[13] "We supped outside the city of Drogobusa, which lies on the bank of the Borysthenes. . . . This river formerly divided Lithuania from Russia." Korb, II, 45.

a man was sent ahead to Smolensk to hire a house. That night I spent the night on the estate of the wife of a Smolensk nobleman, /172/ the widow Stankeevicheva, in the village of Tsurikova, 10 versts from the settlement of Pnëvo.

March 9. I arrived at the city of Smolensk at the fourth hour of day;[14] 3 versts away I had descended to the river Dnepr and crossed to Smolensk over the ice. I entered Smolensk by the Dnepr gate. Smolensk is 30 versts from Tsurikova. In Smolensk I stayed at a townsman's home near the shops. The city of Smolensk stands on a hill over the Dnepr; it is all of stone and has a fine fortress. Smolensk has two open gates. One called the Dnepr leads to that river, and the other is called the Molokhov, and other gates that pass through the towers are blocked up. The cathedral in Smolensk is newly built,[15] and it is very large and high, having a height of 3 windows, one of them round. In this church the altars have been pulled down and are unfinished. The wooden church in the Avramiev monastery in Smolensk has an archimandrite; this monastery has a service on Saturday to read the *akafist*[16] of the Mother of God before the Liturgy. The convent of the Ascension is in Smolensk; its newly built stone church is not yet consecrated. There is a father superior in this monastery. The home of the metropolitan of Smolensk has a stone fence and the residence is low and of wood; near it at the gate is a wooden church of the Epiphany. Smolensk has 32 blank towers in addition to the entrance gates.[17] Each tower has many fine brass cannon. The icon of the Blessed Mother of God, the wonder-working icon of Smolensk,[18] hangs on the Dnepr gate, and multitudes of people constantly come here believing that this holy icon works miracles.

[14] Throughout the Diary, Tolstoi counts time in the medieval fashion, by indicating the number of hours from daybreak or from nightfall. Seasonally these hours were of shorter or longer length, and he was never comfortable with the modern twenty-four-hour clock, in which all hours were of equal length. This attitude toward time marks a major division between the old and the new worlds, made possible in the West as early as the thirteenth century by new technological advances in clock making. In general, see Cipolla, *Clocks and Culture 1300–1700*. See also the perceptive comments on the psychological differences between unequal *Horen* and equal *Stunden* in Landes, *Revolution in Time*, pp. 60, 76, and passim. For the seventeenth-century horological revolution specifically, see Macey, *Clocks and the Cosmos*.

[15] The twelfth-century Cathedral of the Assumption (Uspenskii Sobor) was destroyed by the Poles in 1611 and fully restored only in 1772.

[16] This is a song of praise in the Orthodox service.

[17] The walls, originally with thirty-eight towers of brick and stone, dated from the time of Boris Godunov (1596–1602). "This city, the metropolis of the Duchy of Smolensko, seated upon the bank of the Borysthenes, possesses a citadel built of oaken timbers." Korb, II, 46.

[18] This famous icon, attributed to St. Luke, was brought to Chernigov by the Byzantine princess Anna in the eleventh century, and was moved to Smolensk in 1103.

March 11. [Some of] my slaves who accompanied me from Moscow to Smolensk returned to Moscow with the horses. Smolensk has a monastery built of wood named for the Holy Trinity; it has a Father Superior. There is a large and high wooden bridge across the Dnepr from the Dnepr gate, which in all seasons provides water for the defense of the inhabitants of Smolensk. Across the river Dnepr from Smolensk is a large settlement, in the middle of which there is a stone church of the Apostles Peter and Paul, and formerly this was a Roman church. Here there are many shops that have every kind of merchandise. In this area across the river there is a wooden market where foreign traders bring various goods. /173/ In Smolensk there is a great warehouse on the *błona*, that is, on the square, in which there are many great brass cannon and all sorts of military supplies and small arms. I lived in Smolensk until the 18th because the winter roads began to worsen and there was water on the road.[19]

March 18. I left Smolensk on the proper road and spent the night in the village of Iakovichi, 2 [Polish] miles from Smolensk.

March 19. I dined in the court hamlet of Zharkovki, 4 miles from Iakovichi. In this hamlet I spent the night, because the road was too difficult.

March 20. I left Zharkovki to dine in the court hamlet of Krasnoe, 3 miles from Zharkovki, and there I spent the night.

March 21. I left Krasnoe, and dined at the court hamlet of Zverovichi, 2 miles away. I spent the night there because the winter road worsened, and it was impossible to proceed by sleigh. I transferred from a sleigh to a wagon.[20]

March 22. After dinner I left Zverovichi and spent the night in the district village, which is called Vasilevicha, 3 versts from Zverovichi and close to the Polish

[19] The Church of Sts. Peter and Paul is a twelfth-century structure. "The Society of Jesuits had a college here, the Dominicans, Franciscans and Augustinians, all had monasteries, from which they were expelled to make way for the Russians, who now inhabit them." Korb, I, 71. He refers to the acquisition of Smolensk by the Russians earlier in the century. Above, Błona, Polish, village green. This is Tolstoi's manner of introducing neologisms in the Diary. At this point Tolstoi begins to calculate distances in Polish miles, each equal to five versts (see April 11, below).

[20] Tolstoi delayed his departure until the last moment, and had to change his mode of transport with the spring thaw. Peter the Great had hoped to avoid such delays by decreeing a winter departure.

border. On the *23rd* I dined in the village of Vasilevicha and covered the 2 versts to the Polish frontier, to the river Ivata, which divides the Muscovite from the Polish-Lithuanian state. On the Smolensk side of this stream stands the court village of Burtsova, and on the other side of the Ivota facing Burtsova is the Polish king's village of Volkov (Wolkow). It is 14 miles from Smolensk to Burtsova. This day I crossed the border and spent the night in the hamlet of Romanovo, 2 miles away. This hamlet is prince Slutskii's (Słucki), but for defense it is entrusted to the voevoda of Troitskii (Troki?), the pan Oliakhovski (Olachowski).[21] The inhabitants of the hamlet are of various faiths. There is a blessed Greek Orthodox and a Catholic church, and there are quite a few Jews. The Orthodox church is named for the Holy Trinity.

March 24. After dinner I left the hamlet of Romanova and arrived at the seat of the Lithuanian hetman Sapega (Sapieha),[22] in the village of Koteleva, 2 miles from Romanova. That day I left the village of Koteleva, to spend the night at the seat of the great Lithuanian hetman Sapieha, in the hamlet of Gorki. The hetman Sapieha took this hamlet of Gorki as a dowry to his son Grigorii from the pan Polubenskii (Polubienski) for his daughter. In this hamlet of Gorki /174/ there is one Orthodox church, two Uniate churches,[23] one Catholic church, and a Jewish temple. It is a large hamlet with over a thousand households of various faiths—Orthodox, Roman, Uniate, and Jewish. It is one mile from Koteleva to Gorki. In the hamlet of Gorki on the ***25th of March,*** that is, on the feast of the Annunciation, I heard the Divine Liturgy in the Orthodox church of the Assumption of the Mother of God. I stayed in

[21] Pan (Pol.), noble, lord, gentleman. Beginning with Tolstoi's entry into what was Poland-Lithuania in his day, place names and proper names are given in Polish, with Russian form (transliterated) given only the first time a name appears in the Diary. "A nameless rivulet marks the frontier between Lithuania and Muscovy." Korb, II, 48.

No one traveled through Eastern Europe without commenting on the Jews. "Up to the time we had seen no Jews in Prussia; but they are in great numbers in Poland, and, above all, in Lithuania." Korb, I, 41. "The inn was kept by a Jew, and as it appeared indecent to have mass celebrated under his roof, we resolved to sanctify this Sunday in the place where we were to dine, named Sodin, alias Boguslaw; but as our inn here was also kept by a Jew, the sacrifice was omitted." Korb, I, 53. "A Jew baptised at the Church of the Holy Cross; the sponsors were Cardinal Radzioski and the wife of the grand Chancellor of Lithuania. The neophyte received the name of Michael." Korb, II, 62. "A dangerous riot that arose between our train and the Jews that lived in that village detained us beyond an hour; a stone thrown by a Jew knocked out the right eye of one of the grooms of the chamber. Several on both sides were injured." Korb, II, 65.

[22] The Sapieha family led the Lithuanian faction in the politics of the state, and General Sapieha (identified by Korb, I, 45) virtually ruled the eastern regions.

[23] The Uniates in Poland were those Orthodox Christian communities that accepted the Reconciliation of Florence-Ferrara, 1439, and the authority of the pope, while maintaining Eastern liturgical rites.

the home of a townsman of the Orthodox faith. This day after dinner I left Gorki and stayed at the seat of the above-mentioned great Lithuanian hetman Sapieha, in the hamlet of Gorodetskoe, 2 miles from Gorki, and stayed at the home of the nobleman pan Teterski. There is a Uniate church in this hamlet.

March 26. I departed Gorodetskoe and dined in the village of Gubino of the hetman Sapieha, one mile away. This day I spent the night in a royal estate, in the village of Gubari (Gubary), in Mogilev (Mohylew) district, 2 miles from Gubino.

March 27. I left Gubary after dining and spent the night in the royal estate in Mohylew district, the village of Zhdanovichi (Żdanowicze). Beneath this village of Żdanowicze flows the river Bas, which was high and therefore crossed with great difficulty. It is one mile from Gubary.

March 28, that is, on Palm Sunday, I dined in the above-mentioned village of Żdanowicze, and then spent the night in a royal estate, the village of Voinovo, 3 miles from Żdanowicze.

March 29. I departed Voinovo and stayed in the hamlet of Lupanovo (Łupanow), 3 miles distant; in this place the road crosses the river Dnepr to the left bank. This hamlet of Łupanow is across the river from the city of Mohylew.

March 30. Crossing the river Dnepr on a ferry, I arrived in the Polish king's city of Mohylew. At the crossing there was a great *konfuziia* (Pol. *konfuzja*), that is, confusion on the part of Mohylew's officials, because they were apprehensive, having no orders to transfer Muscovites across the river Dnepr into Mohylew.[24] Because of this confusion I went to the *ratusha* (Pol. *ratusz,* Ger. *Rathaus*) with the passport of the Great Sovereign where, upon looking at the passport, the burgomeister gave me a pass to the upper city. In the upper city, having looked at my passport, they gave me a pass to the court /175/ of a certain person in authority, pan Burba, who was sent by hetman Sapieha of Lithuania to Mohylew. This Burba looked at my passport and ordered me, my slaves, and my things to be transferred across the river Dnepr, and ordered me to stay in the suburb, and not in the city itself, but I was allowed to enter the city for a time should the need arise. I stayed in the suburb at the house of a townsman of the blessed Greek faith. The city of Mohylew is large, and there are large settlements around it, and gardens in the settle-

[24] The Austrian delegation also had difficulty entering Mohylew. Korb, II, 50.

ments. Mohylew is much larger than Smolensk. An earthen fort runs from the river around the settlement and back to the river again. The upper city is also earthen and very high; there are two stone and two wooden passage gates, but no towers over them. Merchants live in Mohylew. The stone city is called the royal *ekonom* (Pol. stewardship), that is, royal or courtly, but the Poles simply call the city the royal kitchen. The inhabitants of Mohylew who are townspeople are all Orthodox.

Mohylew has a holy monastery called the Brotherhood,[25] and monks live there. A stone fence surrounds the monastery and the cathedral inside is sizable and well built. Another holy monastery in the city is named for the Savior and has a wooden church. In the settlement there are three stone churches and eight of wood, and, in all, eleven holy churches; and 2 versts from Mohylew there is a monastery that has a fine stone church. Beyond the city is the Nicholaev monastery where Orthodox monks live. This monastery has a fine stone church. Many Hebrews live in Mohylew and they are rich and have fine homes. There are 20,000 town dwellers' homes and 10,000 Jewish homes in the city and the settlements. In this city the streets are paved with natural stones, and there are many shops in which all kinds of fine goods are for sale; and the rows of shops are made of stone. There are a few Catholics in this city, and they have only two churches, which are not very luxurious: one is made of stone and is very old; the other one is wooden and the Jesuits serve in it, and the stone one is called Farao,[26] and parish priests serve in it; the Catholic church in the suburb is wooden; Roman monks live at this church. The altars in Roman churches are done in the Roman fashion, and Roman /176/ churches have a place where the clergy stand and sit.[27]

[25] The Mohylew Brotherhood was founded in 1620. The Orthodox brotherhoods (*bratstva*) were social, charitable, and educational fraternities that were founded throughout Lithuania in the late fifteenth and early sixteenth centuries, modeled on and in competition with the communities of Catholics and Lutherans in the eras of the Reformation and Counter-Reformation. Many of them opened schools, modeled after classical academies, through which Western standards of education reached the East Slavic Orthodox world, eventually even Moscow. See Okenfuss, "The Jesuit Origins of Petrine Education," pp. 106–30.

[26] Early in the Diary, Tolstoi uses this word with some frequency, and he later indicates that it designates a cathedral; it is from the Greek for Pharaoh and came to signify a large home or court, and by extension, the major church or cathedral. Later he writes "Thara" (Pol., *faraon,* Pharaoh).

[27] Tolstoi here introduces a subject that will preoccupy him throughout the Diary—the physical appearance of Christian churches. Those familiar with Catholic churches will recognize the "place where the clergy stand and sit" as the sanctuary area; it is nonexistent in an Orthodox church, which typically has three apses at the eastern end of the church, set off from the body of the church by the icon-screen, the iconostasis. Through the central doorway in the iconostasis, the royal or tsar-door (sometimes called the Door of Paradise), one looks into the *bema,* which contains the altar. To the left or north, there is the prothesis (Russ. *zhertvennik*) containing the altar of preparation; to the right or south, there is the diakonikon (Russ. *riznitsa*), where vestments, liturgical vessels, and books are kept; it thus corresponds to the Western sacristy. The significance of this passage, then, is that Tolstoi has discovered that in Catholic churches the altar stands in the correct place to the eastern end of the church,

This day I was at a Carmelite church; the altar there had two doors, just as Eastern churches have, to the south and north, and they are painted with the images of Melchizedek and Aaron. Between these two doors there is an altar, but there are no holy gates. In this church there are five other altars; this church is decorated with holy icons, and the decoration of the altars is good, as in Eastern churches. And on top of them are four-pointed crosses, and there are belfries, but the bells are small and they ring them; and they ring them with poles, very much as they do in Orthodox churches in the Ukraine. In this city, bread is very expensive, and there are many foodstuffs and some fresh fish, but all is expensive. The ruler of this town is called the vice-*ekonom*, but he was absent during my stay; he was then in Vil'na (Wilno) with hetman Sapieha.

March 31, that is, Wednesday of Passion Week, I was in the Brotherhood Monastery for Sacred Liturgy; the cathedral in this monastery is large, with eight pillars, and around them is a choir loft. The structure of this church is of fine gilt work. The walls of the church are covered with fine icons, and the iconostasis is carved, gilded, large, and of very fine workmanship. During Passion Week in this church the whole iconostasis and all the holy icons were curtained with crimson-colored cloaks, and on these cloaks the passions of Christ are well painted.[28] The service in this church followed the Greek custom very decorously, and the holy icons were fine and richly decorated. The church is dedicated to the Epiphany. In this church on both sides are chapels, one dedicated to the Descent of the Holy Spirit, and the other to the Nativity of the Mother of God. This day I was outside the

---

but it is not hidden behind Royal Gates, and furthermore, the prothesis and diakonikon are absent. The reference to "four-pointed crosses" below is meant to distinguish the Catholic cross from those of Orthodoxy, which have six points, the last two being Christ's footrest; since the middle of the sixteenth century in Muscovy, this bottom crossbar was often rendered as a crescent, symbolizing victory over Islam, with the conquest of Kazan' and Astrakhan'. A convenient and lavishly illustrated introduction to the subject is Faensen and Ivanov, *Early Russian Architecture*.

Here, too, Tolstoi begins his serious examination of the rituals of Christianity in the West. In analyzing Tolstoi's comments on the Liturgy, I have been guided primarily by the scholarly literature on the normal form of observance, the Liturgy of St. John Chrysostom. The best brief outline is in *A Dictionary of Liturgy and Worship*, ed. J. G. Davies, passim. More detailed is Solovey, *Byzantine Divine Liturgy*, readable and concise. And finally, most detailed and with full commentary on the differences between Greek and Russian practices, see Kucharek, *The Byzantine-Slav Liturgy of St. John Chrysostom*. On clerical vestments I have used Davies's *Dictionary*, and Pocknee, *Liturgical Vesture*, as well as variations noted in Kucharek. Also useful was von Gardner, *Russian Church Singing*, vol. 1, *Orthodox Worship and Hymnography*.

[28] Tolstoi refers to the practice of covering all holy images with crimson cloths during Holy Week to symbolize Christ's death and descent into Hell. On Easter, the day of the Resurrection, these shrouds are suddenly joyfully removed, since "Christ is Risen, He is Risen Indeed!"

town at the church of the Resurrection of the Lord; this church is of wood, and its iconostasis is gilded, carved, and curtained for Passion Week as in the Brotherhood Monastery, in memory of the Passions of the Lord. The same day I was at a stone Catholic church, where the service was led by the parish priests, that is, by white clergy;[29] this is a large church named for the Assumption of the Mother of God; this church is built in the Roman fashion, and it has three poorly adorned altars. On the right side of this church is the tomb of a lord covered with the shroud of Christ. This tomb is made like a bed, covered with various materials with a curtain in the corners, around it are many mirrors, small and larger, and on the wall is one large mirror and from afar the perspective resembles a human form.[30] Around /177/ this tomb are many oil lamps that are lighted when required. There is a small organ in the choir of this church. In Mohylew there is a newly built Jesuit stone *kliashtor* (Pol. *klasztor,* cloister), that is, a largish monastery, and like many of these monasteries it is built of stone.

April 1, that is, on Thursday of Passion Week, I was at the Church of the Resurrection of Christ; at this time in this church there was no washing of the feet in the manner of the Greek faith, nor was it done in the cathedral. In the Liturgy in the *ektenia* they recalled the ecumenical Orthodox patriarchs and the metropolitan of Kiev. The vestments of the priests include short chasubles and long white cassocks with embroidered skirts.[31]

April 2, that is, Good Friday, I attended vespers at the Brotherhood Monastery in a warm church; this warm church had no dome, but a flat ceiling; the iconostasis and the whole structure are very fine in this church, which is built in the name of the holy evangelist John the Theologian. At this time, as during vespers, they sang *stikhovna*[32] and the priests bore forth the shroud of Christ above their heads and proceeded to the large Cathedral of the Epiphany, and there were five

[29] Tolstoi here distinguishes the "white" or parish clergy from the monastic or "black" clergy.

[30] Although it was not uncommon for princes or hierarchs, that is, the upper clergy, to have their tombs in Orthodox churches, the prohibition of graven images in the Eastern Church meant that Tolstoi had never encountered a tomb with a likeness of its inhabitant.

[31] Tolstoi here explores differences between the Eastern churches. He finds this particular church puzzling because one essential part of the Liturgy for Holy Thursday, the Washing of Feet, is absent. The *ektenia* is the prayer during the Liturgy in which the names of rulers and their families, and of the hierarchy, may be mentioned, followed by the refrain, "Lord have mercy." The priests, since they wore long white albs and short chasubles, rather than the dalmatic, the long outer vestment of the Eastern Church, dressed more like Catholic clergy.

[32] This is a collection of verses sung after the personal ektenia in the vespers service; *stikhovna* (Gk. *stichos,* verse of a psalm).

priests in vestments and three deacons in vestments. As they bore the holy shroud, the ringing of bells was very loud; the shroud was painted on white satin, and they placed it in the great cathedral before the holy gates. Under the shroud in the great cathedral was a table covered with linen instead of a coffin, and there was a canopy over the shroud with inscriptions and lamps, but no other kind of decoration. And as they came into the great cathedral they sang the verse "come and be satisfied" and all kissed the shroud. Then the preacher spoke a sermon from the pulpit on the crucifixion and burial of the Lord, but they did not carry the shroud around the church on Holy Saturday.

By royal privilege the city of Mohylew is a free city, but the *ekonom* does not actually rule the townspeople of Mohylew, but is their judge in all things. Arriving from the direction of Moscow the river Dubrovka flows on the left side, and it joins the Dnepr beneath the very walls of Mohylew. /178/

April 3, that is, on Holy Saturday, I attended the Liturgy at the cathedral in the Brotherhood Monastery. The dark curtains had been removed from the iconostasis, and the church was finely decorated.

April 4. At the fifth hour of night on Easter the bells for matins began to ring for the Orthodox church in the Brotherhood Monastery, and at that time I was there for matins. Near the monastery and by the city gates and on the walls cannon were fired as the matins singing began. There were great volleys at the other Orthodox parish churches at that time on this important day. The inhabitants of Mohylew do not bring eggs to matins on Easter.[33] I heard the Easter Liturgy in the cathedral of the Brotherhood Monastery. The Sacred Liturgy was served by the abbot and by six priests and three deacons, all in gold vestments of great richness. All the holy icons

[33] Korb gives a fascinating account of the Russian Easter, which helps to explain Tolstoi's comment on eggs.

> The following custom prevails among the Russians. From the feast of Easter until the day of our Lord's ascension, when they meet one another, no matter where, even in the public places and streets, they salute with the acclamation, "Christ is risen!" When men or women are thus saluted, they immediately reply, "He is risen, indeed," take the egg which the person usually offers at the same time, and are bound to give the kiss of peace and receive it. . . . This custom of saluting and kissing admits of no distinction of rank or lot in life, of no remembrance of quarrels. If the red egg be offered, no magnate will refuse the solicited kiss to the vilest of the populace, no matron will excuse herself through modesty, no maiden out of bashfulness; it would be held a sin either to reject the proffered egg or reject the kiss. Moreover, they celebrate with continual drunken orgies the festival of Easter, which is preceded by a long period of austere fasting. Nor are the women more abstemious than the men.

of the iconostasis were alit, its gilting was all alit even to the very top row. And as they began to read the "Apostol," three bursts were fired from many cannon. The "Evangelie" was read by the priests and deacons who were serving; in all, ten people read the gospel, two of them at the altar before the holy gates, one priest in the church, four at the four pillars, and the three deacons from the western door to the *amvon.*[34] And during the reading of the "Evangelie," at every exclamation the bells tolled six times and each cannon fired once; and when the reading ended the cannonade was great. When they began to sing the song of Jerusalem, the cannon each fired once, and 24 renowned townsmen with large green wax candles entered from the north door and stood opposite the altar until the departure of the Sacred Gifts [the Eucharist]. At that time the cannon fired three times. They fired again at the Words of Christ and at the time of the song of joy, and at the appearance of the body and blood of Christ there was a great cannonade at the Brotherhood Church and throughout the city by six cannon, and at the end of the Holy Liturgy the cannon fired three times. And when the *artus*[35] was brought, the 24 men with candles surrounded it; then there was a great pealing of bells, and simultaneously the firing of one great cannon. On Easter the inhabitants of Mohylew of the Greek faith /179/ have the custom of not going out; rather they stay the whole day in their own homes. During this time the shroud, as a symbol of the tomb of the Lord, rests on a table in front of the holy gates in the churches. This day I went to vespers at the Brotherhood Monastery; six priests and three deacons were in vestments, and at vespers the preacher on the pulpit spoke the sermon very well.

April 5, that is, Monday of Easter Week, I was at the Liturgy at the Nikolaev monastery. Its church is of stone, with a large gilted iconostasis; there, when they read the "Evangelie," the Song of Jerusalem, the words of Christ, and at the Eucharist, they fired from cannon, and 14 townsmen stood before the holy gates with large fine candles. And on this day there was in Mohylew a procession, and they walked with the Holy Cross from all the holy churches to the church of the Resurrection of Christ. In

---

> They are often the first to become raving mad with immoderate draughts of brandy; and are to be seen pallid, half-naked, and shameless in almost all the streets. (Korb, I, 99–100)

"[On Easter] and for fourteen days thereafter, practically everyone—notables and commoners, young and old—carries colored eggs. In every street a multitude of egg venders sit, hawking boiled eggs decorated in various colors." Olearius, p. 100.

[34] In the Roman Mass the Epistle corresponds to the *Apostol,* and the Gospel to the *Evangelie,* the writings of the Evangelists. The ambo is the raised platform in front of the iconostasis from which the ektenia, Evangelie, and sermons are read.

[35] Greek, *artos:* this is the leavened kissel bread blessed on the first day of Easter (Palm Sunday) and distributed to the people on Saturday of Holy Week.

this procession the priests walked in vestments and in the caps they always wear, and before the Resurrection Church they read the "Evangelie" verse, and the preacher spoke the sermon before the church on the pulpit in white *mitkalina* and in an *epitrakhil.*[36]

April 6, Tuesday of Easter Week, I was at Mass at the Resurrection Church, close to the city. This church has a fine iconostasis and decorations; in the right choir is an icon of the miracle-working Mother of God. This day I was at the home of a Mohylew townsman named Zachary Antufiewicz. This townsman has a sizeable home built within a stone court, and his structure and furnishings are fine, and he has many silver vessels. Another Mohylew townsman named Kaskowicz invited me to his house; he lived beyond the city beyond the river Dubrovka; this house was a fine wooden dwelling. All the Mohylewans who received me were of good birth and very rich. This day I left Mohylew on my journey, crossed the river Dubrovka on the bridge beneath the city, and spent the night in the forest, 2 Polish miles from the town. In all I spent 8 days in Mohylew.

April 7. From this camp I left for dinner in a seat of the Crown hetman, the Polish pan Polotski (Połocki), in the village of Bulyzhichi (Bułyzycze), 2 Polish miles from the camp. I spent the night in the borough of Polovchin, 2 miles from Bułyzycze; it belongs to the Lithuanian-Polish pan Slushkii (Słuszki). This /180/ borough has an Orthodox church and a small home belonging to the hetman.

April 8. From Polovchin I went 3 Polish miles, dined, and passed the hamlet of Teterino in the woods. It belongs to a Lithuanian *kanclerz,* the son of Prince Oginski.[37] This borough has 3 Uniate churches. This day I spent the night at the seat of the Lithuanian *unter-kamer* Milski, in the village of Krutaya, 2 miles from the Polish camp, having passed the village in the woods.

[36]These are, respectively, the Roman surplice and the Roman stole; Greek, *epitrachelion.* Tolstoi has previously identified this as an Orthodox monastery, and he notes the Roman-styled vestments of surplice and stole on the preacher.

[37]37. Here and later Tolstoi uses Polish court ranks to identify nobles. To provide a more readable text, they are listed here, and only the Polish form is included in the Diary hereafter.

Russian *kantsler,* Polish, *kanclerz,* chancellor
podskarbiia, podskarbi, treasurer
podstolie, podstoli, assistant pantry or table master
podkantsler, podkanclerz, vice-chancellor
podstarosta, podstarszy, vice-elder
podchashiia, podczaszy, cup bearer

April 9. I arrived to dine at the seat of the Lithuanian marshal, in the village of Ellian, 2 Polish miles from the village of Krutaya. This day I passed close to the seat of the *podskarbi* of Lithuania Sapieha, the hamlet of Bobr; this is a large hamlet, and there are many rich Jewish homes in this populous place; the *podskarbi* has a home here, a small low wooden structure. From Ellian it is 2 Polish miles here. This day I spent the night at the seat of Prince Sangushka (Sanguszka), in the hamlet of Krupen (Krupiec), 2 miles from Bobr, 4 Polish miles from Ellian, and before reaching that hamlet I crossed the river Bobr by bridge.[38]

April 10. I stopped to dine in Borisov povet (Borysów *powiat,* district), at the seat of the Polotsk (Połock) military governor, the pan Słuszki in the hamlet of Naga, 2 miles from Krupiec. In this hamlet a foreigner from the Empire came to me and said he was traveling to serve the Great Sovereign in Moscow. This day I reached the seat of the above-mentioned governor of Połock, the hamlet of Lozhnitsa (Loznica), 3 miles from Naga, and I went 2 Polish miles further to sleep in the forest, 5 Polish miles from Naga.

April 11. I arrived to dine in the city of Borysów, 2 miles from the camp where I slept; in all, from Mohylew to Borysów it is 24 Polish miles, or 120 Muscovite versts, and from Moscow to Borysów 730 versts. The city of Borysów has an earthen fort; there are no buildings inside except for the court of the military governor of Połock, the pan Słuszki, because the town of Borysów is his seat. The settlement around the fort is not large, and its inhabitants are of the Orthodox faith. A river flows beneath Borysów, called Bereza (Berezina); there are many Jewish homes in this town. In front of the settlement is an Orthodox monastery. The cathedral church in it is dedicated to the Resurrection of Christ. Seven monks and an abbot live in this monastery. In this monastery in the week of St. Thomas I heard the Sacred Liturgy.

In Borysów I stayed in a townsman's /181/ home; there are no Uniates in Borysów. There is a Catholic church; it is wooden and prebends, that is, the white clergy serve in it; in this church I was at a Roman service; the church is dedicated to the Holy Mother of God; in this church on the left side there is a small closet that the Poles call the sacristy; in it the priest dressed for the service in front of me. At the beginning he put on a white linen alb, just like a Greek alb, and then he donned a stole,

---

khorugv', chorazy, ensign or standard bearer
gusarskaia khorgv', husarz, cavalry ensign
pantsyraia khorugv', pancerz, ensign of armor
kashtelian, kasztelan, casteller
korunyi lovchii, lowczy koronny, crown huntsman

[38] Korb identifies the towns as Bobr and Krupke; II, 52.

which is not sewn or of the measure of an Orthodox stole, and then he put it on crossing himself, and he girded himself with a girdle, but not with a flat thick cord, and on his left arm he put on a narrow maniple dissimilar to the Greek one; on the right arm he did not don a maniple, and he put on a chasuble, which the Poles call an *ornat,* not like the Greek chasuble; the vestment is like an archbishop's *sakkos,* only not sewn on the side and not buttoned, with very short sleeves; and on all the clothes crosses are sewn.[39]

And having dressed, he emerged from the sacristy, having vessels in his hands, and then those of the Roman faith present fell on their knees before the priest. A server in a white alb carried a book, which is called in their language a missal, and in Slavonic a service book, and he put this book and the holy vessels on an altar, on which they conduct the *mish* (Pol. *msza,* the Mass), that is, they serve the Mass. It is spread with a piece of linen just like the *liton,* and in that place is a stone that the Romans have for the *antimins,*[40] and having spread it he fell on his knees, and opening the tabernacle on the altar, he took another chalice and covered it with a golden coverlet, raised it high, and turned with this chalice to face the people. Then all the Catholics there fell on their knees; at that moment the organ in the choir played. And he placed this chalice in the tabernacle from which he took it (in this chalice they have the sacred sacrament) and he began to conduct the service. During the service they sang in the choir in the Latin language; during this service he poured into the chalice wine and water from the various vessels, and then they took the offering from a silver box and placed it on the paten, but the paten, a small dish of gold, had nothing imprinted on it; and he read a prayer, and at the word "Christ" he raised or elevated high the offering without the paten, raising it with his hands above his head, so that all present could see it; likewise, he raised or elevated the chalice on high. At this elevation the Catholics there all fell on their knees at the word "Christ"; this priest served the whole Mass with awe, and, turning to the people, he blessed them with his hand and wished peace to all; in the Latin /182/ language he said the Lord's Prayer and read many other prayers, and breaking off a piece of the offering, he placed it in the chalice and covered it, but did not put it down; and then standing at the altar he fell on his knees several times, kissed the altar, and consumed the offering. Then from the chalice or from the cup he drank all, and rinsing the chalice, he again drank all. Two youths in white albs were with him in the service as sacristans, and they knelt at the altar and rang little bells, giving the people the signal when it was time to fall on their knees. Then the priest, having consumed

[39]Concerning these vestments, the alb is the *stikhon,* Greek sticharion; the stole, *epitrakhil,* is the Greek *epitrachelion;* the Greek cuffs, *epimanika,* differ considerably from the Roman maniple; the chasuble, *riza,* the Greek *phelonion,* differs from the *sakkos,* which is the Greek hierarch's outer vestment. On the topic see Pocknee, *Vesture.*

[40]The *liton* and *antimins* are, respectively, the corporal, the linen cloth under the chalice, and the flat plate on which the chalice rests. Tolstoi is describing the traditional Catholic Mass.

all from the chalice, wiped it and its rim with a linen cloth and placed the paten on it, and covered it, and, turning to the people, he raised his hand over the people. He again placed the chalice with the reserved hosts in the tabernacle, in which they previously had been, and they took the service vessels back to the sacristy; and the other priest then sprinkled the people with holy water.

While the officiating priest was disrobing, another priest in vestments and chasuble came out from the sacristy with other vessels; and on the same altar at the moment the first Mass ended he said another like the first. The altar on which the Mass is served is set upon a 3-tiered platform, and it is long and narrow and rectangular. On this altar is placed a tabernacle in which is placed the chalice with the *sakrament* (Pol.). On this tabernacle is the image of the Crucifixion of Christ. The altar is covered with fine brocades, with a simple linen cloth over them, and atop that a *liton* and in it a stone. And the altar in a Roman church is placed near the wall, and they do not walk all around it, and the Gospel does not stand on the altar.[41]

In this church on the altar is an image of the Blessed Mother of God with the Holy Infant, painted just as the image of the Smolensk Mother of God, but the child is on her left arm;[42] this image is of fine workmanship and similar to Muscovite painting. On this holy icon on the image of the Blessed Mother of God the left eye and cheek and nose is all black, as if painted over with ink; however, this darkness appeared gradually as a sign. The priest whom I questioned about this miraculous dark sign said that the holy icon formerly was in an Orthodox church in a place called Gumnazh (?), 3 miles from Borysów; when the Great Sovereign, the Muscovite tsar Aleksei Mikhailovich, Autocrat of all Great, Little and White Russia, conquered the city of Borysów,[43] this icon was brought from that place to Borysów and placed in the castle; and when the Moscow governor generals retreated from Borysów /183/ to Moscow, the holy icon of the Mother of God was transferred to the blessed Orthodox monastery of the Resurrection; and there the holy icon stayed for five years, and there was no black spot on the holy icon; but when the city of Borysów by treaty

[41] Tolstoi is describing the difference between the simple sacrificial altar of the Orthodox world and the altar of the Roman world. In Russian the word for altar, *prestol,* has special significance, in that it means both throne and altar; only a priest may approach it through the Royal Doors into the Holy of Holies, where the Mysteries occur behind the veil of the iconostasis. It has been suggested that this very secrecy of the sacrament in Orthodoxy led to a popular disinterest in the Eucharist, and a corresponding increase in veneration in icons. "Icons gained what the Eucharist lost." Fedotov, *Russian Religious Mind* II, 356–57.

[42] The legend of this icon was noted above when Tolstoi visited Smolensk itself. The icon is of the Hodigitria type, in which the Christ-Child sits on his mother's lap; He wears the philosopher's robe and holds a scroll in his hand. Normally Christ sits on His mother's left side, as in icons of the Tenderness type, so that His head might rest over her heart. Icon painters, however, touched their copies to the original to ensure an unbroken succession of identical icons, and for Christ to touch Christ in this manner, the image was often reversed. On the icon type, see Onash, *Icons,* plates 69, 83.

[43] Tolstoi recalls the Belorussian campaign of 1654.

The Mother of God of Smolensk (early fifteenth century).

was granted back to the Polish crown, the Romans took this holy icon from the Resurrection monastery to their Catholic church; and when the icon was taken to the Roman church, at that moment on the icon the small black spot in the size of a Muscovite kopek began to appear, and having appeared at that time, that spot remains to this very day; and many have tried to cover over that spot with colors, and many masters, iconographers, and painters have attempted to cover the spot on this holy icon, but they suffered from injured arms and were yet healed by that holy icon, so that no one now tries to correct that spot. In this church is a grey stone, and in it was the mark of a human foot, as if a man had stood and formed the footstep in some kind of soft material, and they say that this stone was found in a forest long ago, and it was brought to Borysów with the above-mentioned icon of the Holy Mother. Six silver candlesticks stand on the altar of that church, and in them are large white candles that they light during the service.

This day I crossed the river Bereza from Borysów on a ferry, and stayed the night on the bank.

April 12. Leaving the Bereza, I dined, and passed the seat of the military governor of Połock, the pan Słuszki, in the borough Zhidino (Zydyno), 4 Polish miles from Borysów. That night I stayed at the seat of the *podstolie* of Mazovetski (Mazowiecki), the pan Pronskevich (Pronskiewicz), at the village of Zabolot'e (Zablocie), 5 Polish miles from Zydyno.

April 13. I dined at a tavern called Gorodishche (Horodyszcze), 3 Polish miles from Zabolocie, and that night I stayed at the city of Minsk, 4 Polish miles from the tavern, but in Russian 70 versts, and from Moscow to Minsk is 800 versts. The city of Minsk, a seat of the Polish king, is surrounded by an earthen rampart. Pan Zavisha (Zawisza) the Elder, lives in it. During my stay in Minsk he was not there, being at his seat. His home in Minsk is a castle, built of wood, large, low, and of squared timbers. In Minsk the pan Glebovich (Glebowicz) has a large stone home; it stands empty with no inhabitants. The city /184/ of Minsk is much smaller than Mohylew; there are many stone buildings in Minsk. This day I was at a Uniate monastery where Uniate elders, men and women, live. The monastery has a large stone church, which has a fine dome, and such domes are seldom encountered in Polish stone structures. The church is furnished in the fashion of an Orthodox church, but the iconostasis is not luxurious, but the icon frames are large; the elders who serve in this church are called Basilians,[44] that is, of the Rule of Basil the Great. In this church on the altar is an imprinted *antimins* similar to an Orthodox

[44] Russian, *Vasiliane,* which is the monastic order of the Uniate church. The monastic rule of the fourth-century Basil the Great was the most widespread in the Orthodox world, including Russia. See Olearius, pp. 250, 268.

antimins.[45] These Uniate elders accept the pope in Rome as their head and pray to God for him in the service. This same day I was in a Bernardine cloister[46] that has a simple church. Those of the Catholic order of St. Bernard wear a hair shirt on their naked bodies, without an undershirt, and they walk barefooted upon the logs. There are many stone houses in Minsk, and in the shops where they trade, the markets are of stone, and there are quite a few goods. Minsk has an Orthodox monastery dedicated to the apostles Peter and Paul. The monastic church is a large and really fine stone structure similar to the cathedral in the Mohylew Brotherhood monastery. This monastery has an abbot and a few brothers; monks also come here. Around Minsk flows the small river Vislovitsa (Svislotch), and on its banks is a mill with four stones, and across the river is a fine wooden bridge.[47]

April 14. I attended the Divine Liturgy at the Peter-Paul monastery.[48] The monastic church has eight stone pillars, but the iconostasis is not very richly done. On the sides of the church are two chapels, and in them are well-painted icons with very rich silver covers.

April 15. I went to the Liturgy at the same monastery; this time in the large stone church of the apostles Peter and Paul a casket was placed in the middle of the church, and it was covered with a cherry-red satin pall with a cross sewn on it; on both sides of the casket were benches, and on each bench stood three large candles in gilded candlesticks; and at the head of the casket two candles as well as offerings were placed in a glass; and I was told that in this monastery there is the custom every Thursday to place this casket there in memory of the deceased. After the Liturgy the abbot read the Requiem at that casket, and two priests in vestments were with him; both abbot and priests wore chasubles of black velvet. And /184/ the people of the Orthodox faith there in the church all stood with candles.

This day the Romans celebrated, according to the new calendar, the memory of Mark the Evangelist, and had a *protsessiia* (Pol. *procesja*, procession), that is, a walk with a cross, and they walked from the Dominican cloister in this order: in front was an Higumenos,[49] and then two Bernardines, and they bore the cross with the image of the Crucifixion of Christ on it; then came the Dominicans who carried the crucifix, and the procession went out of the city to the church and then back to the city; the *kanonik* (Pol., canon), that is, a sort of protopop, walked with them,

[45] Above in Borysow, Tolstoi had noted that the Roman paten, which covers the chalice, bore no inscription. Here he does see an inscription on the *antimins*.

[46] These are the Bernardines, Cistercians, after Bernard of Clairvaux, 1090–1153.

[47] "The river Suislowiz intersects the city and flows into the sea at Riga." Korb, II, 53.

[48] This is the Greek cathedral, founded in the sixteenth century.

[49] The Russian *Igumen* denotes the Father Superior of a monastery.

and he wore a light blue mantle on a field of gold brocade, and the procession arrived at the Dominican church, and as soon as they entered, the organ in the choir began to play. In this church on a small altar stands an icon of the Blessed Mother of God of Russian painting; the Dominicans say Mass in front of this icon on a special side altar at the pillars; and the above-mentioned *kanonik* passed from that church to the one where he started and then brought the cross back. There were many men and women in that procession. And on that day Romans ate no meat.

That same day I was at the Franciscan cloister; these Franciscans wear a black hair shirt, as do the Bernardines, and a belt of knotted cords, and not all wear beards, and their life is nameless:[50] they may own nothing, and they live on alms, and forever walk the streets asking for alms. And the decoration in their church is the same as in other Roman churches; but in all Roman churches the image of the Blessed Mother is more decorated than other icons. This day I was also at the Jesuit cloister, where live the freest of all the Roman orders, who only are saved from evil by preaching for Christ.[51] In Minsk there is a Uniate church where Uniate elders called the Basilians live; their church is of stone. The Dominican cloister is stone, the Bernardine church and the Jesuit church are stone, but the Franciscan church is wooden and not very large; a stone convent houses Benedictine nuns. This day I visited the cloister with the *panin* (Pol. *pani,* lady, but here, the abbess of the nunnery) of the Bernardines and the *panin* of the Benedictines. Bernardine nuns wear black, and on the body instead of a shirt they wear a heavy hair shirt, and they are girded with a cord with knots, and are barefooted in winter and in summer, and they enter the church by a secret stairway built inside the wall, and they stand in the choir, looking into /186/ the church through small slits in the lattice so people cannot see them. In my presence these Bernardine nuns played the organs in the choirs and sang very nicely. They conduct vespers and matins without a priest, but a priest does come to say the Mass.[52] The Benedictine nuns wear a white habit, with white attire on their heads, and are very well attired, and in church they also enter through a wall secretly, and stand in a concealed place, so that no one can see them. These Benedictine nuns play on the organs, and before me sang most marvelously. I stayed two days in Minsk.[53]

April 16. I left Minsk and stayed 3 miles from Minsk, passing the Cherkass (Czerkasy) tavern.

[50] That is, they renounce their former identity when they enter the Order.

[51] This is, of course, a very Russian interpretation of the Jesuits. Tolstoi's idea of monasticism hardly covers these monks who do not live lives of self-mortification or abstinence, but only teach among the laity.

[52] It is inconceivable in the Orthodox church, whose ritual was monastic in origin, that the Hours would be observed without a priest.

[53] "We arrived at the city of Minsk, in which the Jesuits, the Dominicans, the Franciscans, the Bernardines, have their colleges and monasteries." Korb, II, 53.

April 17. I dined at the tavern, passed the seat of the *podkanclerz* of Lithuania, Prince Radziwiłł, at the borough Kaidanovo (Kajdanowo); this borough Kajdanowo is two miles from the camp where I slept. Kajdanowo is a stone place with towers and a stone fortress, and there are many rich homes there. Here there is an Orthodox church of wood. This night I arrived at the seat of pan Zhitemski, the *podkanclerz* of Lithuania, at the village of Zasol'e (Sasiulle), 3 miles from the camp.

April 18. I dined at the seat of Radziwiłł, mentioned above, in the village of Zhukov Borok,[54] 3 Polish miles from the village Sasiulle, and dined on the bank of the river Nemolt (Niemen). This day I crossed the river Niemen and stayed the night in the town of Mir, 2 Polish miles from the river Niemen, and from Minsk to Mir it is 13 Polish miles, and 65 Russian versts, and from Moscow 865 versts. The town of Mir is the seat of Prince Radziwiłł, the son of the podkanclerz of Lithuania. The fortress is earthen, and in it are stone Uniate and Catholic churches where white clergy serve; the town has four stone passage gates; the townsmen's homes in the town are rich, and there are many Jews. The place is not large, but there are many well-built homes. And the town is well situated, but it has no river beneath it; near the town is an earthen fortress, and there is a large stone building inside, and there are round towers at the corners, and the gates to this building are through very tall stone towers, and the building is four-cornered. In the tower over the gate is a Roman church of fine construction, and between the towers instead of walls are fine palaces, very tall on two sides, indeed, three stories high. This building is paved with stone and water flows around it. From the town of Mir it is half a verst to a large place in an enclosed pine grove; this is the menagerie of the above-mentioned Radziwiłł. In this menagerie are many deer, elk, antelope, wild goats, /187/ and other animals. Radziwiłł's stone house has a *vakhta* (Pol. *wachta,* watch), that is, a guard, soldiers in his pay; there are in all 80 at Radziwiłł's court, and stone arcades circle the palace.

April 19. I left Mir, dined in the village of Polonka, 3 Polish miles away. This village is the seat of the military governor Belski (Bielski). This day I slept at the seat of the cavalier pan Pattsa (Pac) in the hamlet of Khvostovich (Chwostowice), 3 Polish miles from Polonka.

April 20. I dined in the hamlet of Chwostowice; in this hamlet is a wooden Uniate and a Catholic church, and attached to the latter is a stone palace; and in it is a miracle-working carved icon of the Blessed Mother of God with the Christ-Child, and this image Radziwiłł brought from Rome, and it is called the "Orphan." On this holy

[54] "At Schokorora we crossed the river Niemen. . . . Afterward we went on to Mira, which belongs to Radziwil." Korb, II, 54.

icon are three cavalry insignia, given or affixed to it by the pan Niaditski (Niadycki), a Knight of Malta. There are 8 silver lamps in front of this image. This night I stayed in a forest, having gone 2 miles past the hamlet of Polonka, now 5 miles from Chwostowice. This is the seat of various nobles. Formerly in this place Prince Ivan Khovanskii battled the Poles, when the Poles fought the Muscovite troops of the Liakhovichii regiment of Prince Ivan Khovanskii.[55]

April 21. I dined in the city of Słonim, 3 miles from the camp and 13 Polish miles from Mir, and 65 Muscovite versts, and from Moscow to Słonim it is 930 versts. The city of Słonim is largish, with fine buildings, but none of them are large. It stands on the river Schar (Sčara). There are many Jewish homes in the city; the city is the seat of the mother of the Lithuanian hetman pan Sapieha. Her home is in the city; around the home is an earthen fortress, with a large ancient wooden mansion, but it is decrepit. In this city are three Roman cloisters, a convent of the Bernardine order, a Dominican monastery, and in a third live canons who wear white like the Dominicans, and a short white cloak on top, like a short mantle. All these cloisters have large stone churches, but the best church is in the convent. The Bernardine monks also have a stone monastery in this city. I stayed the night in Słonim.[56]

April 22. I dined at the seat of the *podstarszy* of Volchinskii (Wołczynski), the pan Zukowski, in the hamlet of Ivashkovich (Iwaszkowice), /188/ 4 miles from Słonim. Beneath this hamlet I crossed the river Zelva (Zelvianka) on a ferry; there I spent the night, 2 Polish miles from Iwaszkowice, having passed the village of Menirich (Meniricze).

April 23. Passing the village of Petuchowo, I dined at a tavern 3 miles from the camp, 2 Polish miles from the village Petuchowo, which belongs to the pan Kurch (Kurcz), the military governor of Brest. This place has a stone church, a wooden one, and a wooden manor house. The house is large, surrounded by large ponds, and from Meniricze to Petuchowo it is 2 miles. This night I stayed at the seat of the *podczaszy* of Lithuania, the pan Krispa (Kryszpa) in the hamlet of Mścibow, 2 Polish miles from the tavern where I dined. Mścibow is the seat of Prince Oginski, son of the chancellor. There was a fair in Mścibow that day, and a multitude [attended]. From Mścibow to Vislovich (Wislovice) [it is] 2 miles.

[55] Ivan Andreevich Khovanskii, boyar and personal friend of Tsar Aleksei Mikhailovich, is best known for his sympathy for the Old Believers. He campaigned in Belorussia in 1660, was defeated, and lost his army of 20,000 men. He was executed for leading the *strel'tsy* revolt of 1682. See Crummey, *Aristocrats*.

[56] We arrived at the city of Slonim; here there are both Dominicans and Jesuits." Korb, II, 55.

April 24. I dined at the seat of the *chorazy*[57] of Brest, the pan Shelski (Szelski), in the hamlet of Jatowka, 2 miles from Wislovice. I spent the night in a pine forest, 3 miles from Jatowka.

April 25. I passed the royal seat, the hamlet of Narva (Narew), one mile from the place I slept; the river Narew flows beneath Narew, and I crossed it by bridge. This river separates Lithuania from Poland. And I dined at the seat of the crown chamberlain pan Branitski (Branicki), in the hamlet of Plenniki, 2 miles from Narew and 3 miles from the camp. This night I stayed at a royal seat in the village of Belsk (Bielsk), 2 miles from Plenniki. Bielsk is large; it is evident that previously this was a large place, since many spots along the streets are paved with stone. And for many years a road has passed through this place to the stone bridge, and passing here is yet another road, also paved with stone. There are many inhabitants in this hamlet, a few of them of the Orthodox faith. In this hamlet are 4 Uniate churches and one cloister of the Romans, in which the Carmelites live. The townsmen of this hamlet are wealthy.[58] While I was in Bielsk, a Hussar ensign was there. From Słonim to Bielsk it is 22 Polish miles, or 110 Muscovite versts, and from Moscow to Bielsk it is 1,040 versts. /189/

April 26. I dined at the seat of the chancellor's son, the nephew of hetman Sapieha, at the hamlet of Bontsk (Bocki),[59] 2 miles from Bielsk. I stayed the night at the seat of pan Osolinskii (Ossolinski) in the village of Charma (Czarme?), 3 Polish miles from Bocki.

April 27. I arrived at the river Bug, which I crossed by ferry, and I dined at the village of Kremen, and there I spent the night; [the village] belongs to pan Lisinski. From Czarme to the Bug it is 4 Polish miles. The Bug is large, much larger than the Moskva, and very fast. The village on the Moscow side of the river is Kramilovich (Kramiłowicze), and Kremen is on the other shore. Both belong to the seat of pan Lisinski.

[57] As noted above, this is a military rank, *chorazy,* ensign or standard bearer (Russ., the Cossack rank of *khorogv'*). Elsewhere (see below, April 25) I use the English form, ensign, for readability.

[58] Korb, too, noted the wealth: "So we dined in the royal city of Bilseck. Bzaniski is starost for General Sapieha. Besides a monastery of Uniat Basilians there, the Carmelites, too, have a foundation of forty thousand Polish florins; the Polish florin is worth six Pfennings." Korb, II, 56.

[59] Spellings vary. "At night we came to the city of Bodki,—others write Bodsky; a little, winding river of the same name runs past this place." Korb, II, 57.

April 28. I dined at the seat of the military governor of Połock in the village of Zamkovo, 4 Polish miles from Kremen. I stayed at the seat of this same man, the elder of Warsaw, pan Kraspinski, in the hamlet of Vengrovo (Węgrów), 2 Polish miles from the village of Zamkovo. From Bielsk to Węgrów, 13½ Polish miles, or 67½ Muscovite versts, and from Moscow to Węgrów [it is] 1,107½ versts. This place separates Podlasie from Mazowsze. Mazowsze is distinct from Węgrów and belongs to the Hungarian king; this place is large, the wooden homes are luxurious, and the inhabitants are all Hungarians of the Roman faith. There are also many Lutherans and Calvinists in Węgrów. There is a large stone Catholic church, much larger than the Muscovite cathedral. It is very old and richly decorated. The place is on a large pond, but there is no river.

April 29. I dined at the seat of the pan Oborski, the *kasztelan* Ossolinski, in the village of Dobre, 4 Polish miles from Węgrów. I stayed at the seat of the *łowczy koronny* pan Lovetskii (Lowiecki) in the village of Pustelniki, 3 P. miles from Dobre.

April 30. I dined at the seat of the crown ensign of armor, the pan Grebowski in the village of Okuniew, 2 miles from Pustelniki. I spent the night in Warsaw, 3 miles from Okuniew; from Węgrów to Warsaw, [it is] 11 Polish miles or 55 Muscovite versts. From Smolensk to Warsaw, [it is] 161 Polish miles, 805 Muscovite versts, and from Moscow to Warsaw, 1162½ versts. Warsaw is a large place situated on the left bank of the river Visla (Wisła). The Wisła is large, and it flows from the south to the north. In Warsaw there are no settlements /190/ around the city and only one royal castle on the bank of the Wisła; this castle is of stone and well built.[60] There are many churches and cloisters in Warsaw, all Catholic; and there are many large fine stone senatorial homes.[61] Warsaw sits right on the bank of the Wisła, and there are many fine gardens; people and all sorts of goods are brought across the Wisła to Warsaw by ferries. The Wisła is as large as the Volga where it flows beneath Yaroslavl'. While I was in Warsaw I stayed across the river in a suburb called Praga on the Muscovite side. In this suburb the homes are of wood. I stayed here because one could not find an inn in Warsaw proper, because at that time they were holding an election, in which the Poles choose their king, and in Warsaw at that time were all the great senators of the realm of both peoples, of the crown of Poland and of the principality of Lithuania; and indeed it was even very difficult to find an inn in Praga where I stayed. On arrival I sent

[60] This is the Zamek Krolewski, which had been embellished as the royal residence in the previous century.

[61] "All the Polish magnates and ambassadors of crowned heads live in palaces in the suburbs." Korb, II, 58. Tolstoi himself makes this observation below on May 1.

word of myself to the present Muscovite resident, the clerk Aleksei Nikitin.[62] At news of my presence, this Aleksei left Warsaw to meet me at the inn, where I was staying in Praga, on the bank of the Wisła across from the royal castle of Warsaw.

The Wisła falls into the sea that the Italians call the *Mar-Baltiko,* under the city of Gdańsk; the Wisła is plied by large ships with grain and all kinds of goods. When a king dies in Poland, the cardinal-archbishop of Gniezno is in command in Warsaw.[63]

May 1. I crossed the Wisła from Praga to Warsaw proper in a boat, and from the shore I entered by way of the stone stairway that leads from the bank to the upper city, and arriving at the castle, I was at the royal court. The royal Polish court is not large; it has four sides, and instead of a wall there is a four-story-high palace; it has no porch that juts out; rather, a staircase leads [directly] into the court, and there are four passage gates under the palace. Guard soldiers stand on the walls of this palace, and the soldiers' weapons /191/ hang on the walls. At the doors of the palace two soldiers stand in Germanic dress with spears or halberds. At this time at the court all wore black because of the death of the Polish king, Jan Sobieski. Through these walls one enters the palace, which is large and all draped with black cloth; in this palace along the wall on the left side is a large platform three steps high, and this platform is covered with silken velvet and golden lace. On this platform is the casket in which the body of the Polish king Jan Sobieski rests. The casket is covered with golden velvet, and there are golden lace and a fringe and gilded silver nails. Around this casket on the steps of the platform are placed 30 large silver candlesticks, in which tall white wax candles burn. At the foot of the royal body stand two guards with halberds. Above the casket is a golden crown, and under the legs of the casket is a golden, sectioned cushion, on which a golden box shaped like a human heart is placed; in this box near the deceased royal body is the extracted heart, and the royal heart will be buried in Warsaw,[64] but the royal body will be taken to

[62] *D'iak* Aleksei Nikitin was the Muscovite resident in Warsaw 1696–1700, pursuing Russian interests during the interregnum that followed the death of John III Sobieski (1674–96), and prior to the election of the new king, Augustus II, Elector of Saxony, who reigned 1697–1733.

[63] Korb, II, 58–60, identifies Cardinal Radziowski. His nineteenth-century translator added, "The Primate of Poland, Archbishop of Gnesen and Posen, was the highest dignitary of the old Polish kingdom. He enjoyed the privilege of wearing scarlet like a Cardinal; and was, *virtute officii,* Regent of the kingdom, with the title of Inter-Rex, during vacancies of the throne."

[64] It was buried in the Church of the Transfiguration, which Sobieski had built in 1693 to commemorate his glorious victory over the Turks at Vienna a decade earlier.

On September 7, 1699, a year and a half later, the remains of Jan Sobieski were still not interred. "The late King's body embalmed lay still provisionally at the Capuchins; we went to see it, and also the rooms which he had built in the monastery of those fathers, in order to retire there from time to time from public cares for a brief space." Korb, II, 61.

Krakow and there interred. At the moment I entered this palace three priests on three altars were saying the Mass, that is, the Requiem for the soul of the dead king. The three Roman priests all wore black vestments; over the casket, in which the royal body rests, was placed his portrait, painted on canvas in a carved golden frame. Beside the royal palace is one more large palace that the Poles call the senatorial cottage; in this house the Polish Sejm meets,[65] and it has large windows; the window panes are glass, but all are broken; the windows were smashed at a discordant meeting, and there is discord in all affairs among the drunken Poles; and the palace where the king rests is quite far from this palace. While I was in Warsaw, the wife and children of the deceased king were absent; they had left for Prussia, for it is the custom among the Poles that when the king dies, and when they are having an election to choose a new king, they send the wife and children and relatives of the dead king away from Warsaw.

This day I was at a church called Thara, that is, the cathedral;[66] it is large and rich; in this church, on the left side on the wall, hangs an image of the Crucifixion of Christ, done in a fine carved manner; the hair on the head of this image /192/ is similar to black human hair, and the Poles say that if this hair were clipped, it would grow back.[67] In this church, in the choir over the west doors, are very large organs, as large as one finds anywhere. In this church are many altars on all sides, and they are well and richly adorned. This church is not far from the royal palace, and there

[65] In Poland the power of the nobles, the *szlachta,* was centered in its duty to elect a king, and in the parliament (*Sejm*), which the king was obligated to convene. Its upper house, the Senate, was appointed through nomination to a ministerial post, bishopric, *palatinus* (*wojewoda;* Russ. *voevoda*) or *castelanus* (*kasztelan*). Members of the lower house were elected by the local nobility of the countries (*powiaty*), territories (*ziemie*), and palatinates (*wojewodztwa*). Thus the government had the elements of a mixed constitution, at least in theory. In fact, actual politics more resembled those of an oligarchy, in which four clans—the Radziwiłłs, Chodkiewiczes, Sapiehas, and Pacs—sought to dominate each other and, consequently, the rest of the country. All of them appear in the Diary as major landowners. At the moment Tolstoi visited, Poland was in fact in the middle of a civil war, which resulted in 1700 in breaking the power of the Sapieha family. The Polish commonwealth thereafter was more constitutional in form, but of course Tolstoi knew nothing of this; he tells us inadvertently of the power of the Sapiehas and mentions the other leading clans, including the Lubomirski, Ossolinski, and Oginski. The best recent introduction to the clans and the constitution is Kaminski, "The *Szlachta* of the Polish-Lithuanian Commonwealth," pp. 17–45.

[66] This is the large Church of the Holy Cross (Kosciol Sw. Krzyza), by Giovanni Bellotto, 1682–96. Korb, II, 61, notes that "Not far from the church dedicated to the Holy Cross there is a chapel called the Muscovite Chapel, because it was built by two Czars that were made prisoners in days of yore, and buried there."

[67] At first glance, the phrase, "the Poles say . . . ," might be interpreted as a manifestation of Tolstoi's anti-Polish prejudice, visible above in his suggestion that they cannot meet in parliament without drunken brawls. In fact, throughout the Diary, Tolstoi is quite careful to use second-hand narration—"the Poles say," "they say," "the Italians say"—to report miracles or curious happenings he does not personally witness.

are many large, well-built stone townsmen's homes beneath the royal palace. In one wall below the townsmen's homes are many fine stone market stalls in which all kinds of goods are in abundance. Beneath the markets are great stone cellars where various grape wines are for sale, which the Poles drink often and in quantity, and they buy wine at a considerable price. Many foreigners come to Warsaw from various states.

In Warsaw the homes and all buildings in the castle are of stone, and there are many fine four-story buildings, and all are built with the walls right on the street. The castle is all paved with stone, and there is a tall *ratusz* in the middle; there are no senatorial homes in the castle, as townsmen live there. Beyond the city, close to the Wisła, is a large stone cloister with a fine, large stone church; Dominican monks of the Roman faith live there. At the gate of the castle is a very tall column, hewn of stone, and on it is a portrait of Vladislav (Wladyslaw), who was a king of Poland long ago; it is made of brass and gilded; in his left hand is a cross, and in his right a bared sword. The senatorial homes outside the city are large and of stone, because the upper city is not large, and one could not find room for more than three or four of them there.

For the *elektsiia* (Pol. *elekcja,* election) a bridge on boats was built across the Wisła, and a guard stood on the bridge because there are many arguments among the Poles at election time, and also among the Lithuanians, and there are many fights and murders between Poles and Lithuanians; and many stay on that bridge to argue and to drink; they agree so little among themselves that by their arguing they have lost much of their state. And indeed when these drunks drink, they do not grieve and do not repent even though they are doubled over [from drinking]. And when there is no election in Warsaw, there is no bridge over the Wisła. From this one can understand the reasoning, or rather the drunken stupidity, of the Poles, for on these river ferries many people, cattle, and things useful to man are lost in high winds and turbulence /193/ on the river, and the Poles do not have good ferries for transport. Likewise, it causes great hardships; many people, even in emergencies, cannot cross the river because of strong blowing winds and great waves of water, and necessities cannot be transferred across the river, and so they must endure great hardships. Polish leaders know this, but because they would rather enjoy themselves, they have not built a bridge across the river below Warsaw to help their people. And in my opinion, to love ferries only to meet upon them, and for drunks to fight there with swords, and for no other reason, they lose their souls like flies.[68]

Merchants, rich men and even their wives, sit in their markets with all sorts of

[68] Contemporaries found the river Moskva was not much better bridged. Korb noted, on his departure, that "we reached the banks of the river of Moscow. The crossing was not quite exempt from danger, for the bridge was only in the middle of the stream, and did not reach the bank at either side; so that the ascent and descent were of no little difficulty. But the dangers of such ill-made bridges seems [sic] little or nothing to the Muscovites, though they swallow up no few people that are deceived by the unexpected declivity." Korb, II, 34.

goods, and they do not dishonor themselves in this. Through the town and to their seats, senators ride in coaches with their wives and daughters, and this does not dishonor them.[69] They harness six good and richly attired horses to a coach. Across from the city of Warsaw, over the river Wisła in the suburb called Praga, is a men's cloister in which the Bernardine order lives. In Warsaw, grain products and all food supplies that are for sale are costly, and dear compared to Moscow.

May 2. Today I was again in the Warsaw castle in the great church or cathedral called Thara and heard the Roman Mass, that is, the Liturgy. At that time several priests were saying Mass, all at the same time, on various altars. And as Mass was served at the large principal altar, the organs played, there being organs on each side of the altar over the galleries; but they did not play on the large organ that stands over the western doors, for it is used only on holy days during Mass, that is, the Liturgy.[70]

This day after dinner I went to see senatorial homes and visited the home of the Lithuanian chancellor pan Radziwiłł. He has a large and very well-built home. The ceilings of his chambers are of Italian work in plaster, like carved alabaster; the chambers are numerous and richly adorned. One chamber is done in silken velvet, two rooms in gold brocade, two in golden silken brocade; and there are many furnishings of all sorts in these chambers.

Then I was outside the city in the garden of the great crown marshal, the pan Lubomirski, where I saw a large and very fine building, many waterways, and, on all sides of this garden, good fountains. In the middle of the garden are built excellent palaces /194/, and among them a bath was built, and surrounding this bath were various fountains of marvelous and rich construction, and in the middle of this bath was the most marvelous of fountains. In the bath and in the palaces built around it, the exterior walls were done of plaster of fine workmanship, like carved alabaster. In many places

[69] In Russia, especially among the upper classes, women were still secluded, whether traveling or at home, and Tolstoi is thus surprised that the wives of wealthy merchants should be seen in the shops, and those of the nobles in open carriages. "Behind her came the Tsaritsa's female retinue in 22 wooden carriages that were painted green and covered with red cloth, as was the horses' harness as well. The carriages were tightly shut so that no one inside could be seen, unless by chance the wind raised one of the curtains." Olearius, p. 73.

[70] Tolstoi has previously mentioned the organs in Catholic churches, and below (see the section on Opava) will discuss church singing accompanied by a whole range of instruments. He is preoccupied with the music of Western Christendom, since one of the major components of the reforms that divided the Russian Church in his lifetime was the new music. The Russian Old Believers could not tolerate this profound western influence on the traditional Russian Liturgy; in the words of their leader, Avvakum, "They observe Latin rules and regulations, they wave their hands, shaking their heads and stamping their feet to the accompaniment of the organ as is the custom among the Latins." See Florovsky, *Ways of Russian Theology*, pp. 104–105 and passim.

the interior walls are decorated with shells and great mirrors placed on those walls, and with other excellently made things, the likes of which are impossible to describe. These palaces have fine stores, a *kofeiniia* of the most glorious plaster work; the furnishings in these palaces around the bath are very fine, with excellent tables, fine armchairs, patterned pictures, and many other sorts of decorations.[71]

May 3. I left Warsaw for the royal lodge of the deceased king Jan Sobieski, 5 versts from Warsaw.[72] His home there is large, built all of stone, with large rooms, and the external walls are all of fine carved stone. There are very many rooms and many passages to the great garden that is built just outside these rooms. These rooms are low, but above them are many more rooms, the walls of which are set with valuable colored panels of fine workmanship. All these rooms have stoves, some of alabaster stone and some fine carved plaster ones of Italian work. Likewise, the ceilings in these rooms are done in carved alabaster and plaster; and in these rooms are many fine pictures, done by marvelous Italian painters. Two rooms have fine slate floors, done in various marbles or in patterned slate; and I was allowed in these rooms only because the king of the Poles had died, and no king was staying there. Behind these rooms is a promenade, that is, a fine wide square that is hung with really fine paintings. Beyond these rooms is a large garden of fine proportions through which many fine clean streams pass, and there are marvelous fountains of various kinds in many places, /195/ and for watering flowers, water stands in large, cast-brass containers of quite fine workmanship. The garden has all kinds of fruit trees, and many shrubs and flowers of all sorts. In the garden there are pomegranate trees and fig trees; these trees are placed in boxes and are set in the earth close to the walls, and over them a roof is built so that in winter these trees are covered and warmed in their winter spot by a stove, and in summer, on warm days, they are taken out and placed where needed. The garden has two fine ponds in which are many fish. Close to the ponds are two marvelous round shelters; the little walls of these shelters are made of cut glass; in and around the little windows are frames of many colored stones, and these shelters are very well built, rich and quite fine, and the whole garden is immeasurably fine. In this home of the deceased king are eight coaches and two carriages of marvelous, rich French work, and on both coaches and carriages are special tandem harnesses of great richness. And while King Jan Sobieski still lived, they said, he loved to live in this home, and built it on this place that he purchased, which now passes to his wife and children.

[71] "We strolled to amuse ourselves to the Lubomirski garden, the bath of which is much praised for its beauty and art. The hermitage there is so artistically constructed that I must not pass it over in silence." Korb, II, 60. Tolstoi above introduces a neologism, *kofeiniia,* from the Polish *kawiarnia,* a coffee shop.

[72] This is the Italian villa built by Sobieski, 1678–94, from plans by G. Belotto, in Willanow (Villa Nuova).

May 4. I was visited by the Muscovite resident, the clerk Aleksei Nikitin, and he brought me a travel certificate from the primate; and he said to me that I should visit the papal nuncio, who is sent here by the Roman pope from Rome and who lives in Warsaw to direct spiritual matters; I was to get from him a certificate of permission to travel and to stay in Italian regions. With these words from Aleksei, I went to this papal nuncio at his court, where a Roman priest met me and, inquiring about my nationality and rank, immediately told the nuncio about me, and he received me very warmly. His palace is handsomely decorated;[73] the first living room from the passage is all in red cloth, and the entrance way has fine wallpaper. The other room is of crimson velvet, with golden lace sewn on the velvet, and sewn on this velvet is a band with golden heads on a field of crimson. Across from the door on the front wall is a platform; on this platform is placed the nuncio's chair, covered in crimson velvet; over his chair is placed a canopy, also done in crimson velvet. In this room are many other chairs also covered with crimson velvet with gold galloons and fringes. In this room the nuncio himself met me, /196/ wearing black dress, as is the custom of Roman clerics; on top of his dress a large golden chain hangs around his neck, and on it is a diamond cross, on which there are many large diamonds; and the outer garb is black, silken velvet; and he spoke to me in Italian through a translator, and he promised to send to my house immediately a travel certificate for Italy, for which I thanked him. I left him, and he himself led me to the passage and dismissed me from his porch, and all those with him were clerics, and no secular persons were with him. The house in which he lives is not large, and the rooms are not vast. This same day the nuncio sent to my house the travel document I had requested of him.

This same day I left Warsaw, having lived there five days; I crossed the Wisła on a bridge that was built on boats for the election, and I went to the court of the resident of Moscow, the clerk Aleksei Nikitin, and from there I went half a verst from Warsaw to see the place the Poles had prepared for the election.[74] They built a rampart in a field, and around [the rampart] a ditch was dug. There were four entrances to the rampart, and here ambassadors came from the districts and authorities came from Hungary, and the whole embassy was at the rampart. On one side of the rampart a large counting shed was built, which the Poles call a *shopa,* very much like a cattle barn. In truth, in all affairs the Poles resemble cattle, in that they can perform none of their state matters without fighting and arguing; therefore, in all matters they want to repair to a field, so they can endlessly fight and perish in that barn without reflection. They made many benches there on which the senators sit; on the first one sits the *primas* (Pol. *prymas,* primate), the archbishop of Gniezno, and next sit the

[73] This is the palace of the prince-primate in the Senatorska. Korb, II, 59, identifies "the most illustrious lord, Monsignor Avia, the Nuncio Apostolic."

[74] This is the election plain (Pole elekcyi Krolow), the infamous scene of the bloody elections in the sixteenth through eighteenth centuries. Below he describes the meeting tent, the *shopa* (Pol. *szopa,* shed or barn).

bishops in order of rank, military governors, and other senators, and across from the archbishop sits the grand marshal of His Majesty's nobles, who determines the votes with decorum, insofar as all are not drunk.[75] Having seen this place I departed on my assigned journey and stayed in a field one mile from Warsaw.

May 5. Having passed the village of Daramba, I dined in the field 3 Polish miles from the place I had stayed. This night, having passed the seat of the archbishop of Gniezno, I stayed in the hamlet of Mstolovo where I dined, 4 Polish miles from that place. This hamlet has a large stone church. Not far past this place is the large stone home of that archbishop /197/ of Gniezno, very finely built; around the house is a large garden surrounded by a great stream.

May 6. I dined at the seat of pan Siratskii (Siracki) in the hamlet of Narova, 4 miles from Mstolovo; this place is large, and that day it had a market. Here the pan Siracki's home is a large stone building, and there are three large stone Roman churches. This day I stayed at the seat of the archbishop of Gniezno, in the village of Chernitsa (Czernica), 2 miles from Narova. Leaving Narova I met the suite of the Austrian ambassador, who was going to Warsaw for the election. The suite consisted of 6 coaches and many carriages; behind the suite I met the Austrian ambassador himself, who conversed warmly with me. This ambassador is a cleric, a bishop of Vienna; four other men in another coach of six horses followed him, and there were no other leaders with him.

May 7. I dined at the seat of the bishop of Kuiavski (Kujawy) in the hamlet of Volbora (Wolbórz), 4 miles from Chernitsa (Czernica). The bishop's home here is a large stone building. There is a large stone Catholic church, and the hamlet is large. I spent the night in the city of Petrokov (Piotrkow), 2 miles from Wolbórz.[76]

[75] There is reason to believe that Tolstoi was personally abstemious, judging from the anecdotes that tell of Tsar Peter forcing him to indulge. This must be the basis for his harsh comments on the Poles, unless he saw drinking directly affecting the process of selecting a new king. The Russians were, of course, famous for their drinking, and no traveler failed to describe their debauchery. One of the finest collections of such stories is in Olearius, pp. 142–46.

[76] Korb, II, 63, identifies the towns as Velbor and Petrikow. Tolstoi mentions the stone construction of even tiny European villages. Moscow, apart from the Kremlin, was still largely a city of wooden buildings, and the rest of Muscovy was even more so. "The homes in the city (except for the stone residences of the boyars, some of the wealthiest merchants, and the Germans) are built of pine and spruce logs laid one on top of another and crosswise (at the ends). . . . The roofs are shingled and then covered with birch bark or sod. For this reason they often have great fires. Not a month, nor even a week, goes by without some homes—or,

This city is a royal seat and rather large. The royal residence is a large stone building; the town has three stone cloisters and a large stone church called the Thara, and there are many rich townsmen's homes. The elder in the city is the military governor Sendomirski, and his stone house is in the city. The custom of this town is that when a king dies, the town is locked up until a Polish king is chosen. From Warsaw to Piotrkow it is 20 Polish miles, or 100 Muscovite versts, and from Moscow to Piotrkow, 1262½ versts.

[May 8 —missing]

May 9. I passed a royal seat, the hamlet Radomsko, 1 mile from where I stayed. In this hamlet is a large stone church called Thara, that is, a cathedral, and a large stone cloister in which the order of St. Bernard lives; the structure and furnishings of these churches are rich. The town elder is the pan Mechinskii (Mieczynski). I arrived to dine at a mill, built on the river Bart.

May 10. I dined at the Chenstokhovskii (Częstochowa) monastery, 3 miles from my camp; from Warsaw to the Częstochowa monastery it is 32 Polish miles, 160 Muscovite versts, and from Moscow to Częstochowa it is 1324½ versts. Częstochowa is a small royal seat, but many wealthy people live here. There are two stone churches, but no castle. A half-verst away is a stone cloister of the Blessed Mother of God, built on a high stone mountain. In the church of this cloister is placed an image of the Mother of God of the evangelist Luke, a miracle-working icon. Wanting to know for certain about this icon of the Holy Virgin and about the miracles it worked, I referred to a printed history in the Polish language.[77] In this cloister live Romans of the order called the Paulicians or the *Pavliki* hermits, that is, of the order of St. Paul. They wear a white habit, do not cut or trim their beards, but only clip the moustache. Theirs is a hard life. The cloister is large with a marvelous stone church; on the outside are

---

if the wind is strong, whole streets—going up in smoke. Several nights while we were there we saw flames rising in three or four places at once. Shortly before our arrival, a third of the city burned down, and we were told that the same thing happened four years earlier." Olearius, p. 112.

In part the difference between Russian wooden and European stone construction was one of poverty versus wealth, at least in a relative sense. On the other hand, Russia was, in medieval and early-modern times, timber rich compared to Europe, and thus she simply built with the material readily at hand. Europe was always threatened with deforestation, and until the coal revolution of the eighteenth century, economic development, to say nothing of construction, was limited by fuel and timber supplies. See Braudel, *Structures*, pp. 363–67.

[77] Below, at the conclusion of the section on Częstochowa, Tolstoi notes that books about the shrine, as well as copies of the icon, were sold on the spot.

The Mother of God of Częstochowa. (Courtesy of the Black Madonna of Częstochowa Shrine, Eureka, Missouri.)

many fine stone carvings. Around this cloister is a large moat faced with natural white and grey stone; the cloister's fence is also stone. The cloister has one stone gate. At the gate always stands a guard of 20 soldiers with arms. The stone church in this cloister is very large, built by fine Italian masters. The vaults of the church are stone, covered with plaster of marvelous work; many very fine paintings are hung on the interior walls, and painted on these pictures is the life of St. Paul of Thivei, and on the right side of the door of this church is a *kaplitsa,* that is, a chapel of St. Paul of Thebes.[78] In this chapel all the walls are of marble or slate, done as large columns with capitals, as if they were made of finely constructed wood; and in the chapel the platform is all marble. On that same side is another chapel, six steps high; in this chapel all walls are of gilded brass, and beneath this chapel five steps descend. There is the chapel of the Holy Guardian Angel; the possessed are brought to this chapel, and Roman priests exorcise them; during my stay in this chapel a Roman Catholic woman lay there, possessed and tormented by demons, and I saw a monk reading prayers over her. The monks of this cloister say that none leave this chapel uncured.

From this church is a pathway to the left past the porch to the church where the miracle-working image of the Blessed Mother of God painted by the holy evangelist Luke is located. This holy icon is of the same size as the icon /199/ also painted by Luke the Evangelist, which stands in the cathedral in Moscow and which is known as the Vladimir [Mother of God]. This holy icon of Częstochowa is placed in the Catholic church high over the altar, and it is concealed by a silver frame that can be removed from above, and a well-wrought image of the Descent of St. Luke adorns this silver case. This holy icon of the inclined head is painted on a walnut panel, and around it is much silver.[79] It is wondrously done; on it is a cover of silken velvet, on which is sewn much regalia, that is, ornaments of diamonds, rubies, and emeralds, of golden chains, and of large pearls around that holy icon, of many great panels of gold and silver, on which various images are impressed and carved. Under this holy icon lie two maces with stones which were placed here by some Polish hetmans. In this church and on the walls around this holy icon are many decorated swords with gold mountings and with stones. In front of this holy image on both sides are placed six large silver candlesticks, and also five large cast-silver lamps in which lamp oil burns continuously. In this church all the walls are covered with Persian brocades; the vaults are done of plaster of fine craftsmanship and all are gilded. They uncover this icon during singing and when people come to pray.

In this and other large churches they place large fine organs. Beneath this church is a large room in which church vessels and icon covers and all churchly things are kept. In the front of this room is a Roman altar on which they say the Mass, that is,

[78] *Thivei,* Greek, Thebes; above, *kaplitsa,* Polish, *kaplica,* chapel; Tolstoi adopts and uses this Polish term throughout the Diary.

[79] This is the famous Black Madonna (Regina Regni Poloniae), in the monastery since 1382. The church had suffered a major fire in 1690. The icon type is Hodigitria, with the Child in his Mother's arms.

the Liturgy. Beneath the walls in this room are large boxes and tables of fine joiners' work, and they are engraved and gilded quite finely, and in these boxes and on the tables are a multitude of chasubles for the priests, done in golden brocade and strung with pearls and stones and with fine ornaments. On these tables are large silver censers and large silver candleholders and vessels of gold and with stones—of these a great many. There are a multitude of large gold and silver crosses with stones and with fine ornaments. In this room is a vessel or a Eucharist-holder [monstrance] in which the Romans place the sacred Host. This vessel is large, all of gold, with stones, diamonds, rubies, and with emeralds and fine ornaments, in height more than an arshin of the most marvelous carved work, in which there are many fine stones: diamonds, rubies, emeralds, and among these stones at /200/ the top is placed one very large diamond of a size one rarely finds in the whole world. Around this vessel are many marvelous seed pearls, and this vessel is most precious.

In this cloister is a fine pharmacy in which I saw all sorts of medicines, and this pharmacy was well furnished. There are 70 members of the order who live communally and eat daily in the refectory; the dining hall is large and really fine, without vaults, but with a flat carved ceiling of marvelous workmanship; there are fine tables and chairs, as well as tablecloths and hand towels; there are many vessels of pewter and brass, and spoons and knife handles and forks of silver. And here the foodstuffs, the clothing, and all the needed housewares are really fine. In this cloister every monk has his own cell, and they seldom go about together. The stone cells are built in a row and are marvelous but small; there are fine wide stone passages between the cells. In this cloister is an academy where the higher sciences are studied, even to philosophy.[80] And they hold disputations in a long special large hall, upstairs next to the church, which holds the miracle-working icon of the Mother of God. This hall has a great window, and the hall is well furnished. This cloister was built in ancient times, being here some 360 years, since its founding, and it has 200 households subject to it. In its church are great riches, given by the parishioners, multitudes of whom come always to this cloister from all directions, and many people come here from distant Christian regions.

From this Częstochowa cloister it is not far, less than half a verst, to another small stone cloister, which is called *novitsianskii* (Pol. *nowicjat,* novitiate), and anyone who wishes to enter the order of the Częstochowa monastery must first live in this novitiate monastery for a year or two, and then they are accepted into the great cloister. During my stay 20 newly consecrated monks were in the novitiate. Close to the great cloister is a large settlement, with large shops and many stores. The whole

[80] This phrase, "even to philosophy," occurs several times in the Diary. It is a reflection of the vertical curriculum of all colleges and academies of the day, when students, from Harvard College to Kiev, passed through a rigid sequence of studies. Typically they began with three forms of grammar (Latin, of course) and two of humanities (rhetoric and poetics), before proceeding to philosophy. In a full university, students would study "to theology and the other higher sciences (meaning medicine and law)." See Okenfuss, "Jesuit Origins."

settlement and its rows of shops are all of wood, and there are many goods in the shops, including many printed books in Latin and Polish; in these shops are sold images of the Mother of God, called the icon of Częstochowa, done on copper and canvas and on wood in various sizes, to anyone in the shape they want, square or round.[81] /201/

May 11. After dinner I left the settlement at the monastery of Częstochowa, which Poles call Iasnaia Gora (Jasna Gora), and went to the novitiate; the stone church here is dedicated to the blessed martyr Barbara. This is a fine stone building, well decorated by fine carpenters' work in coastal walnut woods and boxwood. Beside this church is a chapel named for St. Nicholas of Mirliki [Myra] the Wonder Worker, where I saw many holy relics and other holy things in shrines.[82] I left this cloister and spent the night at the mill of a priest, Lechowski, 2 miles from the great monastery of Częstochowa.

May 12. I arrived at the border of the Empire;[83] at this spot between the imperial state and the Polish kingdom the border is a marsh, and it is unmarked. Beyond the marsh on the Austrian side is the village of Kamenits (Kamieniec Polski), 3 miles from the border. From Warsaw to the border it is 35 Polish miles, 105 Muscovite versts, and from Moscow to the border 1367½ versts. And crossing the imperial border this day I traveled the land of Silesia; here the great city is called Breslavl (Breslau), which I passed by some 20 miles, and I dined at an iron works in the village of Kuźnica, which was 3 miles from the camp where I stayed. This vil-

[81] This concludes the lengthy and awe-struck account of the monastery at Częstochowa. "Dinner in Zaporowa, supper in the city of Jschestokow. The monastery here is enclosed with a very strong wall, and is always garrisoned with Polish troops. Monks of the order of St. Paul inhabit it. Their provincial, a man advanced in years, received the Lord Envoy with extreme politeness, and, introducing him to the richly-provided pharmacy of the monastery, presented him with Hungarian wine. . . . Out of particular devotion to the Mother of God we performed our devotions here; for there is a miraculous image of the Most Blessed Virgin venerated here, which still retains scars and marks upon the face which were made by a peasant with a whip, and is renowned for numbers of miracles. It was given by Ladislaus, Duke of Oppeln. Afterwards we inspected the treasury of the church, which is exceedingly rich in relics. There is a veil (*velum*) of St. Philip Neri; a miraculous cross that belonged to St. Charles Borromeo, which is very efficacious in cases of obsession. In our presence an obseded [*sic*] woman bellowed horribly during mass." Korb, II, 63–64.

[82] Throughout the Diary Tolstoi points out all shrines to St. Nicholas, his own personal saint and that of many Russians. "Today the Muscovites celebrate the festival of Saint Nicholas, whom they revere as the head of all the Saints." Korb, I, 109.

[83] As Tolstoi enters the Empire, we give preference to Czech or German spellings of proper names. Thus the first imperial city would otherwise be given as Wrocław.

lage of Kuźnica belongs to a Silesian townsman who lives in Breslau and is named Shpiler. This iron factory is of medium size, having 2 furnaces and much iron ore. This day I stayed at an imperial city called Ternovyia Gory [Ternowskie Gory], 2 miles from the iron works.[84] In this place are no Polish forts, nor ramparts, nor walls around the settlements, but only a small ditch. This place is not large, but the many inhabitants are wealthy. Around this place are townsmen's fine stone homes, and shops in which there are many goods. There are one large and 2 small stone churches. There are no nobles' homes here; only townspeople live here. In this town I hired a wagon to the town of Opava. I sent my horses, on which my slave and I had ridden to Ternowskie Gory, back to Moscow;[85] from Warsaw to Ternowskie Gory it is 39 Polish miles, 145 Muscovite versts, and from Moscow to Ternowskie Gory it is 1412½ versts.

May 15. I arrived to dine in the city of Ratsybur (Racibórz),[86] 4 miles from the hamlet of Ruda and 10 imperial miles from Ternowskie Gory, or 50 Muscovite versts.[87] The city of Racibórz is of stone, and its homes /202/ are stone. Racibórz is much larger than Ternowskie Gory. There are many wares of all kinds here. Its fortress, or upper city, is of stone; in it lives His Imperial Majesty's count. His home is a large stone one, as is the church in the fortress. Surrounding the count's home is a large garden, and through the fortress and around the houses are many flowing streams from the river called Odra, which flows below the city of Racibórz, which I crossed by bridge. In the middle of the town are two fine fountains, the waters pouring into great vats; all the needs of the homes are supplied from these vats. In this town are many finely built townsmen's homes.

This day I stayed in the city of Opava, 4 miles from Racibórz, 74 imperial miles from Ternowskie Gory, or 75 Muscovite versts,and 18 imperial miles from the border; and from Moscow to Opava it is 1472½ versts. Opava is a great stone city, and many streams flow through the city, which is finely built of stone, with large churches, fine homes, too, and palaces four stories high—homes of fine architecture, many of them finely painted with figures. At the large church in Opava is a stone column, and on it an image of the Blessed Mother of God, life-size, and quite finely done. On the bottom of this column are four images of angels, well carved out of huge stones. Close by is a round fountain and water from it flows in four places; above the fountain is a beast, and on it a fine carved image of the Savior. Opava is an imperial city

[84] The area had been, since the thirteenth century, a mining center and the economic heart of Upper Silesia.

[85] Having dismissed part of his entourage in Smolensk, Tolstoi now sends home the remainder, as well as his own horses.

[86] This is a ninth-century town, incorporated in 1299, and an important center of trade and handicrafts.

[87] Tolstoi here introduces the third measure of distance, the imperial mile, which he counts as five versts, the same as the Polish.

in the Silesian land; it is ruled by an imperial count, a *litenant*[88] or privy secretary of the Imperial Council. From this city the emperor collects 100 efimki annually from each merchant house, and the count, who rules this city, collects 6 efimki from each annually. This city of Opava is very large and populous. In this city of Opava, as in Racibórz, four imperial soldiers were stationed with me during my stay. In this city of Opava are many rows of stone shops and a sufficiency of all wares, and they are not too expensive.

May 16, that is, in the seventh week of Easter, according to the Roman calendar, they celebrated the feast of the Holy Trinity. This day I stayed at the abovementioned city /203/ of Opava because this day they had a great festival, and wagons did not travel on this day and could not for fear [of sinning]. This day I was at the church in the Jesuit cloister, where they said Mass at the great altar. This is a large stone church, finely carved, but the wealth inside the church is not great.[89] The Mass was said by a Roman priest with six servers, and during Mass they played music on the organs and violins in the choir loft, and on other instruments, on trumpets, on kettledrums and on drums. Green boughs cut from various trees and shrubs, and many flowers were placed in large pots on both sides of the altar in this church; and they do not read the prayers of genuflection in the Roman church on Pentecost. On this day in this church many Catholics received the body of Christ, some at the beginning of the service, some at the end; the one priest who served the Mass gave the Eucharist to the laity; then after the Mass was ended and the Eucharist had been given to all the participants, a Jesuit preacher appeared, standing on the pulpit, but this was not the priest who said Mass; this Jesuit preacher presented to them the words of John the Theologian, written in the Holy Gospel, "For I go not away, the Comforter will not come unto you,"[90] and this sermon was conducted to prepare the hearts of men to receive the Holy Spirit, and he spoke so well that all listening to him were touched in their hearts, and quite a few cried.

In this town is one great marketplace, all made of stone, with large, well-constructed buildings, and here there are 3 fine fountains, and there is a large stone Roman church, which is called Thara, that is, a cathedral, and close by on a church porch are balusters, and behind them is placed commandingly, as if on a hill, an image of the Savior, carved of wood and like the Lord Jesus praying to God the Father, before his Passion, and saying, "Father, if it be possible, let this cup pass from me."[91] In front of this image of the Savior is a carved wooden image with a chalice and the cross. Here are the images of the holy apostles—Peter, James, and John—sleeping, and also carved of wood. The city of Opava is much larger than the Polish capital of Warsaw, and is much better built.

[88] *Litenant*, Ger. *Leutnant*, lieutenant.

[89] This is the Provost Church of the Virgin Mary (Chram Panny Marie), fourteenth century.

[90] John 16:7.

[91] Matthew 26:39.

This day I was at vespers, that is, at evening prayer, in the church I have mentioned, in which I was at the Liturgy. Once again there was a sermon, and a different Jesuit was on the pulpit, /204/ and not the one who had preached after the Mass; this sermon pertained to the Acts of the Apostles: "The Holy Spirit came in tongues of flame, and the Apostles began to speak in foreign tongues."[92] During vespers in this church, they played music in the choirlofts, as they had during the Mass. As I was coming from Racibórz to Opava the great Hungarian mountains were three miles away on the left side; they were as high as the clouds.

May 17. In the morning I left Opava, having hired a wagon, and I dined at the Moravian border, 3 miles from Opava, and the Moravice river divides Moravia from Silesia, and Moravia is an imperial possession. And I stayed at an inn in the village of Gortura, and left to go into Moravia, and went as far as the city of Ul'munts [Olomouc] by high stone mountains, and the road wás all of stone. Both Silesia and Moravia appear better in terms of grains than Poland. From the Polish border to Moravia it is 21 imperial miles.

This day I arrived to stay in the village of Boron (Beroun), 2 miles from Gortura. A mile from this village Beroun I passed a little town, which is called Dvorets (Dvorce); the town is built of stone, and it is 4 miles from Opava.

May 18. I arrived to dine in the city of Olomouc, 3 miles from Beroun, 8 imperial miles from Opava, or 40 Muscovite versts, and from Moscow to Olomouc it is 1512½ versts. One imperial mile on this side of Olomouc is a cloister on a high mountain.[93] Here live the Catholic order called the Carmelites. In this monastery is a large stone church, and in the church from the altar-platform upwards all the walls and vaults are done in fine Italian plaster work. In this church on one altar rest the relics of the martyr Victor, brought from Rome. I was at this monastery during the Liturgy.

[92] This is a paraphrase of Acts 2:3–4.
[93] This is possibly Svatý Kopeček.

II

May 18, 1697–September 18, 1697

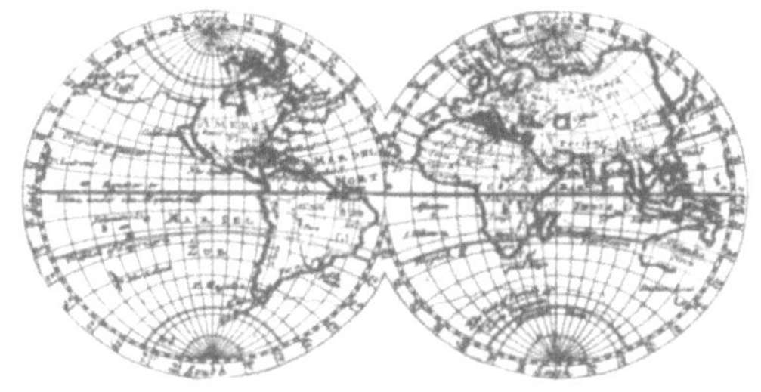

The Empire · Vienna
The Alps · Venice · Padua

/321/ The city of Ul'munts (Olomouc, Ger. Olmütz) is large and finely fortified with stone, and around it rather large waters pass in ditches.[1] The city is built with two thick stone walls. In this city is a castle, that is, an upper city, of fine stone. There are many fine Western monasteries and churches of stone construction. The homes of the inhabitants of this city are large fine stone buildings; they have many high rooms, four stories in height. In the large city on a square is the *ratusha* (Ger. *Rathaus*), that is, the large stone customs building; on the gates of this Rathaus is built a large marvelous clock;[2] this clock strikes the passing of the hours with a musical harmony, and when this clock begins to beat the hour people carved out of wood appear and beat on the bell with their hands. Below them are two men carved of wood, and they blow on trumpets at the same time. And from one side of this clock people who are also carved of wood walk out, and from the other side of this

[1]Olomouc had in the Thirty Years War given way to Brno as the regional capital of Moravia, but it was still an impressive city.

[2]Tolstoi refers to the fifteenth-century town hall, which has an impressive tower adorned with Anton Pohl's astronomical clock, destroyed in the fighting of May 1945 and rebuilt.

Tolstoi's fascination here and elsewhere with mechanical clocks is understandable; I know of none of the type in seventeenth-century Muscovy, and none later, either. Although Muscovy had already entered the period of the Naryshkin Baroque in the 1680s and Renaissance bell towers and churches were already built or under construction (the new buildings in Moscow's Novodevichii monastery are a case in point), the intricate and often fanciful clock tower was not part of that phase of Westernization. See the excellent work by Hughes, "The 17th-Century 'Renaissance' in Russia," pp. 41–45, and "Western European Graphic Material," pp. 433–43. See also Gimpel, *The Medieval Machine*, pp. 147–70, who points out that where the Roman church eagerly accepted the clock of the merchants who knew "time is money," the Greek Orthodox church could not accept the new technology: "Until the twentieth century Orthodox priests never allowed a mechanical clock to be installed in an Orthodox church."

clock they ride out on horses, also carved of wood, so that the walkers appear from behind a wall. All of these people are of fine craftsmanship. In the castle of this city the great stone home of the bishop is of fine architecture.[3] While I was in Olomouc the bishop was not there, because not long before my arrival in Olomouc he had died. Around this city are many fine gardens, in which there are many fine passing [streams of] water.

In this city the large Jesuit monastery is a fine stone building; in this monastery is an academy of the fine higher sciences, with very many students who study the various sciences; many of these students are honorable, of the upper sort of people chosen by the states to study in this academy. Students study as far as philosophy and also up to theology and the mathematical sciences. In this /322/ monastery is a rich church, and I was in this church at the time of vespers; they played in this church on a fine organ and on many other instruments. This city has a marvelous fortress of rough stone built at the foot of a hill. Beyond the city of Olomouc is a great stone monastery, in which Roman monks who call themselves Kamenduly (Cápuchins?) live; people do not see them, and they stay in the church and live in silence.[4] This same day I left the city of Olomouc and arrived to spend the night in the hamlet of Gralets (Kralitz), two miles from Olomouc. Along this road from Olomouc are many large homes finely built of stone.

May 19. I passed the little stone city of Vyshkov (Vyškov/Wishau), I dined in a tavern.

[3] Tolstoi begins to expand his language of appreciation: *arkhitekturoiu*, literally "according to architecture"; examples of buildings to which he applies the term suggest that Tolstoi's own definition of the word would be "according to any consistent principle of architectural style."

Although Tolstoi will later acquire many Italian-based terms for architectural and artistic features, Polish remains the basis for many of his neologisms:

arkhitektura, Polish, *architektura*
proportsiia, Polish, *proporcja*
pliats, Polish, *plac*, It. *piazza*, Ger. *Platz*
kartina, Polish, *kartina*, It. *cortina*
kunsht, Polish, *kunszt*, Ger. *Kunst*

The general conclusion, of course, is that Tolstoi fully participated in that internationalization of the Russian language that is the hallmark of the late seventeenth and early eighteenth centuries.

[4] This identification is uncertain, but the allusion to austerity suggests the Capucians, the Franciscan order founded by Matteo di Bassi in the 1520s. It could also be a Trappist order, since that branch of the Cistercians, dedicated to perpetual silence, had been founded in 1664 at La Trappe in Normandy.

May 20. I arrived to dine in the hamlet of Birints (Brno), three miles from the tavern. Along both sides of this road are the fields, and along the road grow many grapes and Voloskii nuts[5] and black plums and other fruit trees of various sorts. This same day I arrived to spend the night in the city of Nikol'shpurk (Nikolsburg/Mikulov), one mile from Brno, and from Olomouc to Nikolsburg it is ten imperial miles, and 45 Muscovite versts, and from Moscow to Nikolsburg it is 1,607 and a half versts.[6] The city of Nikolsburg belongs to the imperial state, and three stone fortresses are in it. The upper city is on a high hill, and it contains a large stone building and a stone Jesuit monastery. In the court in the upper city is a large stone building with the imperial coat of arms, and in it they store Hungarian wine; in its cellar is one immeasurably large barrel, which holds 800 pails[7] of wine; another barrel in this same cellar is only a little smaller and it too contains 800 pails. There are iron hoops on these barrels, and the barrels are hung up on thick iron chains, so that they do not rot from below on the platform. When they pour a liquid into these barrels, they climb above them by a stairway, which is built over them of good materials. They treated me to some Rhenish wine from these barrels. In this same cellar are very many other large barrels.

Also in this upper city is a large and very fine garden. In this same city are two fine fountains, and in the lower city [are] three fountains. In this city are many well-built large stone homes, and even the simple homes are all of stone, and there are no wooden buildings in this city. There are many wares of all kinds in this city. There are many Jewish homes in Nikolsburg and in them many Hebrew inhabitants. In this city and around it in the fields and along the roads grow very many grapes, and from these grapes the inhabitants of Nikolsburg /323/ make their own wine. On the side of this city is a very high stone mountain, on which I walked, and I saw on it, in grottos, the images of the Passion of Jesus Christ carved of wood of fine work; all of these images are made life-size. At first they made Christ in prayer, the image of the Lord Jesus during His passion when he prayed, saying, "Father, if it be possible, let this cup pass from me."[8] A little higher up this mountain, they have made three images of the apostles Peter, James, and John as if they were sleeping; then a little

[5] *Voloskii*, presumably from Polish *Wołoski*, Walachian (modern Russian *Valakhskii*). I have rendered it as Walachian elsewhere in the Diary, although in modern usage "Romanian" could be used. There is an alternate reading, but it is not as satisfactory: *orzech włoski* in Polish is a walnut, literally "an Italian nut"; but the Russians refer to the walnut as the *gretskii orekh*, the Greek nut. Below, Tolstoi uses *voloskii* to refer to carriages and to wines, and if he meant "Italian," he would say so.

[6] Tolstoi skirted east of Brno, passing by Slavkov (Austerlitz), a site of considerable interest to one of his famous descendants, Leo Tolstoi.

[7] *Vedro*, a bucket or pail; twenty-one pints. See the page on weights and measures at the front of the book.

[8] Matthew 26:39. The site is the Station of the Holy Rood, above the town, with its chapel built in 1630.

higher is made the image of Christ sitting in the dungeon; a little higher up is an image of the Lord Christ dressed in a crimson robe; then a little higher up is the image of the Lord Jesus in a crown of thorns with a reed in His right hand; then still higher is the image of Christ carrying His cross; higher, in a field on this same mountain, is built a *kaplica,* that is, a small church, named for Mary Magdalene. Then on the very top of this mountain is placed a carved image of the Crucifixion of Christ; on this same mountain is a cave, and the covering stone is made to look like the tomb of Christ. Then on this same mountain is made the image of the Resurrection of Christ, and this whole structure is of fine carved work in wood, and it is painted with artist's colors. At the place where they have made the cave and the cornerstone is an image of the tomb of the Lord; there is a garden, which is fitting because the tomb of the Lord was in a garden, and set in this place are fine fruit trees of various kinds.

On this same mountain is built a stone church named for St. Sebastian; within this church stands his carved image, just like when he was martyred for Christ: his bound body has been shot through with arrows, as have his arms, legs, and stomach; and this holy image of him is made of very fine workmanship. In this same church, on the altar behind glass, is placed a carved image of the martyr Sebastian in dress, also done of marvelous workmanship, and a little way down from the top of this mountain stands a dried-up tree, on which among the twigs stands a rather small icon of carved workmanship of the great martyr Catherine, and the size of the case of the icon is octavo. The inhabitants say of this icon that they do not know from whence it came and by whom it was brought. Many times the Jesuits have attempted to bring that image into the church, but by the unseen hand of God the image was again carried back to that tree, and it always returns to the same twig.

May 21. I left the city of Nikolsburg, and crossed the border of the Moravian and Rakotskii (Rakoczi)[9] lands, on which stands a stone castle called Droznagof (Drasenhofen). In this castle is a large stone home /324/. This castle is the estate of a free baron, and in this place is the little river Drozna, a Pol. mile from Nikolsburg, and I arrived to dine in the hamlet of Bolkershtof (Wulfersdorf). In this place the buildings are all of stone; from Wulfersdorf to Nikolsburg it is 3 miles. And in this place the Passion of Christ is built in front of the settlement. The first, as in Nikolsburg on the mountain, shows the praying Lord and His sleeping disciples; the second—the Lord Jesus bound and bared and beaten, and His hair pulled; the third—the placing of the crown of thorns on the head of the Lord; the fourth—the

[9] Strictly speaking, this is the border between Moravia and the province of Lower Austria (Niederösterreich). Tolstoi's name is that of the Hungarian noble family, the Rakoczi, which in the seventeenth century (under George II Rakoczi, 1648–60) and eighteenth century (under Francis II Rakoczi) had led and would lead the Hungarian liberation movement that was centered in the Transylvania they ruled.

Lord carries His cross to the mount and is struck with stones; the fifth—they crucify the Lord on the mount, and beneath the cross is depicted the removal from the cross, and on her knees is His Most Pure Mother; sixth—the placing in the tomb, and on top is placed the stone, and on the stone is carved the image of the Savior in a crown of thorns with a chain around his neck. This same day I left the hamlet of Wulfersdorf and arrived to spend the night in the village of Votkershter (Wolkersdorff), 3 miles from Wulfersdorf.

May 22. I arrived to dine in the imperial capital, in the city of Vienna, 3 miles from Wolkersdorff, and from Warsaw to Vienna it is 79 imperial miles, which in Polish miles are very great, but in Muscovite [measure] they count 395 versts, though it is more; and from Moscow they count in all 1702 and a half versts to Vienna, to which by my reckoning I add another 300 versts or more, and in all the total is more than 2,000 versts. Vienna is a large stone city, the buildings in it are large, of stone, old, rich, and tall, five stories in height; there are palaces and no wooden structures. The city of Vienna is very populous; there are many rows of shops and stores in it, and many fine wares of all kinds. The Viennese inhabitants ride in coaches, and their coaches are fine and rich, and also a great many drivers' coaches stand along the streets, and the coach horses are fine. In this city are many western monasteries and churches of stone, built of fine craftsmanship, and there is not a single monastery or church of the Greek faith in it. There is much bread and all kinds of supplies, and meat and fish, and all kinds of poultry, but the price of everything is expensive, and dearer than in Moscow. This city of Vienna is the imperial capital, and in this city the great imperial home is a fine stone building of great age.[10] At the time I arrived in Vienna the emperor was not there, but he was at his estate, 4 imperial miles from Vienna, with all of his household. Of children the emperor has three sons: the elder son is Joseph, who is king of Hungary; the other son is Karol, who is prince of Ustria (Austria), and the third is but a boy, and there are three daughters.[11] /325/

In Vienna is a great and very tall stone cathedral, built in the name of the archdeacon Stephen, done of ancient fine workmanship with many carvings. Formerly at this church stood the tomb of a Turkish sultan, but now this tomb has been thrown

[10] This is the Hofburg; portions of the old Imperial Palace date to Gothic times.

[11] The reigning emperor was Leopold I (b. 1650, reigned 1658–1705), second male child of Ferdinand III and his first wife, Marianne, daughter of Philip III of Spain. Leopold, like his father, was married three times, in 1697 to the third, Magdalen Theresa (1655–1720), daughter of Philip William, first Elector Palatine of the branch of Neuburgh. Leopold sired ten children, of whom, as Tolstoi notes, five survived: Joseph I (b. 1678, reigned 1705–11; king of Hungary, 1687; king of Romans, 1690); Charles VI (b. 1685, reigned 1711–40; king of Austria, king of Spain, 1703); and Mary Elizabeth (1680–1741), governess of the Netherlands; Mary Anne (1683–1754), wife of John of Portugal; and Mary Magdalene (1689–1743). The third son mentioned by Tolstoi, the one who was "but a boy," would die in childhood.

down from the church, and a cross has been placed in that spot.[12] Beneath this city of Vienna flows the river Danube in five streams, but the very middle of this river flows immeasurably quickly. Across this river Danube and across all the streams are wooden bridges on high wooden columns. On this river Danube are many mills and they are fastened to the shore with iron chains; in these mills they grind all grains, and there are many grist stones. And when the water in the river Danube rises, these mills and grinders are attached by those chains to the shore, and when the water falls they are released from the shore farther into the water.[13] Of the five streams of the river Danube, two are beneath the walls of the city of Vienna. Close to the river the imperial zoo is built, and in this zoo are many beasts of all kinds. On the bank of the river Danube, just before Vienna, is a great stone imperial residence; around this imperial residence are built many country houses of the German senators, great stone buildings with many fine gardens, and they are very large and with rich decorations; around the gardens are fine stone fences, and in the gardens are fine palaces of marvelous construction carved of white stone. In Vienna I stayed beyond the river

[12] I did not locate the origins of this story. On the east end of the cathedral stand very old stone figures, one of them a Crucifix on a pedestal known among Viennese as "Christ with a toothache," and this may be Tolstoi's cross.

[13] Tolstoi's comments on water wheels do not reveal whether or not they were completely new to him. In fact, he had already lived through the first phase of Russia's hydraulic revolution.

References to mills in Russian sources date to Mongol times, but only in the sixteenth century is there reliable evidence for mill construction in Muscovy. A Pskovian attempted to build a dam and mill on the Volkhov River at Novgorod for Archbishop Makarii, but it was destroyed by the spring flood. Only after the acquisition of the Ukraine in the middle of the seventeenth century did mill construction achieve major proportions; the non-Russian Ukraine, previously part of the Polish-Lithuanian state, was apparently much more advanced, with a full network of mills on the tributaries of the Dnepr, and at least one floating mill at Kiev by 1684. Beginning in the 1650s the patriarchate built paper mills, and the Dutch, Vinius, Marselis, and others developed Russia's metallurgical industries, based on the technology of water mills.

See Danilevskii, *History of Hydroengineering in Russia,* pp. 5–20.

These seventeenth-century accomplishments in Russia, however, were modest when compared to even the most backward parts of Europe since the thirteenth century. The floating mill that Tolstoi describes here was ingeniously crafted to exploit the most rapid flow of the river while permitting navigation, and it had been perfected at Toulouse and then spread across Europe. Most mills, as Tolstoi suggests, were for grinding grain, but all premodern Europe reverberated with their sounds, hammering hemp, fulling cloth, making paper, tanning leather, and operating saws, hammers, beaters, and bellows for industries as well. Modern hydroelectric power had its origins in these same mills, many of which operated into the twentieth century. So widespread were they that modern historians are inclined to view them as evidence of a unique Western attitude toward technology and the exploitation of nature, an attitude lacking in Russia and most of the non-European world in medieval and early-modern times. See Gimpel, *Medieval Machine,* p. 128, and Braudel, *Structures,* I, 353–62.

Danube in a suburb, close to the city walls in a guest court under the arms of the Golden Ram, close to Vienna.[14] The city is well fortified with three walls.

May 23. I was in Vienna in the cathedral of archdeacon Stephen at the time of Mass. The Mass at that time was conducted by an *apat* (Ger. *Abt*, abbot), that is, Father Superior, and with him were 4 deacons. During the Mass, music was finely played on various instruments, and with the played music they also sang very well and in harmony, and there were 74 musicians and singers. These musicians and singers did not stand in the choir-loft. Down below in this church, on a high pillar, is a large place, just like a store-room, with windows on all sides; around the windows are many fine gilded carvings. The emperor stands here when he hears Mass in this place. Also in this church, close to the altar, is a place upholstered in golden velvet, and in this place they set a fine armchair, and over this chair and over the whole place is a fine canopy, that is, this is an archbishop's place, and the archbishop stands on this spot. This church of St. Stephen is very long and quite wide; in this church are many /326/ carvings of white stone of fine old work, and also there are many decorations of fine marble. At the chief altar in this church stand four silver arks, and parts of the relics are those of the archdeacon St. Stephen; these silver arks are made of marvelous minted work.[15]

Then I was at the imperial residence. This home is very large and four-cornered, and built all of stone. It has many rooms and is very high—six stories in height is this imperial residence. Along its sides are 14 lamps, and candles burn in them all night; likewise, in Vienna all the inhabitants' homes have lamps on the street, in which oil burns all night, and these lamps in Vienna give a great light all night in the streets and lanes. The imperial residence is built right at the city wall, and when the Turks were beneath Vienna they stood so close to this imperial residence that it was possible to fire at them with an arquebus, and up to half of the imperial chambers were smashed from Turkish cannon fire; and in the places where these cursed Busurmans did their undermining, the city walls and all stone buildings for some 300 sazhens in length were torn apart, but now all of these destroyed and torn-up places are rebuilt. Around this imperial residence is another great imperial stone building for horses, built in the ancient fashion. In Vienna, by the senatorial residences, is a famous home of the marshal's son-in-law, which is called Indetenbrekht (?).[16] This residence is built in the proportions of the finest, marvelous architecture, and the work is fine.

This same day I was in a monastery of Roman monks who are called *Avgustiane;*

[14] That is, he lived north of the city in Donaustadt.

[15] St. Stephen's is indeed long and wide; the cathedral is 345 feet long, the central aisle is 92 feet wide, and each of the two side aisles 73 feet wide.

[16] Tolstoi above describes the devastation of the recent attack on Vienna in 1683, when Kara Mustafa besieged the city until the unexpected arrival of Jan Sobieski and other allies of

these monks go about barefooted and, except for their leader, they do not talk with people. The emperor comes secretly from his residence through a wall to this monastery. This monastery is very wealthy; in the church of this monastery is a fine imperial throne, like the one in the cathedral of St. Stephen. And when the emperor does not deign to come to this monastery he hears mass in a church which is built in his imperial residence.[17] In Vienna on a square among the shops is a great and very tall column of alabaster and of gypsum of the most marvelous Italian work, such as one seldom encounters anywhere in the world; for the construction of this column the imperial treasury spent a huge sum: 1,100 golden chervontsy. On the top of this column is placed an image of the Holy Trinity of marvelous carved work, and in the middle of this column lower down is placed a statue of the emperor Leopold, done of alabaster,[18] [and because it is] beneath the image of the Holy Trinity this likeness /327/ shows the emperor on his knees. At this column is also an image of the Blessed Mother of God, in front of which is always a burning lamp every day there is a *procesja*[19] to this column, that is, a walk with the holy cross, and I was able to see this procession. In it walk an arch priest and four deacons, and 14 men walk in yellow, patterned silk caftans, carrying turned black croziers in their hands, and on the tops of these croziers are circles like those on the large fans [carried over the Sacrament]; on these circles are pictured the images of the Crucifixion of the Lord, and the Blessed Mother of God, and other saints. Many fine large candles were carried in this procession. There were also many large candles placed around the column, and in all there were 74 imperial musicians. This procession always comes to this column from the church of the Holy Apostles Peter and Paul.[20]

---

the Empire. For an account of the significance of the Turkish threat and of the European "crusade" that repelled it, see Wolf, *Emergence of the Great Powers 1685–1715*, 2–3.

Throughout the Diary, I retain Tolstoi's colorful term for Islam and the Turks; almost always he precedes it with "cursed" or "damned"; it is from the old-Russian *Besurmenin*, Musulman, and Tolstoi uses both spellings, *Busurman* and *Basurman*.

The riding school above is not the familiar Spanische Hofreitschule, which was built in 1729–36, but the old Stallburg (1558–65). My inquiries in Vienna yielded no positive identification of the Indetenbrekht.

[17] Above this is the Augustiner Kirche, 1349, the site of the Te Deum after Jan Sobieski's liberation of Vienna in 1683. Tolstoi does not mention the famous Heart Vault of the Hapsburg family. And here is the Burgkapelle, 1447–49, later baroqued and now used by the Vienna Boys' Choir.

[18] This is the Dreifaltigkeissäule, the Trinity Column in Graben, also known as the Pestsäule. It was built in 1687–93 by Leopold I after the plague year of 1679. Perhaps 100,000 or more people had died during this particular outbreak of the plague. Population losses due to the Black Death and due to the siege of Vienna by the Turks in 1683 had left the city severely depopulated at the time of Tolstoi's visit.

[19] Tolstoi uses the Polish form for procession rather than the German *Prozession*.

[20] This is the Peterskirche, which would be reconstructed in 1702. Tolstoi is describing a ceremony of thanksgiving for deliverance from the plague of 1679, a ritual initiated by Leopold I.

May 24. I went to stroll in the shops, and there are many wares of all kinds in the shop-rows, especially much silver, and large fine things both cast and carved, and marvelous turned and engraved work. While I was in Vienna there was a fair, and they traded on three *pliatsa* (Ger. *Platz,* square), where I saw a multitude of expensive wares in small canvas stalls: diamonds, rubies, and fine pearls, and many other costly gold things with stones of marvelous work. On one of these three Platze or squares is a Jesuit monastery; close to this monastery in the middle of a square is a marble column, on which is placed the carved image of the Blessed Mother of God dressed in the sun, and the moon is under her feet, as the holy apostle John the Theologian writes in the Apocalypse.[21] On this same square are two fine fountains, from which flows fine clear water. On the second of these squares also stand a column and two fountains.[22] On the third square is the large stone Rathaus, and leading to it are two fine broad stone stairways;[23] in the middle of the wall of this Rathaus is placed the likeness of a maiden, carved of white stone with covered eyes in the image of Justice, as if to judge, without gazing on a man's face, what is true. On this same square is a stone column, and on it are hung from all sides the executioner's weapons. In this place, at this column, they hold trials and executions.

This same day the Muscovite envoy dined with me, the foreigner Adam Adamov Veit,[24] and after dinner we rode over to walk in the imperial gardens. Adam rode in his /328/ coach, and I hired myself a coach for the day, and paid one efimok for it, and with the coach two fine drivers were included. This imperial garden is half a Muscovite verst from the city of Vienna,[25] and it is very large and finely constructed. The shrubs and fine flowers in it are placed in marvelous array. There are many fruit trees of various sorts in this garden, and they are arranged in proportion, and there are many other trees with their branches entwined, and the leaves on them are identically trimmed, and pomegranate and lemon trees in great fine stone pots are placed in various places. The view is very fine. Likewise, many shrubs and

[21] This is the Mariensäule, and above, probably the Kirche Am Hof. "And there appeared a great wonder in heaven; a woman clothed with the sun, and the moon under her feet, and upon her head a crown of twelve stars"; Revelation 12:1. The column was erected and rebuilt in the seventeenth century; it asked the Mother of God's intercession when the Empire was threatened by the Swedes during the Thirty Years' War.

[22] Tolstoi's route suggests the Platz Freyung.

[23] He is at the site of the Altes Rathaus, on the Hoher Markt, the court of justice and place of execution in Vienna until 1703.

[24] Adam Veit, of Dutch origin, had long been in Russian service, being a captain of a foreign regiment in Moscow at the time of the *strel'tsy* uprising of 1682, and, now Tolstoi notes, ambassador to the Empire.

[25] The distance indicates clearly the site of the Belvedere, which Hildebrandt began to construct in the 1690s. In Tolstoi's day, of course, Vienna was still a walled city so that he had to leave the "city" at the present-day Ring and ride to the countryside. Tolstoi errs in calling it the imperial garden, as it was being built for and by Prince Eugene of Savoy, the Hapsburg's most famous and successful general of the day. He would enjoy his most dramatic victory over the Turks just five months hence, at the battle of Zenta in September.

flowers are placed in various fine pots and arranged according to the principles of architecture.

In this same garden, instead of columns are many likenesses of men and women finely worked in brass. In the middle of this garden is a fine stone fountain, from which flows pure water equally from eight places; in the middle of this fountain are five likenesses of the sirens, that is, men from their heads to their waists, and from the waists down are tails like those of fish.[26] These sirens are made of white stone, and from all of them flows water. Also around this fountain are many likenesses of reptiles of white stone, from all of which water flows. On the sides of this fountain are two other large and well-designed fountains, from which water spurts aloft from 9 places. On the sides of these two fountains are two small fountains; also near to the wall is a fine fountain of fine parts; in this wall are seven places in which a person may sit, and opposite each place is a fountain, from which water splashes into those places. On one side of this garden a square is built, and one climbs up to that square by a stairway; this is a great stone stairway, done of fine work. Around this square they have finely arranged fruit trees of the same size. Along the side of this square is a stone wall of fine and marvelous work, such as one seldom finds in the whole world; this wall is adorned with valuable small stones and shells and other such things; from one place in this wall water flows as a fine fountain. From this place a rather large hill is made, and on that hill is a pond 50 sazhens long and 12 sazhens across; it is all inlaid with white stones. Here they have built the great imperial residence, a four-sided building, and from all sides it is enclosed by fine galleries, large and /329/ high; the length of the wall of this building is 100 sazhens, and its width is 50 sazhens, and this residence is partitioned into three chambers. This court is three stories high; beneath these chambers is one grand chamber, called a *teatrum*, in which comedies are presented for the amusement of the emperor.[27]

May 26. I was at a *shpital* (Ger. *Spital*), that is, a hospital or a house for the ill. This hospital is built outside the city of Vienna in a suburb, on the other side of a tributary of the river Danube; in this hospital is a very long room, and in this room, opposite the doors, a man's bones are placed beneath glass in an icon-case, arranged into a likeness [of a man] and held together with brass wire. These are the bones of the man who first began to build this hospital.[28] In this same room around the walls

[26] This is the famous Fountain of Mermaids (rather than of Sirens); to this day it is the central fountain between the upper and lower Belvedere palaces. Such hydraulic works were unknown in Russia until Peter began to build them in the early eighteenth century.

[27] Tolstoi again refers to the Imperial Palace, which raises the suspicion that he is talking about Schonbrunn Palace (which Fischer von Erlach had begun in 1696), but the distance from Vienna and the Mermaid Fountain both clearly indicate the Belvedere.

[28] Other Russians in Tolstoi's lifetime had reacted to the sight of a skeleton with more emotion; here is the story, as reported by Olearius, p. 132.

> Although they admire and value physicians and their art, nevertheless they will not employ the means of learning better cures that are generally resorted to in Germany

are placed many beds of fine joiner's work, and around each bed is placed a green curtain, and on each bedstead is placed good bedding. They are covered with white sheets, and on each bed is a good blanket. On these beds lie the sick, and by the head of each sick person is a tankard with a drink, and the tankards are all pewter; each sick person also has a white towel. This hospital is just being built by the imperial treasury. Alongside of this hospital is a good pharmacy for the drugs for those sick people, and doctors are attached to it; and the druggists and chemists in this pharmacy are assigned to it, and all are kept at the emperor's expense. In the middle of that long room in which the sick people lie is a kaplica, that is, a small church, where the Roman monks conduct a Mass for the sick daily early in the morning. And here they have set the tables on which the sick eat; and on the other side of this long room is a small garden, and placed in it are grapes, and this is why they built it: when a sick person begins to recover from his illness, he may stroll in this garden because of its coolness. They accept into this hospital the sick of every rank without cost; they only inquire if the sick person has no means of his own, and these they accept into this hospital, and they rest and are treated with great care; they also admit into this hospital traveling foreigners who fall ill, and they keep these sick people in this place until they are completely cured; and when they are completely healthy, they are free to go wherever they wish without paying; no one takes anything from anyone in this hospital, and they do this because of their Christian faith

---

and other countries, such as the dissection of human corpses and the study of skeletons. To everything of the kind they are extremely hostile. Some years ago an experienced barber, a Dutchman of jovial disposition, named Quirinus, was in the Tsar's service. He had a human skeleton hanging on the wall above a table in his room. Once he was sitting before the table playing the lute, as was his habit, when the streltsi who then always guarded the foreign quarter came toward the sound of the music and looked in through the doorway. When they saw the bones hanging on the wall, they were frightened, and especially since they saw the skeleton stir. Accordingly, they left and let it be known that the German barber had a skeleton hanging on his wall, that moved when he played the lute. The rumor reached the Grand Prince and the Patriarch, who sent others with instructions to look into the matter attentively. These people not only confirmed the testimony already given, but added that the corpse danced on the wall to the sound of the lute.

Very astonished at this, the Russians took counsel and decided that the barber must surely be a sorcerer; he and his skeleton would therefore have to be consigned to the flames. When Quirinus learned that such a dreadful end was being planned for him, he sent a leading German merchant who enjoyed the favor of the magnates to Prince Ivan Borisovich Cherkasskii, to give a veracious report and frustrate the design. The merchant said to the boyar: "The barber certainly ought not to be accused of sorcery on account of the skeleton, for in Germany the best doctors and barbers use them. Then, if some living person breaks a leg or is wounded in some part of the body or other, it is easier to know how to go about curing him. The bones moved because the wind blew in through the open window and not because the lute was played." After this the sentence was rescinded. However, Quirinus had to leave the country, and the skeleton was dragged out beyond the Moscow River and burned.

and for the saving of souls.[29] In Vienna it is the custom, twice each week early in the morning, for the senators' and nobles' sons to ride outside the city to the fields /330/ to study military affairs, where they learn to fight with swords, lances, pistols, and other weapons.

May 27. In Vienna there was a great procession, that is, a walk with the cross. In this procession were the emperor, the empress, and all their children, and I saw the emperor, the empress, and all the children. This procession is held in Vienna every year on the feast day of the Body of Christ [Corpus Christi], according to the custom of the Western church. On the evening of this procession, His Imperial Majesty and all his household came from their walk into Vienna and spent the night at their court outside the city. This procession began on May 27 in this manner. First, a multitude of people collected at the church of Stephen the first martyr, and from this church they walked by ranks: first of all came the artisans of every trade with their insignias (gonfalon),[30] and the insignias were carried by seven men, and behind the insignia walked all the artisans two abreast and hatless, and behind them came the townspeople, and then the people of the merchants' ranks, and each had a rosary in his hands.

In the sixth hour of day the emperor came to the church of St. Stephen.[31] Before him rode the senators and those close to him in their 6-horse coaches; and there were 9 coaches, and the coaches and saddles were not decorated very much, but the coach horses were fine, and 4 persons sat in each coach, and in other coaches more or fewer. Behind these coaches rode the kettledrummer and two trumpeteers, and behind them was the emperor's son, the young Karol; in this same coach opposite him sat his uncle; behind this coach rode the elder son of the emperor, Joseph, the king of Hungary, in his own coach; in the same coach opposite him sat his uncle. Both of these uncles of the emperor's children sat with them hatless in the coaches. Behind

[29] This would seem to be the hospital across the Danube on the Taborstrasse at the Karmeliterkirche; the chapel below would be the little church of the Brothers of Charity on Taborstrasse, the Kirche der Barmherzigen Brüder, dating to 1614. It would seem that Tolstoi stayed near it, on the old route from Vienna north. On Russian medicine, see Alexander, "Medical Developments in Petrine Russia," pp. 198–217. On the equation of medicine with sorcery in seventeenth-century Moscow, see Olearius, pp. 147–48.

[30] These are the processional banners that identified each guild or corporation.

[31] Tolstoi here begins a lengthy and detailed account of the procession on Corpus Christi. Such processions were literally the embodiment of the recognized social hierarchy. Foreign ambassadors, as representatives of monarchs and nations, arranged their suites to enter capitals or courts with exactly the same attention to rank; see, for example, Olearius, pp. 56–57, or a half-century later, Korb, I, 83–84.

On the Church's attitude toward processions generally, and on the significance of the order of procession, see the excellent summary in Chadwick, *Popes and European Revolution*, pp. 32–38.

Maria Pötsch, St. Stephen's Cathedral, Vienna.

him rode the emperor in a coach, and alongside of him on his left side sat the empress, and opposite them sat the sister of the empress, the widow of Michail Vishnevetskii (Michael Korybut-Wisniowiecki), the deceased king of Poland, and now her new husband will be the Kurfurst of Lotaring (Lorraine). Alongside the imperial sister in the same coach sat one man close to the emperor. Behind the imperial coach rode the elder daughter of the emperor; in the same coach opposite her sat the two younger imperial daughters; in the same coach at the doors sat their *mama*. Behind this coach 80 men close to the emperor rode on horseback, very smartly, and their horses were fine. Behind them came 13 coaches, each with 6 horses; in these coaches sat the senators' wives and maiden-daughters, 4 or 5 people to a coach, in good and very rich attire, adorned with very many large diamonds. Behind these coaches rode two regiments of knights in red cloth caftans with fine lace and also with fine carbines. All rode marvelous bay horses worth a hundred rubles apiece or more; the saddle blankets on /331/ all the horses were yellow. Around the imperial coaches walked soldiers in gold and in black dress with lace, tall men selected for their height. Along the right side walked soldiers with fine halberds and on the left side with *drabants* (Ger. *Trabant,* halberds), and the halberds and Trabanten were of fine craftsmanship, inlaid with gold, and all their lances were covered with velvet and with lace. The imperial coaches, with windows, resemble those of the Walachians; and the coaches are covered with black leather with black studs; and the saddles on the horses are not gilded, and the drivers sit on the horses and not up on the coach boxes; and the horses on all imperial coaches were large and very fine, all bays, and six horses to every coach. The emperor himself wore black unadorned attire, but on his shoulders was a golden chain, and on it hung a golden dove[32] and a diamond cross; and both of his children, Joseph and Karol, were in black dress; his elder son, Joseph, the king of Hungary, also wore a golden chain. The empress and his daughters all wore black but they wore many large diamonds.

And when the emperor arrived at the church of St. Stephen and took his place, they walked in the procession from the church. First came two sick people, and before them they carried a banner; then came Roman monks called the Augustinians whose habit is black and who were barefooted, but their soles were bound with thongs; behind them were the half-dead, that is, those [monks] who keep silence;[33] then came the Benedictines, who wear a black habit on top and white below; then came the Capuchins in grey robes and unshaven beards. Then came the Franciscans, also in grey habits, and then the Dominicans, who wear a black habit on top with white under their overshirts; and each order carried its banner before it. Behind these monks, also carrying banners, came the notable secular people, the merchants, and between them two Jesuits, and behind them they carried a banner, and behind it several small lads walked in green caftans with white shawls on their shoulders; these children are chosen from those born out of wedlock. Behind them are also small children in blue attire; these are the orphans themselves who have no

[32] Tolstoi may mistake the imperial eagle.

[33] These are presumably the Trappists.

fathers or mothers and who have nothing to live on. They are given food and drink, clothes, and shoes at the emperor's expense. Behind them walked the students from the schools, the honorable ones, and behind them they carried two banners; after these banners walked 8 deacons and two priests in gold attire; behind these priests walked an Abt, that is, an archimandrite, and in his hands he held a cross, and in front of him they carried a crozier, and on his head was a cap made after the fashion of the Western Church.

Then more lay people walked, and behind them they carried two banners, and behind the banners another Abt walked, and behind him /332/ they carried four banners together, and behind them walked the nobles and all the chief people of the imperial household. Then came the kettledrummers and the trumpeteers, and behind them the singers, and they walked singing; behind the singers were those close to the emperor, and four doctors, and behind them the senators; behind the senators were the senators of advanced years, honorable people, 38 in number, and they carried large lighted candles of white wax. Behind them walked 12 priests and 6 deacons, and all carried holy relics in silver vessels. Behind them walked the bishop, who carried the relics of Stephen, the first martyr; behind him walked the cardinal, and around him they carried 12 large lighted candles, made of white wax. In front of him 2 deacons walked with censers and they carried his cap; four people close to the emperor carried a fine canopy, made of gold velvet, four-cornered on four cast silver poles over his head. This cardinal carried in a vessel the body of Christ in the custom of the Roman Church, that is, the consecrated offering. In front of this cardinal walked one man with a bell, and he rang that bell so that the people, standing along the streets, could fall on their knees before the *sakrament*.

Behind the cardinal walked the emperor's younger son, and behind him the elder son, Joseph, the king of Hungary. Both of these imperial sons carried large lit candles. Behind them walked the emperor himself with a golden candle; on either side of him walked his retinue, counts, and no one led him by the hand. One of his relatives walked on the emperor's right side, and he had the golden chain, and the uncles walked alongside the emperor's children. The empress walked behind the emperor; she was led on her left hand by a marshal, and over her they carried a fine canopy. Behind the empress was the emperor's sister, who was mentioned above. Behind her walked the emperor's elder daughter, and then the two younger daughters. The sister of the emperor and all of the emperor's daughters were led by their left hands by elder senators, honorable persons, and senators' children carried round canopies over all of them, and the trains of their dresses were carried behind them by children—minors. Behind the emperor's girls walked maidens, the daughters and the wives of senators, and over each of them they carried a fine round canopy, and each had a rosary in her hands. And, having walked about the city in this procession, they came to the carved column, which was mentioned above in this book, the one placed on a square.[34]

At this column they conducted a spiritual litany. There, for the emperor, they put a

[34] This is the Pestsäule in Graben, mentioned above.

rug, and on this rug they placed an armchair, and in front of the chair was a bench covered with velvet. And having arrived at this place, the emperor and all of his household knelt down, and infantrymen, 4 regiments in fine dress with /333/ weapons stood around the column. The commanders of these infantrymen were all in gold caftans with diamond buttons. And from this column they again returned to the great cathedral of the archdeacon St. Stephen and walked around that church, but the Romans walk on the right side. And when the Cardinal entered that great church, at that moment, in the church, music began to play on three organs, and on violins, on *violgalbakh* (viola da gamba), on harps, on *shtor'akh,*[35] on zithers, on flutes, on trumpets, on kettledrums, on reeds, and on drums, and on many other various musical instruments, and such was the noise that it was impossible to hear the human voice. And the emperor, having entered the church, bowed and returned his candle and left the church in the same manner as he had entered it, and in front of him were his children. And outside the church he sat again in his coach and they went to the court outside the city, and, having dined at that court, he went again to walk in the village from which he had come. At the time of the procession, bells ring in all the churches in Vienna, but not in the great bells [of St. Stephen's] in Vienna. The imperial children—the elder is Joseph, king of Hungary, 19 years old, and the younger is Karol, the prince of Austria, 16 years old.

In all, my stay in Vienna was six days.

May 28. I left Vienna, having hired a coachman to the little city of Mestre in Italy,[36] which is in the Venetian province on the sea coast, and I gave to this coachman, to conduct me and the people with me, 8 golden chervontsy per person, and this day I arrived to spend the night in the hamlet of Dreisekhkirkh (Traiskirchen). In this hamlet, 4 miles from Vienna, the homes are built of stone.

May 29. I arrived to dine in the city of Naishtat (Wiener Neustadt), 4 miles from Traiskirchen. This is no small town and its buildings are all of stone. This same day I arrived to spend the night beneath the Alpine mountains in the village of

[35] Drobinina (see introduction) identifies the *shtorta* as the Italian *storto,* German, *Krummhorn.*

[36] In the seventeenth century it was possible to hire a coachman (Ger. *Fuhrmann*), the basis for Tolstoi's term here, *furman,* but more commonly known by the Italian *vetturino.* These individuals, with a general reputation for dishonesty, would contract to convey a person or group from city to city for a set price, including usually meals and night stops. "You may hire a chaise at Mestre for Vienna and give the *vetturino* fourteen or fifteen ducats for your passage, all charges included, or from seven to eight ducats without including all charges. This route occupied twelve or thirteen days." Mead, p. 336, citing the experience of Thomas Nugent, whose *Grand Tour* was published in 1756.

Nunklits (Ternitz), 3 miles from Neustadt. One mile before this village I passed the little stone town called Neikirkh (Neunkirchen).

May 30. I left the village of Ternitz and rode between high stone mountains; on the right side on a high hill on the very top I saw a stone monastery, and in it live the Roman monks,[37] the Capuchins, and on the high hills and in the middle of the mountains are stone buildings and quite a few dwellings. Also fine water flows between these mountains. And I arrived to dine in the hamlet of Shotvein (Schottwein), 1 mile from Ternitz. In this spot is a stone imperial castle, and here they inspect all travelers and are mindful of [merchant's] wares and the duty [owed by] coachmen, which the coachmen get from trading /334/ people; but from me and from the coachman who was conducting me they did not take anything, because I had travel documents from the tsar and His Imperial Majesty.[38] In this hamlet the coachman who was conducting me changed the axles and the poles on the carriages and the carts, and hired oxen for the carriages and the carts, on which to drive on the mountains, for it is impossible in this place to ride in the mountains with horses, and the coachman hired these oxen at his own cost.[39] And from this place clouds were visible on the mountains, and above the clouds one could see the mountaintops, and other clouds obliterated the mountains; and other clouds rose high up the mountains, but still they were lower than the tops of those mountains. From Vienna to these mountains it is 12 imperial miles, but 60 Muscovite versts.

This same day I arrived to spend the night in the hamlet of Peglibok (Payerback, neighborhood of Semmering), 3 miles from Schottwein. I rode this day through very high mountains. Oxen pulled the carts, but I and the people who were with me walked on foot, and in all the oxen led the carts and the carriages one mile to Ostrozhka (Österreich), and this Österreich divides the Austrian land from the German.[40] From Vienna to the German border it is 13 German miles, but 65 Muscovite versts.

Through these mountains the road is very miserable and difficult. Along the road are uncountably numerous sharp rocks, and the road is very narrow, and the mountains immeasurably high and rocky, and the road narrow; one can ride on it in a cart,

[37] Following Tolstoi's route we were able, with the help of a friendly Austrian farmer, to identify the Peterskirche on a stone outcrop above the town of Ternitz.

[38] The imposing castle of Orth/Donau stands high above the village of Weisenbach. Almost every early-modern traveler commented on these searches of their luggage. It was an endless vexation, since "it is impossible to know what goods are forbidden in different countries." Mead, *Grand Tour*, p. 157.

[39] This was the chief reason for hiring a Fuhrmann. It was his duty and expense to change from horses to steadier oxen before crossing the dangerous mountain paths that follow.

[40] What Tolstoi calls "Germany" we would call Styria, the German Steiermark, the province of southeast Austria, which was an old iron-mining area (see below). The column that divides the two provinces is in Semmering.

but with great fear because the road does not go through the mountain, but along the edge of the mountain. This road is positioned halfway up the mountain, and along one side of this road are immeasurably high stone mountains, from which many large stones fall on the road and hit the travelers and their beasts, and along the other side of the road are very deep abysses, in which a large river flows very quickly.[41] From the rapid flowing of this river there is an incessant great noise just like at a mill, and many travelers fall into these abysses from the road with their carts and horses and are even killed and are drowned in that river, and beyond that river also are immeasurably high mountains. When someone rides through these mountains on that road, he is ceaselessly in deadly fear until he gets out of these mountains. On these mountains much snow always rests, for because of their immeasurable height it is cold there, and the rays of the sun never fall there between them.

In the German land are many wooden domestic structures. The German people of the male and the female sex are not well formed and are wretched. Many settlers wear coarse caftans, and the female sex /335/ wears a particular style of dress, which is very short, goes only to the knees, and on their heads the women wear a tall cap, thin, overlaid with sheepskin. Around the neck they wear a broad linen collar, like the collars worn by the Jews and Jewesses who live in Poland.

In Germany the water is not healthy for human use, so I drank no water in all of Germany and crossed all of Germany without consuming anything to drink because of this dire necessity. From this water many of the male and the female sex have very great chins around their necks, and even large tumors on their throats, and because of this many of them even speak with great difficulty; and this illness happens to them because they always consume this water for drinking and for cooking. And thus from an early age they get these tumors on their throats and a growth on their necks and they grow until the death of the person, and no one can cure them by any means, and with such illnesses people live to the very border of Italy, and beyond the border in Italy there are few of them.[42]

May 31. I left Payerback; I arrived to dine in the hamlet of Kimberk (Kindberg), 2 miles from Payerback. This same day I arrived to spend the night in the city of Prukdenmurk (Bruck an der Mur), 3 miles from Kindberg.[43]

This day I rode through the Alpine mountains. On the right side were very high stone mountains, and on the left side was a very large deep ditch, in which flows a very fast river, and on the other side of this river are stone mountains as high as those on the right side. Throughout these mountains are very many dwellings, and

[41] This is the valley of the Mürz, which Tolstoi saw during the spring thaw.

[42] A century earlier Fynes Moryson noted, "In this Country of Styria, many men and weomen have great wens [tumors] hanging downe their throats, by drinking the waters that run through the mines of mettals." *An Itinerary Containing his Ten Yeers Travell,* I, 143. These were goiters caused by a lack of iodine, a problem of mountain peoples.

[43] At Bruck the traveler leaves the valley of the Mürz for that of the Mur.

these homes are fine stone buildings, and also there are many stone monasteries. The local inhabitants, the Germans, do not shave their beards. Bruck an der Mur is a rather large stone city, and there is a castle in it on a high mountain. The towers and the walls are stone, and in the city all the buildings are also stone. Beneath this city flows a river, which they call the Mur, over which I crossed below the city on a bridge. At this bridge are three stone granaries, and in these granaries 24 millstones grind grain; here too is an iron factory, and not just one, but in Germany there are very many iron factories.[44] Among these high mountains are very many wooden and stone houses halfway up the mountains and also at the bottom and on the tops of the mountains. Before reaching the city of Bruck an der Mur, I crossed the river Rentsykh (Thörl), which flows between the mountains over the rocks.

June 1. I arrived to dine in the city of Liunk (Leoben), 2 miles from Bruck an der Mur. Leoben is a large city, and the homes in it and all the buildings are of fine stone. Under this city flows the river /336/ Mur. This river is rather large, and alongside this river I drove along a rather large road. On this river along the road are many dwellings. This same day I arrived to spend the night in the village of Trantof (Kraubath, near St. Michael), 2 miles from Leoben.

June 2. I arrived to dine in the hamlet Knitifort (Knittelfeld), 2 miles from Kraubath. In this hamlet is a stone castle, and this hamlet too stands on the river Mur. This same day I arrived to spend the night in Aufonfolt (Auffenwölz), 3 miles from Knittelfeld. A half mile before reaching this village I passed a rather large city, which is called Liudemburk (Judenburg).

June 3. I arrived to dine in the village of Gandmark (Unzmarkt), 3 miles from the village of Auffenwölz. This same day I arrived to spend the night in the hamlet of Naimurk (Neumarkt in Steinmark), 3 miles from Unzmarkt.

June 4. I arrived to dine in the village of Girt (Hirt),[45] 3 miles from Neumarkt. A mile before reaching this village, I passed the city of Frizikh (Friesach). In this place are two stone cities, with water around the castle. In this city lives a *biskup* (Ger. *Bischof*), that is, a bishop of the Roman Church. This same day I arrived to spend the night in the village of Terfan (Tiffen), 2 miles from Hirt.

[44] In Bruck one can still see the evidence of the former millraces. The Steiermark had long been a vigorous center of the iron industry; see Braudel, *Capitalism*, p. 276 (*Structures*, p. 374).

[45] Hirt is still a tiny village one kilometer north of the crossing of the river Gurk.

June 5. I arrived to dine in the village of Mautpruk (Mautbrücken), 4 Polish miles from Tiffen. Two miles before reaching this village, I passed the stone city of Sentfant (Sankt Veit). In this city are two fine brass fountains, from which constantly flow streams of pure water. In this city are many fine German horses for sale. This same day I arrived to spend the night in a tavern, which is called Bukanets (St. Ruprecht), 3 miles from Mautbrücken. This tavern is built close to a large lake, which is called Benedektsin [now the Ossiacher See].

June 6. I arrived to dine in the city of Filekh (Villach), 2 miles from the tavern. Villach is a large city of the imperial region; in it is a stone monastery and four stone churches, and its homes and all its buildings are of stone, and there are many large homes. Beneath this city flows a great river, which is called Drakh (Drau/Drave); this river is much larger than the river Moskva.[46] I spent the night in this city because the coachmen, who were carrying me, were inhabitants of this city and had homes in this city. Also, I was glad to rest from the great labor, which I had endured on the road, crossing over those great stone mountains, and not only when I rode over those mountains, but also when I walked on foot I had always a fear of death before my eyes. In this city of Villach seven years before my arrival, there had been a trembling of the earth for two and a half hours, and from this trembling stone churches and many stone dwellings were destroyed, and now a new building is to be seen in some places, but in others up to now /337/ the destroyed building is still not repaired; and many of those homes that were not destroyed in the trembling have cracks in the rooms, which even now are visible.

June 7. Having left the city of Villach by half a mile, I came to a stream, which flows from the mountains, and it has warm water in it, and many sick people bathe in that water and are freed from illness, and healthy people bathe, seeking better health, and there I too washed myself in health and then was kept healthy by the right hand of God on High. This water is warm in its own nature, but it does not burn.[47] And having passed this stream of warm water, I arrived this day to dine in the hamlet of Oblasten (Arnoldstein), 2 miles from Villach. This same day I drove through very high stone mountains. They were the same as those mentioned above, with large and very tall stone mountains on one side of the road, and on the other side deep green chasm, and one constantly hears the great noise of the rushing water below. In many places one can see the bottom of that chasm, and it is a fearful thing to see. In the above-mentioned hamlet on the mountain at the top is built a fine stone

[46] It is not an especially large river except during spring thaw.

[47] The *Warmbad* south of the town of Villach is still a major and enormously popular European spa.

monastery, in which live Roman monks—Benedictines.[48] This day I arrived to spend the night in the hamlet of Tarftsil (Tarvis, Tarvisio), 2 miles from the hamlet Arnoldstein. This same day I rode with great difficulty in a narrow path through the mountains, and such a miserable path I have not seen on the entire road.

June 8. I arrived to dine in the hamlet of Pantafel (Pontafel, Pontebba), 2 miles from Tarvisio. This day I again traveled between high stone mountains. This hamlet is on the imperial border with Italy, with the Venetian domains. The river Pontafel divides the imperial land from Italy; this river is not large and not deep, and it flows through rocks. In this hamlet a stone bridge has been built over this river, and in the middle of the bridge is a stone tower, and on the tower on the imperial side is the Empire's coat of arms, and on the Italian side is placed the arms of the Venetian principality—the lion in the image of the evangelist St. Mark. In this hamlet and all along the river live on the one side those [people] of the Empire, and on the other Italians of Venetia. I stayed in this hamlet on the imperial side; there the Italians looked at my travel document, which was given to me in Moscow, and those from His Imperial Majesty in Vienna, and at my other traveler's certificates that I had brought with me from Poland; also, they inspected me for any trading wares, but they found none; and they looked to see if there were any sick people with me, and all with me were healthy, so they gave me a travel certificate to the first Italian city of the Venetian province.[49] /338/

From Vienna to the Italian border is 55 imperial miles = 275 versts, to which I add by my reckoning another 150 versts or more, because the German miles are very great. And I traveled from Vienna to the Italian border in 12 days; I had seen many deathly frights on the road and endured hardships and difficulties from that miserable road. This same day, having crossed the border, I entered Italy between the same great stone mountains, as were in the above-described narrow and miserable places. From the border I went one mile, and came to a castle, and this stone

[48] The former Benedictine monastery, dramatically poised on a stone outcrop in the center of the town, is now in ruins.

[49] The bill of health was mandatory. Thomas Coryat, in the early seventeenth century, wrote that "The Venetians are extraordinarily precise herin, insomuch that a man cannot be received into Venice without a bill of health, if he would give a thousand duckats." Ray, later in the century, noted, "When you depart from any city, you must be sure to take a bill of health out of that office that is kept everywhere for that purpose, without which you can hardly be admitted into another city, especially if it be in the territory of another prince or state. If anyone comes from an infected or suspected place, he is forced to keep his quarantain (as they call it), that is, be shut up in the Lazaretto or pest-house forty days." And finally, Thomas Nugent (1756) writes, coming back to Italy from Styria, "You must be provided with a passport of health, otherwise you will be forced to go back, or obliged to perform quarantine for forty days." All cited in Mead, *Grand Tour,* pp. 154–55.

castle is right on the road in the mountain. At this castle they detained me, not permitting me into the castle, and they inquired, from which state did I come and where I was going, and did I have with me a travel document from His Imperial Roman Majesty, and there I showed him the travel document of my Great Sovereign, which was given to me by the Diplomatic Office, as well as the imperial and royal Polish travel documents, and having looked at me outside the city the captain took them, carried them inside the city and reported to the general, and then he brought those documents back to me and returned all of them, but kept for himself the certificate, which they had given to me at the Italian border mentioned above, because they always take such certificates from travelers, and they gave me leave to enter the castle, and allowed me into that castle freely. At that castle along my route stood soldiers with weapons; this castle is very small, and having passed it, I traveled this day by the very narrow and troublesome path between the narrow mountains, and arrived this day to spend the night in the hamlet of Reshent (Resiutta)[50] of the Venetian state.

June 9. From the hamlet of Resiutta I went one mile, and came out of the great narrow stone mountains, and I had traveled in these mountains by that miserable path for 11 days, and the measure of these mountains is 46 imperial miles, and 230 Muscovite versts, but I count more than 300 versts. On all of these mountains are many inhabited places, and I arrived this day to dine in the hamlet of Ashpital (Osoppo), 2 miles from Resiutta, and before reaching this hamlet, I traveled past the city of Vintsekh (Venzone) of the Venetian province. When I got out of the mountains, there were many grapes and gardens on both sides of the road, and the walls around the grapes and the gardens were stone. This same day I arrived to spend the night in the Venetian city of Sanktisdanil (San Daniele del Friuli), 3 miles from Osoppo. Along this road are very many fine vineyards and gardens on both sides of the road.

June 10. I arrived to dine in the village of Gradishkut (Gradisca), 2 miles from San Daniele. Before reaching this village, I rode across the river Taiamen (Tagliamen) in two places, and this river is not wide /339/ and not deep, and it flows along the stones with unspeakable quickness. This same day I arrived to spend the night in the village of Kardinal (Cordelons), 2 miles from Gradisca.

June 11. I arrived to dine in the hamlet of Shetselei (Sacile), 2 miles from Cordelons. This is a stone hamlet, and all of the homes are built among the grapes, and the homes are old. This same day I arrived to spend the night in a city of the

[50] Beginning with Tolstoi's entry into Venetia, place names are given in their Italian form, with some exceptions noted below.

Venetian state, which is called Kundiian (Conegliano), 2 miles from Sacile. All this day I rode through fine vineyards and gardens. This city is large and it is placed on a high stone mountain; in it are two stone castles, and the houses in it are of marvelous construction, all of stone. The houses have fine gardens, in which are a multitude of grapes and fruit trees: lemons, pomegranates, and other such, and the grapevines are around the trees in various fine figures. ***June 12,*** I left this city by half a mile and crossed on the mountain the river Piiava (Piave) on a ferry in two places. This river is large and very swift, and I arrived to dine in the city of Triviz (Treviso) of the Venetian province, and it is 3 miles from Conegliano to Treviso. The city of Treviso is large, and in it all the buildings are of fine stone, and there are many marvelous gardens and fine running water in them. From Conegliano to Treviso on both sides of the road are large and very fine gardens, in which there are many large homes, built of stone and of wood.

This same day I arrived to spend the night in the city of Mestr (Mestre), 2 miles from Treviso. This is a city of the Venetian state, and it is built on a naval wharf, from which one goes to Venice by sea, and there is no overland route to Venice from this city. From Treviso to Mestre the road is fine, and on both sides of the road are fine and marvelous gardens; in these gardens are many marvelously constructed palaces. In these same gardens are many grapes and all kinds of fruit trees: lemons, pomegranates, *tsukat,* almonds, olives, chestnuts, peaches, plums, various kinds of *dul,*[51] pears, apples, walnuts, cherries, sour cherries, and all other kinds of produce. At many of these homes they have built marvelous kaplica, that is, small chapels. All of these cities from the imperial border to Mestre and Mestre itself belong to the state of the Venetian republic.

From the imperial border to Mestre to the naval wharf is 20 imperial miles and 100 Muscovite versts, but it is really 150. From Vienna to the wharf is 75 German miles, but in Muscovite it numbers 325 versts, to which I add 200 Muscovite versts or even more. From Moscow to this naval wharf is 2,027 versts plus another one hundred and fifty, but by my reckoning it could be almost 1,000 versts more.

Mestre is a large stone city, and there are many large homes built /340/ of stone in

[51] Some fruits mentioned by Tolstoi remain unidentified. Fasmer's etymological dictionary derives *dulia* from Polish *gdula,* a kind of pear, which is helpful except for the fact that Tolstoi follows it with *grusha,* pear. I use the form "various pears" to indicate that both appear in a list.

Tsukat I have left untranslated throughout. Fasmer derives it from German *Sukkade* or *Zukkade,* or the Italian *succada,* all meaning juice, which leaves the fruit unknown. Possible Polish forms include *cukaty,* from sugar, *cukier,* or *cykata,* citron, and this could be Tolstoi's word, except that later he uses the more common *tsitron* in the same series. Dal's Russian dictionary and the *Slovar' sovremennogo russkogo literaturnogo iazyka* define it as candied fruit or candied fruit peel, a dessert of the boyars in the seventeenth century, but the context makes this implausible. In Italian *zucca* is pumpkin or any other squash, and, perhaps in the context of other fruits, a melon, but this too seems out of place in this series.

Finally, although it appears only later in the Diary, Tolstoi also lists a fruit or nut called *shkot* or *shtot;* I have found no translation of it.

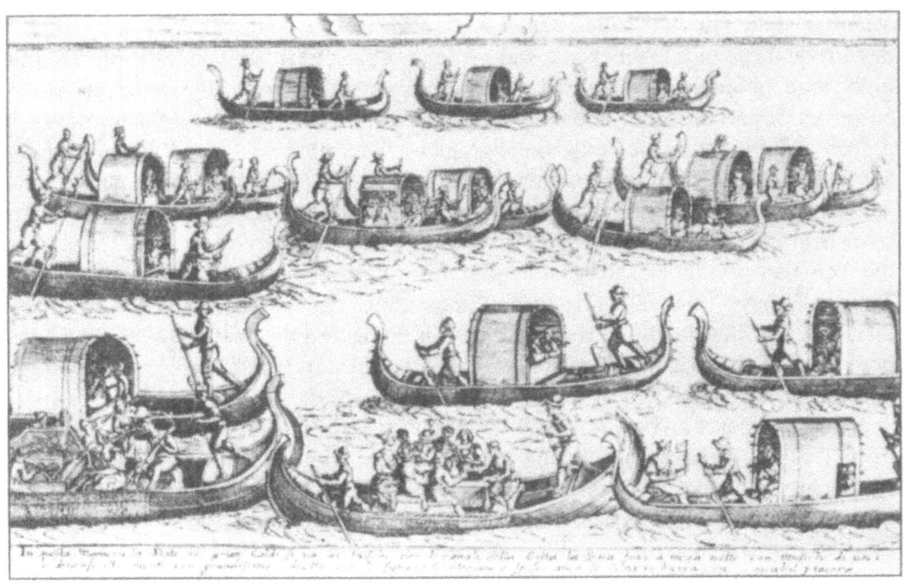

Summer Nights on the Lagoon.

it. This city is full of gardens, with many streams of running water in them; from this city to Venice one travels by sea in *barkakh* (It. *barca,* barque, launch), in *piotakh* (It. *peata,* barge), or in *gundulakh* (It. *gondola*); and the manner of building these vessels I will describe at length below. And this sound, which runs from the city of Mestre to the sea, is not wide or deep, and it is very difficult to breathe because of this water. From the Italian border to Mestre the Venetian female sex in the cities attire themselves in very disorderly clothing, and wives and maidens do not cover their heads, but always wear their natural hair, but in the city of Mestre the female sex is dressed finely in Venetian attire. From Mestre to Venice and from Venice to Mestre at all hours many people, men and women and girls, constantly travel across in the above-mentioned vessels. From Moscow to this wharf I traveled in five weeks; during these weeks I stopped over many days in many places, from which I count, with all the stopover days, six weeks, but from Vienna to the naval wharf I went in 16 days.

In Mestre I lived three days until I could rent myself a house in Venice, in which I could stay in Venice with all the people with me.

June 15. In the city of Mestre I went from the inn to the naval wharf with the same coachman who had brought me from Vienna. This inlet of the sea is at Mestre itself; here we unloaded from the coachmen's carts, and I placed all of the people and all the things I had with me in the barque and rode to Venice; I passed two checkpoints on this inlet without being inspected, but at these Venetian points they [usually] inspect all traveling people for forbidden wares. Along the coast of this inlet a stone kaplica, that is, a small Roman church, is located; in this kaplica stands an image of the Blessed Mother of God, and in this kaplica all travelers give alms according to their means, and going from the inlet to the sea, we raised the sails on the barque and sailed to Venice very quickly. The place of Venice stands on the very sea, and entering into a street in that barque, I came right to the courtyard, which I had rented for my stay. This is a large house, with many rooms in it, all built of fine stone; in this courtyard is a fine well, in which the water is pure, and it is always fine.

Venice is a very large and marvelous place, and it is twice as big as the imperial capital of Vienna. Around Venice there are no town walls or passage towers or walls. The domestic structures are all of stone and most marvelous and very large, and such expensive and well-built homes one seldom encounters in this world.[52] In Venice along all the streets /341/ and along all the lanes everywhere is sea water, and they ride to all the homes in boats, but for one who wishes to go by foot, there are also fine footpaths along all the streets and lanes to every home for walkers, and every house has two gates, one to the water street and the other to the land path. And many streets and lanes are divided into two halves: a water route, and one on land. In Venice there are no horses or cattle at all, and no coaches, carriages, or carts at all, and they do not know sledges. In Venice along the streets over the water are built a multitude of stone and wooden bridges. Those who wish to know about Venice in detail I refer to a reading of a history of Venice printed in the Italian language; here I shorten my account of Venice because I lack the time, and so that I will be able to describe here something of the marvelous things that one encounters in Venice.

In Venice is a stone church of the blessed Greek faith named for the great martyr George; this church is an ancient building, and in this church are holy icons of Greek painting, and the Greek metropolitan Meletius lives at this church, and with him white clergy and monks of the Greek order, and archdeacons and deacons who

[52]Tolstoi refers, of course, to the scores of nobles' *palazzi* along the Grand Canal of Venice and elsewhere. This paragraph, written upon arrival, makes it clear that he, like all first-time visitors to Venice, was properly impressed by the unique physical properties of the island city, by its combination of land and waterway, and by the absence of vehicular traffic.

One can compare Tolstoi's arrival in Venice with the "fictional" arrival of Rhedi in Montesquieu's *Persian Letters:* "My dear Usbek, I am now in Venice. One may have seen every city in the world and yet be surprised, on arriving in Venice, to see a city whose towers and mosques astonishingly spring out of the water, and whose innumerable people live in a place more appropriate for fish.

"But this heathen city lacks the world's most precious treasure: fresh water. Here it is impossible to accomplish a single legal ablution, and the place is held in abomination by our holy Prophet, who never looks down on it from heaven except in anger." Letter 31, pp. 55–56.

are all Greeks.[53] In Venice is a stone cathedral of the Roman faith, in the name of the holy evangelist St. Mark. This is a very large church built of marvelous craftsmanship, and in it are many marbled and other large columns. In this church, the Venetian Catholics say, are now all of the relics of the evangelist Mark: but where they rest, no one knows except one procurator. But the Greeks all say that the relics of St. Mark the Evangelist are not in this church, but the Venetians give great reproach to anyone who says that his relics are not in this church.[54]

On the outside of this church over the western doors on the porch roof are set four likenesses of horses, made of brass and gilded, of the size of a small German horse, and all are of the same size. These horses are made of marvelous workmanship, and formerly they were in Constantinople, and stood at the Church of Holy Sophia, and when in antiquity the Venetians conquered Constantinople, at that time they took these horses and brought them to Venice and in eternal glory they placed them at the Catholic cathedral of San Marco.[55]

Close to this church right by the altar is built the home of the Venetian prince,

[53] The Greek church of St. George (San Giorgio dei Greci) was the center of Tolstoi's religious and social life in Venice. The church dated from the fifteenth century. After signing the Union in 1439, the Greek metropolitan of Kiev, Isidore, requested permission to build a church in Venice. The Senate agreed in 1456, but the Greeks continued to conduct services at the church of St. Blaise. Isidore, incidentally, precipitated the establishment of an autocephalic Russian Church: when Moscow learned he had signed the Uniate convention for Russia, they expelled him.

In 1498 the Greek community asked the Council of Ten for permission to form a confraternity on the imitation of other minorities, and it was granted. In 1511 they asked permission to build a church dedicated to St. George, protector of soldiers; eventually they petitioned the pope directly, and an extraordinary permission was granted by Clement VII in 1526. Land was acquired, a small church was erected in 1527, and the present edifice was built between 1539 and 1573.

Tolstoi visited the Greek community at the moment of its greatest strength, and shortly before its greatest scandal and its demise. The Meletius that Tolstoi met was the metropolitan of Philadelphia, Meletios Typaldos (1685–1713), who would, a few years later, embrace Catholicism and demand a profession of the Roman faith from the priests at St. George. The Greek community protested violently, and in 1710 demanded the intervention of none other than Peter the Great himself. In 1712 the ecumenical patriarchate excommunicated Typaldos; the local Greeks refused to recognize the Roman priests, abandoned the city, and emigrated to Trieste, Livorno, or elsewhere. This latter episode, however, postdated Tolstoi's stay in Venice, although Tolstoi would observe some less-than-Orthodox religious practices even before the furor over Meletius arose; see Manoussacas, "Aperçu d'une histoire," pp. 9–23.

[54] The relics are said to have been brought from Alexandria to Venice in 829. Tolstoi wants to know whether Catholics or Orthodox Christians possess the relics.

[55] The five-foot horses probably once adorned the arch of Nero, afterward of Trajan; Constantine sent them to Constantinople, from where Doge Dandolo brought them to Venice in 1204. Napoleon would take them to Paris in 1797, and in 1815 Emperor Francis would restore them to their former position.

whom the Venetians call in their language *printsipa* (It. *principe*). This residence is built of fine craftsmanship, is all of stone, and in the rooms of this residence are many stone carvings of marvelous Italian work, and around the residence are also many fine carvings. These rooms are built around a courtyard and instead of being walled off, these rooms /342/ are built as offices for conducting all kinds of business. On this princely court, great stone gates are built from the palace to the square, which is called the Piatsasanmarka (Piazza San Marco); inside these gates sit many scribes like the Muscovite scribes of the square, who write petitions and all other necessary matters that someone might require. Goods for eating, that is, bread and all foodstuffs, meat, fish, and all poultry are plentiful in Venice, only all are expensive for Moscow; there is especially a great quantity of all kinds of fruits and of the vegetables, which they use for food, and they are very cheap, and all year round in summer and in winter there are fruits, that is, grape clusters and vegetables, and they are always in abundance; likewise, there are flowers all year round, and they sell many flowers every day, because the Venetian women and girls use flowers in their attire and around their heads, and around their dresses.

In Venice, there are no ovens in the homes' living quarters,[56] but they only build fireplaces in the living rooms, and in them they build fires, and they have ovens only in cook houses, where they bake bread and pastries and all things needed for eating.

At the prince's residence on the right side is the sea, and in this place stands a great galley, colored with red paint, and cannon are placed on it in the customary manner, and also masts and spars with sails, and oars, and all kinds of instruments are in readiness on it. On this galley sit many *galioty* (It. *galeotti*, helots), that is, laborers, sentenced for evil deeds, who are committed to eternal labor to this galley, and all of these workers are always in restraints.[57] From this galley some of these workers are transferred to other galleys, which go to Morea to war with the Turks, but this red galley never leaves this place where it stands; but when it happens that the Venetian prince walks somewhere close to this galley, then, to honor the prince, they fire from the cannon and greet him in this way.

Venetians of the male sex wear black clothes, and the female sex also love to dress themselves in black; but Venetian men dress appropriate to their rank. Those first people who are called procurators and *schliakhta* (Pol. *szlachta*), that is, nobles, wear under their jackets a very short black caftan only to the waist, of velvet or taffeta, or of some brocade, and around the hem they sew on much black trim, and they wear tight underwear and black stockings and shoes, and their outerwear is also

[56] Tolstoi refers here to the large Russian-style domestic oven that was used both to prepare food and to heat the home. As late as the nineteenth century, domestic ovens were rare and often prohibited in European cities as too dangerous a fire risk.

[57] This is not the ceremonial Bucintoro encountered later in the Diary, but a jail or holding station for convicts who would be assigned to other galleys. In early-modern times about a third of Venice's galleys were manned by convicts. See Lane, *Venice*, pp. 366–69, 415, and passim.

black and long, to the ground, and wide with very long and broad sleeves, just like the ones formerly sewn by Muscovites of the female sex for summer. And they trim the right lapel of this outer garment with silk more than three vershoks in width, with wool on top, and on the left shoulder /343/ they wear a black cloth purse more than an arshin in length, and half an arshin or a little less across.[58]

They clip their heads and beards and mustaches, and they wear large and very fine wigs, and instead of a hat they wear a black cloth cap, trimmed with black sheepskin, and they never put it on their heads but only carry it in their hands.

The merchant people wear an undergarment just like that of the above-mentioned noble sort, but on top they wear black and red cloth cloaks, but many others wear black silk and taffeta and velvet cloaks for lightness. And of those of the trading people who so wish, many wear French dress, but all the merchants wear wigs, and they wear fine good hats with pins, and almost all of them use the black color in their clothing. Those of the female sex and maidens of every rank dress themselves very finely in a particular Venetian style of dress, and they conceal themselves with a black taffeta [veil] from the top of the head to the waist, but many others dress in the French manner. In women's costume they use colored brocade of silk, and the women folk in Venice are very well formed and upright and politic (*politichen*), tall, thin, and fine in all ways, and they do not willingly do handiwork, but spend their time in idleness.[59] There are always a great number of traveling people in Venice: Spanish, French, German, Italian, English, Dutch, Swedish, Scottish, Armenian, Persian, and all others, who come here not only for the business of trade or for

[58] Tolstoi's reference to "special dress" indicates that he knows that public attire in Venice was governed by detailed sumptuary laws.

Tolstoi correctly considers the procurators and the nobility together, for although nobility in Venice was hereditary, there were no hereditary differences in rank within the nobility. The procurators of San Marco were a special magistracy originally concerned with administering the endowment of San Marco, but it became a desirable communal office since it assured both life tenure and ceremonial honor. They and other magistrates were required to wear the red, purple, or violet robes of their office. But ordinary mature nobles wore plain black robes or togas (Tolstoi's "outerwear") over their jackets and tights. Various organized social clubs, called *compagnie delle calze,* were so named because each distinguished itself by fancy multi-colored hose and tights. The right, or outer, lapel of the robe was decorated with trim, as Tolstoi notes (a *vershok* is $1\frac{3}{4}$ inches). Finally, paintings of Venetian nobles often show the long soft shoulder bag or pouch unique to the city's upper classes (the *arshin* equals the Russian "yard," or 28 inches).

On a more general level, one should note that variations of these outer robes or togas, the equivalent of the Russian kaftan, were until early modern times the principal dress of all—men, women, and children. They survive to the present in the robes worn by clerics, judges, and academics, but the story of their evolution into official attire, and into a distinctive dress for children, is the history of modern society and of childhood itself. See the classic by Ariès, *Centuries of Childhood,* chap. 3.

[59] The dress of non-noble merchant classes was not as closely regulated as that of the nobles, and considerable variation could be seen. Tolstoi was not alone in noting that social

study, but also just to stroll around and for all kinds of amusements. In the present year no Turks are here, because they have a war with them; but formerly, they say, there were many Turks in Venice, and for the Turkish trading people a large stone house was built, with a multitude of rooms in it, and now this house stands empty. And of Greeks in Venice, who live in residences and who do business by bargaining, there are more than five or six thousand, and also many Arabs, Hungarians, Indians, and Croats.[60]

And of all the peoples there are especially many Jews, who have their own special place in Venice, enclosed by Hebrew houses of the same kind, and there are two gates to this place.[61] In those places are built their two stone hospitals, and their homes are very rich, built all of stone and immeasurably high, to a height of eight or nine stories, and there are almost ten thousand Jews in Venice, and the Hebrews here are very rich, and have a great trade, and many Jews go to sea in their own ships. One Jew may have seven or eight ships of his own, and most of all they trade in expensive goods, diamonds, sapphires, emeralds, rubies, Burmese seed pearls and pearls, gold, silver, and other /344/ similar things. The Jews wear black attire, its form like that which Venetian merchants wear, and they wear fine wigs, cut their beards and mustaches; but only for recognition they wear a scarlet cloth cap, so that it is known that they are of the Hebrew race. Any Jew who does not wish to wear a

---

life was more important to Venetian women of quality than needlework or other domestic occupations.

Concerning the dress of Venetian women, an earlier seventeenth-century traveler noted: "The women wear gownes, leaving all the neck and breast bare, and they are closed before with a lace, so open, as a man may see the linnen which they lap about their bodies, to make them seeme fat, the Italians most loving fat women. They shew their naked necks and breasts, and likewise their dugges, bound up and swelling with linnen, and all made white by art . . . . And they cast a black vaile from the head to the shoulders, and necks, and breasts, may easily be seene"; Moryson (1605), cited in Erlanger, *The Age of Courts and Kings*, p. 64. Tolstoi calls Venetian women "tall," but does not mention that "they seem a foot taller than the men because they walk on high leather-covered blocks of wood"; ibid., and illustration, after p. 168. On the whole subject of dress, see also Molmenti, *Venice*, part III, *The Decadence*, vol. I, pp. 204ff.

[60] Venice was probably still the most cosmopolitan city of the day, and although her Renaissance domination of Mediterranean trade had long since ended, she was still a major market. Lane dates the decline in Venetian trade to the decade after 1602 and sees no major upswing again until the 1730s; Lane, *Venice*, pp. 402–403, 419. The Fondaco degli Arabi, the Arabic emporium, stood on the Campo dei Mori (of the Moors), in a far district near the church of the Madonna dell'Orto. In 1645 one encountered "Jewes, Turks, Armenians, Persians, Moores, Greekes, Sclavonians, . . . all in their native fashions"; Evelyn, *Diary*, II, 449.

[61] Venice gave us the word "ghetto." Not far from the Arabic quarter mentioned above was the *ghetto vecchio*, the name derived from the foundries for casting (*gettare*) metals, which formerly occupied the site. Until 1527 Jews were forced to live there exclusively, and their homes were indeed eight stories high into the seventeenth century. See Lane, *Venice*, pp. 299–304.

scarlet cap must pay to the treasury of the *rzeczpospolita*[62] 5 ducats per person per year in Venetian money (this is 2 golden chervontsy), and then he is free to wear a black cap. Many Jews in Venice dress in the French mode, and their wives and the Jews' daughters dress finely and very richly in the Venetian and the French mode, and many wear diamonds and Burmese seed pearls and other fine stones and expensive buttons. The Jewish people in Venice, the male and the female sex, are well formed, and the Hebrews may never have any kind of weapon on them.

The Greeks who inhabit Venice are rather wealthy, and all the Greeks dress in clothing like that worn by the Venetian trading people; and few people dress in the Greek fashion in caftans, but their wives all dress in the Venetian fashion, but others in the French mode. The Greek people in Venice of the male and female sex are not of a beautiful likeness and are very untruthful in all matters, and they are hardly firm or constant in their blessed Greek faith.

And no Venetian, noble or merchant, who goes about in the customary Venetian costume wears a sword or any kind of weapon on himself, but they only have on themselves, secretly, under their clothes, a small *shtyleta* (It. *stiletto*), resembling a sharp-pointed knife; but those who wear French dress have swords with them. And when a Venetian who carries a sword must go to his prince or to a chancellery or to the senate, he must leave his sword in the passageway.

In Venice they sell meat and fish and all fruits, that is, produce, by weight in funty (pounds), which are called *lira* in Italian, and they trade in all foodstuffs and poultry all day on the square by the sea close to the Cathedral of San Marco.

In Venice the air causes distress, and there is a very foul wind from the sea water.

June 16. I was in the blessed Greek church of the great martyr St. George. This church is a good stone building. The icons in it are local.[63] On the right side of the imperial gates is the icon of the Savior, and beside it is the icon of the Wonder Worker, Nicholas, and on the left side of the imperial gates is the icon of the Blessed Mother of God, and beside it the icon of the martyr George; and in the northern and southern doors [of the iconostasis] there are no gates, as is the custom in the blessed /345/ Greek churches in Moscow and in all Russia; only in these doors there are narrow curved wooden grates as high as a man's waist. And the holy icons in this church are all of good Greek painting, and in the altar [apse] of this church the Greek wall paintings are also good. In the imperial gates, too, there are no gates,

[62] Tolstoi here uses the formal title of the Polish government to apply to the Venetian commune, commonly known after 1462 as La Serenissima. Lane, *Venice*, p. 252.

The usage suggests the word "republic," but I retain the Polish form throughout, because later (July 10), he adopts the form *respublika* (It. *repubblica*), which I render as "republic."

[63] Local here does not mean locally made, but those revered especially in this church. The local icons are the lower tier, the dedicatory icons of this particular church. As Tolstoi will later note, the upper ranges of this iconostasis were not yet in place. See Fedotov, *Russian Religious Mind*, II, 358–62.

The Greek Church of St. George, Venice (From the Museum of Icons and the Church of St. George.)

only a red silk curtain, and on it a cross is sewn. In this church stalls are built along the wall, so that one person can stand in each place. The church chandelier in this church is a large silver one, and there are many large lamps and silver candleholders. In this church over the western doors is built a large choir loft with a railing of wooden grates. Beneath this choir are two storerooms, also set off by wooden grates; in one of these storerooms, on the right side, stand nuns of the Greek order, and in the other and in the choir stand the Greek wives and girls. In this church they conduct the Liturgy and vespers and matins in the Greek language. The Greek monks wear cassocks and hoods, but few wear cloaks or cowls; and the nuns dress just like the nuns in Moscow. In this church the iconostasis is low, and the walls are painted over the imperial gates and over the northern and southern doors. Built into the wall are rather large cases, and into these cases they place holy relics in many silver arks behind glass. In this church on the altar there are no upper or lower raiments, only two covers above.[64]

The priests in this church are Greek white clergy, unmarried, and they cut their beards and mustaches, and at every service, when the priest serves without a deacon, they always read the Gospel standing at the imperial gates, turned to the west.

[64] In the twentieth century the gilded iconostasis reaches the ceiling, but the style of painting on the upper tiers clearly indicates that they were done since Tolstoi's visit. There are indeed two cases to the right and left of the iconostasis, deep enough to have held relics, which now contain icons, but it is apparent that they were originally designed, as Tolstoi notes, as reliquaries. The final statement suggests that the altar itself is draped in the Roman fashion.

The Dedication Icon of St. George (Cretan school, fifteenth to sixteenth century). (From the Museum of Icons and the Church of St. George.)

When a deacon is co-serving with a priest, then the deacon reads the Gospel on the throne on the left side of the church at the wall, high over the church's side door, with his face to the south. For the *proskomidiia* (Gk., *proshomida*) they read over a single large communion bread, on which five four-pointed crosses are imprinted. At the time of the Sacred Liturgy, when the priest or the deacon says the ektenia, at that time small children at the altar sing the "Kyrie eleison," and after the song of Jerusalem they all sing again at the altar, "It is fitting" (Lat. *Dignum et justum est*), but at the word "Christ," the priests and the Greeks do not genuflect. And when the great recessional occurs, all prostrate themselves to the ground and kneel down; also when the priest says, "Holy, Holy, Holy" (Lat. *Sanctus, Sanctus, Sanctus*), all fall to the ground; and when there is the exit with the Gospel and with the Sacred Host, little boys in surplices and girded with cinctures carry the Gospel and the Sacred Host.[65]

The metropolitan has vestments just like a Russian metropolitan, only instead of a cap he has a mitre with a cross, and he serves just like a Russian /346/ metropolitan, only he does not always dress in the same way: on feasts of the Lord and the Mother of God and the great saints, he puts on his vestments in the middle of the church, but on feasts of the significant saints [those who have a feast day], he dresses at his own seat; and his seat is built in the church on the right side of the altar, and there are places for all the people who come to the church on the side of the altar; and the priests and deacons stand in these places and sing the Mass and vespers and matins also alongside of the altar, and there are no special choir places. And when the metropolitan serves Mass for the repose of the deceased, he dresses at the altar; and sometimes this Greek metropolitan Meletius serves the Liturgy without the archbishop's vestments, in only a chasuble and without a mitre, as a simple priest.

And in the hours before the Liturgy they never read in this church; during the sacred service they do not curtain off the imperial gates. They sing the Song of Jerusalem from the choir place, and they sing "It is fitting" at one choir-place, and the Eucharist they also sing from the choir place; and the two lads who serve with the priest at the altar in surplices walk in front of the altar and close the curtains on the imperial gates; and when they read the Acts of the Apostles during the Sacred Liturgy, the priest stands at the imperial gates and faces west. At the conclusion of the Mass, they say neither the psalm "I will praise the Lord at all times" nor the verse "My mouth is filled," which are recited after the prayer said "Behind the

[65] Tolstoi continues his examination of the Greek church in Venice. He notes that the clergy is unmarried; in Russia the parish or white clergy were required to be married; he regards their trimmed beards as unorthodox, and they were at variance with Russian practice. In the church of St. George there is a kind of pulpit built in the north wall over the doorway from which they read the Gospel, and this was alien to Tolstoi. The *proskomodia* is the act of preparation of the main bread, the lamb, and its inscription of five crosses varies from that Tolstoi knew previously. The roles of the children suggest Western altar boys, again alien to Tolstoi's conception of an Orthodox service.

Ambo"; and they read the absolution during the Liturgy when the body and blood of Christ appear. They say the "dismissal blessing in the name of the Lord" at the altar. During the entire Mass, monks of the Greek order do not take off their hoods; they only take off their hoods when the priest says, "Holy, Holy, Holy," and at the appearance of the Most Pure Mystery.[66]

This same day I was at the naval wharf, where I saw many ships and various kinds of vessels, and there are many *batimentov* (It. *bastimenti*),[67] that is, vessels, of all kinds there.

June 17. I was at the Greek church and heard the Liturgy, and there the monks and priests and all the Greeks were very kind and greeted me with every courtesy.

June 20, that is, on a Sunday, I again was at the Greek church at the Sacred Liturgy. This day one priest served the Sacred Liturgy according to the custom described above, and the metropolitan during the Sacred Liturgy stood in his place on a carpet in archbishop's *sakkos* with fringes and in a black cowl, and he held in his hands a crozier like the crozier of a Muscovite hierarch. During this Sacred Liturgy, after "It is fitting," they brought me a large candle of white wax from the hierarch and an icon of the great martyr St. George printed on parchment /347/ and finely painted. I accepted the icon and the candle and gave him who brought them to me a golden chervonets, as was within my means. At the end of the Sacred Liturgy the metropolitan himself said a public prayer; in saying this prayer the metropolitan stood in his place, and not in the middle of the church. His vestments were a stole and an *omofor* (Gk. *omophorion*),[68] with a hood on his head, but the priests and deacons with him were not in vestments, and the metropolitan said the ektenia on

[66] The same topic is continued. Russian hierarchs do not wear the mitre, and in fact Russian Christianity, as early as the fifteenth century, viewed them with suspicion; in the Lives of Muscovite saints, demons were depicted wearing "Lithuanian conical hats"; Fedotov, *Russian Religious Mind,* II, 180. Above, Tolstoi describes the stalls along the walls on either side of the altar. Metropolitan Meletios will shortly profess Catholicism, and here Tolstoi notes the introduction of several Roman practices. A Russian metropolitan would not celebrate the Liturgy as a common priest; the Eucharist proper would be conducted behind the closed Royal Gates; the Greeks in Venice omit the recitation of Psalm 34, "I will bless," etc.

[67] The name Tolstoi uses evokes the image of the "large, veritable castles on the sea," the fighting and cargo ships of Venice since the thirteenth century; other names include *navis, buzus,* or *banzonus;* see Lane, *Venice,* p. 46.

[68] The omophorion is worn by Byzantine bishops. It is a six-inch wide band of embroidered silk, worn around the neck so that the ends nearly reach the ground in front and back, and as Tolstoi notes, it is worn over the *sakkos,* the short, half-sleeve tunic, resembling the dalmatic, worn by hierarchs.

the prayer himself; during the Sacred Liturgy, when the priest said the prayer "Behind the Ambo," the metropolitan sat in his place. The metropolitan's beard is unclipped, but his mustache is cut; and many Greeks in this church sit in their caps and in skullcaps during the Sacred Liturgy, and all through the Mass they stand in skullcaps. This same day I was in a Roman cathedral on the seacoast, and Jesuits live at it; this is a large church, and it is made as a circle, that is, round, and there are many riches in it.[69] In this church the floor is of slate, and it is done in the pattern of various slates. In the iconostases of all the altars are large alabaster columns of the most marvelous work, and also along the walls is much fine alabaster work.

June 24, that is, the feast of the birth of John the Forerunner,[70] the metropolitan served the Liturgy in the above-mentioned Greek church, and with him in the co-celebration were seven priests. At this time in the middle of the church they placed a platform two steps high and covered with a carpet; on this platform was placed a gilded armchair of fine carved work, upholstered with silken velvet with golden *galun* (It. *gallone,* galloons) and with fringes. And opposite this chair in front of the imperial gates the image of John the Forerunner was placed on a lectern, and over this image of the Forerunner they set a canopy on four silver poles, and at the corners they placed four tall silver candleholders, and in each was a candle of white wax, finely painted, lighted, and covered with the same canopy.

The priests vested themselves before the arrival of the hierarch into the church; the vestments of all the priests were white silk, and there were no shoulder covers or lower skirts on the chasubles, and the archdeacon and deacon both awaited the metropolitan in the church in vestments, and their surplices were white silk, bound at the sides with ribbons. When the hierarch entered the church, the archdeacon and the deacon met him at the church doors with *kandilami* (It. *candela*), and, having entered, the hierarch spoke according to custom in the Greek language and began to don his vestments, and the priests who co-served with him dressed him; the hierarch did not have any subdeacons or subclerks with him, but there were only three young lads in surplices, who every day co-serve /348/ with the priests. And I have already written at length above about the vestments of the hierarch. And when the hierarch entered the church, he kissed the holy icons, and they sang "It is fitting," in the Greek language; and when he was vesting, the archdeacon and deacon incensed him, and when the hierarch was dressed, they immediately began the Liturgy and did not read the hours. And the priest began the Liturgy at the altar, first co-serving

[69] The identification of this round church on the sea is not positive, but it is probably the octagonal Basilica della Salute, built by Baldassare Longhena (1604–82) to commemorate deliverance from the plague of 1630. The elaborate floor design and the rich columns at each of the six side altars seem to confirm the identification.

[70] Tolstoi used interchangeably "the Forerunner" and "the Baptist" for St. John, and I retain his usage as it occurs.

with an archdeacon who spoke the first ektenia standing before the imperial gates, and the other deacon standing in a line with him; and, having finished the ektenia, they bowed to the hierarch, and the archdeacon and the deacon went to the altar, one in the north and the other in the south door, and thus did one archdeacon or the deacon speak all of the ektenia, with the other standing with him. After the ektenia they sang "Kyrie eleison" at the altar; when they began to sing "Blazhenni" (the Blessing), the serving priests went to the altar, but the two priests remained by the metropolitan.[71]

At the exit with the Gospel, the archdeacon carried the Holy Gospel, and the other deacon walked before him with a candela and carried in his hands the *trikiri* (Gk. *triharion*, the bishop's three-candle holder).[72] The hierarch, kissing the Holy Gospel and holding up the *trikiri*, went to the altar, sang "Come let us bow," and, arriving at the altar, he incensed the altar, but did not incense the church, and through the whole Liturgy they did not extinguish the *trikiri*, but the deacon held it in his hands. At the time of the "Three Holies"[73] they sang "Holy God" at the altar, and the metropolitan blessed them, only without a cross. The hierarch did not go up to the elevated place, but the serving priests walked with him to the altar during the "Three Holies." The deacon read the Acts before the imperial gates, standing in front of the image of John the Forerunner, which stood under the canopy; during this the hierarch sat on a stool in the imperial gates. The archdeacon read the Gospel on the throne facing south, and meanwhile the metropolitan stood in the imperial gates with his face turned toward the people. After the Gospel, and after the Song of Jerusalem, the hierarch blessed the people with one candle. During the Great Recessional the hierarch was at the altar, and all the serving priests exited with him. The archdeacon walked with a candela and carried in his hand the *amothorius* (antidoron),[74] and the deacon carried the *diskos* (paten); behind him a priest carried the *potir* (chalice) and other priests carried the holy relics in arks, and the deacon who carried the *diskos* said nothing, but the archdeacon spoke. During the Great Reces-

[71] Tolstoi here is concerned with the positions assumed by the co-celebrants of the Liturgy, especially during that part of the Liturgy of the Catechumens that corresponds to the Gradual in the Roman Mass. The blessing "Blessed is he that comes in the name of the Lord (John 12: 13)" is usually spoken from the apsidal throne, the bishop's ornamented seat behind the altar.

[72] This is the three-candle holder that recalls the Trinity, and which the bishop holds in one hand (the *dikiri*, or two-branched holder, being in the other) when he blesses the people during the Liturgy.

[73] The Three Holies is the Trisagion, Thrice Holy. "Holy God, Holy Mighty One, Holy Immortal One, have mercy on us" is the verse sung by the people after the cantors have intoned the variable hymns of the day, during the Liturgy of the Catechumens, after the Little Entrance.

[74] This is a misprint; the antidor is the blessed bread that is distributed to the congregation in the Byzantine rite. Antidor, Greek *antidoron*. In view of the correct use of antidoron on the next page, this seems the best reading, but there is an alternative: an *artophoron* is a coffer intended to hold the consecrated bread for the communion of the faithful.

sional all of the bells in the belltower rang. During the Song of Jerusalem the metropolitan himself incensed the altar, but the archdeacon incensed the church, standing at the imperial gates, and when they arrived at the imperial gates from the Great Recessional, the metropolitan took the paten and the chalice into the imperial gates and spoke what is customary for a hierarch, and having spoken he took them to the altar. /349/

All during the Liturgy, even at the dispensing of the Divine Mystery, they curtained off the imperial gates, and at the holy dispensing the serving priests and deacons began from the right side. And when the hierarch was serving, and co-celebrants were with him, they had no service book during the service and did not say the prayers in the Liturgy; but the hierarch said only the appropriate prayers, and the priests listened with heads bowed, and he spoke so loudly that it was possible to hear him.[75] At the time of the appearance of the Sacred Host, there was great bell ringing on all the bells, and they held six large, white, lighted candles before the imperial gates, and after the Prayer Behind the Ambo,[76] they put them out. Then the hierarch sat in his place in the church and distributed the *antidor* (antidoron) to the serving priests and to all the people while sitting. When the metropolitan left the church, he asked me to visit his cell, and since he requested it, I went to his home. In his first cell all the walls were covered with colored wool velvet, and there were many armchairs covered with leather. In another cell were many books in cases on all the walls. The third cell was all covered with crimson silk, and there were many armchairs in it covered in green velvet; at the front wall a carpet was spread, and placed on that carpet was a fine armchair, where the metropolitan himself sat, and I sat on another armchair close to him, and he greeted me with great affection. Then they brought fine confections in great silver cups and he treated me to them, and he brought me white grape wine in a small fine glass goblet; then, dismissing me, he escorted me to the stairwell with great friendliness.

[75] Tolstoi's comment that it was possible to hear the celebrant calls to mind the controversy over church singing in seventeenth-century Muscovy. The Russian church had long used a practice in which different clerics could read or chant prayers simultaneously, garbling the service and contributing to the experiential as opposed to the doctrinal thrust of Russian Orthodoxy. In the middle of the seventeenth century, first by Patriarch Iosif in 1651 and then by the controversial Nikon, the principle of *edinoglasie* was introduced, in which one voice, priest, choir, or deacon read or chanted at any single moment. These same reforms also introduced the sermon, which Tolstoi also notes in Western churches. See Lupinin, *Religious Revolt in the XVIIth Century;* von Gardner, *Russian Church Singing, I,* 135–46.

[76] The Prayer Behind the Ambo is the dismissal blessing at the end of the service, part of the Thanksgiving after Communion. In the Roman Mass it is the *Dominus vobiscum;* in the Byzantine Liturgy a longer prayer begins, "O, Lord, you bless those who bless you and you sanctify those who trust in you; save your people and bless your inheritance." It is intoned aloud. See Kucharek, *Liturgy,* pp. 722–30.

June 26. I was at the armory court, which in Italian is called the *arsinal* (arsenale);[77] this court is very large and built of good stone; and when I came to this court, I had to tell the *generale-maggiore* who was in charge of this court about myself. This maggiore allowed me to enter the arsenale and had me shown everything in this court that was appropriate for a traveling foreigner. The gates to this court are well made, and in front of these gates is a large stone platform, and around the platform is a fine iron grate; on both sides of this platform are placed two large lions made of white stone of fine carved work; and in these gates stood the guard, quite a few soldiers, who prevented me with their sabers from going into the court, and with my saber I returned [the salute] to these soldiers, as is the custom. I entered the courtyard, and inside in two places are built large palaces two stories high. /350/ The wall paneling in the palaces is all of painted wood; in these palaces along the walls are placed a multitude of marvelous weapons of all kinds, all arranged in figures, in circles, and in all sorts of designs: *pistolety* (It. *pistoletta*), *karabiny* (*carabina*), *mushkety* (*moschetto*), swords, also armor, breastplates, and all things appropriate to 15,000 serving cavalrymen. And for infantrymen, who are on galleys and on other vessels, for 25,000 men; and the weapons here are always clean and ready, and they constantly inspect and clean them, but there are no very fine weapons in these palaces. At this same court are warehouses where cannon stand, and I saw 34 large cannon, and also many small and middle-size cannon and also many *mazzher* (prob. It. *moschettiere,* musket), from which they throw *granaty* (It. *granata*) and bombs; and the cannon balls and grenades are all arranged in fine patterns. In the same court is a large palace, where they cast brass cannon; in the same court they build all kinds of vessels: ships, penal ships, *galeottas, marciliane,*[78] and all other vessels for sailing the sea, and at all times in this court there are 2,000 workers to build naval vessels, and these workers are never allowed to go anywhere from this court,[79] and they issue a salary annually of 25,000 Venetian ducats to these workers, and a Venetian ducat has in it 15 altyns in Muscovite money. Also at this court is a great stone cellar, and in this cellar is a great stone vat, and into the vat from behind a wall pours a red grape wine, and from this vat they strain the wine through cloves, and every day they distribute a measure to those

[77] The Arsenal (corrupted Arabic word *darsin'a,* house of industry, shipyard), founded in 1104, had two famous antique lions at its entrance in 1697. They were brought from Piraeus (Athens) in 1687 as war booty after the reconquest of Morea by Francesco Morosini; the other two lions would be added in the eighteenth century. The elaborate gateway is from 1460, and the two palaces stand on either side of the Ca'di Dio.

[78] The *galeotta* was a small long-ship, a light galley used in coastal waters. The *marciliane* were cargo ships, some as large as 240 tons, which carried the Adriatic trade; they were being phased out in the seventeenth century as too difficult to defend. For information on naval affairs, see Lane, *Venetian Ships and Shipbuilders.*

[79] That is, they were not allowed to travel, for fear that their skills would be used by another state.

shipworkers. In this same cellar are many barrels with white and red grape wine for the same workers, and they carry the wine to the workers in large tubs. At this same court I saw two gondolas, that is, small naval vessels carved and gilded, with roofs covered with golden velvet; these gondolas are similar to the cossack boats on the Volga. The Venetian prince goes to ride in the sea in these gondolas, and he also rides in them in processions. In this same court stands a galley, that is, a penal vessel of middle size, neither large nor small;[80] it is made of fine gilded carved work with a roof. I was on this galley, and this galley is inlaid with designs; along the sides are benches, and in the middle is a carved and gilded place for the Venetian prince. Annually, on the day of the Ascension of the Lord, the prince of Venice goes to sea three versts from Venice in a procession to wed the sea, whereby he throws a golden ring from this galley into the sea. This galley is made of very great richness and of fine craftsmanship. /351/

June 29. I went to sea with my master captain, George, surnamed Radzhi (Raggi), with whom I studied naval affairs, and I was with him on two ships. This same day I was in a monastery,[81] in which live Roman monks—the Georgians—who wear a black habit on top and a white underneath, just like the Dominicans. The monks in this monastery are all of honorable, noble birth; there is a large stone church in this monastery, built with a generous hand; the columns in this monastery and also on the outside of the church are marble; in this church the altar platform is also marble, set with alabaster tiles in patterns. In this church are many of the most marvelous stone carvings, and in this church in the choir is a large and very fine organ, and the whole structure of the church and the monastery is marvelous. This same day I was in another monastery in which the Roman monks, the Capuchins, live, and they wear a grey habit, made of coarse cloth, and they always walk barefooted. These Capuchins never eat meat. Within this monastery is a large stone church; there are one hundred monks in this monastery. The monks do not cut their beards, and they live one monk to a cell and drink nothing but water, and they have no possessions except books. In this monastery they showed me many holy relics in

[80] This is the Bucintoro, from which annually the Doge wedded the Adriatic by throwing a ring on Ascension Thursday. The ship was destroyed by the French in 1797. A description of the ceremony is given below when Tolstoi witnessed it.

[81] Although the identification is not absolute, the first of these two churches seems to be San Giorgio Maggiore; the name may account for Tolstoi calling this old Benedictine center "Georgian." Begun by Palladio in 1565, the façade and the elaborately patterned marble floor in the sanctuary and on the altar platform conform to Tolstoi's description. The identification is confirmed if indeed Tolstoi returned there a week later (see July 8, below) to see the library.

The second church in the paragraph is probably Santa Maria della Salute, 1631–87, mentioned above, but this visit brought Tolstoi to the Seminario Patriarcale (by Longhena, 1670), which houses the origins of what would become the vast cultural collections of the Venice Seminary.

arks, among which they showed me with especially great honor the hair of the Blessed Mother of God. In this monastery I was in the library, where I saw a multitude of books, more than 2,000 in various languages, printed and handwritten.

July 1. I was at the court of a Venetian woman at which they make fine gold and silver brocade and silks of all kinds. These masters make brocade very quickly and well, and the price is cheaper than the Muscovite [brocade]. This same day I was in a monastery of the Carmelites.[82] In this monastery is a large church, and the outside walls of the monastery are all done in carved alabaster of marvelous Italian work. There are no painted icons in this monastery, but all of them are carved of alabaster and done of the most marvelous work. There are many altars at the walls in this church, and the columns are slate, and the platform in this church is slate. This monastery has a large garden, with grapes and fig trees, and black plums and nutmegs and many cypress trees, where I lingered for an hour or so.

July 6. I was at the home of a Venetian nobleman (Pol. *szlacta*) who was the uncle of the previous Roman pope.[83] His house is a large stone building, and the chambers in the court outside are /352/ very fine. In the middle of these chambers the decor is fine, and in all there are 16 rooms, upholstered in French silk in various colors; in whatever color silk the room is covered, the chairs and armchairs in that room are covered in the same silk. The doors of all the rooms have curtains of crimson velvet and broad gold lace. Two rooms are covered with Venetian velvet, one crimson and the other blue, and the chairs and armchairs are the same. One room is decorated with fine gold wallpaper.

July 8. I rode from Venice to a place called Murana (Murano), a half verst from Venice. Here I saw a place where they make large glass mirrors and all kinds of glass vessels and all kinds of glass figurines.[84] This same day I was in the monastery of the Georgian monks, and I was in their library.[85] This library is a large palace,

[82] The description seems to be of Santa Maria del Carmine, and the attached monastery is probably the present Scuola Grande dei Carmine, baroque, attributed to B. Longhena, which corresponds to Tolstoi's portrait. There is a small cloister, now the Istituto Statale D'Arte, but the large garden he mentions is probably the adjoining large open space of the Campo Margarita. The number of Longhena churches mentioned in the Diary suggests that his Venetian hosts were most interested in showing the newest local architecture.

[83] The former pope was Alexander VIII (1689–91), Pietro Ottoboni of Venice.

[84] The small island of Murano had been the center of Venice's famous glass industry since the fourteenth century, and remains so.

[85] As noted above, Tolstoi is returning to the library and monastery of San Giorgio Maggiore, famous for its cloisters of bay and cypress trees. The great library was recently built by

and in it are 15,000 books, and it is well built; and the cases, in which the books rest, are walnut. In this same library stand two very large globes, one celestial and the other earthly. The circumference of these globes is 4 sazhens. In this library, too, are two other small globes placed nicely behind glass. On the walls in this palace are placed many fine painted pictures, and the whole stone structure of this monastery is marvelous. I was in the garden of the monastery, where I saw many grapes, interlaced on arches over the paths. In this garden are many fig trees, and I had plenty of time to eat from them.

July 9. I went by sea from Venice to an island called Lida (Lido); on this island is a courtyard where soldiers sit.[86] This courtyard is made of stone, and it is one verst from Venice. It is rather large and holds 400 soldiers. A guard is posted at the gate of this courtyard. Soldiers are never permitted to go into Venice for any reason, and when they go to sea, they are taken away in ships or galleys. These soldiers are foreigners of all types, but also Venetians who are sentenced to this station because they are guilty of a crime. Foreigners who have robbed the rich people are sentenced to this courtyard, and they have no one to defend them, they will not be released from this courtyard to the end of their days. Not even the prince of Venice has the power to grant someone freedom—only the whole republic (*respublika*) can do this. And alongside this courtyard is a monastery, where these soldiers go to sing.

July 11. There was a procession in Venice, as Catholics celebrate the Holy Cross of Christ today. Priests, monks, and lay people from all the monasteries /353/ and churches meet in the church of San Marco the Evangelist, with banners and with crosses. The prince of Venice rode this day over the gulf to a monastery where Capuchins live, and from there he returned again by sea to his house, and this is how he went: Before him went a covered gondola, on which 6 flags were carried. In the same gondola rode trumpeteers who blew [their trumpets], and behind them rode the prince of Venice in a carved, gilded *karbas* with a roof.[87] The roof of this karbas is covered in scarlet velvet, and gold is well and richly sewn on the velvet. In this karbas the prince of Venice sat in the middle in an armchair, and in front of him was

---

Baldassarre Longhena (1604–82). The monastery was suppressed in the early nineteenth century, and its treasures were dispersed.

[86] Tolstoi's description does not allow us to distinguish between the Castelvecchio, the ancient Castle of San Nicolo and the nearby Monastery of San Nicolo di Lido, and the newer Castle of Sant'Andrea, with its adjoining Carthusian monastery, Sant'Andrea della Certosa.

[87] A *karbas* (Russian) is a Russian cargo vessel with high sides, sails, and four to ten oars, used on the White Sea. It is unclear why Tolstoi here uses the Russian name rather than an Italian one, since he was pursuing his naval studies. The procession crosses to Santa Maria della Salute, previously described.

a gilded table, and on the table a gold pillow was placed, and on the pillow an unsheathed sword. Alongside the karbas sailed 4 small gondolas, finely made of carved work and gilded. The roofs on all 4 gondolas were covered in cherry-red velvet, and they were finely sewn with gold. No one rode in these gondolas—they were empty. The ambassador of the pope of Rome sat on the right side of the prince of Venice, and on the left side was the French ambassador, and below them sat the Venetian procurators. On the nose of this same karbas stood 6 men, and they held the round golden velvet sunburst [?] of the prince of Venice. Behind this karbas sailed two more gilded and carved karbases, in which rode the Venetian procurators. When the prince of Venice arrived at his home and left the karbas for land and went to the church of San Marco, they carried two cushions and chairs before him, and behind them walked two captains, and behind them walked the prince himself. Their dress was full and gold in the Venetian mode, and on top of their dress, over their shoulders, was a short ermine cloak. On [the prince's] head was a golden cap of a particular fashion; with him on his right side and on his left side were the papal and the French ambassadors, and behind him they carried the unsheathed sword and the sunburst. Then all the procurators walked two abreast. All of them wore red silken attire made in the Venetian mode and covered with gold cloaks, and others wore velvet double fringes. Each had a gold velvet purse over his left shoulder; and there were 40 of these procurators. When the prince arrived at the church, they began to say the Mass, with 3 priests. At this time they played the organs and sang in the choir, and during this time all those who came with crosses passed through the church. In this procession I saw many immeasurable church riches. They had made a great mound of silver, and on the top of this mound were the holy relics in fine arks, and over the holy relics was a fine golden canopy on silver /354/ poles at the four corners. When all had passed and the Mass ended, the prince left the church by the same path and in the same ranks as he had arrived. When Mass is conducted in the church of San Marco, which in Italian is called *misa* (Lat. *missa;* It. *messa*), many lamps throughout the church are lighted with wood oil, and indeed many lamps of oil burn in this church continuously.

July 24. Venice had a very great wind and rain from the east, and in this rain was a great hail the size of the egg of a Russian chicken, only not rounded but sharp on the edge. Inhabitants were struck dead by this hail in many Venetian courtyards, and in gardens all the fruit was knocked from the trees, and the trees were felled. So great and dark was the cloud that it was impossible to see anything, just as on an autumn night, and everyone's fear was very great, and it lasted an hour and a quarter; and this wind began in the 12th hour of day, and two Greeks, who were walking along a street, were thrown from the shore and cast into the sea by the wind, where they drowned; and at sea many ships were turned over by that wind. At the same time, one gondola was turned over close to Venice, and in it a notable gentleman of the Venetian senate was riding on business, and he drowned, and his body and those of many others who drowned were brought to Venice today.

July 25. On Sunday was the burial of a Greek of the blessed faith, who was drowned in the sea by the above-mentioned wind. He was carried from his house to the burial on a couch; his body and head were covered in black, like a shroud of the deceased. A rug was placed beneath his body, and under his head was placed a yellow satin pillow. His face was uncovered, the hands were positioned in the Orthodox custom, and in his hands he held a candle made of white wax. In front of the coffin they carried the ark, on which is painted the image of Nicholas the Wonderworker. Behind the body walked many people with candles, and clerics of the Roman faith walked in white dress behind the body with candles, and a Catholic priest walked in a stole, and in front of the coffin Catholics walked and sang, and behind the coffin walked Greek priests not in vestments, but with candles, and all carried lighted candles; and all walked in their hats. They brought his body to the Greek church of the great martyr George, and they placed it in the middle of the church on high, and they stood around the coffin with large candles, and the Roman clergy performed his funeral while seated. When they had completed the funeral and left the church, the Greek priests began to perform the funeral; all wore surplices, and they did not wear chasubles /355/, and they did not open the imperial gates, and the priests did not stand around his body, but in the places[88] where they always stand in the church. And they sang the funeral in the Greek language, but briefly, and they did not sing the verse of the Kiss of Peace. After the funeral, when the people had left the church, they took the dead body to a room, where a doctor removed the viscera from the corpse, and they took everything from inside of him, having cut his belly open. They took his brain from his head, and they interred his insides and brain at the Greek church, where they performed the funeral. In place of the insides in his belly and in place of his brain in his head they poured herbs and spirits of balsam, and they put on a *paskoni* [?] and sewed him up; and when they removed the brain, they sawed the head bone with a saw, as one would saw wood. Thus arranged, they sent his body and bones without the viscera to the Levant, that is, to the East, where he had been born and had his home.

August 7. I was at the residence of the Venetian prince.[89] His home is of stone. First I was in the chamber in which they receive ambassadors. This is a large

[88] That is, they stood in the stalls around the walls on either side of the altar.

[89] The Ducal Palace was the physical expression of the powerful Serenissima: it was the Doge's Palace, the central administrative building, the Public Archives, and the Palace of Justice. Tolstoi describes four rooms:

1. The Sala del Collegio, the most famous and magnificent for its art and decoration, the room in which the Doge sat with the signoria: the Six Councillors (the Savi), the Heads of the Council of Ten, and the Grand Councillor; here ambassadors, already awed by their ascent up magnificent stairways, were received, and important questions of state were discussed.
2. The Consiglio dei Dieci, the room of the notorious Council of Ten, which discussed all

chamber; the ceiling in it is of carved, gilded wood, and among the carvings are many fine paintings. The prince's place is set in the middle of the front wall, and on both sides of his place are benches on which the procurators sit. The walls in this chamber are covered with golden horses [*sic*]. Then I was in another chamber, where the Venetian privy council sits; in this council the Venetian prince meets with just 24 procurators, and the procurators among the Venetians are the first people under the principes, that is, the princes; when a prince of Venice dies, they select as prince one of the procurators of old age. There are no decorations at all in this chamber, only a princely seat covered in red satin. Then I was in the chamber of justice, where I saw their judges. In this chamber three judges sit behind a table, and in front of them rests a book, and a clerk stands at the table, and he holds a paper in his hands. One man, standing in front of these judges, speaks and looks at a notebook, which he holds in his hands, and he speaks loudly; the other *supernik* (It. *supernico?*, *supplicante?*) stands silently and listens to his words, and when he has said as much as he has to, he bows to the judges and withdraws a little, and his supernik begins to speak. The judges heed their words and speak to the clerk, who stands with the paper, and they order him to write the decree, that is, the resolution of the matter and the order; this order is read to both superniks /356/, and justice is decided on the same day. Over the doors of this chamber is a carved-stone representation of a person of the female sex in the image of Justice: her eyes are veiled, so she cannot see whether the person on trial is mighty or wretched, and in one hand she holds scales, that is, the standard of justice, and in the other hand a sword, that is, vengeance for wrongdoing.

Then I was in the princely armory, which has three chambers. In these chambers are many weapons, and they are finely decorated with designs. The Venetians were famous for their arms in antiquity, and they have many fine ones, but there are no very costly ones here. In this same chamber I saw one small cannon, made of red iron, and plants are carved on it, and it is gilded of fine work. In these same chambers I saw 12 fine Turkish arquebuses and many Turkish damask steel blades and

---

extraordinary business in secret (hence its notoriety, and Tolstoi's designation as a "privy council").

3. The Capi del Consiglio dei Diece, the room of the three head magistrates elected from the Council of Ten to read letters and to call assemblies of the whole; unmentioned, but between these latter two rooms was the small chamber containing a Bocca de Leone, the box into which secret denunciations were dropped.

4. Three rooms of the armory, then as now more a trophy room than an actual warehouse of military supplies.

Evelyn's comments are very brief, but he mentions "those gallant Paintings of the final judgement, just over the Dukes Throne, the work of *Tintoret,* & esteem'd amongst the best pieces in *Europe:* On the roof are the famous Acts of the Republick, painted by severall excellent Masters, especially Bassano; . . . Thence into the Chamber of the Council of *Ten,* all of them painted by the most celebrated Masters." Evelyn, *Diary,* II, 444.

The Doge's Palace (Giacomo Franco, 1610.)

Sitting of the Great Council (Giacomo Franco, 1610.)

shields, for which the Venetians are famous, for they took these arms and blades and shields from the Turks in battle. The living quarters of the Venetian prince are above these chambers; the decor in them is very rich.

It is the custom for the notable people of Venice to ride from their homes every day to the prince's court, and all ranks of people are allowed to enter his palace, except for his living quarters; not only men but also women and girls, who so desire, enter and walk about in these princely chambers. Tradespeople come to the passageways and sell pastries, and they carry the loaves on spars, and those who wish will buy and eat them [in public] without shame. And it is very crowded at and around the princely court every day because they conduct all sorts of business, and all the chancellery offices are built at the princely court. Every man who has an urgent matter can approach the prince himself by this method: except for feast days, it is customary for the prince of Venice, along with the procurators, to conduct business on all free days in his palace in a special chamber; when the prince and the procurators enter that chamber, the man who is assigned to stand at the doors opens and locks them, and he does not admit just anybody to that chamber, but he admits petitioners into the chamber in this manner: when the prince and the procurators are sitting in that chamber, a secretary comes out of that chamber and takes petitions, which in Italian are called *supliki* (It. *supplica*), from every petitioner, he writes the names of the petitioners on a list, and he takes their petitions to the prince inside the chamber; and, going by the list, he calls one man at a time into the chamber before the prince; when the petitioner enters the chamber and comes before the prince, the secretary reads the petitioner's petition before the prince; and given a decision based on the petition, /357/ the petitioner is dismissed from the chamber. Then they summon another, and thus they deal with all petitioners that day; and the prince and procurators do not leave that chamber without dealing with the petitioners, however many there are that day.

In the above-mentioned church of the great martyr George, this is the custom: on the first day of August a passageway is built in front of this church; they make *preshpektivi* (It. *prospettivi*) in the gardens, and they are covered in red silk, and on the silk white fruits and all sorts of marvelous designs are embroidered, and the roof and *shprengela* are painted; in the middle of the shprengela[90] is placed an icon of the Most Holy Mother of God of Greek painting, held in a rich frame; the size of this icon is almost an arshin, and in the frame of this icon are many fine stones; this icon is an old Greek painting, and around this holy icon are placed 50 silver candlesticks, in which burn fine large candles made of white wax. Among the candleholders are 20 silver pitchers, and in them are all kinds of flowers and foliage, and this image stands in this place until the 15th of August. There is no procession from this Greek

[90]Tolstoi introduces a neologism, *preshpektiva,* perspective, here in the sense of a stage setting. *Sprengeli* is unsatisfactorily identified, but I suspect this is It. *pergola,* an arbor or trellis. At the Church of St. George I was unable to learn just which icon of the Mother of God was so honored.

The Mother of God Hodigitria by Michael Damascenos, early sixteenth century. This is most likely the icon of the Mother of God carried in procession from the Church of St. George. (From the Museum of Icons and the Church of St. George.)

church for the blessing of the water on the first day of August. They bless the water in the church after the Liturgy; the metropolitan does not bless the water, but rather a serving priest without a deacon.

August 15. The metropolitan served the Sacred Liturgy in the Greek church, and with him in the service were 8 priests and one archdeacon, and the icon of the Blessed Mother of God was taken from the shprengela, and the passageway was removed from the church. The hierarch's vestments were of fine brocade fabric, with crosses on them. At the end of the Liturgy there was a procession: first they carried six white wax candles on tall silver candlesticks, and behind them were 12 students who study in the Greek school; behind them on a sedan-chair they carried the previously mentioned icon of the Blessed Mother of God, which stood in the middle of the church over a passageway; behind the icon walked the priests, and behind them the metropolitan with a crozier; on each side of the metropolitan walked a priest, but they did not lead him by the arm. Over the icon of the Blessed Mother of God they carried a four-cornered canopy, made of gold velvet on four tall silver poles. Behind the metropolitan a Greek merchant carried the Blessed Cross, and with him the Greek trading people walked two abreast; then came all the people with large lighted candles, two abreast, and I was among them in this procession. And thus they walked around this Greek /358/ church three times with the icon of the Blessed Mother of God, and again they entered the church by the south doors. Before the exit from the church into the procession, they did not pray or sing, but they sang during the procession of the Mother of God; and, having entered the church, they said the ektenia and then were dismissed. This same day in the Greek church 30 Greeks were recipients of the most pure and most precious Mystery of Christ; these recipients took the Eucharist before the beginning of the Liturgy, and during the distribution of the Eucharist there was no singing. The priest with the Divine Mystery stood at the imperial gates in only an alb and stole, and he distributed the Eucharist from a ciborium.

August 17. From Venice I went to the city of Padua in a *piota* (It. *peata,* barge), and I hired the peata, in which I was carried from Venice to Padua for 5 Venetian ducats. This peata was of good *sitarskoi*[91] (carved) work, painted outside and gilded inside, with large windows. The drapery was of red silk, and the curtains on the windows were red tafetta for defense against the heat of the sun. In this peata

[91] The Russian editor, Dmitrii Tolstoi, confirms this spelling in the text. Later it is corrected to *snitsarskoi* work; German *schnitzen,* to carve, is an obvious analog, but the source is probably Polish, *snycerski,* carved, *snycerz,* a carver. Tolstoi used a private peata rather than the more common *burchiello,* the large barges that plied daily between Venice and Padua.

I stood on a fine carpet, and when we had crossed the open sea in that peata, we entered a river by which one gets to Padua.[92] The pilot, who carried me in his peata, hired a horse, and the horse was tied to the peata, and the horse pulled me in that peata to Padua. On the river, on which I sailed to Padua, there are locks in four places, and they open and close those locks with instruments on iron chains, because the river has little water, and a peata could not go on it without these locks. Because of the locks, the river has deeper water, and large peatas can pass without obstacle. I arrived in Padua in that peata from Venice in one day. It is 25 Italian miles from Venice to Padua.[93] I stayed in Padua in an *osteria,* that is, in an inn, and stayed in Padua 5 days. Padua is a large place on level ground; close to the city are small forests. The Paduan fortress is of stone and set off from the city afar by earth, and around the walls water passes, and the width of this water is more than 20 sazhens. There are many large stone homes in Padua. One of them has a garden belonging to a Venetian cavalier; it is very large and has many marvelous structures in it.[94] Also in this garden are many lemon, pomegranate, chestnut, walnut, fig, apple, various pear, plum, cherry, sweet-cherry, peach or apricot, various grape—white and black—*tsukat,* paradise-apple, and many other fruit trees of all kinds. In this same garden /359/ are fine fountains, from which streams of fine pure water flow; in the middle of this garden is a stone garret built of fine craftsmanship. Around this garret, trees are placed in the most marvelous workmanship, in such a way that the branches and leaves interlace tightly; and paths are built through the trees of a width so that one person may pass, and, if necessary, two side by side; and one passes to the garret by that path, and if someone who knows [the way] does not lead one along the path through those trees, one cannot get to that garret, even if one walks the paths all day; and when one walks along these paths and gets right to the middle, then one cannot get back out without a guide.[95]

In this garden are fine *prospettivi* of Italian painting; there are many other marvelous things in this garden, the likes of which I do not describe because time is short. There is a large Western church in Padua named for the Catholic saint Anthony of Padua, and in this church, they say, his body rests under the altar. This

[92] On his trip up the Brenta canal Tolstoi fails to mention the numerous villas built densely along its course. Already in the sixteenth century many Venetian families, *borghesia* as well as patricians, fled to the countryside between June 4 and the end of July, and again from October 4 until sometime in November. He is more observant on his return trip below. See Honour, *Companion Guide to Venice,* pp. 240–50.

[93] Tolstoi here introduces the Italian mile, which he attempts to measure against the Russian verst, but confusingly, on September 18 (see below). As a rule of thumb, the Italian mile he uses is very close to an English/American mile.

[94] This is almost certainly the Palazzo Giustinian, the Renaissance summer house built for Luigi Cornaro by Giovanmaria Falconetto in 1524, with extensive gardens laid out for his nephew, Alvise Cornaro.

[95] This is apparently Tolstoi's first encounter with a maze.

The water journey between Padua and Venice. The towing of the Burcello, public transport, and, on the right, a private vessel similar to that used by Tolstoi.

church is built on a fine foundation and is very long and wide, and it has seven large heads.[96] In this church, around the altar, is a fine structure of alabaster and of various colors of slate stones, and the altar-platform in this church is made of various colors of marble of marvelous work. In this church they showed us many relics of the holy apostles and of holy martyrs and many other holy things, among which they showed us a tongue, and they said this was the tongue of St. Anthony of Padua. Around the resting place of St. Anthony, around his grave, hang many large and small silver lamps, of which I could count one hundred and thirty; the rest, which are present throughout the church, I could not count because of the great size of the church. At this church live Catholic monks called Franciscans. In the middle of this church, along the walls, one sees ancient Greek wall paintings.[97]

In Padua is another church named for the holy martyr Justina, whom the Eastern Church commemorates on the 2nd of September with St. Cyprian, who had once been a magician. This church is very large: its length is 70 sazhens and 3 arshins, and its width is 40 sazhens and 3 arshins; it is built on a cross-shaped *fundament* (It. *fondamento*), and it has five large heads. In this church the floor is made of various colors of marble of marvelous workmanship, and around the altar and along the walls is very marvelous work of various colors of slate and also many works of alabaster. There are many marble and alabaster columns in this church, and a multitude of fine figures /360/ made of alabaster of the most miraculous workmanship.[98]

The body of the martyr St. Justina rests under the altar in this church, but it can-

[96] It is no accident that Tolstoi goes first to the Basilica of Sant'Antonio; although St. Anthony lived only a short time in Padua, his shrine had long been the most celebrated in the city, and pilgrims even to the present come from everywhere to visit it. The church has seven principal domes, Tolstoi's "heads," a medieval Russian term for them, distinguishing them from towers or spires ("tents"); see Fedotov, *Russian Religious Mind,* II, 351–53. It is in fact an elaborate structure, with a variety of spires and campaniles as well as domes.

[97] The sanctuary, the Chapel of the Treasure, in which rests the reliquary with St. Anthony's tongue, had just been added in 1691. The nave, transept, and eastern apses are richly frescoed in an antique style, but the work is not "ancient Greek." The tongue of the saint is still on display, and in 1981 his coffin, sealed in 1263, was opened.

Tolstoi's description of Sant'Antonio is sparse; he is unawed by Donatello's high altar and statuary, or by his equestrian statue "il Gattamelata" outside.

[98] Santa Giustina is sixteenth century (1501–32). Justina, virgin and martyr, and Cyprian, converted sorcerer, died in 304; their feasts are celebrated on September 26. The church, the fourth on the site, is a basilica ("cross shaped") with five domes. Tolstoi notes the magnificent carved stalls along the walls, the great choir by Riccardo Taurigni, sixteenth century. Among the "figures," or statues, Tolstoi would have been shown was the recently completed marble masterpiece, the Pietà by Filippo Parodi (1689).

Tolstoi often uses the word "slate" (Russian *aspid*) generically to mean something like "any colored facing stone"; likewise, he uses the word "alabaster" (Russian *alebastr*) broadly, not only for the fine hydrated sulfate of calcium from the region around Florence, nor for specific calcites, but for any architectural stone that could be carved.

not be seen.[99] In this church they showed us a narrow place beneath the church's altar-platform; on the opposite side is another very tight place, and they told me that in antiquity a man and a girl toiled in these places for the sake of Christ. If this is true—that these two people lived in these places—it is most miraculous, for both places are so tight that a person cannot stand there on his feet, but can only kneel down; in these places it is also so dark that there is not even a little bit of light there. In one spot in this same church, they have placed a slate cover like those the Venetians customarily place over a water well, and in the middle of this slate stone an iron grate is placed; and when one lowers an iron rod with a lighted wax candle through this grate into the darkness, one can see many human bones. And they say these are the bones of holy martyrs, and they do not know the names of these holy martyrs because many years have passed; however, they honor these relics as those of saints.[100] In this church, at the altar on the left side high in the wall, is an organ in the choir, the likes of which, they say, one can find nowhere else, and they played on that organ for me during my stay in this church. This organ is wondrous—it is so immeasurably loud that it seems like the church is shaking from the sound of that organ.[101] On this organ is a golden star that shines when the organ is played [as the light] passes along the pipes of the organ; and in the organ hovers the likeness of a bird—a canary or a nightingale. In this organ, when they play all the voices and pipes, not a single instrument remains in all of music that does not echo as if it were played on this organ; at first there are the organ, cymbals, violins, basses, Krummhorns, harps, flutes, viola da gambas, zithers, trumpets, kettledrums, and all other musical instruments. When they push in some of the stops the organ echoes trumpets exactly as if two trumpeteers are blowing their trumpets together, calling to one another, one from afar and the other from nearby; and this organ has many other parts, which I do not describe now because I lack the time.

At this monastery live Dominicans who have finely and marvelously constructed cells for themselves, and between the cells they have marvelous food gardens filled with various shrubs and flowers and vegetables of all kinds. /361/ Under the cells they have built large and very fine cellars, where they showed me many large barrels filled with white and red grape wines. In this same monastery I saw a fine pharmacy in which there are many drugs. In this same pharmacy I saw water that is passed

[99] It is in a crypt beneath the high altar. The present sixteenth-century basilica is built upon the remains of a fourth-century paleochristian basilica, a second built ca. 500 and destroyed in an earthquake in 1117, and a Romanic-Gothic built thereafter and pulled down in the sixteenth century. With these complex ancient origins, the church abounds in such stories and in their physical remains, including paleochristian burial chambers, a spurious tomb of Titus Livius, and the Well of Martyrs mentioned below.

[100] This is the famous Pozzo dei Martiri—indeed, as Tolstoi notes, a six-sided well, like one would find in Venice.

[101] A modern, simpler organ is now on the spot that Tolstoi describes; it is less colorful but has exceptional tone.

through five stone cups by the doctor, and I drank that water at the invitation of the doctor, who told me that it is very healthful, and this water looks very light.

There is a great academy of doctors in Padua which has 1,000 students and more. Honorable people from various states come to this academy to learn the doctor's science, and this academy is closed from the first day of June to September, when it has no science or other activity. The students here have this custom: when a student completes his doctoral science studies, he must take his *inspektor* (It. *ispettore*) in hand and lead him through all of Padua's streets, and many people walk in front of them and cry out "Vivat"; and the student who has completed his doctoral science makes arrangements for a man to walk in front of him and throw money to the people, who cry "Vivat" to that student. The people pick up this money and cry "Vivat, vivat," and all this is done at the cost of the student who has completed his science; then the inspector and the Jesuits crown this student in a church. During that time, the people are not allowed in—only one Jesuit or another monk and his ispettore, that is, his master. And having crowned him, his master gives him, from the academy, a certificate of mastery, as is appropriate to an academy, and he is dismissed with honor.[102] In Padua is an academy where they train horses; they have built a large palazzo there, and in front of it are stables, and in front of the palazzo and the stables is the square on which they train the horses.

All foodstuffs and bread are a little cheaper in Padua than in Venice, and all fruits, that is, produce, is more expensive than in Venice. Padua is a very large place, but not very populous, and it is filled up only with the people who come to Padua for the sciences.[103]

In Padua there is a general's home that is very large and has many rooms; it is built of the most marvelous workmanship and has fine furnishings.[104] The gates to this general's court are built under the arcades, which are built around the courtyard in place of a fence. Over the gates is a tower, on which is built a clock of fine workmanship. /362/ Close to this general's court is a captain's home, also large in size and marvelously built; it has many rooms with fine furnishings.[105]

Between these homes is a very large palace, 50 sazhens and three arshins in length and 30 sazhens and 3 arshins in width. This palace has no vaults or rounded

[102] Presumably Tolstoi has seen this spectacle first-hand. This is one of the more colorful and charming passages in the Diary, in which he captures the sense of public participation in a formal ritual in early-modern society.

[103] See, for example Evelyn, *Diary,* II, 462–80, for the numerous English and Scots studying in Padua in midcentury.

[104] This is the Renaissance portal and clock tower of the Palazzo del Capitaniato, rebuilt by Falconetto in 1532, the palace of the lords of Padua, the Da Carrara family. The clock, with 12- and 24-hour faces, a monthly calendar, phases of the moon, and signs of the zodiac, has a sun that revolves around the earth; it is a few blocks from the university where Galileo taught for eighteen years, 1592–1610.

[105] This is the Loggia del Consiglio dei Nobili, 1496–1523.

ceilings—it has only an iron roof on iron arches. In Italian this palace is called the Justice, for it is a chancellery palace, and in it are placed tables just like the clerks' tables in the Muscovite *prikazy*, and they are enclosed by wooden grates. Many people come to this palace on all kinds of business.[106]

In Padua there is a house in which they make all kinds of cloth, but they are unable to make the finest cloth there. The best Paduan cloth is 14 Venetian lira per arshin, and in Muscovite money 14 lira would be a ruble or less; and they make this cloth in all colors.[107]

There is also a food garden in Padua that belongs to the doctoral academy; it is circular and of fine craftsmanship. They have built 5 fine fountains in it, from which flow streams of fine, pure water. In this garden are many shrubs and roots that are used for medicinal purposes. In many places in Padua, flowing water passes through the city, and built on these waters are mills, which grind all sorts of grain. All wares in Padua are less plentiful than in Venice, and all are more expensive than in Venice.

There are several churches in Padua; all are fine stone buildings, and there are many riches in the churches. Many homes in Padua belong to Venetian cavaliers and were built for their trips to Padua. When someone wishes to wander around, he travels from Venice to Padua; and when these cavaliers live in Venice, their Paduan homes stand empty. Outside these homes they build fine pleasure gardens; in the food gardens they build fine fountains and many other wondrous things, and fine water passes through these gardens in ditches.[108] The inhabitants of Padua are poorer than the Venetians; none of the procurators or cavaliers of Venice live in Padua, although they have homes there, but they come to these homes only for pleasure.

The traveling foreigner who happens to be in Padua must live cautiously, and must not walk alone late at night from house to house, because the traveler will be /363/ injured and at times even killed by a student; however, those who must walk late should do so with weapons.[109]

[106] The Palazzo della Ragione, called the Salone, a "Juris Basilica," 1172–1219, was the hall of justice and the medieval Communal Palace; market stalls have replaced the scribes' tables.

[107] The area is still dominated by fabric merchants.

[108] Although many have been filled in, and their commercial role has been much diminished, Padua is still laced with canals.

[109] Violence at night was a common problem in Padua: "I return'd to *Padoa*, when that Towne was so infested with Souldiers, that many houses were broken open in the night, some Murders committed; The Nunns next our lodging disturb'd, so as we were forc'd to be upon our guard, with *Pistols*, & other fire armes to defend our doores: And indeed the students themselves take a barbarous liberty in the Evenings, when they go to their strumpets, to stop all that go by the house, where any of their Companions in folly, are with them: This costome they call *Chi va li:* so as the streetes are very dangerous, when the Evenings grow dark." Evelyn, *Diary*, II, 471–72. Evelyn's *Chi va li*, of course, has come down to us as charivari (or corrupt, shivaree), the mock serenade of newly married couples, but in general it means here any ritualized debauchery.

While in Padua, I wished to see the fine and marvelous things that are famous the world over, for there is a spring of naturally hot water.[110] And I hired a carriage and drove to this spring of hot water after dinner, and approached it in one hour, for the warm waters are at a distance of 5 Italian miles from Padua; and when I approached these warm waters, I saw many homes, gardens, and fine food gardens built of marvelous mastery on both sides of the road. And when I drew near the warm waters I was amazed when I saw them, for many springs flow on a rather low mountain, and these springs pass in various directions, one in opposition to another, and on the top in the middle of this mountain these streams of warm water flow together into a small lake. From this lake one spring leads along a trough for some distance, and a stone mill for grinding grain is built on this spring. Note the reasoning of the Italians who live here: this water, which is a wonder throughout the world, is not regarded as a gift, but as something for every use.[111]

Other springs of these hot waters are diverted down from the mountain to a house that is built close to these springs. In this house the springs of hot water are conducted to a room, and in the room two large vats are built, and the hot water is allowed into one of the vats, and into the other vat very cold water is allowed; and a pipe leads from one vat to the other so these hot and cold waters can pass and mix, so that people can bathe in these vats. If the hot water were not mixed with the cold water, it would be impossible for a person to dip even a finger into it because of its great natural heat. And thus mixing the hot water with the cold water, people can get into the vat and bathe for their health, for the Paduan doctors say that the natural heat of this water is useful for the health of man. And when the hot water is not mixed with the cold water, one could, if necessary, boil meat in it, and one could without trouble quickly boil a chicken's egg in it. One can see these are springs of hot water, for their water is always boiling, and in these hot waters there is always a thick steam like smoke, and this steam has an oppressive odor to a man's sense of smell, like burning coal or turpentine.

The mountain from which these springs of hot water flow is of stone and it slopes down on all sides. There are narrow slits on it that a human hand can reach through, and from these /364/ holes comes a steam just like that from the hot waters described above, and with the same unhealthy smell, but no heat comes from these holes. And one walks freely on the ground on this mountain, and it and the stones are not hot; but those springs of hot water that are conducted from the mountain down along the troughs and through dug-out places in the earth—in those places

[110]Tolstoi refers to the baths of Avano Terme, still an international spa.

[111]Just as above Tolstoi commented on the ingenious floating waterwheels in Vienna, here he again encounters evidence of the uniquely Western attitude toward nature as something to be harnessed, exploited, and used. Here, Tolstoi says explicitly that others, like the Russians, might regard a mountain spring as a gift of God or a natural phenomenon; these Italians see not merely a warm bath, but a source of energy. This is first-hand confirmation of the insights developed in Gimpel's *Medieval Machine*.

and also close to the mountain there is always heat, just as on the mountain itself, and the farther the waters go from the mountain the more their heat diminishes, and this hot water grows cool just like water is warmed by a fire, and they say that in another place close to these hot water springs there are other springs of hot water in all ways similar to these springs of hot water.[112] Only because of a certain obstacle, I did not drive to those other hot waters. And around the hot water springs that I saw, one sees ancient buildings built on old stone foundations, and newly built small palaces, and in them are a small number of inhabitants.

Then, after having seen these hot water springs, I arrived in Padua the same day and spent one night in Padua, and went back from Padua to Venice in the above-described peata, in which I had ridden to Padua. For the transportation from Padua to Venice I also paid five Venetian ducats, and I rode from Padua to Venice along the same river that goes from Venice to Padua. Around this river from Venice to Padua, along the shore, there are few places that have no buildings or gardens. On the 25 versts on both sides of the river are many stone homes of fine workmanship, and also marvelous gardens and very large food gardens containing many fruit trees of various kinds, among them a great number of white and red grapes of all kinds, and all sorts of fragrant shrubs and marvelous flowers.[113]

And I rode from Padua to Venice just as from Venice to Padua with a horse harnessed to the peata; and in the last hour of the day that I left Padua I arrived at the sea and could see Venice. At that hour the sea water rushed in and remained on the shore; because of this I could not row to Venice in the peata, and at that moment there was no wind, and our peata was carried by the sea water to the shore. Seeing this, I hired a small barque, and transferred from the peata to the barque. /365/ I arrived in that barque in Venice the same day in the 3rd hour of night, praise be to God, in good health. And when I went from Venice to Padua and from Padua to Venice, I dined on the road in osterie, that is, at inns, which are along the bank of the river along which we traveled to and from Padua; and in these osterie all travelers eat and drink whatever they wish—meat or fish or fruit, that is, all produce, and also double wines or even fine anise vodka, which they draw from grape wine, and which in Italian is called *akva vita* (It. *aquavite*), and also red and white grape wines. One eats as much as one wishes. And for those who spend the night in an osteria, there is a bed all made up with bedding and with white sheets and fine blankets, and for everything one must pay the master money according to an agreement. In these osterie there are tables and cards for those who wish to amuse themselves, and there are many of them; but to use them one has to pay the master some money. There is also tobacco for sale, for smoking as well as for snuff, and pipes in which to take the tobacco.

[112] The nearby similar springs are those of Montegrotto Terme.

[113] Here Tolstoi gives a good portrait of the destination of the Venetian's *villeggiatura*, and rightly suggests that they are the site of gardens and orchards rather than large estates; they more resembled suburbs than farms; see Honour, *Venice*, p. 241. See also Molmenti, *Venice*, III, 1, 182ff.

When a peata goes along that river from Venice to Padua or from Padua to Venice and comes to the locks on that river, which I have written about at length above, the master of the peata must pay an established price for each passage, depending on the kind of vessel; and people live at these passages in order to collect that money, and they build their homes in those places, and the gates to those passages are always locked, so that water can pour into the river for the passage of ships, and so that no small boat passes without paying the established toll. On this river they haul boards to Venice from distant forests for every possible kind of structure, and from the forest to the passageway they collect the established toll, and without paying it no one is allowed into the locks.

August 23. I was in Venice in a Western church, in which I saw the relics of the reverend Savva the Blessed, placed under the altar behind a gilded iron grate; his holy relics are undecayed, and on the bones are skin and sinew, but the jaw and neck are decayed by the will of God. And the clothing on the relics are the undergarments and a mantle, which he wore in his life—all complete; instead of a belt around his waist is a thick iron chain, and there is no rust on it. And I was able to kiss this holy reverend father on the right hand. On top of his chasuble his holy relics are covered with a golden satin shroud.[114]

August 25. I was on the naval gulf away from Venice at a convent where maiden nuns called /366/ Benedictines, that is, of the order of St. Benedict, live. In the church in this convent, over the altar, rest the relics of St. Athanasius the Great behind a grate and behind glass. One can see that a human likeness lies in sacred dress, the kind of attire that the hierarchs of the Western church wear, and on his right side is a crozier; and it is impossible to see if these holy relics are complete. The inhabitants there say that only a certain part of the relics of St. Athanasius' bones are here, and that the other parts of the image of his body are made of wood.[115]

[114]Tolstoi refers to St. Sabbas (Saba) of Palestine, disciple of St. Anthony the Great, the Egyptian founder of monasticism, and author of the Palestinian rule, or Rule of Jerusalem, known in Russia in Kievan times, and chief influence on all Russian monasticism. His rule of bodily strength and joyful serenity became a hallmark of early Russian church life. His relics, brought from Constantinople in 992, were first in San Giovanni d'Acri, then placed in the Tiepolo family chapel of the Church of Sant'Antonino in the middle of the thirteenth century, perhaps by Doge Lorenzo Tiepolo (1268–72). Sant'Antonino is quite near San Giorgio dei Greci.

[115]The relics of St. Athanasius (d. 373), champion of the Council of Nicea, are in the Church of San Zaccaria. Tolstoi revisited the church just two days later; see below. I often used Lorenzetti, *Venice and Its Lagoon,* to identify sites in Venice.

August 27. In a convent of the Roman faith the feast of Holy Zacharias the Prophet was celebrated, according to the Roman calendar on the 5th of September. In this monastery a tomb is placed high over the altar, and in this tomb are placed the relics of the holy prophet Zacharias, the father of [John] the Forerunner, whose holy relics I was able to see intact; and on his head was placed a cap, as priests' caps are painted usually on ancient icons, and the relics are covered with a shroud.[116] In this same church on another altar lies the head bone of St. Gregory Nazianzen and the head of St. Theodore *sekiota* (Syceum). In this same church, on a third altar, a tomb is placed, and in it are placed the head bones of the holy martyrs Savin and Pancrat (Sabina and Pancras). In the same church, over a fourth altar, are placed two heads: one of the martyr Martir (Martyrius) and the other of Stefan, the pope of Rome. In this same church, over a fifth altar, a tomb is placed, and in it is the head of the martyr Boniface; attached to this head is the likeness of a human body made of wood.

All of these holy relics were brought to Venice from Constantinople in antiquity, when Venice fought Tsargrad.

August 29. I was in the monastery of the holy apostles John and Paul.[117] In this monastery is a very large stone church, and attached to this church is a kaplica, that is, a small church also made of stone, and in this chapel over the altar stands an ancient Greek icon of the Blessed Mother of God. In size this holy icon is of the height of the icon of the Blessed Mother of God of Lakhern, but a little narrower, and the setting and the frame on this holy icon are all struck of silver. This miracle-working icon was brought to Venice from Tsargrad, and they say that in antiquity this holy icon healed the severed hand of St. John Damascene. In this monastery of John and Paul live Catholic monks called Dominicans, and their habit is white underneath and black on top. In this same monastery is an *ospedale,* that is, a hospital; to this hospital come the sick of various peoples of the male sex. This same day, in the Greek church described above, I saw the relics of St. John the Forerunner in an ark—one finger bone. /367/

[116] The body of Zacharius, father of John the Baptist, is still to be seen, but the other relics have been removed from the side altars. Tolstoi is at the Church of San Zaccaria (1485–1515); he fails to mention the numerous works of art, including the famous Madonna and Child by Bellini. Among its many relics, Tolstoi mentions those of Gregory Nazianzen, patriarch of Constantinople, d. 389; Theodor of Syceum, d. 613; Sabina, martyr under Hadrian, d. 127; Pancras, martyr at age fourteen under Diocletian, d. 275; Martyrius, subdeacon and martyr, d. 335; Stephen, pope and martyr, d. 257; and Boniface, martyr, d. 230.

[117] This is the imposing Basilica di Santi Giovanni e Paolo, 1333–90, entrance, 1430; Tolstoi fails to mention that it is the burial place for the doges of Venice; he does note that it contained a much-revered icon, the Madonna della Pace. Attached to the cathedral, the Ospedale di Santi Giovanni e Paolo still operates as the Ospedale Civile.

The Madonna della Pace, Venice, Basilica dei Ss. Giovanni e Paolo.

[7]207th year,[118] ***September the 10th*** day, I secured myself a place on a ship, on which I was to go to sea from Venice for study pertinent to my business, and I was to be on that ship more than one and a half months from this date, on which I went to sea on that ship from the Venetian *porto,* that is, harbor.

September 12. I left Venice on a ship and spent the night on the ship, and I stayed on the ship beneath Venice until the ***15th of September,*** and on the 15th of September our ship went from Venice and stopped in port opposite the island of Lido, where soldiers are stationed close to Venice, and our ship stayed in that place until the 17th of that month, for there was no favorable wind, and it was impossible to leave the port. And ships leave the Venetian port in this manner: when a ship wishes to leave Venice, the captain of the ship must declare his departure to the *admiral*[119] at the *arsenale;* even then the captain is not free to leave the Venetian port for the sea, but must wait for a barque with people from the *admirale,* and those people who come from the admiral in one or two barques attach ropes to the ship, and lead the ship from the port to the sea by rowing. The captain of this ship must give to those people, who thus conduct the ship from the port, 10 Venetian ducats. And when the admiral's people attach the ropes to the ship, that ship is in the care of the admiral. And if during the time that they are conducting the ship from the port the ship suffers some ruin or destruction, the admiral must pay the captain of the ship; and therefore the admiral looks for the very best weather to lead the ship from the port out to sea, so that he can do it without any harm. And it is impossible for any ship to leave the port by sail, because the place through which ships leave the port for the sea is narrow, unusable to a ship's course, and ships do not pass that place without fear; and it is necessary for a captain who wants to go from that port to sea to request the admiral, without delay, order the ship to be conducted from the port to the sea. But the admiral is never disposed to such a request, and he looks for good weather so that he does not lose a ship and so that he does not incur a great loss. Their habit is to leave the port more often by night than by day.[120]

[118] Tolstoi here includes the year 7206 (1697/98), for this is the first entry of the new Russian calendar year.

[119] Italian *ammiraglio,* but Lane, *Venice,* p. 164, gives the form for the head of the arsenal as *armiraio.*

[120] Tolstoi's troubles while trying to depart from Venice were not unusual. From September to March one needed the services of a tightly organized guild, the *pedotti,* to bring ships through the constantly shifting channel and sand bars. Silting was a major problem in the whole lagoon, and in the seventeenth century Venice had to use pontoons called "camels" to bring larger ships to the city, although Tolstoi does not mention them. Access to the port was controlled by officers at the Arsenal. Inbound ships often had to wait long periods of time at the Istrian city of Parenzo (see below) for their permission and for the *pedotti.* See Lane, *Venice,* pp. 18, 413, 454.

September 18, in the 5th hour of night the admiral's people led us on the ship from the port to the sea in two barques, and we on the ship went under sails on a southeasterly wind, on which in the 6th hour of night we sailed 30 Italian miles /368/; an Italian mile consists of 1,000 sazhens of three arshins [each]; an Italian arshin is smaller than a Muscovite arshin by two vershoks, and every Italian sazhen is less than a Muscovite sazhen of three arshins by six vershoks.[121] At that time the wind changed its direction, but it was between east and south, during which time our ship ran 25 Italian miles in 6 hours. And when our ship came opposite the land called Istria, we turned our ship to that Istrian land and went on an eastern wind, on which in 7 hours we went 28 Italian miles. And on that day, an hour before nightfall, we came to Istria, to the city of Ruvin (Rovinj).[122] This city of Rovigno stands on the sea coast on a high rocky mountain. All of this city is made of stone. In this city is the church of the holy martyr Euphemia the Most Praised, and her relics rest in the church, and I was able to see them; in this same church I saw the finger of the same martyr made of silver and crystal, and the silver belt of this martyr made of silver wire. In this same city at that church is a very tall bell tower, and on top of the tower is placed the image of the martyr Euphemia, cast in brass in human dimensions. In this same city in the outskirts are many olive trees, with much fruit on them. Our ship stayed beneath this city until the ***25th of September.***

[121] Here is an unsatisfactory paraphrase of Tolstoi's only attempt to deal with the Italian mile: an Italian mile contains 1,000 sazhens, and is thus twice the length of a Russian verst (which contains only 500 sazhens, and is equal to a kilometer or 2/3 of a mile). However, the Italian sazhen is 10.5 inches shorter than a Russian sazhen (about 6 feet instead of 7 feet); thus the Italian mile is closer to 6,000 feet than to the 7,000 feet it would be if composed of Russian sazhens. Therefore a verst/kilometer is about 3,500 feet, an Italian mile somewhat less than 6,000 feet (or slightly longer than a statute mile of 5,280 feet).

[122] On this Istrian city, see the following entry for September 26.

III

September 26, 1697–May 29, 1698

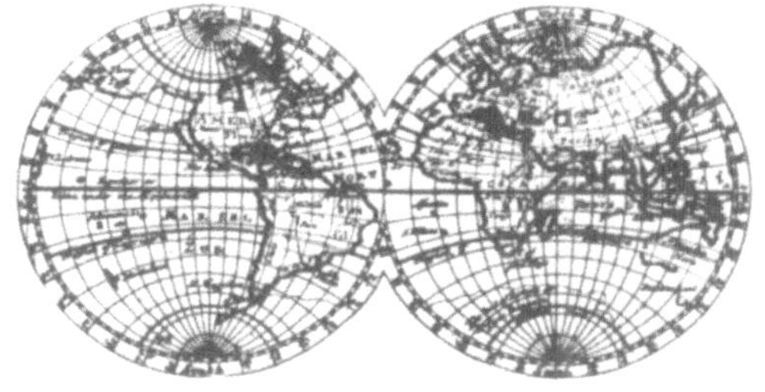

Dalmatian Coast · Venice
Milan · Venice

/505/ The night of ***September 26,*** in the seventh hour, our ship departed Ruvin [Rovinj] [1] by a southeasterly wind. This wind was unfavorable to our set course, and our ship went by tacking, and we made two tacks. In 12 hours it went 50 Italian miles and approached a land called Dalmatia. These lands, Istria and Dalmatia, are the property of the prince of Venice. And when we caught sight of Dalmatia, severe weather began, and a wind blew contrary to our course, and to save ourselves from that weather, in order not to break the mast, we could not follow our course. Because of the strength of the wind, we could not hold the ship on anchor in the sea, and this contrary wind forced us back to port, that is, to the harbor, and when we turned back, the wind began to blow in the sails of our ship. With this wind we covered 32 Italian miles and arrived in the port beneath the city called Pola [Pula] in Istria, 18 Italian miles from Rovinj. In our flight our fear was boundless, because our ship was lightly loaded and so lopsided that cannon from the ship drew water.

The city of Pula stands on the edge of the sea; its buildings are all of stone; in the city is an Orthodox church. Outside the city walls I saw a certain ancient stone

[1] The Italian form is Rovigno; usually, for areas along the Dalmatian coast, I use the modern Yugoslav place names. Because "Italy" and "Yugoslavia" are meaningless terms in the seventeenth century, the reader must be aware that Tolstoi's ship is crisscrossing the Adriatic Sea, which Tolstoi refers to as the Venetian gulf.

Tolstoi, eight months after his departure from Moscow, shows some inclination to pursue the naval studies that were the reason for his trip. Before this he had little to report to his tsar except for casual visits to the Arsenal.

Venice was, as noted in the Introduction, no longer the naval capital of the world: one measure of her decline was the fact that in the seventeenth century Dutch mariners were paying a lower insurance premium than the Venetians. Aware of their deficiencies, Venetians began to propose formal schools of navigation at the Arsenal, and one was finally opened in 1683. Tolstoi thus had opportunities for study that had been unavailable a few years earlier. See Lane, *Venice,* p. 419, and Molmenti, III, 1, p. 20.

building,[2] quite amazingly built like a circle, 172 sazhens in circumference and very high—indeed, to a height of 3 windows, and some 300 windows are found in this structure. They say about this building that in antiquity it was built by a certain caesar, and lions, leopards, bears, and many other kinds of vicious beasts were enclosed in it; and when by the power of that caesar a man was condemned to death, /506/ he was taken to this structure to be torn apart by the beasts, and the caesar watched from the walls of this building and was amused.

Our ship stood in port beneath this city of Pula until the ***28th of September.*** On the 29th at 2½ hours of night our ship left the port with a southerly wind, and we went by tacking. On the first tack in 3 hours we went 6 Italian miles, and the wind changed and became southeasterly, on which we went 24 Italian miles in 6 hours; from this point we turned to the other side, and on that wind we went for an hour and a half, and it became light. In daylight we sailed on that wind 5½ hours, and in all we went 30 Italian miles in 6 hours. We arrived in a port in Istria beneath the city of Fazhana [Fažana], 3 Italian miles from Pula, back toward Venice; and the route we wished to sail was impossible because there was a great wind contrary to our course. The city of Fažana stands on the coast, its buildings are all of stone, and there is a small settlement beyond the city. Our ship stayed beneath Fažana until October 1.

October 1. In the 7th hour of day our ship left Fažana and sailed back to Rovinj, because the winds were contrary to our course, and we went 2 hours toward Rovinj and covered 15 Italian miles, and we fell short of Rovinj by 2 Italian miles. At this point the winds changed in intensity and became favorable to a course toward the city of Ankona [Ancona], to which we wanted to sail, so we turned the ship and went to Ancona. At this time the wind became easterly, what the Italians call *levantine,* on which we covered 15 Italian miles in 3 hours. At this point the wind changed, became southeasterly, on which our ship went 30 Italian miles in 6 hours. At this place we turned again on a southerly wind and went 14 hours with it, and covered in all 15 Italian miles, because the winds changed in strength and were not constant. The lightest wind is called *greco,* then *tramonta,* then *maestro,* then *potente,* and between them are half- and quarter-winds[3]. At times there was no wind at all, and when there was a wind, it was very slight. And on these winds our ship headed toward the city for three hours until night, and we stayed 4 Italian miles from Ancona, because it was dangerous to enter the port—that is, the harbor—because the wind toward Ancona was favorable and strong. We were unable to enter the port before nightfall, and one does not enter a poorly known port at night; we feared that

[2]This is the famous first-century amphitheater in Pula, in modern Yugoslavia. It is every bit as well preserved and amazing as Tolstoi suggests. It is Tolstoi's first encounter with actual Roman ruins.

[3]Tolstoi includes the Italian names for the direction and intensity of the winds: *greco,* northeast wind; *tramontana,* north wind; *maestrale,* northwest wind; and *potente,* strong.

/507/ the ship might be wrecked on the shore or on the rocks. And at that time we lowered all the sails on our ship, and not a single sail remained unfurled. All our sails were lowered because we saw lowering clouds on the northerly winds, and we were cautious that such winds should not come upon open sails, in fear of God, lest the mast break or the ship be destroyed.

In that place our ship stood immobile for 3 hours without sails; and we did not toss our anchor into the sea there, fearing a great *fortuna.*[4] During these three hours there was a terrible thunderstorm, lightning, hail, and great rain, and the great wind became easterly. In the first hour of night we unfurled 2 sails and against our will left Ancona for the open sea; we intended to go straight to sea until midnight, so as not to be close to the shore at night, and after midnight we could again turn toward Ancona, in order to enter the port of the city of Ancona in daylight, and not at night, because that port has shallow water and rocks, and we knew it poorly. And from midnight a great fortuna began, and it did not permit us to return to Ancona; and on northerly winds we raced the whole night from the shore to the sea where we did not want to go. In the morning we still raced, until the 7th hour of day, and we approached Dalmatia and entered a port in the 7th hour, and we had come toward that port for 5 hours and arrived beneath the city called Zara (Zadar; It. Zara). This is the best city in Dalmatia, where a Venetian general lives, and we spent the night there. In the morning we fired three small ship's cannon, which stood above on the rails, and are called *petrieri,*[5] to honor the general. On the stern of the ship we posted the arms of the Venetian republic with lions, which depicted St. Mark the Evangelist, and we stood beneath the city of Zadar until the ***7th of October.***

The city of Zadar is large, with good stone buildings; it stands on the very shore, surrounded by high mountains. The Turkish border is very close to Zadar, and a Turkish city is close to Zadar, because Dalmatia divides the Venetian possessions from the Turkish. From Zadar to the Turkish settlements it is less than 30 miles. Zadar is finely fortified, surrounded by a sea moat and by bastions, and beneath the bastions in many places are large cellars. In these cellars are warehouses for stores of gunpowder, and in other places there are forges and everything else needed in times of siege. In this city on the walls /508/ and on the bastions are innumerable very large brass cannon. The town has no towers except for the entrance gates, and they are not high but level with the city's wall; and on the walls and bastions there are small, round, stone guard rooms, in which there is space for only one guard. In this city, in a Western church, I saw the relics of St. Simon, "who received God."[6] These relics lie in a silver shrine high over the altar. Over this shrine there are 2 human size brass angels who hold the shrine. These holy relics are amazing to the human eye; placed in that shrine, they are all nude, except for a small shroud of black velvet strung with pearls; that shroud covers that necessary part of his body that could not be without a cover. Even now St. Simon has veins and skin on his

[4] Italian, *fortuna,* a storm at sea.

[5] In Italian this is *petriero,* petard, a small gun, a braga or breech gun.

[6] This is the traditional sobriquet of St. Simon, the apostle who held the Christ-Child.

right arm, only he does not have all of his hair or beard or moustache; his insides are all dried out, and on his stomach his veins are intact. On the index finger of the left hand are many decorative rings of gold and silver. In the city of Zara, in another Western church, they say there rest the relics of the 3 martyrs—Vera, Liubva, and Nadezhda.[7] I went in to see them; they said to me that they were under the altar, but it was impossible to see those relics because there was only a small opening, and in the darkness I could not see them.

In this city of Zadar is a small Eastern, Greek church named for the prophet Elias. It is built of stone, and is attached to a Western church. We stayed beneath Zadar until ***October 7th,*** and on that day we left, intending to go into the possessions of the Spanish king to the city of Bari.[8] At the port or harbor of Zadar on October 7 we met with the general-commissar, who left Zadar to winter in the city of Shpaletra (Split; It. Spalato) in Dalmatia. This general sailed on a galley, and we saw that galley pass close to our ships, and in his honor we placed poles with flags on our ship's stern and bow. Then we saluted him on our ship, firing from 9 cannon; then he, reciprocating and honoring us, fired 8 cannon on his galley. Then we, granting him still greater respect, fired from three cannon, and thus we departed. And we went 18 Italian miles from Zadar and stayed the night in the channel that is below Zadar, because the channel is large and the winds at that time were unfavorable, and /509/ we were unable to pass out of that channel in a single day, and we stayed in that place until the ***9th of October.*** We left on the 9th and went without a wind, pulling the ship from the channel in a barque and a rowboat; then the wind became favorable on our desired route to the city of Bari. On this wind our ship moved 5 Italian miles per hour, or $4\frac{1}{2}$, or 3 or less; and so we sailed the whole day and night, and in a 24-hour period we covered, from where we stood in the channel, 80 Italian miles.

October 10. In the early hours of the day the wind was very slight, and our ship could make but 1 Italian mile per hour; and thus we proceeded along the shore until the 11th hour, and as night fell we moved very quietly because the wind was slight at that time.

October 11. We arrived in our ship beneath the city of Korsul (Korčula).[9] This city is a Venetian possession and stands on an island close to the shore; its

[7] These are three sisters—Pistis, Elpis, and Agape (Faith, Hope, and Charity)—second-century martyrs.

[8] Bari, the location of the shrine of St. Nicholas that Tolstoi wanted to visit, is on the east coast of Italy across the Adriatic from Yugoslavia. In the 1690s it was part of Naples, and thus a possession of Spain.

[9] Korčula is on a large island off the Yugoslav coast, perhaps four-fifths of the distance from Venice to the major city of Dubrovnik.

buildings are all of stone, but it is not a large city. It is set on the border of Dalmatia, at the edge of the possessions of the prince of Ragusa, and we did not go as far as the capital city of Ragusa, Dubrovnik, 60 Italian miles from Korčula, because we wanted to go to the city of Bari, in order to be honored to see the relics of the great Miracle Worker Nicholas. Failing to reach the city of Barletta by 80 Italian miles, we turned back in our ship, because on these days there were 5 large Turkish ships, which held some 500 janissaries each, which intercepted the route to Bari; therefore we were not able to see the holy relics of the Miracle Worker Nicholas, but stayed at Korčula until ***October 16,*** when we turned back to Venice via that channel through which we had arrived at Korčula.

In this city of Korčula I saw in a monastery the body of Christ, of human size, on a cross, all carved of wood. They say that this image of the Crucifixion was made by the hand of the holy evangelist Luke, and it is of miraculous workmanship; the legs of the Savior are affixed to the cross with a single nail; the cross, on which the sacred body is depicted, has 4 points. Concerning this holy image, they told me that the head was not made by human hands, but by His divine will. When Luke the Evangelist had made this most sacred image of the body of Christ, he began to contemplate the creation of His divine head: and on that day of contemplation the head remained undone in the morning, but on that night the image of His head had been completed by His divine will. /510/

Opposite this city of Korčula, on the Ragusan mountains in a Catholic church, I saw a Greek icon of the Blessed Mother of God similar to the Mother of Smolensk; and they say that the icon, with divine help, swam from the place where it was to the place where it now stands and where I now saw it, and that it arrived invisibly; and now this holy icon works many miracles.

And when we left Korčula and went 18 Italian miles on a great fortuna contrary to our desired route, and because fortuna prevented us from going farther, we entered a port called St. Ivan. We stayed in this port until the 20th of October, when we left and sailed that day by tacking and went 13 Italian miles, and it became frightening. In the first hour of night the weather became contrary, and from the third hour of that night a strong contrary fortuna arose, and hour by hour blew winds of such strength that seldom do greater winds occur; and that great and strong wind found us between the mountains, and the night was dark, and at that time we were in great fear for our lives, and still that fortuna gripped us hour after hour. Therefore we were in very great fear of death; initially we feared that we would be held from the *arbur,* that is, the harbor, by the great winds; then the fear was that our ship would be cast upon the land or on the rocks in the night. We also greatly feared our ship would capsize, for the winds were contrary to our course and unnaturally strong, and we had set our sails in daylight, as it is customary to set sails on a quiet tack. With the strong winds the ship did not hold its first course but was drawn sideways, and our ship tipped sideways so that the cannon drew water, and the water poured over the ship from the high waves. And we passed the entire night in great and deathly fear, and on the ***21st of October*** we arrived at the port on an island, which is called Liza (Lizze; It. Lissa), below the village of Lizze. We stayed until the ***25th***, because the winds were strong and contrary, and we left that port on the ***26th;*** the wind was contrary but not strong, and from the 25th to the 26th we went 32 Italian miles, and all night on the 26th we went on slightly favorable winds, and in that night and the day of the 26th we went 16 Italian miles. And we arrived in port beneath the city called Trava [Trogir; It. Trau], and stayed /511/ in that port beneath Trogir until the ***28th of October,*** and on the 28th we left Trogir. While we were in the town, the commandant of the city of Trogir came to us on a ship with his wife, and to honor him we fired 3 cannon from our ship.

The large city of Trogir is built as a fortress surrounded on all sides by sea water. It is all made of stone; the bell tower of the cathedral is of fine stone workmanship; in this church rests the body, they say, of the bishop of the Roman church of the city of Trogir, and his body is undecayed because of his holy life, but they did not show the body to me; his name was Ioann, but he was bishop in this city after the Greek faith broke from the Roman.

On the 28th of October our ship went on a favorable wind until the 4th hour of day, but in the 5th hour a contrary wind arose, and it was immeasurably strong. It prevented us from sailing to Istria, for we wanted to sail past the whole Venetian gulf into the lands of the Roman pope into the port beneath the city of Ancona, about which I wrote above. And in a short time that wind changed, became a favorable light wind, and on this wind we sailed until evening, and in the evening a very strong wind, favorable for Istria, arose, and we went on that strong favorable wind until midnight; and after midnight it lessened, although it was still favorable, and on it we sailed until daylight on the 29th. We sailed into Istria beneath the city of Rovinj on the 30th at night, and we spent the night without entering the port because we intended to go to Venice quickly; and on the day of the 29th and the night of the 29th we covered 250 Italian miles from Trogir to Rovinj. Having stayed at Rovinj, at the first hour of day on the 30th we left for Venice, and we arrived at the city of the Roman pope, which is called Orseria (Vrsar; It. Osera), but did not stop there, because the winds were favorable and we hastened to Venice. That day we arrived in Istria and beneath the city of Parentsa (Poreč; It. Parenzo), and there we stayed and awaited a favorable wind on which we could go to Venice.

Ships enter Venice only at the proper moment. They enter into the port of Venice with difficulty, because the place where ships enter is narrow and shallow, and one always awaits the time when the winds are *tramontana,* that is, northerly, /512/ or northeasterly and not strong; and when the sea water by its natural course increases its activity and runs toward the shore, then ships have a free passage into the port of Venice. Therefore we stood beneath the city of Poreč, awaiting that moment, which always comes. *Marcilianas* and large *bastimentos,* that is, ships, wishing to enter Venice stand in the Istrian ports beneath Rovinj and Poreč and beneath other cities; and no ships enter until they have waited the proper time, because many evil things happen to ships and marcilianas and *galleazzas,* that is, galleys, and all ships dread the entrance to Venice.[10] Ships approach the port only when the time is right, and if the wind changes or becomes favorable but too strong, then, without entering Venice, they turn around and return to the ports they did not want to enter; and when a fortuna does not permit a ship to return to such a place, it must stand on 3 or 4 anchors and hold itself firmly in order not to be thrown closer by that strong wind. And even when the wind is not strong but the sea water is diminished [i.e., low tide], then large ships do not enter the port of Venice because they would shipwreck in the entrance because it is shallow. And even when a ship comes to this place on a slight wind, should the sea waters be rising and falling with the action of the waves, and if the ship would rise and fall on those waves, the ship, rising to heights and falling back with the sea's waves would hit bottom and break up; it would be impossible to be saved from the shallow water in that place. As we stood beneath the city of Poreč on ***October 30th,*** a cavalier from Venice arrived at Poreč on a ship called a *piota* (It. *pilota*). Every ship wanting to enter the port of Venice must have a pilota, and without the order of a pilota one cannot enter Venice from Poreč. When this pilota arrived in Poreč, they fired 5 cannon in his [the cavalier's] honor and received him honorably.

The city of Poreč is built of stone above the sea in a pleasant spot, and it is surrounded by gardens of olive trees. /513/ Food in this city, bread and meat and vegetables are half the price of that in Venice, and the homes in Poreč are all of stone.

October 31. Having come to the end of the duration of my journey as agreed on with the ship's captain, I left his ship on the 31st, because the captain did not want to take me to Venice for a small price; and I hired a pilota, giving 40 Venetian ducats for it, in order to go to Venice in this pilota with all my things. And on the 31st I left the ship, but on this day I could not take all of my things from the ship, so I transferred my most needed things onto the pilota, but the rest remained on the ship; and leaving the ship, I spent the night at a house in Poreč. As I left the ship the captain fired 5 cannon from the ship to honor me. On November 1st I left the ship in my hired pilota with the things I had left behind, and I stayed in Poreč until the 2nd, because I waited for a favorable wind and because I had a small argument about my things with the captain who had carried me on his ship. And on the 2nd, between the 3rd and the 9th hour of night, I went on the pilota from Poreč to Venice, and my pilota sailed along with another to Venice, and on the other were Muscovite soldiers and slaves, among them my slave. In the 2nd hour of night a great fortuna pushed

[10] The *marciliana,* noted above, was a large but indefensible Adriatic cargo ship. The *galleazza,* sometimes *galea grossa,* was the great galley used for war with many men per oar, very mobile, and the ultimate achievement of Venetian shipbuilding in early-modern times; Galileo contributed to its physics. See Lane, *Ships,* pp. 70–71. *Bastimento* is a generic name for ship, usually fortified.

us, and our pilotas separated so that soon we could not see each other; and the pilota on which the soldiers and our slaves traveled, upon seeing that foul weather, turned back to Poreč. The pilota on which I was raced from the shore to the open sea, and we could not return to Poreč because of the severity of the winds. All night and day I was in such fear for my life that I completely despaired and could only call upon the aid of God and of the Blessed Mother. I began to say the canon to Nicholas the Wonder Worker, and from that hour the fortuna diminished, and my fear diminished; however, I still had that great fear until noon on ***November 3,*** and all of us in that pilota were constantly showered by the sea's waves, and we were all sitting in water. Nevertheless, on this day at the last hour of light we arrived in Venice, while the other pilota stayed in Poreč until the ***6th of November,*** and on the 6th they arrived in good health. And so, praise to God, I ended my sea journey in good health, although I had seen the fear of death many times. The ship on which I had traveled was called /514/ the *St. Elizabeth.* When I left that ship, the captain, Ivan Lazorević, gave me a testimonial certificate in his hand and marked with his seal; and in it was written:

> Captain of the naval ship St. Maria Elizabeth, Ivan Lazorević, I give to all and in general, and to whomever to know, that in the year 1698, the Muscovite gentryman Peter Andreevich with his soldier Ivan Staburin did board my ship; they wished to learn naval sailing, in ships and various vessels, and to learn naval affairs, that is, *bussola* [It., compass] from me, and in Slavonic, *maiatnika,* with all that pertains to it, including naval charts, on which naval courses are plotted, and also to become acquainted with the names of woods, and sails, and ropes, and all the ship's instruments, and all those things related to navigation, such as maps, and the compass and the names of those ship's instruments; and that above-mentioned gentryman learned our ways at sea well. Then he wanted to see the formation of ships and galleys at the time of a battle, which we could not find on the whole Venetian sea-gulf that year. And this gentryman, being on my ship during strong winds and fearful fortunas, applied himself to the ship's order with diligence and fearlessness, showing himself in all things to be capable in great naval disturbances and winds. I also sent this gentryman and his soldier on the Venetian seas to another ship for better practice. And to see galleys and to spend time at sea in battle I, the above-mentioned captain, had this Muscovite gentryman and his soldier travel on the Mediterranean Sea past Calabria to the islands of Sicily and even to Malta, because there are few galleys on the Venetian gulf and they do not sail often. In this matter I give testimony, that in his knowledge of winds and of bussola, and of maps, and in his understanding of ship's instruments, of wood, and of sails and ropes, on my oath this gentryman is skilled and capable, and upon my faith I sign this certificate with my own hand and impress my seal.

At the bottom of this certificate is written: "Captain Ivan Lazorević, of the ship *St. Maria Elizabeth,* I sign with my hand, as a mark of authenticity." On this certificate the seal of naval captain Ivan Lazorević is imprinted in red wax. I accepted the certificate from him, thanking him for his affection for me.[11]

November 27. An icon of the Blessed Mother of God was placed on the great altar in the Church of San Marco in Venice. This /515/ holy icon is not large, smaller than a little sexto.The image of the Mother of God is half-length, with the Blessed Child painted in her womb, as in the Pecherskii Mother of God, an ancient Greek painting.[12] Venetians say that this icon was painted by Luke the Evangelist. And around this holy icon a multitude of wax candles burn in large silver candlesticks; there are in all more than 300 candles, and among them are placed fine flowers in large silver vases, and fragrant greens are also placed in these vases. This holy icon stood in this place for 8 days, until the 5th of December, and during these 8 days people constantly came to this church by day and night, and this church was never locked. In this church on these days oil burned in lamps in various places, and more than 1,000 lamps were burning; these lamps were decorated with fine figures. There were 2 sermons on each of these eight days in this church; one sermon was at the time of Mass and the other was at vespers; and the preachers who gave these sermons came to this church from various monasteries. Also at this time a cross with the carved body of Christ on it was placed in the middle of the church; and incessantly on this day a multitude of people approached this cross, and all who so wished kissed it.

[11]This certificate of naval study that Tolstoi included in his Diary was meant to convince his tsar that indeed he had lived up to his charge. His ship's master and teacher was obviously a Slav from the Dalmatian coast. Tolstoi does not mention study on shore during this trip; twenty years later the well-known Marko Martinovič would operate a more regular school for visiting Russians at his home port of Perast on the Bay of Kotor (there is a picture of that later group with Martinovič, misidentified as Tolstoi's, in Tolstoy, *The Tolstoys,* p. 50.

This is the first time that Tolstoi mentions by name the soldier whom he took with him, according to the instructions given to the group of *stol'niki* in Moscow. We know nothing of Ivan Staburin's origins or subsequent career. Tolstoi reveals that it was Lazarević who arranged for Tolstoi's grand tour to Naples and Malta the next year, for the expressed purpose of finding Turks at sea with whom he could fight. That journey to the south occupies fully half of the pages of the Diary.

[12]Tolstoi here describes one of the greatest treasures of San Marco, the icon of the Mother of God Orans, known as La Nicopeia, of Victory. Formerly carried by the Byzantine emperor in war, it was brought to Venice by Enrico Dandolo with other spoils of war after the Fourth Crusade (1204). Tolstoi is especially interested because of its Byzantine origin, because Russia, too, had protector-icons of the Mother of God, most notably the one that saved Novgorod from the Suzdalians, and because, as he notes, it resembles one of the oldest and most sacred of Russian icons, the Virgin of the Cave Monastery in Kiev. The reference to its size can be translated as a printer's sheet folded into six leaves.

The Vergine col Putto, detta Madonna Nicopeia, San Marco, Venice.

A Venetian gave these as the reasons: on this day the household of the Holy Mother of God came to Laretto;[13] the other reason was that on this day news came to Venice from the pope in Rome that all Catholics were to fast, so that there might be an eternal peace between all Christian monarchs, and therefore the Venetians kept the fast for all eight days in the Church of San Marco, coming here from all the

[13]On special occasions the icon La Nicopeia was displayed on the high altar. Since the accepted birthday of the Virgin was September 8, her conception nine months earlier was on

churches and monasteries in a procession. And this was the order of their procession: first of all they carried two wax candles in tall silver candlesticks, and then came the cross, and after it 2 more candlesticks with wax candles, and after them came the clergy of the Roman faith, two abreast; and after them came the laity, also two abreast, and all with wax candles, and the candles were all of white wax, for there are no yellow candles in Venice or in all Italy. There were more than 100 persons in this procession, and in other processions more than 500 people. And many in these processions are of the honorable sort of people, and not wanting to show themselves or be recognized, they walk in these processions in special clothes that cover their faces. This is the reason for these clothes: /516/ they intentionally wear them in churches, and he who would wear these clothes puts them on secretly so that people do not know him or who he is, because the clothes mask the head and face. They walk in these processions in these clothes barefooted, and they lash themselves, beating themselves with stringed ropes on the back, baring their backs until their blood flows, and they soak the cords with which they beat themselves in Rhenish vinegar, and for this they carry the vinegar with them in vessels. They do this so that the wounds on their bodies sting from the vinegar, to endure their torment the more for the remission of their sins; and we must endure an amount of bodily torment equal to our great sinfulness. Many men and women, even those of the honorable sort, do this.[14]

December 5.[15] For 2 hours before nightfall there was a procession from the Cathedral of San Marco with that icon of the Mother of God we have mentioned. Many thousands of people were in this procession, and they all walked with large wax candles, and they prostrated themselves before the holy icon of the Mother of God with great faith and with tears. First came the choirboys of the Venetian prince, then the deacons in albs, and behind them they carried the icon of the Mother of God high up in a sedan chair. Under this holy icon on the chair, they had made a great silver mound in three tiers of fine and very rich workmanship. Roman priests carried this icon, and behind them a canon carried a part of the icon's mounting of the Blessed Mother in a container, and another canon carried several locks of hair of

---

December 8, the date which, in the nineteenth century, would be universally recognized as the feast of the Immaculate Conception. Tolstoi is thus describing the week-long vigil of that feast. Tolstoi's Diary is in Old Style, the Julian calendar, which lagged behind the Gregorian calendar by ten days in the seventeenth century, thus the discrepancy in dates.

[14] During the later Middle Ages, the scourging devotion had fallen into disrepute, and gradually the old hooded processions of flagellants became less common. But they could be seen in Italy, Spain, Portugal, and southern Germany into the eighteenth century. See Chadwick, *Popes and European Revolution*, pp. 33ff.

[15] December 5, that is, December 15 by the Gregorian calendar, is the Octave Day of the Immaculate Conception and thus the end of the formal observance of the feast.

the Blessed Mother in another vessel. Behind them the Venetian patriarch carried the milk of the Blessed Mother of God in a vessel. In front of all of these holy things walked the deacons with censers, and they incensed the holy things, and over all these holy things they carried fine golden canopies. This holy procession left the Church of San Marco by the south doors and entered by the west. The prince of Venice and all his procurators were also in this procession; there were many cavaliers and simple people, and they carried the holy icon around the square, which is in front of and around the side of San Marco.

Vespers began on ***December 15th*** at the first hour of night in the Church of San Marco, because by the Catholics' new calendar this was the ***25th of December,*** the feast of the Nativity of Christ, and after vespers they began the Mass. A bishop said this Mass and when it began the prince of Venice approached the altar himself, and he knelt at the altar, and served the bishop, taking the place of the sacristan. Such is their habit every year on the eve of Christmas, /517/ and on the feast of the Nativity each Catholic priest must, by their law, say three Masses at the same altar and with the same chalice. On Christmas Eve there was vocal and instrumental music in the Church of San Marco, and there were 130 singers and musicians.

December 29. I was at the monastery of Sts. Peter and Paul, where the Catholic patriarch of Venice lives. This day the Catholics celebrate the feast of Sts. Laurentius and Justinian,[16] and his [*sic*] body lies beneath the altar of the church in this monastery. The prince of Venice and all his procurators were in this monastery this day. In the church, the patriarch of Venice said Mass with 6 canons, that is, with two archimandrites or abbots, two archpriests, and two deacons; and the patriarch said Mass as if he were a simple priest, and he received the Eucharist and the simple servitors received the Eucharist with him. The incensing occurred four times during this Mass, and the patriarch washed his hands three times. The vestments of the patriarch were thus: first a paramanta (amice) like a Russian monk's; then a white alb, and on it a stole; and then a mantle on one arm; and then a double white taffeta surplice, one side shorter than the other; and his outer vestment was like a sakkos,[17] only without sleeves, but the sides were not sewn; and then a panagia (pectoral cross), a cross with a chain; and then something similar to a diadem, only long and

[16] This is a local feast: the Church celebrates the feast of St. Laurence Justinian on September 5. St. Laurence was born in Venice to the illustrious family of the Giustiniani, and he preferred the monastic life to marriage. In 1451 he was made patriarch of Grado, transferred his see to Venice, becoming the first patriarch of the city, and thus is greatly revered there. He died in 1455.

The feast was formally observed at the Church of San Pietro di Castello (Tolstoi garbles both its name and that of the saint). San Marco did not become the cathedral of Venice until 1807; it had earlier been the patriarchal church.

[17] The *sakkos* is the vestment of a hierarch of the Eastern Church, tuniclike, with half-sleeves and a slit up the sides. The word is also used for the sack-cloth worn in mourning.

narrow and put on the head, and with braids with stones; and then a cap and white satin gloves; and then a ring on the large finger. When he approaches the altar, he takes off the ring and glove, and before dressing he puts on white satin slippers sewn with gold.

January 1 [1698]. In the Greek church I saw the arm of Basil the Great; that holy hand is intact and covered with silver, as with a glove. A glass is placed against the palm, which indicated where I was able to kiss it.[18]

January 6. They blessed water in the Greek church just as they do in Moscow, except when the servers drink, the bishop sits and there are no incensings in the church; and they bless the water twice, first at vespers, and then on the feast of the Epiphany at the end of the Liturgy.

January 27. I was in Venice at the Armenian church where the Armenians conduct their service.[19] Their church is made of stone just like the Roman churches, and the altar is as it is among the Catholics; the icons in this church are painted on canvas; one icon /518/ of the Blessed Mother with the Christ-Child is a Greek work on a board. Wax candles are in silver candlesticks on the altar. The church has 3 altars. The Mass was said by an Armenian monk, whose vestments were a mantle and skullcap similar to a Greek monk's, but he had no cowl and his beard was not shaved and his moustache was somewhat trimmed. Such an Armenian is called an archimandrite. During the service his vestments included a white linen cassock, and then a stole, and then maniples on both arms, and then a gold satin chasuble like a cloak, and around the neck on this chasuble a tall collar, and on his head a cap like a Greek archbishop's. Their service was similar to a Roman's: they use unleavened bread, but the *tseremoniia* (It. *cerimonia*) in the service is like in the Greek church. Serving him this day were 2 deacons wearing albs and shoulder sashes like the Greeks, and 6 men in albs sang the Mass on the steps [in front of the iconostasis]. Before the beginning of the Liturgy they prepared the chalice in the area behind the cross, that is, in the sacristy, but the Armenians call this the "sacrificium." This

[18] In the Eastern Church (and thus at the Greek church in Venice) the feast of Basil the Great is January 1, hence the public showing of his relic on this day. It is June 14 in the Roman Church. Basil, archbishop of Caesaria (d. 373, 379?), was the author of the monastic rule observed in the Orthodox Church: the Basilians.

[19] The well-known Armenian church of Santa Croce degli Armeni of the Mekhitarist fathers, on the island of San Lazzaro degli Armeni, was founded in 1717, when the island was given to an Armenian nobleman, Manug di Pietro, a monk (1675–1749) called Mekhitar (the consoler). I did not locate this older Armenian church.

sacristy is on the right side of the altar. They read the Epistle and the Gospel, and after the Gospel the Creed, and then the song of Jerusalem, and then a deacon brings the chalice to the altar, and placing it on the altar, they serve and take the Eucharist just like the Roman priests, and having received the Eucharist, he distributes Holy Communion. Before the beginning of the Liturgy, the archimandrite incensed around the church, and the deacon incensed six times during the Liturgy, and the incensing was like the Greeks'. When the archimandrite said during the Liturgy, "Love one another," all the Armenians in the church kissed each other on the shoulder. The Armenians stood in the church at the time of the Liturgy in skullcaps, but some were on their knees.

[7]206, March 6.[20] I left Venice by gondola by sea for the city of Mestra, and arriving there we stayed the night in an inn, which is called the inn Capella, that is, a guesthouse.

March 7. I left Mestra in a carriage and arrived to dine at the city of Trivitsa (Treviso), 10 Italian miles from Mestra. This day I arrived to spend the night in a city of the Venetian authorities called Kastello Franko (Castelfranco), 10 Italian miles from Treviso. This city of Castelfranco is a stone fortress of ancient work; it is not large but the walls are very high, like the walls of the Moscow Kremlin; around this fortress there is a moat 20 sazhens wide, faced with stone and filled with water. /519/ The domiciles in this city are all of fine stone work; there is a fine stone church with no small riches. The home of the Venetian cavalier in this city is of marvelous workmanship and very extensive; in it are 2 chambers with walls done very smoothly, except on the top there is some fine carved white stonework, and the walls in those rooms are painted with fine Italian paintings. The fence around the home is of stone, and it has three finely proportioned entrance gates on one wall. Along one side of this home is a large, fine pond filled with clear water. The decorations and furniture inside these rooms are very rich and wonderful, with fine beds and many large, wondrously made mirrors, and in these chambers there are no wallpapers, but the walls are painted with glorious Italian paintings.

Behind this house is a large, marvelous garden with many kinds of fruit trees and aromatic shrubs and a multitude of all kinds of flowers. There are many stone pillars having on them the likenesses of men and women, carved of white stone. There are also many animals, beasts and birds, done of fine workmanship, and all are placed among the flowers to decorate this garden. There is a fine fountain in the center; on the back wall—the wall around the garden is of stone—there is an extensive gate, and instead of a door these gates have 2 thick, stone, four-sided pillars of marvelous

[20] Tolstoi includes the year, as it has been some weeks since he last wrote in his Diary. He here begins a trip to Milan; no reason for the visit is given in the Diary.

workmanship, and these pillars are carved like two horses of white stone of such marvelous work that they seem alive and of the size of a large German horse. On either side of this gate are two hills filled with dirt, 20 sazhens long, and on these hills are stone *altany*[21] of yellow marble and overgrown with grapes. The benches and tables in these altanas are eight-sided and of yellow marble. In this garden are two clean, well-proportioned ponds of fine water, with many fish in them; over the ponds are fine stone bridges, under which a sizeable barque may pass. Alongside these ponds are pavilions that can be taken down quickly. In these houses lemons and pomegranates and other fine fruits, figs, and chestnuts grow all year, and on these trees I saw /520/ fruit on the 7th day of March: lemons and ripe pomegranates, and some were unripe and very green, and some just-formed, and there were also blossoms on the same tree; and thus this tree bears fruit the whole year. For this the pavilions are placed over these trees, so that on cold days they place burning coals in braziers in the pavilions, so that extreme cold does not touch the fruit of these trees, as if they were in a protected grove. In warm times these pavilions are taken down and carried away.[22]

March 8. I left Castelfranco early and arrived at the Venetian city of Shtarelo (Cittadella), 8 Italian miles from Castelfranco. This city of Cittadella is of stone, with a large ancient stone fortress, and set on a slope; around it is a 20-sazhen moat filled with water. This same day I arrived for dinner at the Venetian city of Vitsentsa (Vicenza). This is a fine, large city with a large fortress and stone entrance towers. The town is populous, with many fine stone houses, and with many well-stocked markets. It is 10 Italian miles from Cittadella to Vicenza. There is a very fine stone church named for the Blessed Mother of God, with an altar of marvelous work, as one could scarcely see in all Italy.[23] Having dined in this city, I left and arrived at an inn called the Litora Dekomfina (Torri di Confine); it is 13 Italian miles from Vicenza. I stayed there for the night.

March 9. I left the inn early, four hours before daylight, and went 5 Italian miles, and because of the darkness of night the carriage in which I sat with the

[21] Italian, *altana,* belvedere. The altana is also the roof terrace, usually of wood, used in Venice to escape the summer's heat and for family gatherings in the city.

[22] Tolstoi notes the temperate Mediterranean climate that allows fruit growing year-round and the technology of collapsible greenhouses and braziers that allow man to control the climate. Evelyn, who visited the area at about the same time of year, emphasized the tastiness of the fruit and the preserves made of it, but did not mention the technology. Evelyn, *Diary,* II, 484.

[23] Cittadella, a well-preserved, medieval, fortified town, was built by the Paduans in the thirteenth century to combat their enemies in Castelfranco. Evelyn, *Diary,* II, 481–85, found much of interest architecturally in Vicenza.

driver who was transporting me fell from the road into a deep moat; and there the carriage came to rest, and because of the darkness of night we could not put the carriage back on the road soon, for we had only 2 drivers; and so we had to stay in an inn not far away; it is called Velianova [Villanuova]. Arriving there at daybreak, we left soon and arrived in a city called Verona. This city of the Venetian republic is 13 miles from the inn Villanuova. The stone city of Verona is very large, and it has many large fine churches and homes of marvelous stone work. The town has fine stone bridges over a great water, and there are many such bridges. Verona is populous; around this town are many fine gardens and markets with /521/ many wares. The inns, that is, the stop-over courts, are really fine. I stayed in this city this day until noon, and at noon I went to walk around Verona and to see how the town is built. The town is well constructed, and around the fortress is a strong moat, and this and the other fortresses are well done with a mathematical reasoning and are fortified, that is, strengthened very well. The *pliats* (piazza),[24] that is, the square, in the city of Verona is fine, and all the decorations of this town are marvelous and very fine.

This 9th day of March I arrived to stay at an inn called Kaval'kaselia (Cavalcaselle), 14 Italian miles from Verona, and I stayed there.

March 10. I arrived to dine in the Venetian city of Liunato (Lonato), 11 Italian miles from the inn. This is a small stone town with few people, and it stands on a lake[25] called Liago Dedizhensiago (Dezenzano sul Lago de Garda) in Italian. On this lake is a large stone fortress from which a town called Shtyr (Sirmione) extends; however, it has few people. From this city it is not far to a stone fortress called Undelia,[26] which is an old building; in some places it is crumbling. There are other fortresses on this lake of the Venetian republic. I stayed in the city of Lonato until noon, and after noon I left and spent the night in the city of Bres (Brescia), of the Venetian state, 15 Italian miles from the city of Lonato. In this city of Brescia lives a general of the Venetian republic, and in Brescia they built a large, very fine stone house for him, and it has many miraculous, well-proportioned rooms. This city of Brescia is very large, surrounded by a strong, fine earthen rampart. Above the rampart is a stone wall, and the stone towers along the wall are of fine dimensions, and the whole fortification is quite fine. The town has many fine stone buildings, many markets with all kinds of wares, and also many guns for

[24] *Piazza* is the Italian form; Tolstoi could have heard in northern Italy the German, *der Platz*, but most likely this is Polish, *plac*. In Verona, Tolstoi was struck by the fortress alone; Evelyn was impressed by Verona's antiquities and by the fact that the city had produced "*Cornelius Nepos, Emilius Marcus, Plinie, Vitruvius,* all of them honouring Verona with their birth, as of later date, *Julius Caesar Scaliger* that prodigie of Learning." *Diary,* II, 487.

[25] Lonato is actually inland from Desenzano.

[26] This is probably the ruin of the castle of the Scaligers at Sirmone on Lake Garda.

sale—firearms, arquebuses, which they call *fizii* (It. *fucile*), and fine pistols. In this city of Brescia are many tradespeople of all kinds, and the city of Brescia is praised for its masters of arms and of all manner of iron working.[27] This city has many people. Waters flow through it, and along the streets are fountains in many places. In this city of Brescia, at the entrance from Venice on the right side, is a stone fortress on a high mountain. In this city there are many large /522/ churches of fine workmanship, and they are well decorated. In size, Brescia approaches the size of Venice. This city stands close to high stone mountains, and on them there are many fine gardens, and around this city there are more grapes in the fields than one can say. In this town there are all kinds of foodstuffs. I spent the night here and left.

March 11. I arrived to dine in the borough of the Venetian prince, which is called Paliotsola (Palazzolo), where I stayed in an inn until noon. From Brescia to Palazzolo it is 18 Italian miles. And after noon I left this borough, and arrived to spend the night in the city of Bergamo, 13 Italian miles from Palazzolo. Approaching the city I saw a miraculous thing: around a garden there is a fence of bushes, and these bushes grow like a stone wall an arshin thick and 2 arshins high. Along this wall of bushes the bushes grow like various figures, such as a walking man with a spear, or with a halberd, or with a saber; another is like a man on a horse with weapons; another is like an angel with wings; another is like a woman or a girl dressed in the French fashion; another is a figure like a barque with sails and with ropes; another is just like a Venetian gondola, that is, a boat, with an awning, and on it a man with an oar; others are like fountains of various shapes; others grow in the likeness of animals and beasts and birds of various sorts, and others are like fine vessels. In the corners of this garden the bushes grow just like towers, on top of which grow people in the shapes of soldiers with weapons. This thing is exceedingly marvelous and wondrous, since this bush grows in these various shapes.[28]

Bergamo is large and very fine. Its walls and towers are of stone. The town has good stone churches and many fine stone houses and markets with many goods. A large river called the Arno[29] flows through this city, and across it are large stone bridges. Around the city is built a castle or stone fortress, and in it are many well-

[27] "Here I purchased my fine Carabine of *Lazarino Cominazzo* which cost me 9 pistols, this Citty being famous for these fire Armes, & that workeman, with *Jo:Bap:Franco* the best esteem'd; This Citty consists most in arts, that make Armes, every shop abounding in *Gunns*, Swords, Armorers &c, most of which Workmen come hither out of *Germanie*, of which this is a Staple." Evelyn, *Diary*, II, 489.

[28] It is not difficult to imagine Tolstoi's driver, when the credulous foreigner inquired, responding gravely that yes, indeed, these bushes actually grew in these fantastic shapes. As Tolstoi has previously encountered his first labyrinth, so now he finds the art of topiary, but he appears unaware it is art, not nature.

[29] Bergamo is not on the Arno; Tolstoi must mean the river Adda.

built stone homes. In this city of Bergamo there are a large number of soldiers posted from the Venetian republic for defense, because the city of Bergamo is close to the Spanish frontier. Aside from the soldiers, this city is very populous and well built. I spent the night in Bergamo, and left it. /523/

March 12. I arrived at the border of the Venetian principality with the Spanish state, 10 Italian miles from Bergamo. This place is called Bergamashka (Bergamasco). I crossed the border, and approached the first Spanish city, which is called Kalianiko (Colnago). This city stands on the shore of the great river Ada (Adda) on a high hill. In this city a home is marvelously built over the river Adda, and on the heights of the hills and from the house to the river there is a long stone passage of wonderful work. Along this passage and its handrails are placed gilded patterned pots, and in these pots grow pomegranates and lemons and other fine kinds of trees and wondrous flowers. Above the passage and in front of the palaces many cypress trees are set, and they grow very tall. This home has a fine garden in which they keep many peacocks and peahens. From this place I arrived this day to dine in a Spanish inn called Forna (Villa Fornaci), 6 Italian miles from the Italian border. I dined here and stayed until noon, and after noon I left this inn and arrived this day to spend the night in Mediolan,[30] 14 Italian miles from the inn Fornaci. Approaching Mediolan there were homes along the road, and beginning 4 versts from the city there were many homes on both sides of the road; these were large stone buildings, very fine, with marvelous gardens and many grapes in the fields. Mediolan is a large place and finely built and very populous. I arrived in Mediolan and stayed in an inn called the Tre-rei, in Slavonic the Three Kings.[31] The inn in Mediolan is very good for arriving *forestiere*, that is, foreigners. In this inn they assigned me a room all done in fine colored satin and decorated with marvelous furnishings, with 2 fine beds with satin bedding and covers. The tables were fine, and the armchairs and chairs were marvelously upholstered in velvet. And on the

[30] Milano; from the Roman Mediolanum; I retain the Spanish form as consistent with the politics of the period. During the Renaissance, Milan, like Florence and Venice, was a sovereign state, generally aligned with Florence and Naples against Venice to produce a kind of political equilibrium. It became a Spanish possession when Charles V succeeded Maximilian as German king (1519) and after the death of the last Sforza, Francisco II, in 1535. The French claimed it, regarding the Sforzas as usurpers and basing their claims on a marriage to the Visconti who had ruled Milan from 1277 to 1447. Since 1556, Milan was formally an appanage of the Spanish crown and a fief of the Empire.

The politics of the period are reflected in Tolstoi's language. He uses "the Italian border" as synonymous with "the border of Venetia," but now enters "Spain."

[31] Everyone stayed at the Three Kings, including Evelyn a half-century earlier. It was located in the via Tre Alberghi, was first mentioned in 1476, and was pulled down in the nineteenth century. Evelyn, *Diary*, II, 491. On its reputation as the best hotel, see Sells, *Paradise of Travellers*, p. 143.

morning of my arrival in Mediolan, that is, on ***March 13,*** I hired a fine coach, with 2 fine coachmen; I paid 9 lira per day for it, in Muscovite money 20 altyns, and in this coach I drove into Mediolan, where I could see what I wished without any restrictions.

First I went to the Mediolan monastery of St. Ambrose (Sant'Ambrogio), and a short distance away I saw the fine small church built on the place where St. Ambrose had baptized St. Augustine, his brother, and his brother's nephew, and having baptized them, Ambrose left the church on foot for his home.[32] And now /524/ no one can go to this place by coach or by horse, but only on foot, and so I went on foot along that road to the church where the body of St. Ambrose rests. This is an ancient church; from when it was built in Ambrose's lifetime until now it stands as if without repairs as a Roman church. It is a fine building and has many marvelous things in it. Its size is not at all small, and there are fine carvings in white stone in this church. The body of St. Ambrose rests under the altar, between the bodies of the holy martyrs Gervasius and Protasius; and now, by order of the Roman pope, the relics of St. Ambrose are shown to no one, and no one could say the reason for this prohibition. At the altar, under which the holy relics lie, there are very tall and finely done marble columns that support a cupola of miraculous work over the altar. In this church there is a marble column on which is placed a brass likeness of the serpent made by the prophet Moses in the desert to cure the Israelite people of the snake's bite; and they say that the likeness of the snake was brought to Mediolan by St. Ambrose. This likeness of a snake was broken into 3 pieces, and now the broken places are welded together, but it is noticeable. This likeness of a serpent is two arshins long, and its thickness is less than that of a man's arm.[33] At this church live both white clergy and monks, canons under rule, who are called Cistercians. And they have made a most marvelous and very extensive monastery for these canons. In this monastery I saw many miraculous holy paintings by fine Italian masters, and other fine things, which are there to decorate the church, which I fail to describe in detail for a lack of time.

From this monastery I went to the Church of St. Viktor (San Vittore). This church is of the most miraculous work and most amazing; it is all done in marvelous carved

[32] The Basilica of St. Ambrogio is a fourth-century church, built on the site of a Christian martyrs' cemetery and often reconstructed. It was badly damaged in 1943. The relics of Sts. Ambrose, Gervaso, and Protaso are in a small chapel under the high altar; Tolstoi notes the ciborium, supported by four magnificent porphyry columns, over the high altar. Earlier a Benedictine monastery, it passed to the Cistercians of Chairavalle in 1400.

[33] Evelyn was more skeptical of Moses' serpent: "We revisited *St. Ambrose* Church; the high *Altar* is supported by 4 Porphyrie columns, and under it lies the precious remaines of that holy Man; neere it they shewd us a pit or well, (an obscure place it is) where they say, St. Ambrose baptized St. Augustine. . . . They shew'd us likewise a fragment of the brasen serpent which *Moses* made in the Wildernesse, if you will believe it, it stands on a pillar in the Church." Evelyn, *Diary,* II, 500. See Numbers 21:8–9; and for the destruction of the serpent, see 2 Kings 18:4.

alabaster.[34] This church has one side altar made marvelously of wondrous black marble. This altar, they say, cost 28,000 scudos. At this church a monastery is built in which canons called Olivetans live. This monastery is very extensive and built marvelously.

From this monastery I went to the church of the martyr Akvili (Capella de Sant Aquilino). This church of the holy martyr Akvili, or Akili, is round, in all similar to the church in the Resurrection monastery, which is on the river Istra, only it is much smaller; it is an ancient building, but of fine workmanship.

At this church along the street stand /525/ 12 very tall and large stone columns, each carved of a single white stone in ancient times.[35] It is known that in this place in antiquity there was a certain marvelous building, but it was destroyed many years ago; and in many places these columns are bound with iron; the height of these columns is 5 sazhens, 3 arshins, and the thickness at the base is 4 sazhens around. On these columns, according to history, was built the home of the martyr Maximian, and when Mediolan battled in ancient times and Fedorikus Barbarosa destroyed it, all the buildings in the whole city were wrecked and destroyed; left undestroyed was only this church, in which the relics of the holy martyr Aquilino rest, and these columns.[36] And to this day this church and the columns stand unrestored, and the relics of the holy martyr Aquilino rest in the vestibule of this church over an altar, in a shrine behind glass. I was able to see these relics, and they are undecayed and most marvelous; the tendons and skin on the bones are undecayed on the head and the hands and feet, the parts of the holy body that are visible; the other parts are covered by clothing. On the left foot are a few parts of the metatarsus, where the blood has coagulated, and also on the left side of the neck, where the martyr was stabbed with a knife at the time of his suffering for Christ; even now it appears to be bleeding freshly and profusely. The structure of this vestibule where the holy relics rest is fine and rich, and the whole church is richly decorated.

From this church I went to a church they call the Il-Domo (Duomo) in their language. This church is miraculous and glorious to the whole world. They began this church 312 years ago and it is not yet complete, although they are building it inces-

[34] "Marvelous carved alabaster" is Tolstoi's way of saying that this is an elaborate and ornate baroque church, 1560.

[35] Tolstoi is describing the chapel of St. Aquilino of the Basilica of San Lorenzo Maggiore, parts of which date to the fourth century. The chapel itself had been an early Arian baptistry. Going outside, he sees the sixteen ancient Roman Corinthian columns in the Corso di Porta Ticinese.

[36] In reference to the columns mentioned above, Tolstoi cites a legend that attributes them to the home of Maximian (b. ca. A.D. 240), a general who lived in Milan and ruled the Western Empire while Diocletian ruled the East, A.D. 286. He then mentions the destruction of Milan during Barbarossa's second Italian campaign, 1159–62, when he defeated Milan, asserted imperial claims to it, and drove the Milanese into revolt. Maximian was killed by Constantine, but it is difficult to regard him as a "martyr" in the Christian sense that Tolstoi uses the word.

santly.[37] This whole church is done in white marble, and they have not laid a single brick or simple stone either in the walls or in the arches; but rather the outside and inside are all of slate, which is so well selected and arranged that one cannot tell that the church was not hewn out of a single stone. It is a most glorious work, and no such church, they say, of such great and miraculous workmanship can be found in the whole world, except for the cathedral in Rome. The length of this church is no less than 200 sazhens, and the width is more than 100 sazhens. The church has 92 white marble columns, each as if carved of a single stone. Many of these columns are veiled with fine gold lattices of glorious French workmanship. There are many large and small silver lamps in this church. /526/

In this church over the altar in the arch is a fine, rather small, four-pointed cross of black iron. In this cross, in a silver frame, is placed an iron nail that had been driven into the hand of the crucified Christ Our Savior; and this nail, they say, was brought to Mediolan by St. Ambrose of Mediolan in antiquity. The richness of this church is most miraculous, and it is difficult to speak of the multitude of numerous gold and silver vessels and of all things and of the decorations, which I will describe in detail below. This church is all built on a vault, and that vault is made of white slate of marvelous work. The size of this vault is very large; it is more than 700 sazhens around and 9 steps high.

Beneath this church is a finely built lower church. In the vault on which the church is built, in the middle of the lower church, rests the body of the archbishop of Mediolan, who was called Karlo Borameo (San Carlo Borromeo). This church, in which Carlo's body rests, is not large. Inside the church the walls are all covered with golden velvet; the arch in this church is done of cast silver sheets of the most marvelous work and of very great wealth. Over the altar of this church is the crystal coffin in which the body of Carlo rests. This coffin is very fine, of most marvelous work and great wealth. The body of Carlo lies in the coffin in clothes, dressed like a Roman bishop, and the bishop's dress and cap is in the Roman fashion. The only exposed part of his body is his head, one bone with no skin or flesh on it, and the other parts of the body cannot be seen because it is all dressed; and on his hands he wears white satin gloves and on his feet white satin stockings. And whether there are bones in these clothes cannot be known for they are shuttered; only people of the Roman faith believe very much in Carlo, and they say that his body works many miracles.[38] In this church where the body of Carlo rests, there is a window to the

[37] Founded in 1386, the massive cathedral was consecrated by San Carlo Borromeo in 1577; the dome was not completed until the eighteenth century. Tolstoi is not given to architectural superlatives, but it is not surprising to find them here, for the cathedral, with its 135 statue-topped spires, is spectacular by any standards. Evelyn was equally impressed, comparing it also to St. Peter's in Rome. *Diary,* II, 492–94.

[38] The crystal coffin now rests under the new post–Vatican II main altar. Evelyn marveled over the crystal: "His body, before the high altar, grated & inchas'd in one of the vastest Chrystals in *Europe.*" *Diary,* II, 493. Borromeo, archbishop of Milan, a cardinal at age twenty-three, founder of orphanages and of the modern system of seminaries, was also the

other church, and around this window in the large church is a marvelously done brass grill. This window is to allow light into the lower church where the body of Carlo rests, because without this window there would be no light in that church. At the columns in the large church are 2 great thrones, all of silverplate, and on them are large silver minted boards, set /527/ in places with patterned work. This church also has an untold quantity of lamps and silver candlesticks.

One cannot describe the marvelous workmanship that has gone and continues to go into this church, and I expect that for many years it will not be completed the way they wish to. I refer those who really want to know about this church to a printed history of Mediolan.

The cardinal lives at this church. He has a fine, large home with many rooms in this stone building; white clergy called canons serve in this church, and they regard these canons as cavaliers of the honorable sort of people, and many of them live at this church. In front of this church is a square, and much in this square is similar to the one in Venice in front of San Marco. The home of the viceroy of Mediolan is built alongside the cathedral church. It is very large, with many rooms all built of stone, done of smooth work without carving, but still very good. While I was in Mediolan the viceroy was not there; he had been selected, but not yet crowned.

From this great church I went to a *shpital,* that is, to a hospital.[39] This hospital is very large and built like this: it is four-sided, and one hundred fifty sazhens on a side, and around it are great halls two stories high. As many as 1,000 sick men and women always lie in these halls. They have made good turned beds with clean white bedding for these sick people, and each bed is veiled with a crimson curtain. There are 300 males and 300 females in this hospital to serve the sick; in this hospital they have built an apothecary for the benefit of the sick that has four doctors and 20 pharmacists. There is a garden at the apothecary in which all kinds of pharmaceutical plants and roots are grown, and the garden belongs to the hospital. In the hospital are 14 scribes who have their own particular rooms and who write down the income and expenses of that hospital and who conduct all the necessary business. In this hospital is a large room, and placed in that room is a large round table; around that table are placed many fine chairs. Twice every week, on Mondays and Fridays, the Mediolan senators come to this room and sit to direct all the affairs of this hospital.

---

voice of the Counter-Reformation and the spokesman of the Council of Trent and of the Inquisition (d. 1584).

[39] The Ospedale Maggiore, founded by Francesco Sforza in 1456, was in a massive building known as Ca' Granda, built in the fifteenth to seventeenth centuries to consolidate other hospitals in the city. Its elaborate façade is 260 meters long, and inside is an impressive courtyard. It now houses the university. Evelyn was equally impressed: "Next we went to see the greate Hospital, a quadrangular Cloyster, of vast compasse: in earnest a royal fabric, & has to it of annual endowment 50 thousand crowns of Gold: There is in the middle of it a Crosse building for the sick, & just under it, an Altar so plac'd as to be seene in all places of the Infermarie." *Diary,* II, 495–96.

/528/ This hospital is set up to receive all sorts of income from hereditary estates and from landed property after the owners are deceased. And all donors who for the sake of God give something to this hospital are written down, and they put these persons so recorded in a special room, and these persons are the first to be put into that room of the Mediolan merchant, who began to build this hospital, and who personally completed it not long ago.

Previously a small hospital had been built at royal expense, and now this old hospital is not destroyed, but it has been given to this new hospital for the various needs of the ill, so that the new hospital would be built close to the old one. In this large new hospital they have built churches and chapels in which they say Mass for the sick every day. The rooms of this hospital are well built with marvelous carvings around the windows, and everything is most miraculous. In this matter one can recognize the Catholics' love of mankind, such as one scarcely finds anywhere in this world. In this hospital they give comfort, and the food and drink for the sick is gratis in the name of Christ; also they are treated without cost. From this hospital I went to a church where I saw pictures of marvelous Italian painting, which were bought at a high price; for one picture 20,000 philipa were given, that is, 10,000 golden chervontsy. Around this painting, instead of an icon frame, are broad carved boards not less than an arshin wide, on which in ancient times the history of the Old Testament was carved. This board is of marvelous work. On the walls of this church are also many very fine paintings, and the whole structure is really fine and most amazing. At this church live white clergy who serve the Mass every day.[40]

From this church I went to the inn in which I stayed because it was the hour for dinner. This day after dinner I went to see a great library, and in this library I saw a multitude of books in all languages. Two large globes stand in this library. In this library in a certain room I saw *kunshtov*[41], that is, models of fine workmanship of carved alabaster and various materials and sculpted of plaster. I also saw there the likeness of a man carved of white marble, and I also saw [displayed] on a board all sorts of military artifacts of such miraculous work that no one could describe it. There are a multitude of other things of the most intricate carved work in this library, about which I now fail to write because of time. In a special room of this

[40] I did not locate this church near the hospital. On one end stands the ancient Basilica degli Apostoli with its chapel of St. Catherine. Close by the other end of the hospital is the baroque San Stefano, and next door is the seventeenth–eighteenth century San Bernadino alle ossa; in 1695 a capella ossario was added, and this may be Tolstoi's church, since its recent completion might have led a guide to tell Tolstoi of the high cost of a painting.

[41] Tolstoi here visits the famous Ambrosian Library and Art Gallery. Founded by Cardinal Federico Borromeo in 1609, it was a vast collection already in the seventeenth century. Evelyn found it very impressive, and was able to attribute the Four Elements described below to "Hans Breugill." *Diary*, II, 497–500. Two of the pictures by Jan Bruegel the Elder are still in Milan, two others are in the Louvre. The term *kunshtov* (Ger. *Kunst*, or Pol. *kunszt*) here apparently denotes statues.

library I saw many most intricate paintings on brass, on wooden boards, on canvas, and on various materials, about /529/ the masterfulness of which the human tongue cannot speak. Only because of the high price of these paintings, I write one thing here. Among these paintings there are four objects painted on brass boards one arshin in height and width. On one is painted the *element,* or the element of earth; on another, water; on a third, air; and on the fourth, fire. The *kurfurst* of Saxony, who is now the king of Poland,[42] gave 16,000 gold chervontsy for each of these four things, and because he gave this price, the Mediolans will now sell nothing from this library at any price. And in this library there are many other such painted things, which are expensive. In the midst of the halls of this library is a fine fountain from which spurts fine clean water. In this library I saw a very large book of the mathematical sciences, written in antiquity, but it is not a printed book, and they say that this book was written 300 years ago; and they say that its price is very great, that the English king would give 8,000 golden chervontsy for it.[43] In this library I saw a book written on very threadbare linen in the Greek language, and it is certified that this book was written 1,635 years ago; and there are many other books of antiquity written by the hand of St. Ambrose of Mediolan. There are two other libraries in Mediolan, but they are smaller than the one I describe.

From this library I went to a church in which I saw the coffins of the three Persian tsars who brought worship and gifts to our newborn Christ the Savior. Their bodies, taken from the tomb, were transported 20 Italian miles to Koloni (Colonno) from Mediolan by Fedorik Barbarossa at the time of the destruction of Mediolan, and now their bodies are in Colonno, where I was honored to see them.[44] In this church I saw the gold that the Persian tsars brought as a gift to Christ at the birth of our

[42] The newly elected king of Poland after the death of Jan Sobieski in 1696 was Augustus II (Elector of Saxony), king of Poland, 1697–1733.

[43] About 1630 Arundel, and about 1632 William Petty attempted to purchase some drawings of Leonardo da Vinci for Charles of England. Evelyn tells the story: for a book of sketches, "the Inscription pretends that our King *Charles* had offered 1000 pounds for them." He denies the report, saying that having seen them, he "did not thinke them so much worth." *Diary,* II, 498–99.

[44] There are many legends about the Three Kings, the Magi. The Basilica of St. Eustorgio was built to bury their remains, brought to Milan by Eustorgio II. After Barbarossa's destruction of Milan in 1162, they were taken to Cologne, and that city's famous cathedral was built to preserve them. Evelyn tells the same story: "Passing along we saw St. *Eustorgio* wherein they told us there lay formerly the bodys of the 3 *Magi,* since translated to *Colin* in Germany: they yet reserve the Tomb, which is a Square Stone, on which is a Star ingraven, & under it: *Sepulchrum trium Magorum.* Here is also (as affirmed) some of the money or golden Treasure, which they offered our B:Saviour." *Diary,* II, 496.

The last clause is a mystery; it does not contain a subjunctive, "Where I would be honored to see them," and Colonno is not capitalized as it is two clauses earlier, and thus it becomes the word "colony." Since Tolstoi does not mention travel to Colonno twenty miles distant, I assume his phrase is confused, and he wished he could have seen the relics.

Savior. The gold coin is made like a [Russian] efimok, except its imprint was made in ancient times. In this church I saw a tomb carved marvelously out of white marble, and in this tomb rested the body of the martyr Peter, who was a Dominican and in ancient times was martyred for Christ. In his martyrdom his tormentor ordered his head split in two, and his face was cut away from his skull, and until now both parts of his head rest on the altar, and not with his body in the coffin; and the beard and hair and skin on his head are all intact and undecayed.[45] From this church I went to the inn, where I stayed, because night had come. /530/

On the morrow, ***March 14***, in the morning, I went to the Church of St. Aleksandr (Sant'Alessandro).[46] In this church I saw a most miraculous thing: according to Roman custom, they have built a place where the priest hears confessions, and this is how they made it: at a pillar in the middle of the place is where the priest sits when he hears confessions; and over this place they have set the image of the Savior without Hands, carved of white stone, and on either side are the places where the penitents stand, and over these places they set a viper in yellow stone. These stones are an arshin in height and width; on these stones are depicted footsteps, as if a human foot had made them in a soft new material, impressed in wax or something similar. And they say that this is the impression of the most pure foot of Christ, and these stones were brought to Mediolan from the mountains of Sinai in antiquity. This church of Sant'Alessandro is of the most marvelous work, although it is not completed, and the inside is hung with paintings of the most glorious workmanship. In it the pulpit is made of stone and has many jaspers, chalcedon, other stones,[47] crystals, topazes, and very large turquoises, and also many white and red corals. There is a fine monastery at this church; canons like the Jesuits, called Theatines, live in it.

From this church I went to the castle or fortress in which the general lives with 500 soldiers.[48] I was sent to this general to inquire whether I would be allowed to go into the castle, and he sent to me a certain man in charge who guided me through the castle and took me along the walls to see the fortifications and the cannon and all things. This fortress, that is, the upper city, is of stone with very high walls, and from the ground to the merlons it is 20 sazhens and 3 arshins, and the width between

[45] Of numerous St. Peters, this is presumably Peter of Verona (b. ca. 1205), a Dominican noted for his perfect purity and as an enemy of the Manichean heresy. He was killed by the Manichees on the road from Como to Milan in 1252.

[46] This is the Church of St. Alexander, founded in 1608 and still under construction during Tolstoi's visit. It is famous for the inlaid woodwork of the confessionals and the pulpit.

[47] Here Tolstoi lists two unidentified semiprecious stones: *enemiti* and *isabiki*. The first is possibly hematite, Italian, *ematite*, an oxide in the family of rubies and sapphires, but I am strictly guessing.

[48] Tolstoi now visits the Sforzesco Castle, built in something like its present form by Francesco Sforza after 1450. Upon hearing "Francesco," Tolstoi erroneously attributes it to a "French" king. The corner bastions have a facing that does resemble the Faceted Palace in the Kremlin, and the parallel can be drawn even further, since both were Italianate palaces of the same period.

the merlons is the thickness of the walls, 26 arshins; and the French king built this fortress when Mediolan was under his power. Along the walls of this fortress are many large, medium, and small brass cannon, and the bastions are round and built of faceted stone, just like the faceted State Palace in Moscow is built, and on these towers are many large cannon of fine French work. On one tower is placed the brass likeness of a human head, set high up on an iron rod, to commemorate this: when the Spanish general betrayed the Spanish king and gave Mediolan to the French, and when the general was caught by the Spanish /531/ and they severed his head, they placed it on a stake; and when this head disappeared after many years, they made an image of the general's head in brass, and placed it in eternal memory on the iron rod on this tower. Around the castle is a deep moat filled with water and immeasurably wide; around the moat are very strong earthen bastions, and placed on them are many great cannon. To enter this fortress, they have made strongholds with 8 passage bridges that lead across the water to eight passage gates from a single place, and at each gate stands a guard with large cannon. In the middle of the castle on the walls stand 2 very large cannon of fine workmanship and proportions. This castle is strengthened and fortified as a glorious stronghold from all sides. No Frenchman is ever allowed into the castle. In size the castle is 500 sazhens around, and there are no homes in the castle except for the general's and the soldiers'.

From this castle I went to the city to see a building called the *lazaret* (*lazzaretto*).[49] This house is built beyond the city, close to the moat that goes all around Mediolan. This building is of stone, and along the walls of the structure are halls one story high. There are many of these halls, and because of them the place occupies a large four-cornered space surrounded by these halls. In the middle of the building is a four-cornered church; and this is why it was built: when Mediolan has a pestilent infection, those infected with the plague are taken from the city to this building, and here they are treated and they rest, and those who die are buried in this place. Here I saw a column of white stone, and on one side of it is a small sore from which a yellow stream flows down, and they say this about it: whenever there is a

[49] The city of Venice apparently founded the first of these plague hospitals, giving them the name by which all of them were known. On the island of San Lazzaro degli Armeni was the Lazzaretto Vecchio, and Venetians hold (see Lorenzetti, *Venice*, p. 846) that Lazzaretto was a corruption of *Nazaretum*, from the ancient name of the island, Santa Maria de Nazareth. The more probable derivation is from Lazarus (Luke 16:20), the leper covered with sores.

The most famous description of the Lazzaretto in Milan is in the novel of Manzoni, *I Promessi Sposi*, pp. 482ff. "The Lazzaretto at Milan . . . is a quadrilateral and almost equilateral enclosure, outside the city, to the left of the gate called the Porta Orientale. . . . The two larger sides extend to about the length of five hundred paces. . . . In the midst of the clear and open space within, rose a small octagonal temple. . . . The primary object of the whole edifice, begun in the year 1489, . . . was as the name itself denotes, to afford a place of refuge, in cases of necessity, to such as were ill of the plague . . . which usually appeared two, four, six, or eight times a century."

plague in Mediolan, the sore begins to run—and not just briefly—and it flows just as from a human wound for as long as there is the pestilence. The Mediolans therefore know that there will be a plague this year, because a flowing pus can be seen on this column.

Mediolan is very large, much larger than Venice and immeasurably populous. They say that it has 500,000 inhabitants[50] not including the forestieri, that is, the foreigners, who have come here. Mediolan has /532/ a fine moat around it. There are many wondrous stone fortresses, churches, monasteries, and homes, and no wooden buildings at all. Plentiful waters flow in many places, and on these streams the inhabitants can go wherever they wish in large barques.

The inhabitants are honorable people; their wives and daughters go about in coaches, which have fine drivers. Behind the coaches walk many footmen, as is the Muscovite custom. Mediolan has its own coins, and they change a golden chervonets for 14 lira or for 5 soldos.

The shops and wares in Mediolan are numerous, and there are all sorts of fine goods of ironwork, and weapons: pistols and fine muskets and wondrous swords; but it is very expensive to buy iron goods of quality.

In Mediolan all speak Italian, only with some slight changes. The inhabitants are of good morals and affectionate to foreigners. Bread and foodstuffs are not expensive, and there are many fine grape wines that can be bought cheaply. The males in Mediolan wear a black costume similar in all respects to that of a Venetian cavalier; only with these differences: the Mediolans wear a collar in the back, like that on a Muscovite short kaftan; they do not wear purses on their arms like the Venetians; and the women in Mediolan wear dresses similar to those of Dutch women, and on their heads they wear French attire and they cover themselves with veils.

The streets and lanes in Mediolan are paved with stone, and around the upper city a great square has been constructed. There are no buildings on one side of the upper city, for Mediolan stands close to high mountains. When one arrives from Bergamo at Mediolan, the great mountains are on the right side a half-verst away, and in some places closer; and these great mountains are called the Alps, across which one can cross from Germany to Italy with great difficulty and not without risk. The Mediolan people are by nature dark-skinned men and women; rarely does one see a naturally white [fair-complexioned] person.

A description of what I saw in the great Mediolan cathedral in the repository of vessels:

[50] "Milan is one of the princliest Citties in *Europe*, it has no suburbs, but is circld with a stately Wall for 10 Miles, in the Center of a Country that seems to flow with milk and hony: the aire is excellent, the fields fruitful to admiration, & consequently the Merkat abounding with all sorts of provisions: The Citty has neere 100 Churches: 71 Monasteries: 40000 Inhabitans; It is of a Circular figure fortified with bastions." Evelyn, *Diary*, II, 501. Evelyn's source had said that the city had "above 300,000" inhabitants, and modern encyclopedias give the population as 115,000 in 1714. Ibid., 492, 501.

Eight gold vessels of the most marvelous work, the weight of gold being more than two puds.[51] /533/

A golden board on which is stamped the face of the Spanish king. This board is ¾ of an arshin high and an arshin wide, and the weight of the gold is 60 funt.

A gold chest sent to the Mediolan cathedral by the Spanish king from Madrid. This chest is of glorious work, the gold weighing 20 funt, and in the drawers of this chest are many holy things.

A crystal chest of the most miraculous work in gold, with stones set into the gold: rubies, emeralds, and sapphires. I saw very many silver vessels of patterned work, among them one silver chalice or cup cut of red coral of marvelous carved work, such work as one seldom sees in the whole world. The silver in the molded vessels, candlesticks, and lamps is more than 100 puds.

4 golden vessels, in which the Romans, as is their custom, place the sacred Eucharist, over which they perform the Mass and from which they give the Eucharist to the people. These vessels are of carved work with diamonds, rubies, emeralds, and sapphires.

For the same use, 6 vessels of fine patterned craftsmanship, and made up of various stones, of crystal, of topaz, of jasper, and mounted in gold.

The attire of an archbishop of the Western church, the cap, the chasuble strung with very many fine stones, and also many marvelous priests' attires.

Patterned cloths, of which there are 30, sewn and stitched, with which the altar is adorned on feast days; these cloths are of such marvelous sewn work that there are none better in the world; only in Rome is there a cloth from Mediolan, which was taken to the pope. These cloths are of such gloriously sewn work that someone gave 5,000 scudos for this craftsmanship. No one can describe how gloriously this work is sewn.

There are many other marvelous things in this church, which because of the lateness of the hour are impossible to describe.[52]

And on this 14th day of March, after dinner, I left Mediolan for Venice by the same route that I took from Venice, and I arrived on the ***19th of March,*** that is, on the Saturday of the second week of the Great Fast (Lent).

During my stay in Venice the Roman Easter was on ***March 21*** by the Greek calendar, on March 30 by the Roman calendar, five days before the Greek Easter; and in the present year of [7]206, March 21 was in the second week of Lent. The Romans and Italians call the week before Easter the Week /534/ of Palms, and in Slavonic it

[51] Tolstoi previously introduced the Russian "pound," the funt of about 9/10 of an English pound. The pud contained 40 funty, and equaled 36.113 U.S. pounds.

[52] By seventeenth-century standards, Tolstoi had a thorough introduction to Milan. He missed only one really major attraction that Evelyn and others found "incomparable," da Vinci's Last Supper in the Church of Santa Maria delle Grazie. *Diary,* II, 497.

is Palm Sunday Week. On this day everyone walks to the church carrying palms, finely braided into various figures.

In Passion Week, on the Roman Holy Thursday, the Venetian patriarch in the monastery of the apostle Peter, where he lives, does the washing of the feet in this manner:[53] In the middle of the church they place a table and cover it with white brocade. At this table, on both sides, sit 28 clergymen, 14 to a side, in the vestments of priests and deacons; and the patriarch comes and begins to say the Mass in the fashion of the Western Church. When he blesses the sacrament, he leaves the altar and sits in a chair at the table. They bring him two large ewers with balsam, two large pewter bottles, and two small measures of wood oil, and on this table they consecrate the chrism. Then they bless the oil, and having blessed it, all the clerics who are at the table convey all these things to the vessel repository, and they go there surrounded by candles and church singing. The patriarch distributes this holy oil to all the churches on Good Friday. Then he again goes to the altar and blesses the annual sacrament, and the others of the laity who are in the church to take the Eucharist may take the sacrament at that time, as does the patriarch himself and as do the priests and deacons who serve the Mass with him. Concluding the Mass, he disrobes and puts on a black vestment and sits on the chair, and an archdeacon begins to read him the cursed book of the heretics. Then begins vespers, that is, evensong, and during Vespers there is the washing of the feet: twelve men—sit in white garments in the manner of the apostles, laymen of great age and not clergymen—some of them sickly, and that day they had taken the Eucharist at Mass. And at the moment of the washing, the patriarch is in a cassock and in a stole and wears a cap with ribbons. He washes the feet of each man sitting there, placing them in a pan of water; and having washed them, he kisses the feet; and having kissed them, he dried them. At this time they do not read the Gospel but are silent, for they have read the Gospel earlier [during the Mass]. And when they come to wash the feet they sit in the image of the apostle Peter, and not a word is spoken.

After the washing the patriarch leaves for his house with those whose feet he has washed; and when they arrive, a round table covered with a fine tablecloth is placed there, and the fine viands are placed on it. The wretched ones whose feet he had washed sit /535/ at that table 6 to a side, and the patriarch stands in the middle of them at the table, and he serves them and feeds them. The patriarch himself brings

[53] Tolstoi describes the ceremony in the Church of San Pietro di Castello, the patriarchal cathedral. On Maundy Thursday the Mass is preceded by the Blessing of the Holy Oils, which the Council of Trent had reaffirmed as a symbol of supernatural grace that protects from the contagion of sin. Following the Mass the reserved Host is carried in procession to the Altar of Repose. Then vespers are said, followed by the Stripping of the Altars and the Mandatum, the Washing of Feet. Once the feet of twelve poor men, recalling the twelve apostles, were washed, but St. Gregory the Great noticed a thirteenth, who disappeared after the ceremony. Believing the visitor to be an angel or the Lord himself, he changed the official number to thirteen.

them water to wash their hands, and sets the food before them, and he distributes it, and he himself serves them, and he feeds them fish, and gives them a ducat of Venetian coinage, and in Muscovite money this is 15 altyns a man, and he receives them in his chambers.

The house of the Venetian patriarch is large, and his rooms are finely furnished. Two halls are all done in gold velvet with lace, and four are all in silk, and the other rooms are also well decorated. From Holy Thursday until Holy Saturday, no Romans anywhere ring any church bells, and the clocks do not strike the hour, because, they say, the Son of God is undergoing his Passion.

On Good Friday night in Venice the following happens: At the first hour of night a multitude of people collect at San Marco, and they arrive in processions from eight churches. In these processions they carry the image of the Crucifixion of Christ, and behind each image there are some 500 and even as many as 1,000 people, with large candles of white wax and with cords. Many in these processions flagellate themselves cruelly even until their blood flowed, as I have written above, and they arrive in the Church of San Marco, where all kneel. And then the chief canon from the pulpit shows the people the body of Christ in a glassy vessel, which is kept in Venice in the church vessel repository at the Church of San Marco. He also shows them a piece of wood from the cross of Christ, and then all the people fall on their knees and press their faces to the ground. There were shouts of many possessed people in San Marco this night. The very first procurators of Venice walked in these processions without shame. This night all the canons of the Roman faith of all orders flagellated themselves out of duty; and when the processions ended, at that time they began to read the Gospel in San Marco, and the people did not leave the church all night.

On Good Friday there is also the obligation to walk behind the cross with candles all day from church to church, for 1,000 and more men and women. At this time they wear black clothing, and none wear white; they also cover the face, and on one side is sewn a cross, and on the other is sewn the image of the bones of a dead man. On Good Friday in the Church of San Marco /536/, people kiss the wood of the cross of Christ and the nail from the crown of thorns, stained with the blood of the Savior.

Also on Good Friday, two hours before nightfall, the interment of Christ is performed by the Romans. They make a facsimile of the tomb, and they carry this tomb from the Church of San Marco around the square. The archimandrites, that is, the first people of clerical rank of Venice, carry this tomb. The patriarch was not there at this time. Over this tomb the Venetian senators carry a canopy, and they bring this tomb back to San Marco, and they place it on an area by the wall on the left side of the church. This area is elevated, and the wooden tomb is placed there, decorated with cast silver boards of marvelous work. The church wall where the tomb is placed is covered with gold velvet on a crimson field. When they close the tomb, they place the sacrament in it, and they place at the tomb 6 large candles of white wax, and they seal this tomb with the signet of the prince of Venice.

On the night before Holy Saturday processions from all the churches in Venice come with the sacrament to the Church of San Marco, and they walk around the square at San Marco with a multitude of lit candles. At this time at the square and throughout the city, 2 large wax candles burn in each window of all homes and palaces. The light from these candles glows like the light of day throughout Venice; it is difficult to calculate the number of these candles and impossible to calculate the cost of the wax. These processions go in fine formation and are not disorderly, and they do not stop for the whole night.

At noon of Holy Saturday all the church bells suddenly begin to ring, and the sacrament that has been placed in the grotto and sealed with the signet of the Venetian prince is taken from the tomb, and when the people come to San Marco, it is opened. On the night before Easter a procession leaves every church, and they walk around the churches, and matins begins in all churches after midnight. On the feast of Easter itself, the prince of Venice and all his senators were in San Marco. At that time there was also marvelous singing and instrumental music; they sang and played from six choirs in this church. The altar in San Marco was decorated with the finest array. /537/ At that time I saw all of the church treasure in the church of San Marco: first, the corona or gold crown of the emperor (tsar') Constantine; then four large gold candelabra; then 12 cast gold crowns; then 18 gold headgears with pearls and stones; and these 12 crowns and 18 headdresses were from the daughters of the empress Helena, the mother of the emperor Constantine. And they keep these holy things in the Church of San Marco to adorn the altar. Many large silver candelabra and large silver pitchers are also placed there; and there is a gold censer that was brought to Venice from the temple of Solomon in Jerusalem. On this day in San Marco, music played simultaneously on six organs in different choirs to the same beat.

This day at one o'clock the Venetian prince was in San Marco to hear a sermon, and one of the white clergy spoke from the pulpit in very fine Italian. And after this sermon the prince went to the monastery of St. Zacharias (San Zaccaria), where Roman canons called Benedictines live, and he went to this monastery by sea in a golden barque, and his rowers were finely dressed in velvet kaftans.[54] In front of him they carried his cap, which they call a crown; this cap is covered with silken velvet and many stones: great rubies and emeralds and sapphires. And when the prince arrived and entered the church, evensong, that is, vespers, began. At that time they began to play on one organ and to sing a choral song for the prince of Venice; and after vespers the prince left this church and went to the iron gilded grating behind which, by custom, stands the mother superior with her nuns; and the prince showed them the cap they call a corona. Having seen it, the mother superior and the nuns bowed to the prince, and she brought him a vase finely covered with gold and silver; the nuns also brought flowers on silver dishes to all the senators who were then with

[54] The Easter vespers visit to San Zaccaria was one of the many ceremonial visits required of the doge. Since the twelfth century, when the nuns donated a part of their garden for the enlargement of the Piazza San Marco, the doge annually received his ducal cap from the nuns in memory of the first doge's cap, given by an abbess of San Zaccaria to the republic.

The Doge-Elect Carried Round Piazza (Franco, 1610.)

the prince. Thus, on Easter every year the prince of Venice has to come to this monastery for vespers and must show this cap to the superior and to the sisters, because a former mother superior of this monastery made this cap in antiquity for a former prince of Venice, and it is always kept in the vessel repository of the Church of San Marco.

March 25, that is, on Friday, on the feast of the Annunciation, I was at the Liturgy at the Greek church. The metropolitan served at the church on this occasion. The beginning of this holy /538/ Liturgy was not that which is customary in Greek and Russian churches: he began this Sacred Liturgy like the beginning of the Mass of Chrysostom, and not like vespers, only a single Liturgy without vespers with the blessings, but they had vespers at the regular time. At all masses of the presanctified in this Greek church of St. George, when "My Prayer Corrects" is sung, the priest and the people merely stand and are not on their knees, and they do not bow their heads at all, and not one in forty of them make a bow to the ground. The Greek men and women who are worthy to be recipients of the Holy Eucharist, before the Liturgy receive the Eucharist that remained from the year, and not from the service of that day.[55]

April 21, that is, on Holy Thursday by the old Greek calendar, they held the washing of the feet in the Greek church according to a Liturgy identical and without change from that in the Russian state. The metropolitan washed the feet of the priests. The place for the washing was made on high in the middle of the church and was covered with a carpet; six chairs covered with green velvet were placed on each side of this spot, and the metropolitan's place was set on the right side to the west, and at the head was placed the image of the Savior, and in the place of Judas sat a layman of the Roman faith; such is their custom that they hire a layman for this role, and pay him. His dress was a simple alb, and the metropolitan washes his feet before all others.

On Good Friday the royal hours in this Greek church began later than on this day in Moscow, and vespers this day were at the same time as the service. At the beginning the tomb of the Lord was under black velvet, and the tomb was set on four columns of carved gold and covered with black velvet just like a real coffin. When they began to sing the verse, the metropolitan and the priests walked out the northern doors carrying the image [of Christ] taken from the cross and the shroud, and they placed the image [of Christ] in the tomb. And then there was the kissing [which concludes the Liturgy].

On Holy Saturday, matins were two hours before daybreak. When they sang the "Blessing of the Pure" and the refrains, all who were in that church stood with candles. Then there was the glorification, the shroud on the tomb of the Lord was raised, and the metropolitan and the priests circled inside the church three times, and all entered the royal gates; all the people had large wax candles. They brought the Lord's tomb inside the church because at that time there was great rain and

[55] In addition to the normal Liturgies of St. Basil and St. John Chrysostom, the Byzantine Church also has what is termed the "Liturgy of the Pre-sanctified Gifts." It is celebrated during Lent on certain days when the more common Liturgies are not celebrated. The Liturgy omits the Anaphora, the Eucharistic Sacrifice, the essential party of the normal Liturgies. See Solovey, *Liturgy*, p. 47.

thunder and lightning; when it does not rain on this day /539/, they carry the tomb of the Lord and the shroud around the outside of the church. And when they bring the tomb of the Lord to the altar they read the lessons and the Epistle and the Gospel. The metropolitan himself read, and they say that the canons do not speak and do not break their fast on Holy Saturday, and there is no kissing of the shroud at matins. During all of Passion Week they do not read the Gospel on the hour in this Greek church, and on Holy Thursday they have no absolution. On this Holy Saturday in this Greek church they had the blessing of the oil because they do not bless the oil on Holy Thursday; the metropolitan blessed the oil with six priests, and at the time of the blessing the holy oil was in an amphora, and the metropolitan stood not at the table, on which the oil was placed, but at his own place. Likewise, the priests stood not in chasubles, but only in stoles in their own place, where they stayed all day to hear the singing. And after the blessing all the people in the church were anointed with oil, and then without interruption the Liturgy began. One priest served with a deacon, and when during the Liturgy they began to sing "God is Risen, to Judge the Earth," the bells rang. The bells had not rung all of Passion Week in this church; during the singing they used the clapper.

April 24, that is, on Easter by the Greek calendar, the bells at the Greek church rang for matins three hours before daylight, and matins began a half hour before daylight. Before matins, when the metropolitan was dressing and went with a candle from the altar and sat in a chair in the royal gates, all the people who were then in that church came forward to ignite their candles from his; and they do this to commemorate how fire came down from the heavens on the day of the Resurrection of Christ in the church of Jerusalem. And then came the procession with icons from the west doors; and they again entered the church through the same doors from which they began, and they started to sing the canon, but during this the metropolitan sat in his place with the Epistle on the side of the altar and began the kissing [which concludes the Liturgy]. The clergy did not kiss on the lips, but the laity did kiss on the lips. After matins they had the Liturgy without an interruption; the metropolitan himself said the Liturgy, and with him 10 priests and archdeacons and deacons. During the Liturgy the priests and deacons and archdeacons read the Holy Epistle, and they did not read at the altar, and the metropolitan himself and four priests read individually. After the reading of the Epistle the bells rang at the time of the Eucharist, and after /540/ the Eucharist and at the end of the Liturgy there was a volley from cannon at the church. This day they sang the Liturgy at the 3rd hour of day.

In this week of Easter the metropolitan himself said vespers in this church; he dressed in the middle of the church and read the Epistle at the altar, and the priests read in the church just as at the time of the Liturgy, and at every exclamation they rang the church bells and beat with clappers. When they finished the Epistle, they rang loudly and fired the cannon at that church, and the kiss was just as at matins. When vespers ended, the bells again rang loudly in the bell tower, and the firing from the cannon and from small arms was loud.

May 1. According to the Roman calendar they celebrated the feast of the Ascension, and in Venice each year this is the custom: On the day of the Ascension of Christ the prince of Venice with the whole Senate marries the sea and such was his conduct:[56] He left Venice in a large galley that stood at the arsenal all carved and gilded and covered with silken velvet and gold lace. The patriarch of Venice went on this galley with the prince and all the magistrates. Trumpeters went before them, and leaving Venice from the port called Lido, they went half a verst out to sea. There the principe, that is, the prince of Venice, threw the signet-ring of Mark the Evangelist into the sea on a string. Retrieving it from the sea, he threw another ring without a string in its place; and returning he went to the monastery of St. Nicholas, which is close by, on the Lido island, where the Dominicans live.[57] In this monastery he heard Mass. And when the prince and patriarch and senate sailed close to Lido island, they fired mightily from cannons and from small arms. And when the prince went forth from Venice to marry the sea, then from all the ships and from the Venetians on frigates and galleys and on tartans and other vessels that stand at Venice, there was great shooting from cannon; they fired, giving honor to the prince of Venice. Behind the prince of Venice and the people sailing with him were a great multitude of men and women in gondolas, in peotas and other small vessels, among them

[56] As with the Easter ceremony described above, Tolstoi here tells of another of the popular rituals that were required of the doge of Venice and around which the cycle of life revolved. The ritualistic marriage with the sea on Ascension Thursday was fully established in the Middle Ages, celebrating Venice's dominion over the Adriatic. Arriving at the sea in the sumptuous Bucintoro, the patriarch blessed the sea with holy water, and the doge threw a ring into the sea with the words, "In sign of eternal dominion, we, the Doge of Venice, marry you, oh sea." The prayer during the ceremony is

Keep safe from stormy weather,
Oh Lord, all your faithful mariners,
Safe from sudden shipwreck and from evil,
Unsuspected tricks of cunning enemies.

The legend of the origins of the ceremony begins with a Venetian victory over an imperial fleet, and a submissive Emperor Frederick I Barbarossa kissing the pope's feet in Venice, for which the pope ceded dominion over the Adriatic to Venice in 1177 in gratitude. No such battle and no such victory took place, but Doge Sebastiano Ziani did play host to both pope and emperor. Contemporary prints give the formal title of the ceremony: Il sposalizio del Doge con il Mare. See Molmenti, *Venice*, III, I, pp. 120ff.

[57] The Church of San Nicolo di Lido was a Benedictine monastery for seven hundred years.

Ascension Thursday. The espousal of the sea, Sponsalia Maris Adriatici (eighteenth century).

many richly decorated peotas and gondolas covered with fine velvet and golden lace, and silks and other fine brocades of marvelous work, all gilded with great mirrors; and the insides of these ships were hung with wallpaper, and others with velvet, and others with fine brocades; and the oarsmen were also attired in fine gold and in velvet kaftans.

This betrothal of the sea was begun in antiquity by the Venetians /541/ with the blessing of the Roman pope, Alexander III [1159–81], in this manner: This Pope Alexander, in a certain enmity with the [Holy] Roman emperor, was banished from Rome and came secretly to Venice, where he was recognized and accepted as the pope; because of this, the Roman emperor [Barbarossa] who had seized him began a war with the Venetians and sent his regiments to the city of Mestre close to Venice, where a battle took place between the imperial soldiers and the Venetians. In this battle the Venetians defeated the imperial troops, took the emperor's son into Venice, and refused to return him until the emperor himself came to Venice and made peace with Pope Alexander. In this way the emperor came to Venice against his will, submitted to Pope Alexander, and was pardoned by him in Venice in the church of San Marco. Having taken his son from the Venetians and having gone to the appropriate place, Pope Alexander was sent from Venice back to Rome with his previous honors. And from the time that Pope Alexander became the lord of the Mediterranean Sea, that is, of the White Sea, the Venetians each year conduct the marriage of the sea in memory of this event.

On the above-mentioned princely galley, on which he and the patriarch and senate went to marry the sea, were 60 rowers in fine golden attire.

Many of the Venetians are wise, politic, and learned; however, in their outward behavior they are not affectionate, although they are receptive to visiting foreigners. Among themselves they do not love to make merry, and they do not come together at home at dinner or for an evening, and they are a very sober people and never does one see a drunk anywhere. They have all kinds of drinks, many fine grape wines, and also many fine *rozolinov*[58] and anise waters made of fine substantial grape wines, only they use little of them. Most take as drink lemonades, *simady* (It. *semata,* barley water), coffee, chocolate, and such drinks, from which it is impossible to get drunk.[59]

For visiting foreigners they have stop-over houses, which in the Italian language they call *ostarii* (*osteria,* inn). There are many rooms in these houses, and when a foreigner arrives to stay in the inn, they give him his own room. In this room will be a bedstead, a table, an armchair and chairs, a chest for clothes, a large mirror, and everything else one could need, and each day they prepare dinner and supper for him, and every night they bring a tallow candle and also a lamp with wood oil. And for all of this the visiting man, even though he eats like a /542/ cavalier, pays a Venetian ducat a day, and in Moscow's money, 15 altyns a day. If he has a servant living with him in the same room, he needs to pay 2 Venetian lira per day for him, and in Muscovite money, 5 altyns, and for this payment he receives meals—dinner and supper—enough to satisfy him. And for dinner and supper for all visiting foreigners and their servants there is sufficient red and white grape wine to drink, and this is included in the price; but if one wants to drink after dinner or supper, then he must pay extra. The meals in these inns are good, both meat and fish; and after dinner and supper there is some fruit, and at their meals the Italians use many greens: salads, celery, *kapros* (It. *cappero,* caper), and other such things. In these inns every foreigner who stays there is served by a house worker: they make the beds daily, change the linens weekly, always pick up the room and clean it as needed, and serve for the one price. And when a foreigner leaves an inn, it is honorable to give something to the man who served him without it being requested. There are as many as a hundred people for dinner and for supper every day in these inns. For this purpose these inns have among the rooms a great hall over 20 sazhens in length, and in the hall there are many long, and square, and round tables, and at these tables the forestiere, that is, the foreigners, eat, at various prices. When it is time for dinner or supper, they ring a bell provided for this purpose in this hall. Then all the foreigners come from their rooms to this hall to dine or to sup, and all sit at the table for which

[58] 58. Rossolo is an Italian liqueur, "made from raisins and an aromatic plant of the drosera species." Braudel, *Capitalism,* p. 171.

[59] Tolstoi here describes the *festa* that began with the ceremony on Ascension Thursday and lasted for some days as a fair in the Piazza San Marco. He begins here with a statement of Venetian sobriety and good sense, and with the suggestion that Venetians are more apt to be found in their home environments than at parties; soon, however, he begins to see "the world upside down," the phrase used in Burke, *Popular Culture,* p. 185 and passim.

they have paid. And every arriving traveler stays there freely, as long as he wants, whether a year or more, or only for a day—it is up to him.[60]

There are many shops of all kinds in Venice, and they are marvelously furnished as nowhere else in the world, except perhaps in France. There are a multitude of all sorts of wares fine and marvelous, in Venice. It is difficult to describe the commodities of the Venetian markets, as they are supplied every day with goods. Among the markets and amid the shops there are many fine pharmacies, in which there are all kinds of drugs, and they are so well stocked that it is impossible to describe them. There are many imported goods in the Venetian shops: French, English, Dutch, Turkish, Persian, and all other kinds. /543/

There are many marvelous master craftsmen in Venice—gold and silver smiths, *skitsarei* (It. *schizzare,* to sketch), joiners, sculptors,[61] painters, master stonecarvers, those who mold plaster, and others. There are many fine brass and tin and iron master craftsmen, and there are fine masters of carved and smooth ivory work; there are also masters of fine brass and wooden mathematical instruments,[62] and all of the works of Venetian masters are fine, even those of the arms makers. In Venice they make gold and silver and silk brocades, fine velvets, marvelous thick crimson fabrics and woolens, and various other brocades; and patterned and smooth taffeta, silks and smooth satins, and patterned fabrics and fine patterned silks, and good *oreri* (It. *oreria,* cloth of gold); they also make silk stockings in Venice.

Near two sides of the Church of San Marco in Venice are great squares finely paved with bricks. All of Venice also has streets and lanes paved with bricks. It is marvelous that the bricks do not get soaked from rain or sea water. Around these squares are the great, fine homes of the procurators of Venice; near these homes are fine shops in which they sell fancy sweets and all other confections and drinks: chocolate, coffee, lemonade and such things, and sniffing and smoking tobacco, and in other shops they sell all kinds of goods. The honorable people of Venice come to these shops and sit together and amuse themselves with drinks and confections. One of these two above-mentioned squares stretches out to the sea, and there is a stone stairway from that square to the sea. A large number of small naval vessels, pilotas, and gondolas are for hire there, and anyone who wishes can hire a vessel to go anywhere. On this square are two large stone columns, smooth and round, cut from whole stones and not finished, 6 sazhens or more in height. At the foot of these columns are stone shop stalls. On one of the columns is a stone lion with a Gospel in the image of St. Mark the Evangelist—a fine carved work. On the other column is

[60] Contemporary Englishmen were generally less enthusiastic about the quality of Italian inns. Since Tolstoi has rented a furnished apartment in Venice, his impressions must reflect his earlier travels to Padua and Milan. Although it was possible to find acceptable accommodations in the towns, all agreed the country inns were deplorable at best. See Mead, *Grand Tour,* pp. 84–95.

[61] There are, literally, "masters of figures," *figurnykh masterov.*

[62] Tolstoi alludes to astrolabes, sextants, and the like.

the likeness of the beast crocodile, and on it is placed the likeness of a man in the image of a certain martyr.[63]

On this square close to the gate of the princely court are two short columns; on these columns they executed even the principes of Venice, that is, princes, when long ago they acted contrary to their office. On one of these squares at the Church of San Marco is a very high four-sided belltower, done of smooth work; in it /544/ the steps are marvelously wide and steep, and the bells on the tower are not very large; they peal, and they ring them throughout Venice with ropes. This bell tower is covered with a tent.[64] And instead of a cross they placed there the likeness of a cast brass angel of marvelous work. On this square, too, are booths covered with canvas, and in them Persians and Armenians vend their wares on counters. On this square all day Saturday, they trade wooden dishes, brought from the coast, and trunks and baskets and all kinds of other wooden things. Around this square are many shops in which they make and sell hairpieces; they also make and sell gilded leathers there. On these squares there are often sermons to the people; canons come from the monasteries and give sermons on a tall pulpit that always stands on that square.

On this square all morning and in the evening, Venetian nobles and honorable people arrive and walk around and talk together about all kinds of matters. The square close to the sea is divided into three parts; beneath the princely court walk the nobility and the honorable people of Venice in the morning, because the palace of the Venetian prince shades this square from the sun in the east. On the other side, beneath the palace of the procurators, the honorable Venetian people walk in the evening, because those palaces shade that square from the setting sun. Between these two parts of the square, in the middle, the rest of the people walk freely. On this square of the nobles no visitor and no non-noble Venetians are allowed to walk unless they have to cross the square, which is not prohibited; but it is not possible for anyone to walk along this part of the square at the time that the nobles are walking there.[65]

[63] These are the two granite columns by the Palace of the Doges, erected in 1180; one bears the winged lion of St. Mark, the other St. Theodore on a crocodile. It is a former place of execution.

[64] Tolstoi refers to the tentlike roof, the spire of the Campanielle, as opposed to a building with a "head," that is, a dome. In Muscovy bells were often rung with poles instead of ropes.

[65] Tolstoi here describes daily life on the Piazetta of San Marco, the square bounded by the Pool of San Marco, the Ducal Palace, and the Sansovino Library. While Venetian society was less segregated than that of Spanish Naples (see below), Tolstoi notes little mingling of *borghesia* and nobility. Burke, *Popular Culture,* has shown how the upper and lower orders of society shared a common culture in the Middle Ages and Renaissance, how the upper classes, noble and non-noble, withdrew from that tradition in early-modern times, and how they rediscovered the *volk* only in the era of Romanticism. Tolstoi here captures vividly the middle portion of that great movement, the moment of separateness, of segregation. No such cultural division has yet occurred in Muscovy: there boyars and peasants still shared a common culture. When Tolstoi, and others like him, observed and copied the mores of the West

In the middle part of the square, male and female astrologers sit on high stages on chairs with long tin pipes, and he who wants to know something from these astrologers gives one a certain amount of money, and the astrologer whispers into his ear through that pipe. Many people are in this square all day for amusement; puppets perform, trained dogs dance, monkeys also dance, and other people play with *bandiera,* that is, with flags, and others play with brass plates and one stick very well and all together: one throws that plate high in the air with the stick, and from the height it falls down on that stick; and other people eat fire, and other people swallow large stones and many others do all kinds of tricks to amuse the people, and for this they take money from those /545/ who watch them. On this same square at the time of the fair they erect many wooden shops and trade in them; at this time in these shops there are a great multitude of all kinds of the most marvelous and rich wares. All day at this time, the honorable Venetian people and women and girls in marvelous attire stroll through these shops, as do forestiere, that is, all sorts of visitors, and they walk and stroll and buy what they need at that fair, and at times from caravans.

On this square by the sea they set up large tents and sheds; in these tents men and women dance on ropes most marvelously, as also do girls, among whom I saw one wife pregnant and close to birth, and she danced on the rope most marvelously. In another tent puppets performed a comedy just like living people. In other tents they showed marvelous things, among which I saw a man who had two heads, one in the place it should be, and [he is] called Iakov (Jacob), and the other on the left side and [he is] called Matthew; also that one on the side has long hair, and eyes and a nose and mouth and lips, only he does not speak or eat, but constantly stares; and they say that it squeaks, but that the real head of that man speaks and drinks and eats. And he who wants to see such a man must look at its faces, for they are seldom encountered any longer in Russia; and if someone wants to see him for oneself, he must travel to Italy. I also saw a bull with five legs there, and also a ram with two heads, having 6 legs and 2 tails, and many other natural marvels. And whoever wants to see them pays 5 solda per person in Venetian money, and in Muscovite 3 dengi, for the entrance to everything.

From this square there is a gate to the *markandia,*[66] that is, to the shops of the fine masters; on this gate there is a marvelous striking clock, and above the gate a large bell, and beneath the bell two likenesses of naked humans done of fine brass work, and they hold in their hands large iron hammers. When it is time to strike the hour, these brass human likenesses beat the bell with hammers, as much as the hour requires, so much do they strike. This clock does not have quarter-hours; in all of Italy there are no quarter-hours in striking clocks. Instead of a quarter-hour of the time,

---

European nobility, they would import these notions into Russia: this is the significance of Raeff's essay, *Origins of the Russian Intelligentsia.* See Molmenti, *Venice,* III, I, 143ff, for life on the Piazza.

[66] In Italian this is *mercanzia,* the merchants' quarter.

they have *instrumenty* (It. *strumento*) when needed, and from the right side comes the image of the Blessed /546/ Mother of God, holding the Sacred Child in her hands. She sits in a prepared chair, and from the left side come 3 crafted men in the image of the 3 Persian kings [*tsarei*] with gifts, gold, incense, and myhrr, and the images of the kings bow before the image of the Blessed Mother of God and present the gifts, just as the Persian kings came to honor the newborn Christ. This clock begins to beat the first hour of the evening and beats all the 24 hours until the next evening. In Venice there are many striking clocks in monasteries and on the bell-towers of parish churches.[67]

There are operas and marvelous comedies in Venice that are impossible to describe adequately, and nowhere in the whole world are there such marvelous operas and comedies. During my stay in Venice, opera was performed in five places. The palaces where operas are performed are large and round, and the Italians call them *teatrum*.[68] They built many boxes five tiers high in these palaces, and in one theater there are 200 and in another more than 300, and all the boxes inside the theater are done of marvelous gilt-work; others are covered with thick imprinted paper so that it is impossible to know that it is not the marvelous work of men who sketched them. Everything in this theater is gilded, and the floor is inclined so that one person sitting behind another in the chairs can see the opera; and for these chairs and benches they pay a price, and he who wishes to sit in a special box, he must pay a higher price for the box, but for general admission to this theater the price is all the same. Over one side of this theater is a large, long hall in which the opera is performed. In this hall they sometimes have marvelous *prospettivi* (It., scenery), and in one opera there are 100 to 150 or more men and women in costume. The costumes they wear are of fine gold and silver, and they have many stones: crystals and jewels, and also diamonds and seed pearls. They play in these operas wearing the costumes of ancient history, and such things are presented in this theater for him who loves this history. The marvelous music in these operas is played by 50 different instruments

[67] Tolstoi describes the Torre dell'Orologie, 1496–99, the famous clocktower, topped by a terrace with a great bell struck by two "Moors."

[68] Public theater in Russia, at the time of Tolstoi's departure, was nonexistent. The Latin-Greek academies at Kiev and soon at Moscow were laying the groundwork in their rhetoric and poetic forms, and the court and a few Westernized nobles were experimenting with private theatricals, but no theaters per se had yet been built, and thus it is not surprising that Tolstoi should marvel over the simple device of a sloped floor.

Venice at the end of the seventeenth century was a world center of theater, with some seventeen operating and at least four giving performances simultaneously. Some 388 operas were produced between 1637 and 1700, and they were noted for their elaborate staging, with painted scenery, "perspectives," and the machinery to move it was a Venetian speciality, soon to be exported to Paris and Vienna. I have seen the court theater of the Vasas of Sweden built in the seventeenth century, and there, as in Venice, it is clear that the technology of moving heavy objects on board ships was the technology used in moving scenery on stage. See Lane, *Venice*, p. 432, and especially Molmenti, *Venice*, III, I, 154ff.

or more, and one opera costs 30,000 or 40,000 ducats per year in Venetian money, and each ducat is 15 Muscovite altyns. The comedy in Venice is not as good as the opera, but very amusing. In Venice the opera begins on the first of November, and, having played a little, it stops and begins again at the time of the November carnival at the /547/ end of November or beginning of December; it runs until Lent every evening except Sundays and Fridays. And they begin to play in these operas in the first hour of night, and they end in the 5th or 6th hour of the night, and they never play during the day.

Many people come to these operas in *mashkarakh* (It. *maschera, mascherata,* masquerade), in Slavic, in masks, so that no one will recognize them if they are at the opera, because many come with their wives, and visiting foreigners also come with girls; and because of this men and women put on masks and strange clothes, so that they are not recognized together. Also all through the carnival all the men and women and girls walk in masks, and they stroll about freely, wherever they please, and no one knows anybody. And this is how they always make merry in Venice, and they never want to be without amusement, and in this gayety they sin much and, when they come together on the square at San Marco, many girls in masquerade hold hands with visiting foreigners, and stroll with them and amuse themselves without shame.[69] Also at this time in many places in the square they make music and dance in the Italian fashion, and Italian dances are not very orderly: one skips around another, and they do not hold hands together.

Also many people amuse themselves by tormenting great bulls with Milanese dogs and with other such fun, and they go along the sea in gondolas and barques with music, and they constantly make merry and no one is dishonored being together in this, and no one has any kind of fear doing this; all do whatever they wish according to their own will. This freedom is always present in Venice, and Venetians always live in this ease and without fear, without injury, and without painful obligations. And when the carnival comes to a close, that is, on the last day of the Christmas fast[70] by the Roman calendar, the amusement and merrymaking are great in Venice, but in the last week of the Christmas fast, on Friday, the prince of Venice begins the fun on San Marco square at his own princely court, and there are fine

[69] In these passages describing the world of carnival and the masquerade, Tolstoi captures the essence of early-modern society. In a world of strict social hierarchy, of regulated behavior, and of sumptuary laws governing dress and social interaction, some form of release was needed, and the mask provided it. Masquerade meant equality under hierarchy, license under restriction, and frivolity under formality. Tolstoi captures its essence when he says that it permits all to sin without feeling guilt or shame, without embarrassing consequences, and without hurting anyone else. Most important, the mask allows one to sin "without dishonor," that is, without a loss in status, the very definition of the old hierarchical society. I suppose this is the closest that Tolstoi comes to saying that he held hands with young women in masquerade, which presumably he did. See the comments on the women of Venice, and on his famous Italian lady-friend, below in this section.

[70] *Miasoed* is the time from Christmas to Shrovetide when it is permitted to eat meat.

things on Friday and Saturday and the end of the week, and with this the carnival ends and the Romans begin the Great Fast.

During my stay in Venice during the last three days, on Friday, Saturday, and Sunday, the princely fun was thus: on San Marco Square they made a large place like a pavilion, very high and framed with artificial fires and rockets that burst and burned all together. Then, in the place where they built the fine pavilion and beneath it, they played music on various instruments, and between the poles atop the pavilion they made a high place, finely decorated, on which /548/ a girl sat in fine attire, and on her legs sat 2 young 8-year old girls in fine dress, and attached to them were wings made of flapping, colored feathers; all of these sitting girls, holding *cantychki* (It. *cantici,* song sheets) in their hands, sang very nicely, so that all present were amazed, and the prince of Venice looked on from a window in his palace. The small girls who had wings rose from the place they had been sitting on, and flew on a rope to the window from which the prince was watching, and they sang while flying, and they tossed printed pages to the people in praise of the Venetian Carnival.[71]

Then, in front of the Venetian prince they held three great bulls, and they slashed the heads of these bulls with swords, and with one stroke severed the head of one bull so cleanly that the sword was hardly obstructed and buried itself finally in the ground; and thus did two men sever the heads of two bulls so cleanly, but the third bull's head the man could not sever with a single blow. Then one end of a thick rope was fastened to the top of the San Marco bell tower, about which I wrote above, and the other end was fastened to the edge of San Marco Square at the edge of the sea. Along this rope, from the bottom to the top of the bell tower, went one man on a lion, crafted of wood of fine work just as if alive, and this lion was placed on that rope and fixed to it with instruments, so that the man could not fall off or turn over. Another rope was attached to that lion and taken to the top of the tower, by which rope the lion was drawn to the top of the tower; the man sat on the lion as simply as if on a horse, and nothing attached the man to the lion, and so, sitting on the lion, he ascended to the tower. And with this the year's carnival in Venice ended, and for the remaining three days on San Marco Square there were only people to clean it, all with difficulty; it seemed to me to be a thousand men and women.

In Venice is one home that in Italian is called the *reduta* (It. *ridotto*), built for the

[71] Tolstoi above and below describes two of the rituals of Carnival. First, the flights of angels and, below, of the Turk, volo del Turco, dell'Anzolo; in this ritual, winged girls, in homage to the doge, sailed on a rope to his window, dropping flowers or poetical compositions to the crowd. In the case of the "Turk," an acrobat rose to the Campanielle by means of a device of cords and rings and then descended to a barge moored in the basin. The other ceremony perpetuated the memory of the victory of Doge Vitale Michiel II in 1162 over Ulric Patriarch of Aquileia: he had been imprisoned together with twelve canons of the Chapter, and was eventually set free on the condition that he would, in shameful homage, annually cut the throats of a bull and twelve piglets in public on the last Thursday of carnival. See Lorenzetti, *Venice,* p. 20.

Doge Viewing Bull-Fair from Balcony of Palace.

purpose of playing at cards for gold coins and for money.[72] This home has many large rooms in which there are many small columns, and behind each column sits a man, and on the tables lie many gold coins, singles, doubles, triples, and tens and *efimki* and ducats and scudos, and whoever wants to approaches that table and plays with the man who sits at the table; this particular game is called *baseta,*[73] and the Venetian cards are different. In this game no one is compelled to [do] anything; he plays /549/ or wins, and if he no longer wants to play, he is free to do this. Many honorable people come to this house; and women and girls come to play freely and without dishonor, in masquerade and to play silently, so that neither misdealing of cards, nor fraud, nor miscounting of money can occur. And it happened that I was in this house, and I saw a girl who won 4,000 gold chervontsy on a single card, and taking it departed freely, not wanting to play further, and no one forced her to play more. In a few hours in this house many win and lose thousands. There are times when one man in a few hours will lose or win 20,000 or 30,000 golden chervontsy or more, because on the tables in this house are many thousands of golden chervontsy and other monies; and there are more players and money here at carnival time, because many come here to play without shame in masquerade.

There are many stone and wooden bridges in Venice, among which there is one very large and wide bridge which the Italians call *Arialta* (Ponte di Rialto); on both sides of this bridge are shops in which they sell all kinds of petty goods. Beyond the bridge are large stores in which they sell silver vessels and cloth. Large ships with masts can pass under this bridge, for it is built very high in a single arch and is well built.

The Venetian people are divided into two: those who live on the side of the Ponte di Rialto where the cathedral-church of San Marco is located, and they are called the *Kostelliani* (Castelliani); and those who live beyond that bridge, and they are called the *Nikolioti* (Niccolioti). At times there is a secret animosity between them; and the Venetian senators purposely embroil the base people of the Castelliani and the Niccolioti so that there is no agreement between them, so that there are riots; and there are great fist fights between the base people of the Castelliani and the Niccolioti.[74] From these fist fights on this great bridge are many fatalities; fist fights happen often

[72] This is the famous Ridotto, now on the Calle del Ridotto just down from the Church of San Moise, a public gambling hall opened in 1638 by Marco Dandolo in his palace, which had been the French embassy in the sixteenth century. The Signoria would close it in 1774 because of the fortunes squandered in gambling. See Molmenti, *Venice,* III, I, 171ff.

[73] Italian *bassetta,* basset, is an old card game resembling *faro.*

[74] The *battagliole dei pugni* (battles with fists) between the red-capped inhabitants of the *sestiere* of San Pietro di Castello and the black-clad men of the district of San Nicole dei Mendicoli were ritualized, savage fights to capture a bridge by throwing the opposition over the side. Tolstoi describes the fights but fails to sense their annual nature. They are, in fact, one of the best examples of acceptable violence in early-modern society, the kind of activity replaced by spectator sports in modern times.

Le Pont de Rialto a Venise. (G. B. Brustoloni, *Veduta della citte de Venezia* [1763].)

in Venice, only less in other places, and on the other bridges in Venice fist fights do not happen at all.

In Venice there is a convent in which girls taking orders play on the organ and on various other instruments and sing in choirs so well that in all the world such sweet singing and harmony are never encountered; and so marvelously do they sing that all the listeners are led to amazement, and from the whole world Christians come to Venice, wishing to enjoy /550/ this imitation of the angels' singing. In this monastery which is called *Inkorabeli* (It. *Incurabili*), and [also] in a monastery on the new foundation in which the order of *Medicanki* (It. *Mendicanti*) lives, and in other monasteries, too, girls sing well.[75]

[75]Tolstoi describes two separate places. First, at the Ponte degli Incurabili, so named for a nearby former hospital for incurables, San Gaetano of Thiene in 1522 created an orphanage that became famous for its oratorios. The building was destroyed in 1821. Second, at the Ponte dei Mendicanti, on the Fondamenta Nuove, stands the Church of San Lazzaro dei Mendicanti, 1601–31, a similar institution. He may also, judging by his last sentence, have visited the Ospedaletto or Casa di Ricovero (Almshouse), created in 1527, with its great, oval, spiral staircase, also famous for its children's concerts. See Lorenzetti, *Venice,* pp. 356–57, 383, 536. For a fuller discussion of the concert societies, see Molmenti, *Venice,* III, I, 169ff.

In Venice there are many carriers' boats, called gondolas, and they are all black and covered with black cloth and large window frames, and all gondolas have one rower, and some have two. He who has to go somewhere in Venice or nearby by canals, that is, by streets, goes in a hired gondola; and the cost for a gondola all day with one rower is a Venetian ducat, or 15 Muscovite altyns, and for this sum one is taken wherever one wishes. And Venetian procurators and nobles and notable merchants as well as clerics have their own gondolas, of which in Venice there are almost a thousand. Many of these gondolas are decorated with fine gilt carving, covered with velvet and lace, and with golden velvet and other fine brocades and great window frames; also in them are wallpapers or colored woolen velvets, or other fine brocades and the like. And these gondolas are made in a particular fashion, long and not wide, similar to a [Russian] single-tree-trunk boat, with a sharp bow and stern. The bow is bound with iron, and in the middle is built a pavilion with window frames and covered with fine curtains, and in it are fine benches with cushions, and one rower is at the bow, and the other at the stern. In the gondolas without a second rower, the one rower is at the stern, standing up to row and to steer with an oar, but they do not have a stern oar like our gondolas; however, they do steer neatly even without one.

The womenfolk of Venice are very well attired and given to fashion and not inclined to any kind of business, but they always love to stroll and to be amused, and are weak to the sins of the flesh not only because of wealth, but because having gotten rich, they have nothing further to do with business. And many wenches live in their own homes—of these there are more than 10,000 in Venice—and they do not regard themselves to be in sin or in shame, and they set themselves up as a business venture. Others who do not have their own homes live in special streets in little low rooms, and each room has a door on the street, and when they see a man approaching them, each solicits him over to herself with great diligence. The days when many men approach are days of great happiness for them. From this they suffer the French diseases, /551/ and also they get rich quickly, from those who come to them. And the clergy particularly prohibits this in its sermons, but they do not constrain them. But they treat the French diseases very cleverly in Venice; when a man who has just learned of it tells a doctor, they cut out that disease and in a few days he is cured, so that no one learns of the disease; and a man who goes with this disease without treatment will be under treatment a long time, but it will be completely cured.[76]

[76] In these comments on Venetian society at large, on women and their loose morals, on prostitution, and on syphilis and its cure by surgery, when combined with earlier observations on masquerade, marital infidelity, theater, and gambling, Tolstoi is one of the early authors to capture what would become an eighteenth-century cliché: Venice was the most licentious, gay, festive, and frivolous of the European capitals. See Lane, *Venice*, pp. 433–34.

One can only speculate on the extent to which the fifty-three-year-old Tolstoi was a participant-observer of Venice's female company. He has remarked earlier that women shamelessly

In addition to pharmacists and druggists and medicine men, there are 400 doctors in Venice, and each has his own pharmacy, and they cure all illnesses cleverly, and they go to the sick promptly and cheaply. Among these doctors are many of the Greek faith, as well as Jews; and the respect for doctors is such that they are entitled to the pay of a Venetian nobleman, but the Jewish doctors do not command such pay.

The Venetian schools, in which they study to philosophy and to theology, are fine. There is also a school in Venice at the Greek church, kept by the Greek metropolitan at his expense, and the Greeks teach Greek students in Greek, Latin, and Italian languages, to philosophy and to theology.[77] When a student comes to the completion of the sciences in any school, they crown him in this manner of certification: in a hall or in a church in the middle they place a chair in which this student sits, and along the left side in other chairs sit his masters, and on both sides in chairs sit learned monks and priests, and also all who at that time are assembled, and to all who are there at that time are distributed printed sheets or notebooks called *kompleksii,*[78] that is, the dispute, about which the student will be tested and will testify about all that is printed on those pages. Then this student gives to all present a fine oration about his test and begins to speak about his science, and with him the learned people sitting there begin to argue one at a time, and three men argue with him, and more than three do not argue with him; his teacher defends him in this dispute and himself argues with those outsiders, and thus ends the dispute, and the student is congratulated, and all the learned men greet him enthusiastically.

---

walked hand-in-hand with foreigners in the squares. We do know that he ceased to have any intimate relations with his wife long before her death in 1722, that in his seventies he was known as a tireless old man who danced all night with girls young enough to be his granddaughters, and that in the 1720s, when he was president of the College of Commerce, he was ruled by a mysterious young Italian woman named Laura; business was conducted through her mediation, and she traveled for him. See Tolstoy, *The Tolstoys,* p. 81.

A more general note on syphilis is in order. The disease has been found in prehistoric skeletons, and there were clinical cases before 1492. But the modern visit began in Barcelona from the time of Columbus's return in 1493, and it spread rapidly. Within five years it was everywhere in Europe, known as the Neapolitan disease, *mal français,* the French disease, or *lo mal francioso;* in France the barber-surgeons claimed to cure it by cauterization with red-hot irons, but Tolstoi's notes here indicate that Venetian doctors used a more direct surgical approach. See Braudel, *Structures,* pp. 81–82.

[77] Tolstoi here describes the college at the Greek church of St. George in Venice. In the seventeenth century, thanks to a generous donation in 1648 by a Greek lawyer, Thomas Flanginis, a college was founded. Called the Flanginion, chartered in 1662 but opened in 1665, it was housed in the quarters, built by Balthasar Longhena, which now serve L'Institut Helenique. It had twelve *pensionnaires* and some day students. It was modeled on similar Greek colleges at Padua and Rome, and its pupils could continue their studies at the University of Padua, to the doctorate. It had its own printing press, operated by faculty and students. Some five hundred students attended between 1665 and 1797, and it produced many of the Greek literati of the day. See Manoussacas, "Apperçu d'une histoire," p. 20.

[78] Latin, *complexio;* in rhetoric this is a short summary of the whole matter.

There is a house in Venice in which they study military affairs: how to fight with swords, to play with standards and pikes, and to use muskets in the infantry. In this house the teacher is paid by the Venetian /552/ prince from his council. Because of this payment, any Venetian who wants can study gratis; but any forestiero, that is, visiting foreigner, who wants to study in this house pays that teacher a golden chervonets a month. For this price he may come to this teacher in this house and he studies those subjects, just mentioned above; and one can also come to this house to study and pay 2 golden chervontsy per person per month. For this price the teacher will also come to [the pupil's] house every day, all day, except weekends and feast days, and teach there where he lives.

In Venice is a monk, a master of mathematics and cosmology and related sciences, and his name is Karonelii.[79] He also has a house from the council where he can distribute and print books of the mathematical sciences, and also cosmological maps and such things.

There is a convent in Venice in which this is the order: when a fornicatress or a widow gives birth to an infant, and does not want to feed it herself, she brings it without shame to this convent and gives it to the nuns there, who have a duty to accept it, to give it food and drink, shoes and clothes, and for this the elders receive a fee from the council. When that child reaches the age of seven, the boys are given to the boys' school and the girls to the girls' school, where they are also given food and drink and shoes and clothes without cost. And they collect money for that school and for its dependents; every weekday the children walk throughout Venice in a procession, carrying before them a large cross, and behind it walk the children two abreast, and they sing several verses and carry a box into which in the name of Christ they place the alms that some give, and their teacher walks behind them. Thus walk the boys, and the girls, too, with their instructress behind them; and when any of them comes of age, they are free to become priests, or monks, or some kind of tradesperson; likewise, the girls who come of age can become nuns or get married or become the same fallen women as their mothers, [but] for this they are discharged.

[7]206, ***May 29,*** I left the court where I had stayed, on a frigate, having the intention to leave Venice by sea for various places, and I stayed on that frigate at Venice until June 1.

[79] Vicenzo Maria Coronelli, 1650–1718, minor friar and general of the Order, famous publisher, cosmographer and geographer, held the title of *Cosmografus publicus Sereniss. Republicae*. His historiographic notes on Morea were translated into Russian and published in 1769. On his academy, see Molmenti, *Venice, III, II, 156*.

IV

June 1, 1698–July 15, 1698

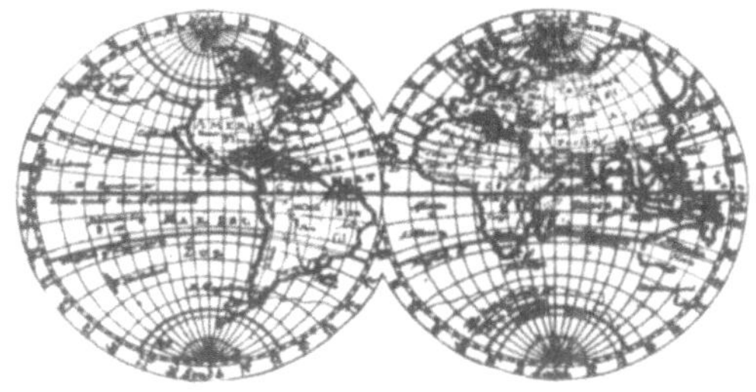

Dalmatia · Bari · Naples
Calabria

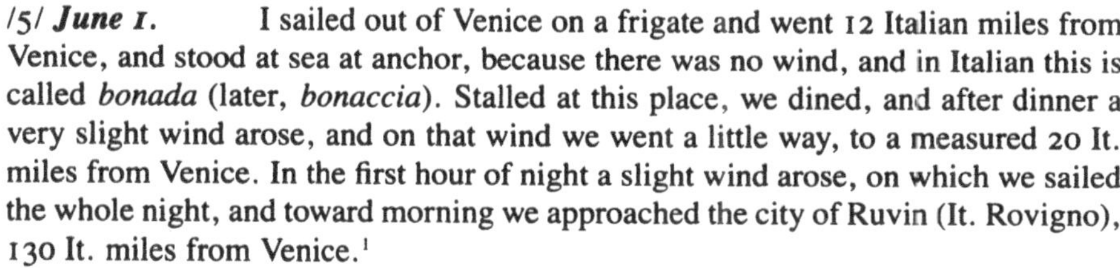

/5/ ***June 1.*** I sailed out of Venice on a frigate and went 12 Italian miles from Venice, and stood at sea at anchor, because there was no wind, and in Italian this is called *bonada* (later, *bonaccia*). Stalled at this place, we dined, and after dinner a very slight wind arose, and on that wind we went a little way, to a measured 20 It. miles from Venice. In the first hour of night a slight wind arose, on which we sailed the whole night, and toward morning we approached the city of Ruvin (It. Rovigno), 130 It. miles from Venice.[1]

June 2. In the first hour of day a slight wind arose, and on it we sailed until noon, and sailed past all of Istria and came even with the first Dalmatian mountains 15 It. miles from Venice. This day after noon there was a slight wind, and on it we sailed until night. At nightfall there was no wind, and three hours before daylight a strong wind arose that was agreeable to our course, and we sailed on it until daylight and in 3 hours covered 20 Italian miles.

June 3. From the first hour of day the wind was strong and agreeable to us, and it did not change from what it was 3 hours before daylight, so we sailed on that wind all day steadily, across from the city of Trav (Trogir; It., Trau), 300 It. miles from Venice. In the first hour of night the wind abated, and by midnight the larger wind ceased and the whole night was without wind, and our frigate stayed in one place.

[1]Tolstoi here begins his grand tour within a tour, an extended trip ultimately to Malta, for the expressed purpose of engaging the Turks in naval combat. He would travel three months, until the end of August, and write almost half of the Diary during this journey.

June 4. From the first hour of day a very light wind arose, and our frigate moved forward a little, and at /6/ dinner a large wind began, contrary to our desired course, and our frigate went by tacking and in Dutch, by *lavirami* (Ger. *das Lavieren*). After noon a great wind arose against us, and the fortuna at sea became very great, and our frigate could neither by *bordami* (It. *borda,* tack) nor by any other means follow our course. Because of this we entered a port called Lizir (Lesina? Hvar?), and we spent the night in that port, 350 It. miles from Venice. There are no dwellings in that port.

June 5. After noon we left that port. The wind was favorable to us and considerable, and on it we raced all day for five hours. At 6 o'clock at night we sailed into Korsul (Korčula; Ital. Curzola), 400 It. miles from Venice, and we stayed in that city of Korčula until the 8th of June. The city of Korčula is a Venetian province in Dalmatia ceded to the Ragusan principality, and it stands on an island. Across from this city on an island on a mountain a monastery is built, which is called Subin Celio de la Madonna in the Italian language, and in Slavonic it is the Taking or the Assumption into Heaven of the Blessed Mother of God.[2] In this monastery is a church of the Roman faith, in which there is an ancient Greek icon of the Blessed Mother of God, painted exactly like the icon called the Mother of Smolensk. Many miracles and other things have occurred from this icon. Both on the seashore and on land at this monastery many cypress trees, large and small, are planted. Beside this monastery are also many bees in hives and in the church walls. Four men of the order of Bernard live in this monastery, and there are no other inhabitants. [The area] from this monastery to the sea is regarded a Venetian gulf, a possession of the Ragusan principality. Around this monastery in the town live Ragusan naval captains, astronomers, and mariners. The homes are of stone, small, and no larger than necessary. Also, they have but little cattle and grain and make do with fruits, that is, with clusters of grapes. Of figs, grapes, pears, peaches, almonds, and walnuts they have plenty, and all speak the Slavonic language, but they all know Italian and they are all called Croats, and profess the Roman faith.

June 8, in the fifth hour of day, we sailed from beneath Korčula; the wind was favorable and considerable, and on this wind we sailed until noon, and at noon the wind became slight, /7/ although in our favor, and on it we sailed all day. In the last hour of day we sailed opposite an island, which is a Ragusan possession and is called Santo-Andrea (S. Andrea, Sveti Andrija). On this island, on the heights, large stone dwellings are built, among which is a chapel, that is, a small Roman church. On this island always lives a single man who has not even a single comrade, and Romans

[2]This is probably the Franciscan monastery, with a relief of the Virgin, 2 kilometers west of Orebic on the Pelješac peninsula.

regard this man as holy, and they tell a story about him, which is not possible to believe, and which no one needs to hear. And this island is not 10 Ital. miles from the capital place of Ragusa, Dubrovnik. And from this island we sailed to Dubrovnik in 3 and a half hours, and in the 3rd hour of night we sailed beneath the city of Dubrovnik.[3]

June 9. This morning I was in the city of Dubrovnik in the Franciscan monastery, and in this monastery they showed me these sacred things:

A nail from the crown of thorns of Christ our Savior.

A cross made from the very wood of the cross of Christ.

A silver coin that Judas took from the Hebrew bishop for Christ, in the shape of a niello, the size of a Cherkassian *chekh* and similarly made, and the impression on it is unrecognizable because of its great age.

A part of a bone from the head of John the Baptist.

A part of a bone from the hand of the holy martyr Catherine.

A part of a bone from the leg of St. Blaise, the archbishop of Sevastia (Sebaste).

A part of the leg of St. Heronimus.[4]

[3] In the sixteenth century the Ragusan republic was virtually independent, and although it paid tribute to the Turks, it was treated as neutral in wartime and thus traded when Venice could not. The city traded in the Adriatic, locally in Bosnia and Serbia, and, after the Turkish conquest of the Balkans, overland in Constantinople; the surviving fortifications attest to the wealth of the principality, won at the expense of Venetian trade. In the seventeenth century Ragusa continued to trade profitably, especially when Venice was at war, but by late in the century her merchant fleet had declined, and the city itself recovered only slowly from the massive earthquake of 1667. See Lane, *Venice,* passim.

[4] During the voyage, Tolstoi will preoccupy himself with the relics of saints fully as much as with naval studies. This is not surprising.

> Because Orthodox are convinced that the body is sanctified and transfigured together with the soul, they have an immense reverence for the relics of the saints. Like Roman Catholics, they believe that the grace of God present in the saints' bodies during life remains active in their relics when they have died, and that God uses these relics as a channel of divine power and an instrument of healing. In some cases the bodies of saints have been miraculously preserved from corruption, but even where this has not happened, Orthodox show just as great a veneration towards their bones. This reverence for relics is not the fruit of ignorance and superstition, but springs from a highly developed theology of the body.
>
> Not only man's body but the whole of the material creation will eventually be transfigured: 'Then I saw a new heaven and a new earth; for the first heaven and the first earth had passed away' (Revelation XXI, I). Redeemed man is not to be snatched away from the rest of creation, but creation is to be saved and glorified along with him. [Ware, *The Orthodox Church,* p. 239.]

From this Franciscan monastery I went to a convent, in which 40 women of the Franciscan order live. Then I was at a newly built Jesuit monastery in which 8 Jesuits live. Then I went to the place where cannon stand on a redoubt, and that redoubt clears the entry to the port gates. Three large cannon stand there; one of them is very large, of fine workmanship, and faceted. There is a small number of small cannon on this redoubt under a shed. Then I was in a palace in which they made the dinari of Ragusan money; there are in all 9 master workmen: 5 cast in silver and 4 do the imprinting. Then it was time to dine, and I left the city on the frigate. This day after dinner I returned to the city and was in the Dominican monastery in which they showed me many sacred things. First a large cross in which there is a large part of the wood of the very cross of Christ. Then a part of the arm /8/ of John the Baptist, on which one finger is missing because that finger is in Rome.

The head of Blaise, the bishop of Sebaste, a bone from the larynx of that same Blaise, and the hand and leg of St. Blaise.

The hand of the holy martyr Paraskovia (Paraskeva), who is called Brigit in Italian.

A bone from the spine of St. Augustine.

A bone from the jaw of the Blessed Polagei.

A bone from the head of the first martyr Stephen and a stone, one of those with which the Jews struck St. Stephen.

A bone from the head of Empress Margarita.

Two bones from the head and two legs of the holy children, killed by Herod for Christ. On their legs are flesh and skin and tendons.

A stone from the tomb of Christ our Savior.

The shroud of Christ, in which at his birth our Savior was held by Mary, His Most Pure Mother. It is very thick, but it is such worn-out material that it is impossible to know that it in fact was once a thick piece of linen.

Two spikes from the crown of thorns of Christ.

A bone from the rib of the holy apostle Paul.

A bone from the head of St. Anne, the mother of the Mother of God.

A bone from the holy apostle Andrew the First-Called.

A bone from the leg of the holy martyr Kanarei (?).

Parts of the hands of the three holy brothers, Peter, Laurentius, and Andrew.

The leg of St. Nicholas the Pilgrim.

Part of the hand of St. John the Golden Mouth, whom the Italians call Chrysostom.

Part of the head of Empress Helena, the mother of Emperor (Tsar) Constantine.

Part of the relics of the apostle Bartholomew.

The head of St. Pagkratius (Pancratius).

Part of the hand of Petronima, daughter of the apostle Peter, and the threads she concealed.

Part of the head of the holy martyr Sergius.

Part of the hand of St. Trofim.

The leg of the holy martyr Zinovius.

The leg of the holy martyress Zinovia.[5]

In this same monastery they gave me two candles that are to be lighted in front of holy icons on a ship or on any kind of vessel in times of great fortuna, that is, a strong wind. From this monastery I went to the principe, that is, to the prince of /9/ Ragusa, at his court. His court is near the cathedral, was built by ostentatious craftsmen, is not large, and has few rooms. First they took me to the room where the Ragusan prince and all of his republic pass judgment and conduct government. This room is not large; it is downstairs, and it is ostentatiously decorated.

Then I went up and entered the room in which the Ragusans select their prince. This room is 6 sazhens long and 4 wide; it is decorated with carvings, and along the walls are benches. From this room I went to the rooms in which the Ragusan prince lives. In the first room stood 8 domestics in red clothing. From this I entered another room, in which the prince himself met me. Behind him was a man also in red dress, and he led me to another room in which a red chair upholstered in red silk fabric is placed, and the room too is covered with the same silk fabric. In this room sat the prince, and he had me sit across from him in an armchair, where I sat with him for a short time. Then, thanking him for his kindness to me, I left him and was taken to the third room from that in which I sat with him. The prince of Ragusa spoke with me in Slavonic. Those who accompanied me to see him did not enter the room in

[5]Tolstoi mentions primarily saints listed in the Orthodox cycle of feasts. Among the less familiar, we can identify: *Paraskeva*, a familiar subject of icons, associated with Friday, and often depicted with the great fathers of the Eastern church, but otherwise obscure. *Pelagia*, the name of six saints in the Roman martyrology; the Orthodox Church remembers Pelagia, virgin and martyr, d. 287 (May 4), and Pelagia, a former harlot of Jerusalem (d. 457). The apostle *Andrew*, noteworthy in that Eusebius says he preached in Scythia, and thus he is known as the Apostle of the Slavs; Orthodox Russians made much of the fact that he was the First-Called, and therefore higher in the hierarchy than Peter. *Nicholas* the Pilgrim, Peregrinus, died in Trani in 1094, and was a young Greek who wandered in Italy. *Pancratius*, Bishop of Turomenia, martyr, third century, is remembered on July 9. *Petronilla* (d. 251), a martyr born in Rome, and legend calls her the daughter of St. Peter. Of many saints named *Sergius*, this is presumably the martyred Roman officer (d. 303?); the Orthodox Church reveres Sergius and Bacchus, martyrs, d. 290. There are four Sts. *Trophimus*, all martyrs under Diocletian or earlier. And finally, the Orthodox Church commemorates *Zenobias*, bishop of Aegea and his sister, *Zenobia*, martyrs, 285.

which I sat with him, because of this Ragusan custom: senators are not allowed to enter where the prince sits with a foreign visitor. And I left the prince, spent the night in town in a house, and did not go to the frigate this day.

The city of Dubrovnik stands on the coast of the sea, beneath tall mountains. This city is the capital of the Ragusan principality. The fortress is of stone, very fine and strong; in front of the passage towers that face the sea is the port, that is, the landing place for ships, and ships enter into that place; here from the town to the wall a strong iron chain is placed and it prevents the entry of all unfriendly ships to this port. In this city of Dubrovnik the stone houses are not large, but this place is not good and is unpopulated.[6]

The Ragusan nobles and senators and merchants receive foreigners with a kind welcome; and Ragusan senators wear black attire with a long kaftan underneath, just like a black cassock, and on top is a long cloak, like a black mantle. /10/

Meat and all foodstuffs are dear in Dubrovnik, and there is very little fresh or salted fish, and at times none at all. There are all kinds of fruit and it is not expensive. Their own money is silver and called a dinarius; of these dinarii they give 132 to a gold chervonets, and they are rounded and the size of a Muscovite kopek.

Principes or princes are newly selected from the senators each month, and they conduct all affairs as a general republic; and the Ragusan holdings extend for 100 It. miles of the coast of the Venetian sea, and across from the capital of Dubrovnik is an island that belongs to the Venetian prince.

The Ragusans never have war with anyone; they give gifts to the Roman emperor, to the Spanish king, to the Venetian prince, and to the Turkish sultan. For guard duty they have 500 infantry soldiers from their own inhabitants.

In Dubrovnik lives a Catholic archbishop who has two bishops under him. In this city I saw many homes struck down and palaces tumbled down; and they say that the whole city of Dubrovnik was demolished by the will of God 30 years ago by tremblings of the earth.[7]

June 10, at the 6th hour of day, we sailed on our frigate from Dubrovnik for the village of Perast on a favorable wind, which was not strong, and going 10 It. miles from Dubrovnik, we saw at sea in front of us two Turkish ships, which are called *fusti* (*fusta,* pirate galley), on which *kursary* (It. *corsaro,* corsairs), that is, predators or naval brigands, sail. And we on our frigate prepared the cannon and all arms for battle, and turned our sails directly toward those corsairs and came close to them so we could fire from the cannon; and those corsairs turned from us toward the coast, and fearing us they placed on their fusta a *bandera* (It. *bandiera*), that is, a flag under the coat of arms of the Venetian republic under the image of St. Mark. Upon seeing this bandiera passing close to them, we did not fire our cannon at this

[6]Tolstoi alludes to the depopulation of the city following the earthquake of 1667.

[7]Tolstoi notes the tribute necessary for Ragusan shipping and again refers to the earthquake of 1667.

close distance. This is the custom of the Turkish corsairs: when they do not want to fight with someone, they raise the bandiera or flag of a Christian sign.[8]

This day, two hours before night, we sailed beneath the city called Castel-novo (Castelnuovo, Hercegnovi). This city is of the Venetian province and 40 It. miles from Dubrovnik. Under this city I came across Muscovites on a ship—Princes Dmitrii and Fedor Golitsyn, Prince Andrei Repnin, Prince Ivan Gagin, /11/ Prince Iurii Khilkov, Prince Boris Kurakin, and others.[9] The city of Castelnuovo is very small, and the fortress and all the buildings are of stone. Our frigate stood beneath this city all day and night.

June 11. At the first hour of day we left the city of Castelnuovo by the channel. The wind was very slight and unfavorable to us. At the sixth hour of day we sailed into a small town called Perast (Perasto, Perast). This is a town of the Venetian state where Croats live—naval captains and astronomers and mariners. The homes are stone buildings, and there are many gardens. From Perast it is 15 versts or less to the villages and towns of the Turks. The town of Perast sits between high mountains, right on the bay. I stayed here until June 19. From Castelnuovo to Perast it is 18 It. miles. Perast is in the principality of Alba, and here there are many Serbs who are of the Greek faith; however, in Perast there is no Orthodox church, but there is a Greek church in a village not far away, and in that village live Orthodox Serbs, and those Serbs are under Venetian rule. Not long ago they escaped from the hand of the damned Busurman, from the rule of the Turkish sultan, and they live among the Turkish villages and cities. These Serbs are a military people, similar in all ways to the Don Cossacks; they speak the Slavonic language and wear Croat clothing. Their wives and daughters are similar to Croat women in their clothing and customs, and they are dishonored by being with men and thus are secluded. These Serbs have sufficient bread and poultry and fruit; they live between great and tall stone mountains, have stone homes, and are very hospitable and considerate to Muscovite people.

In this town of Perast I stayed at the home of a sea captain named Vicencio Buevich (Bujovič),[10] with whom I departed the city of Castelnuovo and whose ship I

[8]This episode shows Tolstoi's eagerness to fulfill the tsar's command that he take part in naval battle if at all possible. The practice of avoiding combat by hoisting a different flag was in fact used by the Venetians themselves, at least in the eighteenth century. See Lane, *Venice*, p. 419.

[9]These are the other *stol'niki* sent abroad at the same time as Tolstoi; they were mentioned on the first page of this Diary.

[10]The palace of Vicko Bujovič in Perast, completed in 1693, was the local naval school, and it is now the regional naval museum, located in the town where Tolstoi and other Russians studied. Not far away is the small home of Marko Martinovič, who instructed another group of Russians twenty years later. See Okenfuss, "Russian Students in Europe," pp. 131–45.

Marko Martinović and a group of Russian boyars, 1711. Although Tolstoi was a student thirteen years earlier, both groups studied in the Venetian outpost of Perast.

was on, and at that time this Vicencio had asked me to stay at his home should I be in Perast. And so I came to Perast, and this captain Vicencio has a cousin, a Roman Catholic *apat* (Ger. *Abt*, abbot), a Venetian also named Vicencio, and his brother accepted me into his home with great honor and regard. I had a room in his house with a bedstead, tables, armchairs, chairs and all else that I needed, and a fine bed was prepared for me. In addition, the captain's brother sent me /12/ fruit and poultry and summoned me to his home and accorded me every respect and great hospitality. This captain Vicencio serves in the Venetian *rzeczpospolita* for pay, and such is his service: he has his own military ship, on which he has 160 Venetian soldiers in the pay of the Venetian repubblica; for his ship and for his service he receives from the Venetian prince and from the whole repubblica 1,600 ducats for three months. The 160 mariners on this ship are kept by this captain for this pay, and they go in this ship endlessly on the sea of the Venetian gulfs in search of Turkish ships. When they spot them, they prevent the Turks from sailing in any ships on the Venetian gulf, and wherever they meet Turks, they try to fight with them; but should they perceive themselves to be weaker and judge that the Turks might overpower them, they still try to seize [the Turkish] ship, and they try to set fire to the gunpowder in their own ship, and to die with their ship, so that their ship and the Turkish ship would burn up together and all of them would perish. And to do this the captain Vicencio swears an oath to the Venetian prince and to the whole *repubblica*.

June 12, that is, on Pentecost, I went from the town of Perast to the village of Riza (Rizan),[11] where Serbs of the Greek faith live, and in this village I heard the Sacred Liturgy in the Greek church. The Serbian priest performed the service in the Slavonic language. The inhabitants of the village of Rizan received me with affection and great respect, and when I left, many people accompanied me to my boat. In this Orthodox church they have several church books of the Muscovite press, and also holy icons of Muscovite painting style (*shtilistovykh*), and the Greeks bring these icons and books here from Moscow.[12]

June 13. I went from Perast in a boat to the city of Katarra (It. Cataro, Kotor), which is a city of the Venetian state. It sits beneath a high mountain at the end of that bay into which we entered with our frigate across from the city of Castelnuovo. From Perast to Kotor it is 6 It. miles. Our captain's ship had been sent to this town of Kotor to deliver the biscuit supply of the Venetian prince, which he had

[11] Rizan, just freed from the Turks in 1687 and brought under Venetian rule, is the oldest town on the Bay of Kotor; it has Roman ruins.

[12] Tolstoi creates a new word possibly based on Italian *stile*, style, but I suspect this may be the Polish, *styl*. Also noteworthy in the passage is the absence of a critique of the Liturgy in Perast, and again, below, in Kotor, suggesting that Tolstoi found their service in conformity with his own and thus anticipating the arguments of Pan-Slavists a century and a half later.

brought from Venice to Kotor in his ship. When we left the frigate for Perast on June 11, the frigate had gone on to Kotor, and I had awaited the frigate in Perast. And when I came to Kotor the governor of that city of Kotor met me at the gates with great respect and conducted me to the Greek church, where I heard the Sacred Liturgy. I went to see this city's /13/ buildings. The governor walked with me and took me to a Roman church, in which I saw, under the altar, a certain woman dressed in the attire of the Dominican order; only her face and hands were visible and they have undecayed flesh and veins and skin. They say that she died 130 years ago. This woman was an Orthodox nun named Anna, and even the Romans say that she was not of their faith; the Romans took her body from the Greeks because the Greeks of this place live under Roman rule. From this place I went to an inn where I dined, and then I left the city. The governor conducted me to the city gates with great affection, and I went from the city after dinner back to Perast by boat. The city of Kotor has a stone fortress and is strongly fortified; half of that fortress runs along the sea on a level place, but the other half circles high up the mountain because of a danger of the incursion of Turkish people by land.[13] Turkish people live quite close to Kotor, 6 versts and closer; and the Turks are always at war with the Perastians and Kotorans, but often they have a truce, and whenever they are at peace, they conduct trade with them.

The above-mentioned Venetian captain, after he has been at sea for a number of months for which he receives payment from the Venetians, is free to go to Turkish places for trade. Arriving at a Turkish city, he resides and trades freely among the Turks; at sea he may meet Turks in ships and fight with them, and then conclude a truce; then he may board the Turkish ships and they board his, whenever they are able to conclude such a truce together; and so in peace, having concluded a treaty between themselves, they depart on their own ways.

Close to Kotor and Perast live free peoples who are called "black mountaineers" [Montenegrans]. These people profess the Christian faith and speak Slavonic. There are many of them and they serve no one; at times they turn against the Turks, and at times they fight the Venetians.

June 19, one hour before sunrise, we sailed from beneath Perast on our frigate up the bay[14] on which we entered, and this day in the fourth hour of day we sailed beneath Castelnuovo. Near this city I went to a Greek church, where I saw holy relics: the hand of the Empress Helena, the mother of the Emperor Constantine; the finger of the apostle Thomas; and the finger of the apostle Barnabas. At this church lives a Greek metropolitan, who has many dioceses among the Serbian

[13] Tolstoi accurately describes the remarkable fortifications of Kotor, which include both a sea wall and a stone wall that climbs high up the mountain over the town.

[14] Here and elsewhere in this section Tolstoi uses *kanala* (It. *canale*, channel or canal) to denote the long and narrow Bay of Kotor.

people under his power. These /14/ Serbs speak the Slavonic language and conduct the holy service in their churches in the Slavonic language, and these Serbs have many Muscovite painted icons and printed books in many places. Not far from this city of Castelnuovo lives another metropolitan of the Greek faith, and he too has many Greek churches among the Serbian people in his diocese. Both metropolitans are placed there by the pious Serbian patriarch, who is of the Greek faith and who dwells in the city of Budim under the power of the Roman emperor. And we stayed all day beneath the city of Castelnuovo, in order to take on fresh water on the frigate, and to add to the ballast (*savorni;* It. *zavorra*) on the frigate, because from the city of Castelnuovo we intended to cross the whole Venetian sea to the city of Barletta or to the city of Bari, in the region of the Spanish crown.[15] We also had to furnish ourselves with cannon and with arms, because in the places we had to pass to reach Barletta or Bari there are always Turks in ships and in galleys, and also corsairs on fusta and on other ships. At this time the *proveditor* (It. *provveditori,* commissioners) of the city of Castelnuovo sent me various wines—bottles of muscatels—but we did not see each other.

This same June 19, in the second hour of night, we left Castelnuovo on our desired course; the wind was favorable but so slight that we could not leave port; and we pulled the frigate with a barque on a rope, and we left the port with difficulty; the wind was also very light on the sea, and so we were able to cover only 10 Italian miles the whole night.

June 20. From the first hour of daylight and all day we went with a very slight favorable wind, on which our frigate could not go quickly; at other hours it was *bonaccia,* that is, windless, during which times our frigate stood in one place and could not move at all. And from sunrise to sunset we went 20 Italian miles, and then the wind became moderate, and from the first hour of night a wind that was not good for our course arose, but it was not a small wind, and on it we sailed the whole night and by daylight we had gone 70 It. miles.

June 21. In the first hour of day we saw, on our left side, a land of the state of the Turkish sultan, which is called Albania;[16] then as we passed that land, we caught sight, on our right side, of a land of the Spanish king, which is called Holy Angel (Monte Sant'Angelo), where in antiquity /15/ the archistrategist Michael worked a miracle, drawing water from a stone. This same June 21 the wind was unfavorable but strong from the first hour of daylight, and we sailed until noon and

[15] That is, they would cross the Adriatic from the Yugoslavian coast to Italy.

[16] This is not Albania on the Balkan side of the Adriatic, but the eastern coast of Italy, in the seventeenth century a part of Naples, which belonged to the Spanish king; thus he can call the area "Hispania" below.

came alongside mountains, on which there is a church named for the miracle of the archangel Michael. Beneath the mountains stands a city of the Spanish crown called Manfredon (Manfredonia). And after noon the wind became slight, on which our frigate moved quietly, and the beaches of the Spanish coast became visible, and on them the city of Barletta or Bari. On that slight wind we sailed until the 10th hour, and then the wind became unfavorable and strong. On it we went from the 10th to the 16th hour, when we sailed into Hispania, below a Spanish city that is between Barletta and Bari and is called Trani. [Across the gulf] from the city of Kotor along the coast are two Spanish cities called Bizheli (Bisceglie) and Mal'sheta (Molfetta). From Molfetta it is not far down the coast to Bari. From the first to the 16th hour of June 21, we went 30 It. miles, and our frigate stood at anchor on the sea below the city of Trani, because there is no *porto,* that is, dock, for ships, in all the cities from Barletta to Bari and even in Bari itself. Ships that come to these cities by sea draw themselves up to the land with their anchors.

The city of Trani stands on the sea coast and has a large stone fortress and stone homes, around which are many gardens and grapevines. From Trani along the coast to Molfetta and around that city, and from there along the shore to Bari and around Bari, there are many gardens and grapevines, and among them many stone homes. We stayed beneath Trani until June 22. The Spanish cities of Barletta and Bisceglie and Molfetta all stand on the sea shore and have stone fortresses, houses, and churches, and the distance between them is not great. Stone towers are built along the shore between them, 100 sazhens from tower to tower; they were built because of the danger of the Turks and the corsairs, because Turkish cities are very close to these Spanish cities. /16/

June 22. Two hours before daylight we went to the city of Bari, where we stayed. The wind was favorable and strong, and in the 3rd hour we sailed beneath Bari, without entering its wharf; we stood across from the city on the sea without an anchor, because this port, that is, this wharf, was unknown to our captain and our *astronom* (It. *astronomo*) and mariners; the captain was afraid to enter, as he might wreck the frigate; it was impossible to anchor on the sea opposite Bari because the sea bottom was rocky, and the anchor would not hold there. And while we stood there, we sent a man to Bari with a *praktiko* (It. *pratica*),[17] that is, with a document, which I had taken as a pass from the Ragusan principality from the city of Dubrovnik. The governor of the city of Bari allowed me to enter, and with his per-

[17]The *pratica* was the pass that allowed one to enter, and it is mentioned in all diaries. Earlier in the century, arriving at Malta, George Sandys was happy to hear that the "Council granted me Pratticke. So I came into the Citie." Cited in Sells, *Paradise,* p. 171. Entering Genoa, writes Evelyn, we "came on shore by the Prattique-house, where after strict examination of the Syndics, we were had to the Ducal Palace, and there our names beeing taken, we were conducted to our Inne." *Diary,* II, 171.

mission I entered Bari, and stayed at an inn, which in Italian is called an *osteria.* This osteria is called the Markendoni di San Marko (Mercanzia? di San Marco), close to the piazza.[18] The governor of Bari sent a man to this inn to greet me and to request that I come to his home sometime. This day after dinner, when the bells rang for vespers, that is, for evengsong, I went to the Roman church in which the relics of the great hierarch of Christ, Nicholas, rest.[19] At the doors of this church I was met by Roman priests who are called canons. This church is of stone, large, and done in the manner of Western churches; in this church the principal altar is dedicated to the Miracle Worker Nicholas, and there are many other altars in this church, as is customary in Roman churches. In this church, too, are many stone columns upon which is built the choir around the inside of the church. Under the altar of this church, in the ground beneath, is built another Roman church, in which rest the holy and miracle-working relics of St. Nicholas. From the large church to this one are two passages with wide stone stairways. In the middle of this lower church is a Roman altar named for the Miracle Worker Nicholas, all of cast silver, on which on all sides are images of the miracles of Nicholas the Wonder Worker in silver. Above this altar is an eight-sided platform (ambo) also of cast silver, two steps high, and on this platform is placed the half-length image of the great Nicholas, cast in silver. His right hand is giving the blessing, and in his left hand is the Gospel, all adorned with fine stones: diamonds, rubies, emeralds, and sapphires. Above this Gospel are three apples, /17/ round and golden, on the image of the miracle of the Wonder Worker; they recall the father of three daughters, who had to give them away to poor marriages, and the three bags of gold Nicholas gave to save these three girls from the deadly debauched sin.[20]

[18] Bari was off the course of most early-modern visitors to Italy; this hotel is not listed in Sells's useful survey of popular inns. Sells, *Paradise,* pp. 143–45.

[19] This is the Romanesque Basilica of San Nicola, 1087, built to house the relics after they were brought to Bari.

[20] The iconography of St. Nicholas is elaborate. He is represented by three loaves of golden bread as the patron of the bakers' guild, by three children's heads as the patron of children, and by the three gold balls or purses of the pawnbroker as the benefactor of the poor. All derive from the story of a certain citizen of Patera who

> had lost all his money, and had moreover to support three daughters who could not find husbands because of their poverty; so the wretched man was going to give them over to prostitution. This came to the ears of Nicholas, who thereupon took a bag of gold and, under cover of darkness, threw it in at the window of the man's house. Here was a dowry for the eldest girl, and she was duly married. At intervals Nicholas did the same thing for the second and third; at the last time the father was on watch, recognized his benefactor, and overwhelmed him with his gratitude. It would appear that the three purses represented in pictures, came to be mistaken for the heads of three children, and so gave rise to the absurd story of the children, resuscitated by the saint, who had been killed by an innkeeper and pickled in a brine tub. (*Butler's Lives of the Saints,* IV, 504)

An Icon of St. Nicholas (fourteenth century). (From Tretiakov Gallery, Moscow.)

Under this altar low in the earth rest the relics of the great miracle-working bishop Nicholas covered with a single marble stone. A single, small round window has been made in this stone, and he who wishes to see the relics of the holy Miracle Worker must go beneath the altar to this window and look down into this round window. A priest descends beneath the altar and goes down to the miracle-working relics with a small candelabra and a lit candle on a silver chain; and through that round window one sees a bone from the leg of St. Nicholas the Wonder Worker, which rests all submerged in holy chrism, which looks just like clear oil. No one can enter into these depths where the holy relics rest, but the canons get the holy chrism[21] for this church in this way: they press a single lip on a silver tube built for this, and they go down to that round window with a candle, and that tube, being filled with the holy chrism that comes from the wonder-working relics, is drawn up and is squeezed into a vessel; and this is done until they have taken as much as they need, and the holy chrism is never depleted. The canons of that church distribute that holy chrism without prohibition to whoever wants it, and gratis; and a large amount of that holy chrism is distributed every day to those who come to pray; however, the flow from the miracle-working relics is never diminished, and there is enough of the holy chrism of Nicholas the Wonder Worker to bless the whole world. At all times a canon keeps this holy chrism in the church in a silver vessel and generously anoints those who come. When someone requests the holy chrism, it is poured into a cruet, where it looks like pure water, and they give this holy chrism to drink abundantly to all who come here.

In this lower church are four other altars on the side of that of the Miracle Worker, two on each side; on the right side by the wall is a wooden carved chest, one and a half arshins in length and an arshin in width, and three-quarters of an arshin high. In this chest a wooden casket is placed, the one in which the relics of Nicholas the Wonder Worker were brought to Bari from the city of Myra. In this lower church are 24 slate columns that support the entrance of the church; and close /18/ to the altar of Nicholas the Wonder Worker is an arch of fine Italian plaster work.

On the right side of this church is a column of yellow slate, which stood by the relics of St. Nicholas in the city of Myra, and when his relics were moved it was brought by sea to Bari and now stands in this lower church. From this column, the Catholics say, miracles now happen to the believers who pray to Nicholas the Wonder Worker, and this column is enclosed by an iron lattice. In this lower church there are more than a hundred large and small silver lamps. This lower church is made in the earth, but the light in it is good; there are four good-sized windows in two of the walls, and on a third wall behind the altar of the Miracle Worker there is another large window. This church is not long, but very wide.

On the right side of the altar is a door that leads to a vestibule built to hold the holy chrism. In this vestibule are many cupboards in which stand many large cruets with holy chrism. In this lower church on the opposite side from where the relics of

[21] This is the famous Manna di San Nicola, which had miraculous powers.

the great Saint Nicholas rest, a large organ is placed along the wall, and on festivals in this church, music is played on the organ and on various other musical instruments. From this church I went back to the large upper church; in this upper church there are fine plaster arches. From the upper church on the left side of the principal altar I went up to a vestibule in which they showed me many holy relics and great churchly riches:

First they showed me a cross, made from the very wood of the cross of Christ, and then a spike from Christ's crown of thorns, stained with the most pure blood of the Savior.

A part of the lip, with which the damned Judas drank the glory of the Lord at the time of our Savior's passion on the cross for His Father.

Some hair of the Blessed Mother of God.

Part of the relics of St. Basil the Great.

Part of the relics of the archdeacon Laurentius; when someone touches the lips slowly, they can feel a considerable warmth, and this miracle I was able to see.

Part of the dress of the Most Pure Virgin Mary the Mother of God, which she wore on her most pure body.

The hand of the holy apostle Thomas; part of the relics of the martyr Sebastian.

The hand of the apostle James, the brother of the Lord.[22]

/19/ Part of the arm of the apostle James the Greater.

The body of a youth, killed by Herod at the time of Christ's birth; part of the head of St. Blaise of Sebaste.

Part of the relics of the martyr Boniface, and many other holy relics that cannot be described here for lack of time.

In this vessel repository, or vestibule, stands a full-size icon of Nicholas the Wonder Worker, of ancient Greek painting, dark from age. In Bari they paint images identical to this one; and this image was brought to Bari together with the relics of St. Nicholas, and he is painted in this holy icon standing, giving the blessing with his right hand and holding the holy Gospel in his left hand, as I wrote in this book above. They say that this image was painted from the Miracle Worker's own face when Nicholas was still alive.[23]

[22] St. James the Apostle, of Cana, was a cousin of Christ.

[23] Tolstoi has just devoted the longest self-contained section of the Diary to his visit to the shrine of St. Nicholas of Myra at Bari, and it is clear that this was the highlight of his trip. In Russia, even more so than in the West, Nicholas was one of the most popular saints. There is a Russian saying, "If God dies, we still have St. Nicholas." In the West he would become the symbol of charity at Christmastime, but in Russia he is the helpmate of the peasant at his work, the protector of the poor and destitute, and the defender of Orthodoxy. In Kievan times he was already seen as the protector of Russia against the infidels, the Tatars, and later against other enemies. Already in Kievan Russia they celebrated the feast of the transfer of his relics

In this vestibule they showed me many beaded archbishop's robes and caps and two beaded pillows that the king of Poland sent as a gift to the church of the Wonder Worker; and they showed me many other church attires. When I wanted to leave this vestibule for the inn where I was staying, the governor of Bari sent a request that I visit him at home, and one canon from the church of Nicholas the Wonder Worker escorted me to his court. When I entered the home of that governor, he himself met me on the stairs, and with great esteem he welcomed me to his palace, where I spent some time with him. Then I returned to the inn where I was staying, and that governor accompanied me to the gate. When I left him the canon escorted me to the inn, and at the same hour the governor and a Spanish nobleman came to me at the inn and sat with me for some hours; then he requested that I dine with him on the 24th of June, and I promised to honor his request.

June 23. In the fifth hour of day I went back to the church of St. Nicholas, where Roman canons awaited me for the Liturgy, and entering the church I brought two containers with bottles for the holy chrism, which flows from the relics of the miraculous bishop /20/ Nicholas. The canons of that church quickly filled the containers with holy miracle-working chrism, and with this great gift, having read the *akafist* (hymn of praise) at the wonder-working relics, I returned to the inn where I stayed.

When I had left the frigate on which I had arrived and its captain, I had paid some golden chervontsy for conveyance to Bari, and the captain fired from the cannon on his frigate to honor me. And this day that frigate sailed from Bari back to Dalmatia to the city of Korčula, but I stayed in Bari.

The city of Bari stands right on the sea, has a large stone fortress, made in fine fashion, with *bel'vardami* (It. *belvedere*),[24] and on the belvederes there are adequate large and small cannon.

In the city of Bari the homes and churches and monasteries are of stone and well built. The governor's home is built at the city wall, right on the sea, in a pleasant place. In Bari an archbishop of the Roman faith lives, but very poorly. The city of Bari is populous, its people are Spaniards who speak Italian; however, between the Venetian's and the Roman's speech there is some *differentsiiu* (It. *differenza*), that is, difference; in dress they wear the Spanish fashion.

The shops and the goods in them are not numerous; there are only a few craftsmen.

---

from Myra to Bari. Icons of his life established not only his charity, but also his asceticism: as an infant he refused to be fed by his mother on the fast days of Wednesdays and Fridays. See the commentary to Nicholas's icons in Onasch, *Icons,* passim. There is much literature on St. Nicholas, but outstanding among it is the story of the growth of the legend around him as told by Jones, *Saint Nicholas of Myra, Bari, and Manhattan.*

[24] Tolstoi here uses the term to indicate a high tower with a field of vision; elsewhere in the Diary, he used it as a gazebo or pavilion commanding a vista, as in a park.

The governor of Bari is a Spaniard from Naples of noble rank, and he wears the cavalier's cross.

And I stayed in Bari until the 25th of June, and hired a carriage; and when I arrived on a frigate and left it, its captain Ivan Karsteli (Carstelli) gave me a testimonial letter concerning my stay at sea and concerning the sciences, and in it is written the following:

> The 22nd of June 1698 in Bari.
>
> I, captain Ivan Carstelli,
>
> by these presents testify, that in the present year the Muscovite gentryman Peter Alekseev together with the soldier Ivan Staburin were on my frigate and went to sea on the Venetian gulf, even to the borders of the Ragusan principality and to Ragusa, to the city of Dubrovnik, and from that place he had the desire to go on my frigate to the city of Castelnuovo and to Perast and even to Kotor, which city borders on the cities of the Turks, and he wished to see the Turks at sea in their military ships, in order to fight with them. And as soon as we departed, we met with /21/ two Turkish fusta, on which were encountered plenty of Turks. And at that hour by the grace of God the needed wind arrived, and with that wind we began to prepare for battle with the above-mentioned Turks, who, seeing their powerlessness, fled to the shore, and because of the shallowness of the place we could not drive them fully to the end. And when we reached the place of Kotor that borders the Turks, where we stayed six days, it was our misfortune not to be able to meet or see a Turkish ship, and because of that we did not stay, but departed. But we entered the Spanish state, even as far as Bari across the whole gulf of the Venetian sea, and we always tried to meet with Turkish ships. But we were unable to do this, and we were aggravated by a naval fortuna, in which the above-mentioned Muscovite gentryman and that soldier were never afraid, standing and resisting the evil fortuna. And then, leaving my ship, they wished to go from Bari to Naples by land, and they had wished to go by ship, but I was unable to sail on my ship into such distant parts.
>
> To confirm for captain Ivan Carstelli, I, naval captain Ivan Lazorėvić, sign in his place, because he is unable to write.

On this authentic certificate the seal of naval captain Ivan Carstelli is imprinted on red wax.[25]

Upon my arrival back in Venice, this certificate was registered in the chancellery of San Marco and signed as follows:

> In good faith I, a public notary, that is, a scribe, as well as a priest for life, Antonius Pasadorski, a Pole of the Dominican order, and naval captain Angelo Kapodorov, saw the above letter, which was shown to me and to the councillor, who recognized

[25] The letter here and the elaborate measures taken by Tolstoi at that time, and later in Venice, to document its authenticity reflect his concern that Peter the Great would know that he had done everything possible to engage the Turks in combat, as he had been instructed in his original charge.

and confirmed it with an oath, and the above-mentioned priest Pasadorski placed his hand on his breast in the manner of a chaplain, that is, a priest, and the above captain of the *Angel* mentioned above, placing the letter in my hands, certified it to be the true and authoritative letter of Ivan Lazorević, naval captain, and also that he knew [him] and had a complete knowledge and understanding of its character and its detail.

Given in Venice this 28th day of October, for which I, Vincencio Vincencio, born a son of lord Jan Geronimus, Venetian merchant and Venetian public councillor, concerning that which transpired, in faith signed it and so signify.

From the chancellery of San Marco I was given a certificate confirming the above-written certificate of the captain, and in it is written the following:

Silvester /22/ Valerio, by the grace of God, Prince of Venice, to all in general and particular, both friends and believers who view this certificate, we are familiar with it. Vincencio Vincencio on the 28th nearest, requested an attestation, that is, the certification of Ivan Lazarevič so named, that he is a notary, and a Venetian scribe of good repute and in high regard, and that that which was written there may be taken everywhere and publicly in good faith [as true]. Given here in our princely palace on the 28th day of October, under index seven, in the year of our Lord 1698.

This certificate, which was prepared in Venice to certify the captain's testimony, is written on parchment. The seal is leaded; on it are these impressions: on one side an image of the holy evangelist Mark, and on the other side it is impressed with the face of the Venetian principe, that is, prince. And the writing on these certificates, both the captain's and on the Venetian certification, are in the Italian language and not in Latin.

Staying in the above-mentioned inn, I paid the innkeeper for accommodations and bed and board 10 karlina (Carlinos) in Spanish money, and they give 24 carlini for a golden chervonets.

In Bari they use Spanish monies, scudi, philipi, carlini, grani, and soldi. In each carlino is 10 grani, and each grana contains 2 soldi.[26]

[26] A few words about Spanish rule in southern Italy are in order. The Peace of Cateau-Cambresis (1559) had confirmed the hegemony of Spain in Italy, excluding the French and giving the Spanish control over Milan/Lombardy, Naples, Sicily, and Sardinia. Although the Spanish monarchs in the first half of the century, Philip III (1598–1621) and Philip IV (1621–65), were not especially able, capable and aggressive viceroys in Milan and Naples retained Spanish rule. There were several rebellions against foreign rule, that in 1637 and more notably that of Tommaso Aniello in 1647, but they were in time defeated.

Thus, when Tolstoi describes towns in southern Italy as Spanish, or when he talks about the way in which the "Spanish" speak Italian, he is simply narrating the status quo as it had existed for a century and a half. A good introduction to the subject is in the first chapter of Sells, *Paradise*.

I have made no attempt in this annotation to convert monetary units of the seventeenth

After dinner on June 23rd I walked around the town walls, and entered the upper city, which in the Italian language is called Castello. I was not allowed into the upper city without the permission of the *castellano,* but he immediately sent for a soldier, who quickly returned to me, opened the gates, and a resident nobleman of Bari conducted me through all the upper city.

In this upper city, inside the town walls, are built the houses of soldiers, who live there with their wives and children. These soldiers in the upper city stand on *gvardi* (It. *guardia*), that is, on guard; and there are 36 soldiers' homes in the upper city, as well as the home of the castellano, and no one else lives in the upper city.

The size of this upper city is very small. The newly built homes in it are very large and fine, with many rooms. Among them is built a kaplica, that is, a small Roman church, in which there is an altar of the Roman saint Francesco. In this building are many rooms, not yet finished, in which they are building ceilings and other decorations of fine craftsmanship. Also in this /23/ house lives the castellano, a Spanish prince of numerous possessions. Not far from the upper city is the very large home of the archbishop of Bari, built right at the cathedral, and the Roman cathedral of Bari is large, but it is not well built. Beneath the altar of this church is an image of the Blessed Mother of God of Greek painting, brought to Bari from Constantinople, and they say it was painted by Luke the Evangelist.[27]

---

century to real values. Here is the statement of the problem given in Mead, *Grand Tour,* pp. 175–76.

> Consider the state of the average tourist's mind on reading the following lucid explanation: "At Venice, and in most parts of that republic's dominions, they keep their accounts in Lires, Soldi and Pichioli, reckoning 12 Pichioli to 1 Soldo, and 20 Soldi to 1 Lira. But the bank reckons by Ducats and Grosses, reckoning 24 Grosses to the Ducat. The current monies are, I. The Pistole of Venice, Florence, Spain, and Louis d'ors worth 29 Lires. II. Another sort of Pistoli, valued sometimes at more than 30 Lires. III. The Pistole of Italy, Genoa, Turin, Milan, Parma, Mantua, Modens and Geneva, worth 28 Lires. IV. The Sequin, worth 17 Lires. V. The Ducat of gold or Hungarian Ducat, worth 16 Lires. VI. The Dacatoon, worth 8 Lires ½. VII. The silver Crown, worth 9 Lires 12 Soldi. VIII. The Silver Ducat, worth 6 Lires 4 Soldi. IX. The Crusado of Genoa, called Genoins, worth 11 Lires 10 Soldi, and sometimes 11 Lires 15 Soldi. X. The Philip of Milan, worth 8 Lires 10 Soldi. XI. The Testoon, worth 2 Lires 14 Soldi. XII. The Julio or 3 d. XIII. The Lira, worth 20 Soldi. XIV. The Soldo, worth 12 Pichioli. XV. The Gross, worth 32 Pichioli."
>
> And this was a mere beginning. In Tuscany one met the sequin, the scudo, the livre, and the paul. The Papal States had a separate system, and so had the Kingdom of Naples, and other parts of the country—Bergamo, Bologna, Genoa, Messina, Palermo, Milan, Turin.

[27] This is the icon Santa Maria di Constantinopoli, ascribed to St. Luke; it was said to have been brought to Bari in 733. Tolstoi saw the Cathedral of San Sabino before it was rebuilt in 1745.

June 24. Early in the morning I went back to the relics of St. Nicholas the Wonder Worker in the lower church, in which under the altar of the Miracle Worker an arch of silver panels of the most marvelous work and great wealth is built. This day I dined in Bari with the governor; at his home I dined with Spanish nobles and canons. This governor treated me graciously, and when I left him he conducted me, with all present and with great affection, to the gate of his home.

I hired a *furman* (Ger. *Fuhrmann*) from Bari to Naples, paying 10 ducats for the carriage. They put my trunk and all my things on the back of the carriage for that price.

In Bari there is a Jesuit monastery and monasteries of various orders. And at the church in which rest the relics of Nicholas the Wonder Worker, there are canons, and there are 42 of them at that church.

June 25. I left Bari in the carriage. And I arrived at a Spanish city that stands on the seacoast and is called Dzhorenatso (Giovinazzo), 12 It. miles from Bari. This is not a large city; its fortress and all its buildings are of stone. Along the road from Bari to this city on both sides are gardens, in which there are all kinds of fruit trees and grapevines, and many domiciles are along the road. I did not stop in this city but went past it and arrived in Mal'zheta (Molfetto), 15 It. miles from Bari. There I stayed in an inn and dined. The city of Molfetto is not small. It has a stone fortress and all stone buildings, and it stands above the sea; in this city there is much *eleio* (It. *olio*), that is, wood oil. Having dined in this inn, I left and arrived in the city of Bizheli (Biseglie). This city stands on the seashore; it has a fine fortress and all stone buildings, and is 6 miles from Molfetto. Not stopping in this city, I passed it and arrived in the city of Trani, 4 It. miles from Bisceglie. Trani stands on the seacoast, and has a stone fortress and buildings. Without stopping in this city, I arrived to spend the night in the city of Barleta (Barletta). /24/ This city of Barletta is 6 It. miles from Trani. Barletta stands on the seacoast, is large, has a fine stone fortress and many fine stone homes, and also has large stone monasteries and churches. In Barletta near one church is a fine stone castle, regular and quartered, that is, equal on all sides.[28] The city of Barletta is populous. From Molfetto to Barletta along the road are dwellings and many olive and grape gardens. From Bari to Barletta all belongs to the Spanish crown.

June 26. From Barletta in the 5th hour of day I arrived at an inn called Deliachirinellia (Cherignola), 18 It. miles from Barletta. Along the road from Barletta to this inn there are no gardens and few homes, only much ripe grain, and in

[28] The Castello, thirteenth century, had been rebuilt with four regular bastions by Charles V in 1532–37. The area is noted for its wines and olives. Tolstoi traveled north along the coast to Barletta, then turned west toward Naples, roughly along the route of the modern autostrada.

fields there are places with many herds of horses and bulls. The cattle there, the bulls and cows, are very large. And the wheat is threshed by bulls. I stayed in this inn on June 26 until the 23rd hour by the Italian clock, and by the Muscovite the 16th hour.[29] In the last hour of that day I left that inn and traveled all night, and in the first hour of day on the 27th I arrived at an inn called *Porta Debovina,*[30] 24 Italian miles from the other inn. In this inn I stayed on ***June 27*** until night. Along the road of this place are many forests, and the road is smooth. From the inn Ponte De Bovino I traveled 2 hours in light and 4 hours in darkness, and stopped on the road, fed the horses a little, and they drank from a fountain, and that fountain is built on the road for the comfort of travelers. Again I departed that place, and arrived in the early hours of morning at an inn, which is called Rotaminarda (Grottaminarda), 24 It. miles from the inn Ponte De Bovino. Along this road are many forests of oak, maple, birch, and aspen. The road is not very smooth, but rocky and hilly. Along this road at night I saw many fireflies, flying along the forests and on the grain and the road. And I stayed in the inn Grottaminarda ***June 28*** from the first hour until the 13th. All of these inns from Bari to Naples are Spanish, and the food in them is very poor, and they have no fish or fruit, that is, grapes, and even for a high price one cannot find fish, and there I was quite hungry. Along the road in the forests are stone homes, where there are always soldiers to protect people from thieves.

June 28 in the 13th hour I left the inn Grottominarda and traveled all night and arrived on the ***29th*** at an inn, /25/ which is called Kardinala,[31] at the first hour of day, and this is 26 Italian miles from Grottominarda.

Along this road are many forests and fields, and the road is hilly, and in the fields they sow wheat, barley, and oats. I stayed in the inn Cardinale until the 10th hour of day, and left and arrived in the last hour of that day in the city of Neapol (Naples). Along both sides of that road are gardens in which there are all kinds of fruit trees, and also many grapevines that are wrapped around great trees. Along this road from Grottominarda to Naples are many dwellings built of stone, and in many places there are guards. A mile or two from Naples on both sides and in the middle of the road are built fountains of fine workmanship, from which flows fine clean water for the use of all travelers.

Two miles from Naples on the left side is a very high mountain, which without interruption has burned since the creation of the world, and in daylight a great smoke arises from this mountain, and at night there is also fire; and so, they say, it always burns ceaselessly and is never extinct for even a short time.[32] Arriving in Naples I stayed at an inn called Allia Koliomba Doro (Alla Columba d'Oro), that is,

[29] Translating Tolstoi's medieval time reference, this would mean since daybreak. Tolstoi's guide travels at night to avoid the worst of the summer heat.

[30] Three sentences later he corrects Porta, to Ponte de Bovino.

[31] West of Avellino and Monteforte is the tiny hamlet of Cardinale.

[32] This is Mount Vesuvius; it is Tolstoi's first sighting of an active volcano.

Beneath the Golden Pigeon.[33] In this inn they gave me a fine room in which there was a fine gilded bedstead and a bed with white sheets; and I paid 10 carlini a day in this inn for food and for the room and bed, with my slave, and I stayed there until the 8th of July.

June 30. After dinner two Spanish nobles came to me; one was a brother of the governor of Bari, and he said to me that his brother had written from Bari by post that I was coming to Naples, and that he should pay his respects to me in Naples. And these nobles asked me if I would go with them in a coach and then walk and look at all the fine things that sweetly meet a man's eye in Naples, and I went with them in their coach. We arrived in front of a Carmelite monastery, and entered the church. This church is of stone, and the insides—the walls and the arches—are all covered with fine alabaster work and the carved alabaster is finely gilded; in this church is a miracle-working icon of the Mother of God,[34] and they say that this holy icon performed this miracle: a woman came and wanted to kiss the foot of the Blessed Child our Lord Jesus /26/ Christ, painted on this holy icon in the arms of the Blessed Virgin, and his Blessed foot lifted itself up, and that is how it appears to this day. This holy image stands over the altar behind a screen, and this most pure icon is opened to public viewing only one day a year; and the Neapolitan viceroy and his wife come to this holy icon every Saturday. In this same church high over the altar stands a cross, and on it the body of Christ the Lord has an inclined head. The reason for the inclination is this: in antiquity, at the time of a civil war in Naples, one cannon ball from a cannon flew at the head of the body of Christ, which was on this cross, and His blessed head turned, and that ball slid past the Savior's head to the church doors, and came to rest there. In that place in the church's platform there is a stone circle, and it is inscribed with Latin letters written in a circle, and the cannon ball now hangs on an iron chain suspended on the wall, and its weight would be 20 funts or more.[35]

In this church, the altar is made of various slates of the most miraculous craftsmanship. In this church are two large organs, and the whole church is marvelously decorated. From this monastery I went to a church; white clergy serve in this church, 100 of them, and every day 100 Masses are said on all the altars. This church was built in the name of the Blessed Mother of God and the true and glorious Annunciation.[36] The altar in this church is made of various marbles of the most mar-

[33] In Naples most travelers stayed at the Three Kings or, less expensively, at the Aguila Nera. Sells, *Paradise*, p. 145.

[34] This is the Church of Santa Maria del Carmine, and the much venerated fourteenth-century Madonna della Bruna.

[35] That is, it weighs about eighteen pounds.

[36] This is apparently a description of the old Santissima Annunziata, which was destroyed by fire and rebuilt in 1761–82.

velous work; over the altar is a golden image of the Annunciation of the Blessed Mother of God, which is valued at 5,000 scudos. In this church the walls and vaults are made of various marbles and alabaster, and gilded in many places, and the whole decoration of the church is most marvelous and very rich; the painting of the holy icons in this church is very marvelous, such as is seldom seen in all Italy. This church receives each year an *entrate* (It. *entrate*), that is, an income of 20,000 scudos from hereditary estates.

In this church they showed me the church's wealth of marvelous workmanship, and a huge amount of silver, and all of this church's silver weighs some 17,000 funts, which is 425 puds.[37] It is in candlesticks, lamps, and in other patterned figures of the most wondrous work, among which I saw an altar of pressed silver, a wondrous ship of pressed silver, also a multitude of other patterned things in silver, which would be difficult to describe because of their numbers.

/27/ In this same church they showed me two fine glass caskets, in which repose the bodies of youths who were killed by Herod for Christ. One body lies naked, complete but without its head, having flesh and skin and veins; the other is also whole, but without a right leg, and it lies in the shirt in which it was killed, girded with red silk. The age of both of these youths is known fairly precisely.

I also saw there the upper skull of the head of the holy martyr Barbara, which produces a fine fragrance.

From this church I walked to the rooms in which they write the revenues and expenditures of the treasures that are collected at that church. In these rooms tables are set, and many people sit at them just as do the clerks in the Muscovite *prikazy;* and they showed me a huge number of gold and silver coins of all kinds in one room.

Then I went to a hospital, which was built at this church's expense.[38] In this hospital there are 250 sick males, and on the other side as many sick females, and at times there are even more. The sick have fine bedsteads and comfortable beds and good curtains, and at each bed they place a small table and vessels from which they drink and eat. To serve the sick in this hospital they keep workers, men for the male patients and women and girls for the females. In the rooms where the sick lie they have made a kaplica, that is, a small church, in which they daily say the Liturgy, and every day 6 priests take turns attending the spiritual needs of the sick. This hospital has a pharmacy, in which there are doctors, pharmacists, and druggists at all times, and they cure the sick without payment because the church pays. The food and all else for the sick are also paid by the revenue of that church, and they cure all the sick and give them drink and food, all without cost in the name of Christ; and he who dies is buried at the church's expense, and those who are made healthy are released without further detention.

Then I went to a cathedral that has a cardinal. This church is long but not very wide, and its decor is good but not overly so; however, its vaults and walls are

[37] Tolstoi calculates that it contains over 15,000 pounds of silver.

[38] This is the precursor of the Casa de Trovatelli, the foundling home supported by the Church. It adjoined the old Annunziata and was notorious for its high mortality rate.

molded of plaster. This church has two large organs; on the right side a large chapel is enclosed with a brass screen, which is of fine cast work and contains much brass. In this chapel rest the treasures, that is, the wealth of the Neapolitan /28/ inhabitants, of the princes, dukes, marquises, and a great number of other honorable people.[39]

Then I went to the church of St. Philip.[40] This church's interior is adorned with various marbles and alabaster, and it is gilded. This church has 12 marble columns, each hewn from a single whole stone. These columns are very tall and thick. The church has two great organs, and the whole decoration is fine.

Then I went to a monastery where canons called the Theatines[41] live. In this monastery is the church of St. Paul. It was damaged by the earthquake eight years ago, and the columns of this damaged church stand broken, and they now stand as a memorial. This church was built in antiquity, and in the year 1580 the present church was built in place of the ancient destroyed one; it is of fine craftsmanship, with gilded plaster vaults. The church has four large organs; it also has many priestly garments sewn with the most marvelous workmanship.

Then I went to a Jesuit monastery.[42] This church is well adorned with various marbles and with alabaster, and the walls and vaults are gilded. This church has two large organs, and they are most marvelous. The whole church is very well decorated.

Then I went to stroll about the city and met the wife of the Neapolitan viceroy; in front of her walked many foot soldiers dressed in fine attire; then came a marvelous carriage with two drivers, and behind the carriage four men carried the viceroy's wife in a *porcheheze* (porte-chaise), which was covered with red velvet. She was dressed in the Spanish fashion similar to the French, with a bare breast and without any cover on her head, and her hair was adorned like a Muscovite maiden's. As I came even with her, I gave the customary bow, sitting in my carriage; likewise, she gave me the customary bow. Behind her came two carriages, in which four girls sat in each, then came two more carriages, and in each of them sat four male servants of the viceroy. Along the side of the viceroy's wife and the carriages walked a large number of soldiers in the attire described above.

[39] This is an uncharacteristically brief account of the Cathedral of St. Januarius (San Gennaro), thirteenth-fourteenth century Gothic. When Evelyn visited on February 1–2, 1645, he wrote, "We were told that this day the Blood of St. Genuarius, & his head should be expos'd, and so we found it; but obtain'd not to see the miracle of the boiling of this blod, as was told us." *Diary*, II, 328. One can only imagine Tolstoi's wonder had he been able to witness the famous liquefaction of the saint's blood that occurs annually on September 19 and again in May.

[40] This is the Church of San Filippo Neri, baroque, 1592–1619.

[41] This is San Paolo Maggiore, 1590; the earthquake of 1688 destroyed the portico of an ancient temple of Castor and Pollux, on which the church was built.

[42] This is the Gesu Nuovo, incomplete when Evelyn visited it in 1645; it too was damaged in the earthquake of 1688. *Diary*, II, 329.

Then I arrived at the home of the nobleman who accompanied me. There we stopped on the street and from the house they brought various sherbets in silver dishes, and also they brought silver plates and spoons, and they treated /29/ me to that sherbet with great respect. Sitting in the carriage I ate the sherbet and again went close to the viceroy's home on the seacoast.[43] The viceroy's home is very large, has many tall rooms, and is very well crafted. At the gates a large number of soldiers stand on guard, and in front of his gates is a large fine square; his home is close to the sea and it looks out upon the sea and on the whole city of Naples. Close to his court on the very seacoast is a building called the arsenal, built for the construction of naval ships. Then, passing the viceroy's home, I went along the coast where I saw many fine fountains built along the shore. We went along that shore and met with many coaches and carriages, in which princes and dukes and marquises rode for amusement, and all the people strolled with their wives and children and made merry. Then I went to the inn where I was staying and saw many most marvelously built fountains in the street. In the streets of Naples are always a great number of people going about in coaches and carriages, and the coaches and carriages, especially those in the Neapolitan style, are without *oselin*[44] and without belts on thin wooden axle rods, and they are very comfortable for riding.

In Naples there are not many good horses and most people go by mule, but horses pull the coaches, and many footmen follow the coaches in the Muscovite fashion. Then I went to the inn in which I was staying, and the noblemen who were going about with me conducted me to that inn and, having bowed to me, they went to their homes.

July 1. Early in the morning I hired a carriage and went to see the quite astounding things one encounters close to Naples. Leaving the city, I saw a wondrous thing: they have made a road under the ground 5 sazhens wide. The height of this underground passage at the Naples end is 6 sazhens, but it is lower at the other end, and the length of this road or underground passage is some 500 sazhens.[45] In the middle of this passage there is a great darkness even in daylight, because this

[43] This is the Palazzo Reale, 1600, by Domenico Fontana. "Then we went to the Vice-roy's Palace, which is realy one of the noblest that I have seene in all Italy." Evelyn, *Diary,* II, 326.

[44] *Oselina,* possibly from the Italian *solino,* collars.

[45] This is the first tunnel that Tolstoi describes. Whereas he wonders at its "astonishing" construction, Evelyn was able to approach it armed with tales of its ancient origins: "We were advanc'd into this noble, and altogether wonderful Crypta, consisting of a passage, spacious enough for 2 Coaches to go on breast, cut through a rocky mountaine (as reported, by the antient Cimmerii) for neere three quarters of a mile; others say by L: Cocceius, who employd no lesse than an hundred thousand men at worke on it for 15 days, we came to the mid-way, where there is an orifice, or Well, board'd quite through the whole diameter of this vast Mountaine, which admitts the light into a pretty Chapel, hewn out of the natural rock, wherein hang divers lamps perpetualy burning." *Diary,* II, 337–38.

road is cut through a great stone mountain, and for light in the middle of this road they have made a small window overhead; however, it gives very little light. This road is all paved with stone. About midway along this road, on the left side when leaving Naples, is a small carved cavern inside which there is a kaplica, that is, a small Roman church, where they hold services for travelers all day. On the mountain through which the road is cut are many gardens and stone dwellings /30/ that are quite large, and in which Neapolitans live. Going along that road 4 Italian miles from Naples, I came to a lake that the Neapolitans call the water of life.[46] This lake is round and quite large and surrounded by high mountains. Arriving from Naples, on the right side on one mountain is carved a niche of a width that one man can pass, and in height it is a sazhen and 3 arshins, and the length of this niche into the mountain is 5 sazhens. In this niche from the earth arises a toxic vapor that will quickly kill any living man, cattle, beast, or bird; and on the ground just four arshins above this infectious vapor a man can enter this niche freely;[47] only he cannot incline his head low or lie down in this niche, because this infectious vapor will envelop his head, and in just a few minutes the man will die, as will all living things. Once that vapor envelops the head nothing can live; and that vapor will not damage other parts of the flesh except the head, and whenever something living dies from this vapor in the niche, immediately they take it away from here and place it in the lake, and in just a few minutes it will return to life and will be as healthy as before. And looking into this niche from the ground four arshins above, one can see that sometimes the smoke becomes thin and bluish like smoke from a house; a fire can go out in this vapor. I examined these things closely. Earlier, taking a dog, I placed it in that niche and that dog struggled a little and yelped and then fell silent and began to breathe painfully, and the sound from his mouth ceased; it went to sleep and sprawled out for a minute; and that dog was quickly taken from the niche and thrown into the water of that lake close to shore where it could not drown; it rested there for a moment, then shook a little, and emerged from the water as healthy as before. Then they set fire to pitch torches with sulphur, and when these torches were burning, they placed them into the niche close to the ground in the deadly vapor, and immediately all went out, just as if a great strong wind had suddenly blown them out, and no trace of fire remained in those torches.

By this mountain lake are stone dwellings that the Neapolitans call baths, in

[46] Even in the seventeenth century Tolstoi is following a well-defined tourist route, in which his visits parallel those of Evelyn a half-century earlier. Here he passes the Lago d'Agnano, the Lake of Serpents. *Diary*, II, 339 and passim.

[47] Tolstoi here describes the famous Grotta del Cane, Dog Grotto, in which carbon dioxide covers the floor to a height of 2 feet; it can stun or kill a dog and will extinguish flames. Whereas Tolstoi describes this as something new to his experience, Evelyn came forewarned: "The first thing we did here, was, the old experiment on a Dog, which we lead from that so mortal Cave commonly nam'd Grotto del Cane or Charons Cave." *Diary*, II, 339. Tolstoi tortured a dog, as did Evelyn, and it was still being done when the Baedeker guidebooks were written in the last century.

which there is a great unending *natural'naia,* or natural warmth,[48] without fire, just as in a bath that would warm many people. Beds are placed in these rooms, and the sick suffering from all kinds of illnesses lie there, even those with the French diseases. They are freed from illnesses /31/, which leave them through sweat because of the *natural'naia* or natural warmth, without any kind of drugs, because in these rooms it is always immeasurably warm, and those lying there sweat very much.[49]

Then I left that place to see other places that were also quite marvelous. First, I arrived at a city called Putsilio (Pozzuoli) 10 It. miles from Naples. In this city, leaving the carriage, I sat in a *filiaga* (It. *felucca*)[50] and went by sea to a place where there is a natural heat in the sea. Approaching one small hill, I left the felucca, and one sailor reached from the sea into the sand of the shore. This sand is always very hot, and the seawater on top of that sand is cool as usual, as it is elsewhere in the sea. A small palace is built on this small hill in which lie many sick people consumed by various illnesses, most in the French way.[51] From this palace there is a narrow passage into the mountain through which a man can pass, and they walk inside bearing candles because it is very dark. Such is the natural heat in that cave that one can scarcely go all the way into it and come out again. This cave is 50 sazhens deep, and a man's breath is so seized that he could live there for four hours only with effort. In this cave, along the walls, they have made places where the sick can stand and sit, but one can only endure it for a short time and then one sweats and must quickly come out. People enter this cave naked. In order to see the sick inside I was compelled to enter that cave, but I returned without going all the way in because I was unable to endure that oppressive heat any longer. During the time that the sick sit in the cave, all of them sing "Santa Maria ora pro nobis," that is, "Holy Mary, pray for us," in their language. They summon the Blessed Mother of God and other saints to their aid with their prayers. Beneath this mountain Nero the Tormentor built in antiquity a stone bath, in which there was hot and cold water from nature, that is, from its essence and not warmed by fire; and these baths are intact, and there is always hot and cold water in them from nature.

Then I went to a place, where, in antiquity, there was a city called Kashtel-di-Baia

[48] The very fact that Tolstoi can put two words in apposition, *natural'naia ili prirodnaia teplota,* suggests that Russian had a perfectly comprehensible way to say "natural heat." In borrowing the Italian, *naturale,* and making a Russian adjective out of it here and below, Tolstoi engages in the linguistic borrowing that is a hallmark of the Petrine era. See the analogous problem of translating the word "attraction" in Boss, *Newton and Russia,* pp. 243–45.

[49] Following precisely the same itinerary, Evelyn wrote, "Neere to this cave are the natural stoves of St. Germain, which are of the nature of Sudatories, in certaine Chambers partition'd with stone for the sick to sweate in. The vapours here are exceeding hot, and of admirable successe, especialy against the Goute, & other cold distempers of the nerves." *Diary,* II, 340.

[50] Tolstoi later corrects this spelling to *feliuga,* felucca.

[51] Tolstoi refers to those who have syphilis.

(Castello di Baia).[52] This city was the realm of Nero the Tormentor, and it was very large, 10 It. miles in circumference. It stood right on the sea, and its fine buildings were of stone, as are those that remain. All of this city /32/ has fallen down, and the place where it stood has grown into a forest, but its ruins can be seen. Here are the palaces and shrines of pagan gods, which were in the city built by that tormentor Nero of damnable memory. Beneath the city is a porto, that is, a harbor for naval vessels, the best in all Spain and Neapolitania. In this place I saw the shrine of the pagan goddess Kaprissoriia (?) carved out of stone in the ground.[53] The shrine has a stone vault and impressed on it are many pagan gods. They were also impressed on chalk or on limestone, but they are indistinguishable because of the many years that have gone by, but it was still most marvelous and wondrous work. The pagan gods are depicted so vividly that I cannot describe them. This shrine was named for the pagan god [*sic*] Venus and was made of plinths, such as are encountered nowhere else. These plinths are an arshin wide and long, and an arshin and a vershok thick, and very strong. This shrine was very large, round, and even now the paintings in many places on the internal walls are quite fine. This shrine was once long but is now all tumbled down, and only a small part still stands, and this shrine was made in the name of the pagan goddess Diana. There were also shrines to other pagan gods, Mercury and others, to whom the damned Nero offered sacrifices, and because of his love of them they are all together in hell. In the place of Nero's city of Castello-di-Baia, which finally was destroyed, a new city was built nearby on the seacoast, and it too is called Castello di Baia.

A stone bridge on many stone columns was built along the sea from the ancient city of Castello di Baia to the city of Pozzuoli,[54] and this bridge was built by Caesar Gaius Galicolus (Caligula) 1658 years ago, and 400 years ago this bridge was destroyed by the sea waves; however, even today several columns rise above the seawater, and vaults between them still have not fallen. The length of this bridge was 3 Italian miles.

There are mountains along the sea from which they throw down earth, and this earth in the sea or in rivers forms a *fondamento,* that is, a foundation under stone

[52] This is the ancient city of Baiae; here Nero killed his mother Agrippina and suppressed the conspiracy of Piso.

[53] I have no satisfactory explanation for this reference. Has Tolstoi heard of the vain and silly Queen Cassiopeia, mother of Andromeda? Here is Evelyn's description of the site: "One of the most delicious places that the Sunn shines on in the World, . . . though as to the stately fabrics there not remaine little save the ruines, whereof the most intire is that of Dianas Temple, & another of the Godesse Venus: This place being heretofore infinitely addicted to Lust and wantonesse." *Diary,* II, 348.

[54] The bay from Baia to Pozzuoli was never spanned by a bridge; the ancient pier juts into the sea from Pozzuoli, and Caligula did build his famous bridge of boats here. Evelyn is more accurate: "13 vast piles of marble onely remaining, a stupendious worke in the bosome of Neptune; To this joynes the Bridg of Caligula." *Diary,* II, 344.

construction, and Neapolitans call this earth "pozzuoliano." This earth becomes as strong as iron or as hard as stone, and this earth is yellowish grey.[55] Close to this place right on the sea is the home of the damned tormentor Nero, a small remainder /33/ of his palace, which was of fine workmanship. In other places the walls have paintings, painted by the muses, and another stone building stands on the seashore. Not far from this building is a stone structure that was built by a Roman senator, Artencius; from there this Artencius called fish from the sea, as many as he needed.[56]

Close by this place, in the earth of the mountain, is the tomb of the mother of Nero the Tormentor. Over the tomb is an ancient stone building.[57] I went toward the water, which is called the Dead Sea. This sea is round, 1,000 sazhens across, separated from the great sea by earth, and the water in this Dead Sea is as salty as the oceans. Below this Dead Sea is a large meadow on which many forests have grown. On this meadow the pagan people cremated dead bodies in antiquity and took the ashes of those cremated bodies to the mountain and placed them in stone tombs that are still visible, having been made of fine craftsmanship with painted interior walls. From these tombs the ancient people took the ashes as holy things to cure the sick. Above these tombs they built stone vaults, and these tombs are 2 sazhens wide and long. Close to these tombs a very large and tall vault is built into the mountain; this vault has 48 great stone columns upon which the vault is built. This vault was built in antiquity by a Roman senator named Liutsio Liulkulo (Lucullus) to hold cold fresh water for the Roman legions to drink. They call this vault the Pisina Marabilia (Piscina Mirabilis) in the Italian language, and in Slavonic, the Water Vault.[58]

Not far from this place is a city called Procheta (Procida) of the Neapolitan kingdom. This place is large and populous, stands on the sea, is made of fine workmanship, and is all of stone.

Then I went by felucca to the city of Pozzuoli and there dined in an inn; and after dinner I went by felucca to Naples, and I had left my coach on the shore in Naples.

[55] The yellow tufa of the region, the result of ancient volcanic activity, is known as *puzzolana* earth, used to make an indestructible cement.

[56] Baia is partially submerged. Here is the story of the fishes, according to Evelyn: "Here were those famous pooles of Lampreys that would come to hand when call'd by name as Martial tells us." *Diary,* II, 348–49.

[57] "The monstrous Murthers of Nero committed on his Mother Agrippina, her Sepulchre yet shew'd us in the rock we enter'd, being cover'd with sundry heads & figures of beasts." Evelyn, *Diary,* II, 349.

[58] The vault generally goes under the name of Lucullus, the subsequent owner of the villa. "Here we walked to those receptacles of water cal'd Piscina mirabilis, being a vault 500 f: long and 22 in breadth, the roofe prop'd up with 4 rankes of Square pillars 12 in a row, the walls are brick, plaster'd over with such a composition as for strength & politure resembles white marble: 'Tis conceivd it was built as a Conservatory for fresh water by Nero, as were also the Centi Camerelli into which we were next led: All these Crypta being now almost sunke into the Earth, shew yet their former amplitude and magnificence." Evelyn, *Diary,* II, 350–51.

Not far from the city of Pozzuoli is an island called Premintoriia de Misino (Promontorio de Miseno).[59] On this island, in antiquity, lived a philosopher-sovereign called Pliniush (Pliny). At the time of the fall of Troy, a Trojan senator named Aeneas, about whom there is a special history, came from Troy to this Pliny on this island. This Pliny burned up /34/ on that mountain across from Naples, which has burned ceaselessly since the creation of the world even to today, and this Pliny did not believe that this mountain really burned but wanted to see the flames coming from the mountain himself and he fell into the mountain and burned up.[60]

Passing that island, I arrived at an island through which a passage has been made, through which water runs. I went through this passage in my felucca, and the length of the passage is more than 100 sazhens, and the width 6 sazhens. Along the sides of that passage are windows for light. This passage is cut through the stone island, and in some places over the passage there is soft earth, and in those places vaults are made of brick. This passage has been made miraculously and astonishingly, and there is always a cool wind in it. There Neapolitan men and their wives and children come in small boats to cool off when it is very hot.

Beyond this place is an island called Nisita (Nisida), on which there is a Neapolitan *kantomatsiia* (Campo Marzio).[61] Built on this island are small rooms for those in the Campo Marzio, and such is a Campo Marzio: when people come to Naples from Levanto, that is, from the East, they are set on this island and not allowed to go anywhere for 6 weeks, and no one visits them, because in the Levanto, that is, in the East, there is often a pestilent infection, from which the Neapolitans guard their state.

Then we arrived at Naples and went to the home of a Neapolitan senator that is built right on the seashore. In this home are very many fine cheerful rooms with marvelous decorations. Among them, in the center, was one eight-sided room that

[59] Evelyn's reference shows a greater awareness of the history of the place: "We proceeded towards the promontory of Misenus renouin'd for the Sepulchre of Æneas's Trumpeter." *Diary,* II, 350.

[60] Earlier in his account, Evelyn had told the same story: Vesuvius is "one of the most stupendious curiosities in nature, & which made the learned & inquisitive Pliny adventure his life, to detect the causes, & to loose it in too desperat an approch." *Diary,* II, 335.

If one recalls Burckhard's notion, in *Civilization of the Renaissance in Italy,* of the revival of antiquity and the general Latinization of culture, one can understand Tolstoi's problem. For him antiquity means the time when Christians were persecuted. Travel can reveal to him the artistic and architectural accomplishment of Rome, but his lack of education in any post-1500 Western sense prevents him from understanding the rhetoric, the poetry, and the thought of Rome revived for centuries in the West. For Evelyn, Rome is alive and present; for Tolstoi it is dead stones.

[61] Tolstoi adopts the etymologically incorrect form *kantomatsiia* throughout the rest of the Diary. In ancient Rome the Campo Marzio was the site of ritual purification, hence the meaning Tolstoi gives. Today, Campo Marzio or Campo de Marte means a parade ground or drill field.

was finely furnished with miraculous Italian paintings. A fine walkway is built from these rooms to the sea, and it is planted with grapes that have grown up to form a roof. From this home I went to Naples, where I saw a very large ancient home on the coast. They told me that this was the home of an ancient Neapolitan king, and now the Neapolitan viceroy has taken it for himself; it had collapsed but now it is newly rebuilt.[62] The architecture of this home is old but fine. Then I went to my inn, where I stayed the night.

July 2. Early in the morning the Neapolitan nobleman, the brother of the governor of Bari, came to me and /35/ took me along in a carriage to the *tribunal* (It. *tribunale*),[63] that is, to the *prikazy* of the Neapolitan kingdom. This tribunale is a large building with many rooms and is five stories high. The rooms are large. Naples has 32 offices, in which there are many judges and clerks; each office has 12 officials. An uncountable number of people come to these offices, and it is very crowded just as in the Moscow *prikazy;* and the judges' and the clerks' tables are laid out just as in the Muscovite *prikazy,* and guards stand at each door, like in Moscow. When I came to this tribunale, more than 100 fine carriages stood there, in which both judges and petitioners had come, since they had business there.

Then I came to a room where 12 judges sit to conduct important state business. One of these judges represents the Spanish king, and he is called the *kapo* (It. *capo*), that is, the head over all others. When I entered this room, this chief judge and all the judges stood up and bowed to me, greeted me with great courtesy, and showed me all the things a foreigner would hope to see. They escorted me out with honor and sent a man along to guide me, and he walked from this room ahead of me, clearing the way through all the people. He courteously led me to the upper rooms, where I saw the ancient books and papers of the Neapolitan state in bookcases; and there were a great many old papers. From the upper rooms we descended to the lower rooms, where the Neapolitan judges serve when two people are judged before the judges: they speak with great courtesy, and do not shout, and the clerks write down their words just as in Moscow.

From this tribunale I went to a monastery, in which friars called Reguliary (It. *regolare*) live.[64] These friars are all of the honorable sort of people; they do not accept those of common people into this monastery. I was taken into this monastery by a friar of honorable birth, a relative of the Roman pope, and he led me to the church. This church was very finely made of plaster and of various marbles, and it was gilded inside in many places. This church was built in the name of the holy apostles. I walked from the church around the monastery and its upper rooms, from

[62] This is probably the palace of the Orsini, dukes of Gravina; see Evelyn, *Diary,* II, 30.

[63] This is probably the Renaissance Palazzo Cuomo.

[64] Regular, in ecclesiastical usage, means belonging to an order, as opposed to the secular or parish clergy. Judging from other comments, this may be the Carthusian monastery.

which the whole city of Naples is visible, and I looked at the fine gardens of this monastery. /36/

From this monastery I went to a convent, where there are 680 nuns, all of them of good birth. This convent also has a marvelously decorated church; among the many furnishings are finely sewn curtains. In this monastery the bodies of the deceased Neapolitan kings are interred.[65] In this church are very large organs of fine tone, which they played while I was there.

From this monastery I went to a monastery in which friars called the Olivetano, who wear a white habit, live. The church in this monastery is quite fine, marvelously decorated, and I saw it from the vestibule. There is a glass tomb in which the body of Our Lord Jesus Christ of most miraculous workmanship rests, and the tomb is done of stone and is colored.[66] At the head of Christ's body is the sitting image of the Blessed Virgin Mary, and on the side the standing image of Mary Magdalene. Beneath her is the likeness of the queen of Naples, who built this monastery; on the other side is the standing image of St. Solomii (Solomon), and alongside is the image of John the Theologian, also standing. At the foot of the body of Christ are two Roman philosophers on their knees. All of these images are of the most wonderful workmanship; one cannot tell that they are not alive. Then I saw a room in this monastery in which they hold comedies, and it is furnished with *prospettivi,* as is customary in comedies. Then I looked at the rooms in which the friars live, and among them I saw one in which they had placed many trees with green leaves, and it was filled with many white and green oaks. They bring children to play in this room of oaks, and one friar is kept there to amuse them.

This monastery is very large, and beneath it are large wine shops in which many barrels filled with various wines always stand. The friars of this monastery eat meat three days a week, and on four they eat fish, that is, on Sunday, Tuesday, and Thursday they eat meat, and on Monday, Wednesday, Friday, and Saturday they eat fish; and when they eat meat they dine and sup in the room where they hold the comedies; and when they eat fish, they dine in their own rooms. In this monastery I saw in a chapel the image of Nativity of Christ carved of alabaster,[67] two arshins in height and width, and it is so unique that one /37/ seldom encounters the likes of it in the whole world; to describe it in detail is impossible, and the mind of man cannot comprehend such work. From this monastery I went to my inn, the dinner hour having already arrived.

This same day after dinner the same Neapolitan nobleman, the brother of the governor of Bari, sent his carriage for me and invited me to come in it to his home. At

[65]This is Santa Chiara, the Pantheon of Naples.

[66]This is the Chapel of the Holy Sepulcher in Monte Oliveto, with the seven life-size figures by Guido Mazzoni, 1489–92; now called Santa Anna dei Lombardi, it was erected by the Olivetano in 1411.

[67]In the Cappella Piccolmini, this is the Nativity altar by Antonio Rossellino of Florence (c. 1475).

his request I went to his home in that carriage, and he greeted me affectionately, as is the Spanish custom. Then we left his home together to see the Neapolitan galleys, and I saw 8 very large galleys, which stood in port close to the viceroy's court, and each had 60 oars, some more, some less. These galleys are finely crafted, their carvings gilded and painted with colors. From these galleys I boarded one galley where the *comito* (It. *comite*)[68] received me honorably. For my arrival he ordered the *galeottos*, that is, the laborers, to wear colored caftans. There are 450 on this galley, all in blue cloth caftans, and every galley slave on this galley is confined by an iron chain on his leg. These galeottas, or laborers, can never leave this galley.

To honor me the comite ordered them to play *shiposhakh* (It. *schioppo*, guns), and the Turks and Spaniards were ordered to blow trumpets. Such is the customary music of the Spanish galleys; and, having seen the galley and thanked the comite, I went to the inn where I was staying, it already being nighttime.

July 3. I hired a carriage and went to a church for music. I was in a church at a Franciscan monastery; it is well built, decorated with various slates with well-painted walls, and the whole interior is gilded. Then I went back to the inn to dine.

This same day I went in the carriage to the seacoast and hired a felucca in which I went along the seacoast to observe the customary pleasures of the Neapolitans, the manner in which Neapolitans amuse themselves in the four months of June, July, August, and September. During these four months, two days each week, on Sunday and Friday, the viceroy of Naples goes out in a fine felucca, which is made of fine, carved, all gilded craftsmanship. Atop this felucca are 3 marvelous lanterns. In this felucca four Neapolitan counts sit together with the viceroy. In front of this felucca is another of the viceroy's feluccas, also finely crafted /38/ and gilded, and the mariners in these feluccas are attired in fine silk caftans. There is no one in the first felucca except the mariners; it goes only to honor the viceroy and they place *bandieri*, that is, flags, beneath his coat of arms in the felucca in which he himself sits; and in front there is yet a third felucca, in which the viceroy's trumpeteers go to play. On the left side of the viceroy is another felucca, in which music is played and sung to entertain the viceroy; on both sides of the viceroy are two more feluccas, in which sit the *ofitseri* (It. *officiale*),[69] that is, the leaders of the infantry for guarding, that is, for defense. Behind the viceroy come many feluccas, in which ride counts, dukes, marquises, and nobles or gentry. In a large number of feluccas also ride all honorable people and the *markanty* (It. *mercante*) ride, that is, overseas merchants, and they amuse themselves, and ride and drink and make merry in their feluccas.

At the same time, six great galleys of the viceroy departed, and they were finely

[68] In modern Italian, *comito*, boatswain; this is the *comite*, in historical usage, the companion of the emperor or governor, often loosely translated as "Count."

[69] In modern Italian, *officiare* or *ufficiare*, to officiate.

decorated. In front came the galley of the general, covered with red silks and cloths; the bandieri, that is, the flags of this galley, were all red. On the stern of this galley are three fine lanterns, and on the bow mast, which is called the *trinketo* (It. *trinchetto*), is another lantern. Behind this galley are four more, also covered with red cloth; on the stern and on the foremast of each galley is a lantern, and the bandieri or flags on these galleys are all white. At the end comes a galley that also has lanterns on the stern and on the foremast. And, coming close to the shore where the viceroy was going, all these galleys stopped on the sea, and from the general's galley they played music on flutes and on trumpets. When the viceroy came opposite these galleys, they fired cannon to honor him, first from the general's galley and then from the others.

The wife of the viceroy came to the shore in a fine carriage, and behind her, in other carriages, came her daughters; they went to their courtyard, which is built on the seacoast, and there they sat on the porch. Below her sat the wives of the Neapolitan principes, three or four old women, and around her stood her maids and relations of the male sex, all finely attired. Likewise in other homes along the shore, Neapolitan wives and maiden daughters sit finely attired on porches and in windows. Along the shore stand many marvelous carriages in which the honorable Neapolitans and their wives and maiden daughters sit in fine dress, and they make merry, eating sweets and drinking fine lemonades. The viceroy /39/ and the principes and all the people passed beneath that shore in feluccas, and when the viceroy came opposite his wife he congratulated and greeted her as well as the other honorable wives and daughters. All the honorable people and the merchants did likewise as they approached the viceroy's wife and the wives and daughters of other honorable men; they greeted them and congratulated them and bowed to them with every courtesy. All the forestiere, that is, all the visiting foreigners, did the same; I also did my duty in this way. And thus do they walk all day, even until night. When the viceroy's wife came to her court, they fired cannon from all those galleys to honor her, just as they had fired to honor the viceroy.

When night fell, the viceroy and all who walked along the shore went to their homes in Naples, and the galleys again fired from cannon, entered the Neapolitan port, and went to their usual places. They fired many rockets from the general's galley, and when the galleys went out from Naples to this merriment, all had been covered with linen, as is their custom. On the general's galley the linen roof was striped. When they returned to the place where they stay, they took the roofs off the galleys and stood roofless, and the galeottos, that is, the galley slaves or rowers, on all the galleys were uncovered. When night fell, they took the bandieri and *f'iamoli* (It. *fiamma*, pennant) from all the galleys and lit the lanterns on the stern and foremast. Likewise they lit the lanterns on the viceroy's felucca as they did on all the other feluccas, because on all the feluccas they have fine lanterns on the stern. And all went home with these lamps. I, in my felucca, approached the shore, and having left it I went in the carriage to my inn.

July 4. I went in a fine carriage to see the home of the viceroy.[70] His home is finely built, is large and has very many rooms, and is 5 stories in height. At the viceroy's gates stand soldiers on guard, and their officers are with them. Arriving at the porch of the viceroy's home, we left the carriage and entered the palace. The viceroy's porches are well made, immeasurably wide and well proportioned; the rooms are large, fine, and decorated with fine Italian paintings; others are hung with silks. There are also fine tables and chairs in the rooms. The windows of the palace are curtained with white taffeta, and great mirrors are placed on the walls over tables in the Spanish manner. Also in these rooms stand fine cupboards /40/ and other furnishings. From the viceroy's palace I went to his courtyard for horses, where I saw 125 horses in the stables, among them many large, fine ones. The furnishings of these stables are really fine. In other rooms I saw a multitude of harnesses and fine velvet tandems, with gold and silver mounts of the most marvelous work. Here, too, I saw 11 fine and very rich carriages, among them two very large and glorious Roman-made carriages of such glorious and marvelous craftsmanship that it is difficult to adequately describe the richness of their workmanship. The price of these two carriages is 10,000 scudos, and they give 2 scudos for every golden chervonets. I also saw other carriages and many barouches there.[71]

Then I went from the viceroy's court to a school where they train horses.[72] The horses in this school are large, fine, and identical; and in the riding square where they train horses I saw their training, and among them I saw a dark-gray horse [trained in] fine school sciences. Then at dinner time I went to my inn, where I stayed. The master of this inn, named Martino, a very rich and good man, was very gracious and helpful to me. This same day I went to a hospital in which I saw 400 sick people lying in beds, and the bedding under them was fine. This hospital is very large and has many rooms; among them is built a kaplica, that is, a church of the Roman faith, in which they say the Liturgy all day for the sick. Under the rooms are built many cellars, and many of the sick lie in cellars because a doctor has prescribed a cool place. The pharmacy in this hospital is large, and in it are enough doctors, pharmacists, druggists, and physicians, all in readiness. A principe, that is, a Spanish prince, and two Neapolitan cavaliers are in charge of this hospital. In this hospital are 200 naturally insane men who live in special rooms and are given food and drink and enough clothing. The inhabitants of Naples say this: these naturally insane men were created by God's will, and so that they are not hungry or in need or abused by others, people are placed in charge of them to compel them to work and to see that they do not fight among themselves. These insane men work in

[70] Tolstoi here revisits the Palazzo Reale.

[71] Evelyn was succinct: "The streetes are full of Gallants, in their Coaches, on horseback, & sedans." *Diary,* II, 353.

[72] "Onely this morning at the Vice-roys Cavalerizzo, I saw the noblest horses that I had ever beheld, one of his sonns riding the Menage with that addresse & dexterity, as I had never seene any thing approch it." Evelyn, *Diary,* II, 330.

the hospital; they carry water from the well, carry firewood and food to the kitchen, as well as the other small necessities they can fetch. And among these insane are some who are mad, /41/ not from nature but from an illness, and these have special rooms and are constrained. The doctors give them drugs, and they are not compelled to work.

While I was at the hospital all the sick and insane were fed; their food was placed in a special room in kettles. Over this food 10 Roman priests sang an *oratsione* (It. *orazione*), that is, a prayer to God for the sick. They distribute this food in small pewter dishes, and they place 6 of these dishes on a wooden tray and carry it to the sick; and the honorable people of Naples carry this food to the sick, and those who serve the sick are those who wish to save their souls. The workers in this hospital are organized so that they receive little for their service: instead the honorable people serve the sick for the sake of Christ. Many honorable people come here, cover themselves with aprons, and distribute food to the sick.

In this same hospital live very young male and female orphans, and there are also insane among these children. These little orphans are cared for in this hospital; they are given food and drink, and clothing and bedding, and all of their needs are well attended.

There are enough workers and directors in this hospital to serve all its needs. And when someone donates food for the sick, a doctor comes and looks at the food, and writes down which of the sick ate it, and how much of each food was eaten, and what food was given during the day or in the evening—all this the doctor oversees with diligence. And for the needs of this hospital they annually collect an *entrate,* that is, an income, of 150,000 scudos from shops, houses, and land. This hospital has been endowed with these shops, houses, and lands by the Neapolitan viceroy, and by all the Neapolitans by the will of the Spanish king.

This hospital has fine gardens for herbs and roots for the pharmacy, and also for the amusement and exercise of the sick, who as they begin to recover from illness can take little walks in the gardens.[73] Those who die of illness in the hospital are buried at the hospital's expense. And all the sick in this hospital are treated and fed, and cared for without payment; all is done for the sake of Christ. In all there are 6 hospitals in Naples, but the others are smaller and have less income than this one.

Then I went to the Neapolitan academy.[74] This academy was built by the *pub-*

[73] In early-modern times, hospital gardens were producing both home-grown spices to flavor food more cheaply than expensive imports from the East, and herbs to soothe the pain of some poor devil lying sick on his back in the infirmary. Salerno, south of the Gulf of Naples, was the thirteenth-century source of this movement to produce at home. These *flora* and the attempt to grow them in Europe are the background for the production of herbals, the books that constitute "Medieval Europe's most original contribution to the growth of medicine." See the account by Goldstein, *Dawn of Modern Science,* pp. 148ff.

[74] Tolstoi visited Naples in the midst of an intellectual awakening centered in the Academy of the Investiganti, revived in 1683, and in the numerous bookstores along the Via di San Biagio dei Librai, one of them belonging to the father of Giambattista Vico. In 1690 the

lichnii (Pol. *publiczny;* It. *pubblico*), that is, the royal treasury, and is very large; /42/ there are 120 large lower and upper rooms; these rooms are built five stories high. In this academy they study to philosophy and to theology and the other higher sciences and anatomy. In this academy there are 4,000 students and more, all who study gratis, whoever comes here, and all the masters are paid by the king. In this academy is a special room for disputes and for the certification of students: whoever completes the sciences so testifies by disputation in this room. This room is semicircular, like a church altar. At the front wall opposite the door is a high place, like a king's place; around it, on both sides, are seats four tiers high, and at the time of disputes the masters, all sorts of learned people, and students sit in these places for that dispute.

Close to this room is a room where they practice anatomy; this room is large and built as is customary for anatomy.

In this academy are 400 doctors and 2,000 pharmacists and druggists and physicians. They live without salary at their own expense, but make their living by conducting their science among the Neapolitan viceroy and the princes, and counts and dukes, and marquises, and nobles, and merchants, and with all the Neapolitan inhabitants.

Then I went to walk on the seacoast, where they were building several amusements for their holiday of July 21 by the Roman calendar. Between the many fountains along the shore they erected columns and covered them with panels, and at festival time these structures are all draped and covered with silks and other decorations, and with flowers and fruits. Along this place will be a procession, at which they will have fine music, vocal and instrumental, and during the festival various grape wines, red and white, will flow from the fountains instead of water, and the needy will take this wine, whoever wants it, without returning it. I did not stay in Naples for this festival because I was in a hurry to go to the island of Malta, and thus did not miss the time at which I had to depart for Malta.

Then I went to the home of a Neapolitan prince, who received me affectionately and treated me to various sherbets. I sat at this prince's home until night with some Neapolitan cavaliers; and when I left this prince, he /43/ conducted me to the porch, and yet other cavaliers conducted me to the carriage with large candles made of white wax. From this prince's house I returned to the inn where I was staying.

July 5. After dinner a Neapolitan cavalier sent his carriage for me and invited me to the home of a Neapolitan nobleman to see an execution—how one per-

---

Academy of Infuriati was revived, and reorganized as the Academy of Uniti in 1692; in 1698 the Academy Medinaceli was founded, but throughout the 1690s the Inquisition was active, with Vico's friends its victims in 1692–93. Vico himself studied with the Neapolitan Jesuits in the 1680s. See the introduction to Vico, *Autobiography,* pp. 31–36, and the first section of the autobiography itself. Tolstoi provides further comments on academic life on July 6, below.

son would be put to death; and in the carriage I arrived at the home close to the *pliatsa,* which is the piazza of the viceroy's home. On this piazza, at some distance from the viceroy's court, a wheel was placed upon a log, two sazhens high or a little higher, and from all sides this wheel was propped up with logs, so that it stood firmly, and they put up a small ladder from each side. On the piazza, at the wheel, a multitude of people gathered to watch the execution, and two hours before nightfall 30 soldiers arrived, and placed themselves around that wheel so that the people were not clustered close to it. Then a man, carrying in his hands a letter and a trumpet arrived. And having blown the trumpet he read the letter about the crime that had been committed and about the matter for which a man would be executed. From the place where the evil-doer sat, and over to the wheel itself, this man trumpeted and read the letter, so that all would know why this evil-doer was being executed.

Behind this man walked several soldiers, and with them 3 leaders, captains from the *tribunale,* that is, from the office in which they judge capital crimes. Behind these captains came a man in white dress with a white hood on his head. His face was all concealed, but the hood was slit across the eyes so he could see, and he carried aloft a large cross on which the image of the body of Christ was carved. Behind him, also in white attire and hoods, were 20 Neapolitan inhabitants of the most honorable sort of people, and they were all covered so that no one could recognize them. Behind them came the man who was condemned to death, wearing a white shirt and trousers, and on his feet were stockings and shoes. After him came the executioner, girded with a small cord that he held, and the condemned man carried a small cross in his hands, on which was depicted the Crucifixion of Christ. On either side of the condemned man walked a priest of the Roman faith in the same white attire and in hoods, and one of these priests was his spiritual father. Walking with him, these priests talked with him constantly, in order that he might confess his sins and be in the hope of salvation and not fall into despair. These priests kept the wheel that was prepared for his torture hidden from him, so that he would not see it and faint.

When they /44/ brought him to the wheel, and to the ladder by which the condemned get to the wheel, the condemned man fell on his knees, and his cleric bent over him and whispered into his ear for a quarter of an hour, so he would not despair of the mercy of God. Then his cleric raised him up, kissed his head, and left him; and the executioner took him and led him up the ladder to the wheel and went after him; another man also supported the condemned man and helped him up the ladder, so that the condemned man in his fear would have the strength to go up the ladder to the wheel. When they led him to the wheel and placed him backwards upon it, they turned his head to the left side with his right temple upwards; they bound his eyes with a kerchief, and they bound his hands and feet tightly to the wheel, and also they bound his head to the wheel; and up the other of the two ladders from the opposite side climbed the confessor of the condemned man; he held a cross in his hand. When the executioner bound the condemned man to the wheel, this cleric sat on the wheel over him with the cross and unceasingly strengthened him with words, so that he was not frightened of death, and so that he might die in hope and not in despair. When the executioner covered his eyes with the kerchief, the cleric, protected by his cross, descended from the wheel. Then the executioner took a large iron hammer and for a long time he waved the hammer with both hands over the head of the condemned man, and he struck the condemned man on the right temple and he broke his head even to the brain, and again he struck strongly with the hammer to his forehead, and again he broke his head, from which a great quantity of blood poured forth. Then he struck with the hammer upon his breast and then upon his private parts, and then upon his knees, and once again on his head and thus with the hammer did he beat him to death. And taking his stockings and shoes from him, the executioner descended from the wheel, and during the time that the executioner bound the condemned man and beat him, the confessor of the condemned man and all those who were in white attire and hoods knelt around the wheel on the ground and prayed for the soul of the condemned man, that God might forgive him his sins.[75]

This condemned man was by birth a Roman, who served a captain in Naples as a menial, and on July 3 in the viceroy's palace he quarreled with a viceroyal servant. In the viceroy's palace he beat this servant to death, and, having been caught on July 5, he was executed on the evening of July 6. His body, taken down from the wheel, was cut into quarters /45/ and strewn on a field a mile or so from Naples, so that all would be frightened to kill anybody in the viceroy's palace.

Then I left the nobleman's home and went to my inn in the last hour of day.

July 6. In the morning I hired a carriage and went to a Jesuit monastery. In this monastery the inside of the large church is all decorated with fine carved alabaster. Then I went to the room where the Jesuits dine. This large room is well decorated with carpenter's work in walnut wood, with many tables covered with fine clean tablecloths, and the bread placed for them to eat was fine, whole-grained and very white. Then I left this room to see a fine fountain, which is done of flint and of seashells of fine workmanship. Then I went to a pharmacy where 5 rooms are furnished with many very fine pharmaceutical drugs. Then I went to a small church, which was built of marvelous craftsmanship in the midst of the monks' cells; the walls and vaults in this church and the altar are done of crystal in fine gilded fretwork. In this church three continuously burning lamps are set in the wall and they are set in large, round crystals, and the flame of the lamps is seen through the crystals, and the church is lighted from them, and there is no soot in the church from these lamps. From this church I went to the rooms where the Jesuits sew and wash clothes. This room is large and well furnished with cupboards. In these rooms there is a small church, well decorated. In this church they showed me many holy relics,

[75] In an essay, "On Crime and Punishment," pp. 23–27, I have argued that Tolstoi's careful notes on this occasion, and above, when he described Christian charity at the hospital—have a general significance for the idea of "Westernization" in Russia.

among which I saw a bone from the head of a certain martyr. In this bone was a large iron nail, by which this martyr was killed at the time of his suffering for Christ, and so it remains in this church. From this church I went to a library, where I saw many books in three rooms, and among them they showed me a large book—a history of Muscovy printed in the Latin language. On the pages of this book the cities of Moscow, the Kremlin, and the Kitai- and the Belyi-gorod are imprinted, and the towers and rivers and streets are indicated in the Slavonic language in Slavonic letters. The whole Muscovite state is described in this book.[76] I also saw two large globes in this library, one celestial and the other earthly. From this library I went to the new library, which is not yet finished. This hall is very large; its interior walls are all done of carpenter's work in walnut, done in cabinets in which they will place the books. Leaving /46/ this hall, I saw three circles in the rooms: one circle announces the hours of day and night, another the days of the month, and a third circle shows the declination of the sun; and the instruments by which these circles move are worked by ropes from the other side of this monastery, far away from the striking clock. Then I saw the rooms in which they hold disputes, and also many schools in which students study. In this monastery there are 150 students and more. Then I went to a cellar where there is wine; there I saw three large cellars, in which there are many barrels filled with various fine wines. There are more than 2,000 of these barrels of wine. Then I left this monastery; the Jesuits escorted me to the carriage. The revenues of this monastery are 18,000 scudos per annum.

I arrived at the Carmelite monastery,[77] in which there is a miracle-working icon of the Blessed Mother of God and the image of the Crucifixion of Christ, whose head was turned aside by a cannon ball, about which I have written earlier in this book.

In this monastery, on this July 6, there is a festival by the Roman calendar and the miracle-working icon of the Mother of God was uncovered, and I was able to see it. In this church I heard vocal and instrumental music; and then at suppertime I went back to my inn.

The custom in Naples for festivals is like that in Moscow. At the church where they celebrate, trading people set up shops and sell sugars, all kinds of confections, fruits, lemonades, and sherbets.

This same day after dinner Neapolitan noblemen came to my inn and requested that I go with them in their carriage to see the various sciences, which are studied by the children of Neapolitan honorable persons, and I went with them to a court that is maintained by the Jesuits. This court is long but not wide, and has many rooms in it; and it is well built, four stories high. In this court there are always some 100 stu-

[76] This is almost certainly a copy of the enormously popular von Herberstein, *Rerum Moscoviticarum Comentarii*, with some ten Latin editions to 1600 as well as several German translations. He was in Muscovy in 1517 and 1526. See Baron, "European Images of Muscovy," pp. 17–22.

[77] Tolstoi is returning to Santa Marie del Carmine. The festival La Bruna, one of numerous such fetes in Naples, is celebrated July 16–17.

dents, at times a few more or less of these children of honorable inhabitants of Naples, and they never accept any non-nobles. In this court they first study how to read and write, and Latin, and [then] various sciences. There they learn to fight with swords in the Spanish manner and without stilettos, here they also learn to play at bandieri, that is, with flags; here /47/ too they learn to dance various dances, to ride on horses, and here they also learn to gallop on horses without using stirrups, and to do fine tricks. The students study all these sciences every day except Sunday and holidays. And when someone gives his son to this court to study the sciences, he must pay the Jesuits who maintain this court 9 scudos per month. For this sum the student will get food and drink, such as is fitting for honorably born people, and his bed will be fine, and he will study all of the above-mentioned sciences for this price. The students in this home live in various rooms; those who are age 10 and younger live in the lower rooms; those aged 13 or 14 live above them in special rooms; and those to the age of 20 are also in special rooms. And thus the students are divided into 6 groups.

When I entered the room in which they learn to fight with swords, to play with flags, to dance, and to gallop on horses, the teacher had his students fight with swords for me here, and also to play with flags, dance various dances, and gallop on a horse that stands in this hall and is built of wood; and the saddle on it is similar to a German saddle. This horse is of the size of a large German horse. And these students surprised me very much by the way young children aged 10 or 12 were fighting with swords, playing with flags, and dancing; they are very skilled in these sciences, and it was even more astonishing how in this hall four fine youths of honorable fathers galloped on that wooden horse, and did marvelous tricks with such ease that it is impossible to describe it in detail. Then I went to those rooms in this building in which the students live; in these rooms each person has his own bedstead and bedding, all covered with green fabric, and each bed has its own curtain, also of green. In these rooms long tables are placed, at which the students play with balls for amusement. Then I went to the room where these students eat. In that room are many tables on which are placed fine white tablecloths and plates, and knives and forks and spoons—all very clean, and the towels are also always white. And then I went from this room to the courtyard, and there those students who had concluded their *alektsi* (It. *lezioni,* lessons) for the day played with large balls in the Italian fashion. On my departure the Jesuits and students conducted me from this courtyard with respect and affection.[78] /48/

[78] One of the first cracks in the monolith of Renaissance Latin-Classical education was the movement in the last quarter of the seventeenth century to provide an alternative education for young nobles. No longer were they to sit on the same school benches and memorize the same subjects as sons of clerics and merchants. In England the educational writings of John Locke are part of this movement. On the continent such new schools were often called knightly or *Ritter-Akademien*. The new curriculum can be deduced from Tolstoi's comments: it included not only the traditional Latin, but also martial arts and social graces; eventually it

Then I rode to the seacoast where customarily the Neapolitans spend all day riding in carriages with their wives and daughters. In this place there is a Carmelite monastery, in which on the 6th of July, by the Roman calendar, there is a festival. Here I met with the Neapolitan viceroy as he rode along the shore in a carriage; opposite him in the carriage sits his captain, a Roman nobleman; behind the carriage walk his people, attired in colored satin caftans in the Spanish fashion. And I bowed to him as he sat in his carriage, and he honored me with a bow. Behind him his servants rode in a carriage, four of them to each carriage.

Along the seacoast, across from the Carmelite monastery in which they were celebrating a festival, they had prepared a fireworks display of rockets, which I was able to see. I came to the court of a Neapolitan senator, who is called the *capo-di-tribunale,* that is, the chief justice. And this senator sits in the tribunale in the stead of the Spanish king. From this court I watched as they ignited the fireworks; and there were many climbing rockets, and also many rockets attached to boards, which shot off like infantry fire. The other tricks were also fine. Then I left that house from which I had watched, and went to the inn where I was staying.

July 7. After dinner a Maltese cavalier and a Neapolitan marquis came to me and took me for a ride in their carriage, and I went with them to the home of a great Neapolitan duke who is a judge in Naples. His great home is built on the seashore in a beautiful palace; the palace is being newly built and is as yet uncompleted, but it will have many spacious rooms. The decor in these rooms is really fine, with fine Italian paintings and great mirrors, around which are painted flowers and fruits of the most glorious artistic work, and there are also marvelous decorations in other rooms. This duke has children, three small sons—the first 12, the second 8, and the third 4 years old. These three sons played on cymbals by reading the notes to entertain me, and they danced well in the French manner and most marvelously, and even the four-year-old sang by the notes and danced in the French manner. Then I went to the garden in which there are many fine fruit trees and flowers, and this garden is well constructed. In this garden are many glorious fountains, done of the most miraculous work, from which flows clean water most /49/ uniformly. From this garden I went to the inn where I was staying. This day our Muscovite princes Mikhail and Andrei Khilkov hired a carriage and left Naples for Venice; but I stayed in Naples because I wanted to go to the island of Malta.

The city of Naples is under the power of the Spanish king and stands on a level place on the sea, close by one high mountain on which the fine Neapolitan stone

---

also added mathematics and modern history and politics, and thus it was important for pioneering the "new subjects" of schools for other classes in the eighteenth century.

One can trace their beginnings in the Western Mediterranean world in the early chapters of Artz, *Development of Technical Education.* I have outlined their introduction into Russia in Tolstoi's lifetime in "Technical Training in Russia," pp. 325–45.

fortress is built.[79] Around the mountain all of the homes and gardens of the Neapolitan inhabitants are fine. The whole city of Naples is of stone, built of fine workmanship, with passage gates built of fine proportions, and all the homes in Naples are of stone construction, and there are none of wood. The palaces of the Neapolitan inhabitants are especially fashionable, not as in Italy; elsewhere many of them resemble Muscovite palace construction. The furnishings in the palaces are fine, adorned with velvet and other such materials, and most love to decorate with fine paintings and with great mirrors, and they place tables against the walls and hang mirrors over them. For entertainment they keep in their homes cymbals and other musical instruments, except organs; they keep organs in churches but not in homes. They place fine cabinets of Neapolitan work in their rooms, and in them they place for decoration fine things made of various materials and of glass.

In Naples lives a viceroy, that is, a subject-king under the power of the Spanish king, and the Spanish king in Madrid sends this viceroy to Naples for 6 years. If a viceroy is useful to the inhabitants of Naples, he may stay in Naples more than 6 years at the request of the Neapolitans; he may not be of use to the Neapolitan inhabitants, but will not stay less than 6 years in Naples. And they send very honorable people of the highest birth to Naples as viceroy. He whom the Spanish king intends to send to Naples as viceroy must first go from the Spanish king in Madrid to the pope in Rome as ambassador, and live with the pope in Rome 2 years without assistance, at his own expense, and then he may go to Naples as viceroy. This Neapolitan viceroy receives great respect from the Neapolitans, who have him as their king and serve him in all things, and his income is 300,000 scudos a year. The Neapolitan viceroy sends whomever he pleases as governor to those cities that belong to the province of Naples, such as Bari, and Barletta, and Manfredonia, and others. /50/

The comrade of the viceroy in Naples is the general sent from the Spanish king in Madrid to command the land and naval troops, and this general lives in Naples. They have built him a fine home with many fine rooms, and a guard always stands at the general's courtyard, that is, a captain with soldiers; however, this general grants the viceroy great respect, but does not really regard him as his master; and also this general occupies a place in the meetings of the Neapolitan dukes, the elders of the honorable people; but the viceroy is himself the head of everything.

There are 500 soldiers in Naples. These soldiers stand guard at the viceroy's court, also at the general's court, and at other places where they should be, and they walk throughout Naples by day and night to see that there are no fights or murders, nor any kind of stealing anywhere.

In Naples the viceroy and all honorable people wear whatever fashion they choose, but most love the French style; but the old Spanish fashion is worn by the

[79] This is the Castel Sant'Elmo, begun in the fifteenth century by Robert of Anjou, the fortification high on the hillside over Naples. Tolstoi here begins his general description of the city.

mercante, that is, the merchants, and other base people and the servants of the senators and noblemen.

Spanish [male] fashion is peculiar: all black and very short, with very tight trousers, with open sleeves and over all a black cloak. The women and girls of Naples wear French attire, and on their heads is also French attire; but some walk with uncovered heads in the Spanish fashion.

The Neapolitan males are warm and receptive to forestiere, that is, to foreigners, but the female sex and the girls have modest morals and are secluded, as is the Muscovite custom.[80]

Honorable people in Naples, including their wives and daughters, ride in carriages and do not go by foot; among the Neapolitans it is dishonorable to walk. And the males in Naples do not ride on horseback, neither the old nor the young—all ride in carriages and coaches, and there are a great quantity of coaches and carriages in Naples.

The Neapolitan inhabitants often assemble together and live very lovingly, and when they dine at home they treat each other with sherbets and lemonades, and they drink a little grape wine, but no vodka at all, nor do they smoke tobacco, but snuff never leaves the hand of any Neapolitan and a great many of them use it—men, women, and girls.

Drunkenness and the sin of fornication in Naples fall under great shame and under fear, and the Neapolitans are not only loathe to talk about these things, but also to do them. /51/

In Naples proper there are 160 fine monasteries of various orders, and counting those beyond the city, some 300. There are more than 400 parish churches in Naples which are very finely decorated and immeasurably rich.

Of people in Naples, they say, there are some 600,000, including servants and tradesmen of all ranks.

There are few good horses in Naples, since most people go about by carriage or coach with mules, but all workers do their work on horses. There are many shops and stores in Naples, with enough of all kinds of wares, and there are many foodstuffs—meat, fish, and all kinds of poultry; but the fish are all from the sea, and there are no river fish; also in Naples are all kinds of fine fruits, very cheap, and the lemons in Naples are very large, of such size as nowhere else in all Italy, and very cheap.

In Naples are many fine gardens with fruit trees and flowers, in which there are many fine fountains with clean water. Along the streets and the homes are a multitude of fountains in Naples, and they are made of fine workmanship altogether. The streets and lanes in Naples are wide, all paved with square blocks of hard grey stone, evenly and very finely.

[80] "The Women are generally well featur'd, but excessively libidinous"; Evelyn, *Diary*, II, 353.

There are many craftsmen who make little boxes and other things from tortoise shell and inlay them with gold and silver, and also with seashell and with bone; they also make large tortoise-shell coffers of quite fine craftsmanship.

In the homes of senators and nobles in Naples the silver is very rich; dishes and plates and washstands and wash-tubs are plentiful in every nobleman's home, as are silver candlesticks and cups.

In Naples lives a cardinal who has under his *regiment* (It. *reggimento*) the archbishops and bishops, and the abbots of the Neapolitan region. His home in Naples is near the cathedral and is very large, with many fine rooms and furnishings. This cardinal has many in his household; and all of the Neapolitan honorable people have households. Behind their carriages, /52/ when they and their wives go riding, footmen walk just as they do customarily in Moscow.

In Naples lives a papal nuncio, that is, an ambassador. His home is on a large street, a marvelous and well-decorated palace. This is the home of a Neapolitan senator given to the papal nuncio, and this senator is paid a price each year from the royal treasury for its use; and when that nuncio goes from Naples to Rome, that home is returned to the senator who owns it.

All of the better inns in Naples, that is, the travelers' courts, are built in a row along one street, but there are small ones elsewhere. Forestiere, that is, arriving foreigners, are few in Naples because of its great distance.

Neapolitans wear short wigs of a peculiar fashion, but the majority like to wear their natural hair; and those who wear wigs do them up like natural hair. It is difficult to know who is wearing a wig, but the base people cut their hair almost bald, leaving only a little hair on the temples, and they do this because of the great heat: in Naples in wintertime it is very warm, and snow never lies on the ground, because Naples is in minus temperature 30 days a year and is close to the equator, being only 43 degrees of latitude, and in summer the heat from the sun in Naples is immeasurable.[81] Naples sends to the treasury of the Spanish king in Madrid 50,000 ducats annually, and the Spanish king receives no other revenue from Naples besides this. Under the power of the Spanish king there are 6 other places that have viceroys, and Naples' viceroy is in second place.

And not having been in the general's *karavana* (It. *carovana,* caravan), and not having been ambassador in Rome, one cannot become viceroy. This is their custom: he who wants to be viceroy must first be in the general's *garmada* (It. *armata,* fleet), and then ambassador to the pope in Rome, and then he may be viceroy, as I have written above in this book.

There is one Greek church in Naples, and Uniate priests serve there, those who united the Greek faith with the Roman. There are no real Greek churches in Naples,[82]

[81] That is, Tolstoi says that Naples has only thirty days of below-freezing weather. He uses the word *temperamenta* instead of *temperatura*. His latitude is wrong: Naples is at 40°51′.

[82] The Russian is "*a samikh Grecheskikh tserkvei v Neapole net.*" Tolstoi returns to the idea of "real" Greeks of the true Greek faith below in Messina, entry for July 13.

and there are no Greeks who are of the Greek faith in Naples who live in homes, but only those who come here to trade.

July 8. I hired a felucca from Naples /53/ to the island of Malta, and from Malta back to Naples and for a stay in Malta, and gave for it a price of 100 Neapolitan scudos, that is, 40 gold chervontsy, for 15 days.[83] On this felucca were a pilota and 8 marinaro. And on July 8 I left Naples for Malta by sail, and in other places by oars, and after noon we came to a place called Pola (Puolo), 24 It. miles from Naples, and there we stayed 4 hours, standing off in the felucca. And having stood off, we left that place and went for two hours until night and arrived in the waning hours of daylight beneath a village, which is called Dol'narano (Nerano),[84] 16 It. miles from the inn called Pola; and we spent the night beneath the village of Nerano. Along the seacoast from Naples there are many dwellings built of stone with fine gardens, and among these structures on the coastal mountains are built many stone towers on high places, the towers being 100 sazhens apart or more. A *guardia,* that is, a guard, looking at the sea, always stands on these towers, so that no Turkish people can approach Naples undetected.

July 9. From beneath the village of Nerano we went by oars because there was no wind at all, and we rowed until noon, and at noon a favorable wind arose and we set three sails and raced on. After noon we quickly came opposite the city of Salerno. This city stands right on the sea; it is a Neapolitan province and a large place. This city has a governor from Naples and is 60 It. miles away. Then we came across from the city of Aropelia (Agropoli), also a Neapolitan province, 90 It. miles from Naples; the city stands on the seashore beneath mountains. Then we came opposite another Neapolitan province, which is called Kostelia Deleboda (Castellabate), 95 Italian miles from Naples. This city also stands beneath mountains on the seacoast. Then we came opposite the city of Liatserona (Acciaroli), a stone fortress, which also stands on the seashore at the foot of mountains. This city of Acciaroli is a Neapolitan province, 110 It. miles from Naples. And in this spot we stayed for 4 hours until night; and we spent the night there because we could not reach another porto, that is, harbor, in daylight, and it is impossible to go along the shoreline at night, because the guardia, that is, the guard on the towers that are built along the seacoast, will fire at feluccas that pass close to the shore, since they are afraid that Turkish ships may pass secretly in the night. /54/

[83] Tolstoi here leaves Naples for the south, with the expressed intention of engaging the Turks in naval combat, something he was unable to do in the Adriatic.

[84] This is a small town, reached after sailing around the southern tip of the Gulf of Naples, P. Camponella.

July 10. At the first hour of day we left the city of Acciaroli and sailed until the 8th hour on oars and sails, and at the 8th hour of that day we sailed beneath the city of Kamaroda (Camerota). This is a city of the Spanish king, 45 Italian miles from Acciaroli, and it stands on the coast at the foot of mountains, and its buildings are all stone. A Neapolitan principe holds this city. We stopped beneath this city and stayed half an hour. Then we left by rowing because there was no wind, and we sailed opposite the city of Poliugasta (Policastro). This city stands on the seashore beneath the mountains, and belongs to a Neapolitan nobleman, and it is 16 It. miles from Camerota. With the city of Policastro, Calabria begins. Eight It. miles from Policastro is the Spanish city of Maratea, which stands on the seacoast beneath mountains. The buildings in this city are all stone. Then an hour before night we arrived beneath the city of Shkalea (Scalea), which stands on the coast near a mountain; it is not a large place but all of stone. From Maratea to Scalea it is 18 Italian miles. This city is in Calabria in the region of the Spanish king. We stayed the night beneath this city.

While going from Maratea to Scalea I saw in the sea not far from us a huge fish, which is called a whale, which swam for a long time above the water and sprayed sea water upward many sazhens high. The fish was the size of a large barge, 30 sazhens or more in length, and immeasurably thick; and when it played above the water and raised its tail upwards, its tail was the size of a house.

July 11. A half hour before daylight we left Scalea, with a favorable wind, and ran with two sails. At the first hour of day we ran opposite the city of Trizuli, 8 It. miles from Scalea. This is a small city, which stands at the sea beneath mountains, with all stone buildings.

Then we arrived opposite the city of Mazhara (Maiera), one Italian mile from Trizuli. This city also stands on the shore and is a small city built of stone. Then we came opposite the city of Cherelia (Cirella), 1 It. mile from Maiera. The city of Cirella stands on the seacoast, beneath mountains, and its buildings are all stone. This is not a large city, and all these cities of the Spanish king are in Calabria.

Then we came opposite the city of Diamanta (Diamante), 3 Italian miles from Cirella, which stands on the coast on a mountain, and its buildings are all stone. /55/ This too is a city of the Spanish king in Calabria, and it is held by a Neapolitan nobleman. This city is sizable, and around it are many gardens of olive trees.

Then we came opposite the city of Belliavoda (Belvedere). This city is in the Calabria of the Spanish king and stands at the sea; it is 6 It. miles from Diamante, and is of stone. Then we came opposite the city of Liushitralia (Cetraro). This city of the Spanish king is in Calabria, stands on the very sea, is all of stone, and is 14 It. miles from Belvedere. This city is not large, but is built on a pleasant spot. Between Belvedere and Cetraro is one great mountain,[85] on which there are many fruit trees, and much fine fruit is grown on this mountain, such as is seldom found elsewhere in

[85] This is the mountain called the Montea.

Italy. Then we came opposite the city of Feshkarda (Fuscaldo), 14 It. miles from Cetraro. This is also a city of the Spanish king in Calabria, and it stands on the shore on a high mountain, is built all of stone, and around it are many forests on the mountains.

Then we came opposite the city of Pavlo (Paola), also in Calabria, also of the Spanish king, which stands on the coast on a hill in a fine place, and its buildings are all stone. Around this city on the mountains are many forests, and beneath the city and mountain is a large bridge, 70 sazhens or more in length, leading to the gates of the city. This city is 3 Italian miles from Fuscaldo.

Then we came opposite the city of Santoliutsela (San Lucido), also belonging to the Spanish king in Calabria, which stands on the coast below mountains, with all stone buildings. From Paola to San Lucido is 4 Italian miles. Around it on the mountain are fields in which they sow wheat.

Then we arrived opposite the city of Shumufrinta (Fiumefreddo), 10 It. miles from San Lucido, which stands right on the seashore, on a high stone mountain in a pleasant place, also in the Calabria of the Spanish king, and it is built all of stone. On one side, on a high stone mountain, are built large fine palaces of fine proportions. Many fishermen live near this city.

Then we came opposite the city of Belliamunda (Belmonte). This is a city of the Spanish king in Calabria, and stands on the seacoast under the mountains, with all stone buildings, and its fortress is on a high mountain; around this city are stone mountains, with no fruit trees at all. This city of Belmonte is 7 Italian miles from Fiumefreddo. /56/

Then we came to the city of Liabantea (Amantea), 1 It. mile from Belmonte in the Calabria of the Spanish king, which stands at the sea on a mountain, with all stone buildings, and it is a large place. In this city lives the governor, a Neapolitan principe. We sailed beneath this city in the last hour of day and spent the night there.

On the coast in all of Calabria between these cities, which sit on the seacoast and beneath mountains, are stone dwellings, gardens, and fields, where they sow wheat on the mountains. The city of Amantea has an ancient stone fortress high on a stone mountain, and beneath all these cities the mountains are very steep, so that no creature could go up from the sea. Around this city are gardens and dwellings right on the seacoast.

July 12. Two hours before daylight we left Amantea by rowing, and then by sails and again by oars, and we passed the city of Liupitsa (Pizzo). This city stands on the seacoast below mountains, is all of stone, and is also in the Calabria of the Spanish king. It is 40 Italian miles from Amantea.

Then we came opposite the city of Trubea (Tropea), also in the Calabria of the Spanish king, 18 It. miles from Pizzo. This city stands on the seacoast, its buildings are all stone, and it is large; around it on the mountains are forests and fields where they sow wheat. We did not stop below this city, but sailed on around noon.

Then we sailed to a city called Choia (Gioia Tauro), 25 It. miles from Tropea, also a city of the Spanish king in Calabria, which stands at the sea beneath mountains, and around it on the mountains are forests and fields where they sow wheat.

Then we sailed to the city of Liubonara (Bagnara), 14 It. miles from Gioia. This city is in the Spanish king's Calabria, stands on the very seacoast beneath mountains, is all of stone, and is a small city; around it on the mountains are forests and fields where they sow wheat.

In the second hour of night we came to the island of Sicily, where a tower built on the Sicilian seacoast for defense and with a very high lantern was visible from afar. The light is placed there so that those who wish to go to Sicily at night by sea can /57/ find the right route, by looking at that lantern. From the city of Bagnara to the island of Sicily it is 12 It. miles. When we arrived at the place at which the island of Sicily was on the right side and Calabria on the left, we spent the night under the village of Tornadafora (Torre di Faro), in which village fishermen live. From that tower, on which a lantern with lights stands at night, to the village of Torre di Faro it is 3 It. miles, and we spent the night beneath this village, being afraid at night: our felucca broke from its anchor and was carried to sea, where with great difficulty and fear we saved ourselves, and again moored ourselves there with two anchors.

July 13. Early, an hour before sunrise, we left that village, and in the first hour of day we arrived beneath Misina (Messina), 12 It. miles from the village. During this time we passed the shore of the island of Sicily, where on the coast all the way to Messina are many dwellings, all built of stone, and also many gardens along the shore. Between the island of Sicily and Calabria the sea is very narrow, in all 6 versts, and in some places it is wider or narrower.

The city of Messina stands on the island of Sicily on the seacoast. The city of Messina is a large place, all built of stone. Arriving in our felucca, we stopped beneath the city, where a Messinian came to us and said that no one could leave our felucca for the shore, until a cavalier, established for this purpose looked at my *pratica,* that is, my traveler's certificate, which I had brought from Naples. And I stayed on the felucca for four hours awaiting the order of that cavalier, who slept a long time this day; and when this cavalier looked at my travel document, he gave me permission to go from the felucca to the city of Messina. But according to their custom, all of my weapons and those of the sailors were taken to that cavalier's court for guarding; and this cavalier's court is built on the seacoast. Every forestiero, that is, every foreigner, who arrives in Messina must anchor his ship at this place beneath this court. And then, having received permission from this cavalier to enter the city, I took a room in an inn or lodging house, which was called the Francesco Aurora, where they gave me a room with chairs, a bedstead with bedding, and a table. Across from the city of Messina on the other side of the sea in Calabria stands the city of the Spanish king, Ridzho (Reggio). /58/

This city stands on the coast beneath mountains and is large, with all stone buildings.

The city of Messina is the first place on the Sicilian coast, and it is very large, with many marvelous dwellings, and also many fine churches and monasteries, in which live friars and nuns of various orders, all of the Roman faith. In Messina there is one Greek church named for the great martyr Catherine, and another Greek church named for St. Martin. These two churches have the real Greek faith, and there is a third Uniate church named for St. Nicholas. In this church the altar is done as in Greek churches, but the platform at the altar is like a Roman church. The icons are Greek, and over the altar is a Greek image of Nicholas the Wonder Worker.

The large stone city is done in the new fashion with bastions and a fine fortress, with one side to the sea and the other to the mountain; and there are 8 small fortresses, that is, castles, in Messina from the mountains to the sea, also done in the new style with fine fortifications.

By the sea is a house is built which is called the arsenale, where they make all kinds of naval vessels. Along the shore for many sazhens are great four-story palaces of marvelous workmanship, and throughout the city the homes and palaces are well built. The city of Messina is very populous, and there are many wares in the shops and stores, and also many large and small red *karaiakov* (?),[86] and lots of artisans in Messina as well. Messina and all the cities on the Sicilian coast are under the power of the Spanish king, and the people in Messina are Spanish and all speak the Italian language.

In Messina lives a viceroy, that is, a delegated king sent by the Spanish king, just as in Naples, and the authorities in Messina are all Spanish.

In Messina there are many Spanish nobles and honorable people who live in homes, wear clothes of Spanish style, and whose wives and daughters go about in the Spanish way. The honorable people ride in carriages and the mercante, that is, the merchants, walk on foot. The *moneta,* that is, the money, in Messina is a special Sicilian silver and brass, not the same as in Naples, and except for the island of Sicily and Malta this money goes nowhere else. There are all kinds of foodstuffs in Messina, meat and fish, and bread and fruit, that is, grapes, and not expensive; and they exist in plenty.

The peoples of Messina are various: Frenchmen and Greeks and Gypsies /59/ who make merry and live by their age-old blacksmithing skills, and who live without homes, sitting along the streets uncovered and working.

Opposite the city of Messina in the sea is a tower, and on it stands a lantern up high. This lantern is always lighted at night for those arriving in Messina, so they can see where the port is. The Spanish people in Messina are proud and unfriendly to forestiere, that is, to foreigners. The home of the viceroy in Messina is large, built on the seacoast, and, as in Naples, a guard stands at his gate. There are only 400 soldiers in Messina, who live at the viceroy's palace, and the *ufficiale,* that is, the leaders of the troops, also live in the viceroy's palace.

[86] The (?) is in the Russian text. I suspect a misprint or a misreading from Tolstoi's manuscript. In Italian *baracca* means stall or booth, which fits the context.

At the entrance gates to Messina a stone pier is built, and on it stand 8 large iron cannon with their muzzles pointed to the sea; on this pier stands the guardia, that is, the guard. In Messina a large house is built on the coast, and it is called a *lazzaretto,* a stone building. In this lazzaretto are many rooms, and this is why it was built: when by the will of God there is a pestilent infection in Messina, or some other illness contagious to the people such as *febramalinga* (It. *febbre-maligno,* malaria) or *franki* (It. *mal francese,* syphilis) or such ailments, then the sick of Messina are taken to this lazzaretto and are cured. People who arrive in Messina from the Levant, that is, the East, are kept in this lazzaretto for 40 days, and they do not go into the city and no one comes to them, because they are afraid, because in the East they often have pestilent infections.[87]

On one side of the city of Messina a fortress is built called Tsitadelia (Cittadella). The first fortress from the sea in Messina is built strongly of fine craftsmanship. In this fortress are 700 large and small cannon. This fortress is built in the new style with *bal'varami* (belvederes), very strongly and well. Beneath Messina the porto, that is, the harbor for naval vessels, is very large and suitable to receive all kinds of ships.

July 14. We left Messina early in the morning. The wind was unfavorable, so we went by rowing: then a good, favorable wind arose, and we went by sail. In all we were 20 feluccas sailing together, but then an immeasurably great wind arose, and it began to drive the feluccas from the shore to sea, and in a short time the feluccas were all dispersed, so that one could not see another. We were in very great fear because our feluccas were not roped together as is customary, and we were thrown far from the shore out to sea, and we were saved from sinking /60/ by the power of God, and we ran into the city of Liashkaleta (Scaletta), 12 It. miles from Messina. This city stands at the sea on a mountain, its buildings are all stone, and it is on the island of Sicily, and Calabria remained on our left. From Messina to Scaletta, along the seashore on Sicily and on the mountains and beneath them, are many stone dwellings, and monasteries are on the mountains by the sea. Then we arrived at the city of Matsia (Zanclea?), 2 It. miles from Scaletta. This city also stands on the island on the sea between the mountains, and its buildings are all stone; but it is a small place, and around it are small forests on the mountains and small fields where they sow wheat.

Then we arrived opposite a Sicilian city called Santoliia (Ali Terme?), which stands on the coast between mountains, but its fortress is on the mountain. The place is small, with all stone buildings, and it is 4 It. miles from Zanclea. Around this city on the mountains are small forests and fields where they sow grain. Between the cities of Zanclea and Ali Terme are large homes, and some stone buildings are on the coast and on the mountains.

Then we came opposite a city that stands on a mountain at the sea, also on this island of Sicily, and called Savana (Savoca), a rather large place. This city is between large mountains. Its buildings are all of stone, and it is 6 It. miles from Ali Terme. Around this city, on and at the foot of the mountains, are many stone dwellings. The mountains have small forests, and the fields in which they sow wheat are small. Then we came opposite another city on Sicily called Santolizina (Sant Alessio), 6 It. miles from Savoca. This city stands on the shore beneath high mountains, is surrounded by many stone buildings, and its buildings are all of stone; around it on the mountains are small forests and smallish fields where they sow wheat.

Then we came opposite the city of Alliadora (Letoianni Gallodoro), 4 It. miles from Sant Alessio. This Sicilian city is on the coast beneath mountains, which have small forests and fields where they sow wheat.

Then we came opposite the city of Dalormina (Taormina) on Sicily, 2 It. miles from Gallodoro. This city stands on the coast on the heights of a tall mountain. The city is not large, but it is very beautiful, built on a pleasant spot with many fine stone buildings, and around it on the mountains are small forests and fields where wheat is sown.

Then an hour before nightfall we came beneath the city of Liatretsa (Trezza), on /61/ the same island of Sicily, which stands on the sea beneath mountains; it is a very small place, with all stone buildings. This city is 30 Italian miles from Taormina. Beneath this city of Trezza is a porto, that is, a harbor, for all kinds of naval vessels. Around the city are small forests and fields where they sow wheat. We spent the night beneath this city; this day at sea we had a great wind, both favorable and unfavorable to us, and its blowing often changed, and the wind was exceedingly strong, and we were in very great difficulty and in a fear of death of it.

July 15. Two hours before daylight we left Trezza on oars, and at daybreak we came opposite the city called Kataniia (Catania), 10 It. miles from Trezza. The city of Catania is very large, stands on the shore on a level place, also on Sicily and its fine buildings are all of stone; it is surrounded by wheat fields. When we were across from this city, a favorable wind arose, and we raised the sails and sailed quickly.

Then we came opposite the city of Liandina (Lentini); this is a very large place, twice as large as the city of Naples,[88] standing on the mountains 8 Italian miles from the sea on the island of Sicily, and 20 It. miles from Catania. In this city are build-

[87] Tolstoi was overly appreciative of the cures effected by plague hospitals; almost certainly the survival rate was better outside the *lazaretto;* one recent authority has suggested that if a hospital had a low mortality rate, it was because hospitalization was normally delayed, and those who reached the hospital were already "a select and more resistant group of the population." For a general introduction to the subject, see Cipolla, *Fighting the Plague,* p. 65 and passim.

[88] [Sic]. The city was nearly destroyed in the earthquake of 1693.

ings all of stone, and it is very populous. The principe de-Batera, that is a Prince Baterinskii, rules in this city, and he serves the Spanish king.

Then we came opposite the city of Avosta (Augusta), 20 Italian miles from Lentini. This city is also on Sicily and stands on the seashore on a level place beneath the mountains; it is a largish place. On both sides of this city are built two fine fortresses, and the whole city is built of stone. Beneath the city is a porto, that is, a fine harbor for naval vessels, in which ships and galleys and all kinds of vessels may tie up. Around this place on the mountains and plains are fields in which they sow wheat. Seven years earlier in this city there was a shaking of the earth,[89] and at that time a Maltese galley stood in the harbor, and on it were 40 Maltese cavaliers and sailors. At the time of the earthquake this galley overturned and all 40 cavaliers and sailors were killed, and not one of them was saved.

Then we came opposite the city of Sirakoza (Siracusa, Syracuse), 20 It. miles from Augusta. This city stands on the shore on a level /62/ place, also on Sicily. This city is large, with all fine stone buildings, and it is built in the new manner, all of stone with belvederes, and with a fine fortress. Around it, in level places, are many fields where they sow wheat, and beneath the city is a porto, that is, a harbor. From Augusta to Syracuse along the shore in level places and on the mountains are many stone dwellings. Beneath the city we saw two Maltese galleys that always go along the Mediterranean Sea from Malta to Sicily and from Sicily to Malta, and around the island of Sicily. These galleys look for places where they can find Turkish people, and when they find them they fight with them, if they have the strength, in whatever vessels the Turks might be, because the passage from Sicily to Malta and from Malta to Sicily is free to Christians. However, there are always many Turks in these places, in galliots, galleys, ships, tartantellas, fustas, and in other vessels; and there are even many Turks in those places, where one crosses from Sicily to Malta. From Sicily to Malta it is 80 Italian miles over the sea.

Then we came to a city also on Sicily, which stands on a level place at the sea close to the mountains, with all stone buildings, a small city, 20 Italian miles from Syracuse. Around this city on the mountains and on the level places are many fields where they sow wheat, and there are also hay fields. We spent the night beneath this city. In this city live many fishermen who catch large and small fish in the sea, and salt them in tubs, and others dry the salt fish and sell them in Messina and in other cities on the island of Sicily. Beneath this city we met a felucca in which Spanish traveled, and they told us that it was dangerous to go to Malta because they had seen 4 Turkish ships close to this city; also, the inhabitants of this city told us that they always saw Turks close to their city, and on July 16th they saw three Turkish ships beneath their city; these Turks ply the Mediterranean, that is, the White Sea, and look to capture Christians, going from Sicily to Malta, and Turks are always on the Maltese route, and they exploit it.

[89] The earthquake of 1693 also severely damaged Augusta.

V

July 16, 1698–August 12, 1698

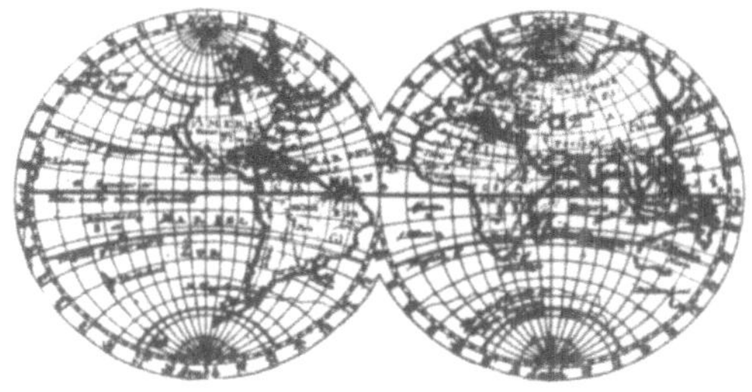

Malta · Sicily · Naples

On ***July 16,*** having set out early, we went from the island of Sicily to Malta by sea, and Sicily was on our right.

Then we came opposite a city called Manikara (Vendicari), eight Italian miles from the city of Adavole (Avola). This city on the Sicilian island stands on the seacoast halfway up a mountain, and all its buildings are stone; around it are fields where they sow wheat.

Then we arrived at a small island, which the Spanish call Capo-Pasato (Capo Passero), but the Turks call this island Capo-de-Oro, that is Head of Gold. The Turks call it this because the Turks often plunder near it. On this island the Spanish have built a stone tower in which 15 Spanish soldiers on guard live with their wives and children, and these soldiers are sent from the city of Palermo on Sicily, and they are changed annually. Turks who approach in ships and in other vessels are unable to do harm to these fifteen soldiers, because the tower in which the soldiers dwell is well fortified. From the above-mentioned city of Vendicari to the island called Capo-Passero, that is, "Cape Passage," is 12 Italian miles.

On shore I found two Maltese galleys, and arriving at the galleys I boarded one which was called the *Nunciata* in Spanish, and in Slavonic, under the flag of the *Annunciation* of the Most Holy Mother of God. On this galley the captain and the knights of Malta received me with great honor, and readily ordered that all my things be put on that galley; then they treated me to coffee and said that I was to go with them on that galley to Malta. I did not /114/ wish to do this, because the galley planned to stay in harbor at this island for another eight days.

And at the hour when I was on that galley, news reached the captain of the galley that three large Turkish ships were approaching, each of them with 60 cannon; and they were heavily manned. Thereupon both galleys entered into a secure place near the island, because they could not go out to sea for a lack of men; in all on the galleys were ninety or one hundred soldiers and twelve Knights of Malta, and 300 galeottas, that is, galley slaves, who row with oars, with six men to an oar. And these galleys stood protected by the island and awaited the Turkish ships; the captain placed my felucca on guard three versts in front of the galleys. And having thus arranged and armed the naval vessels, they were prepared for battle; and we stood in this manner until 12 o'clock of that day, when we sighted Turkish ships ten versts away. Then those ships moved a little on the sea and came opposite us, and the captain sent people from the galley in a small barque to observe carefully; and those people returned and said to us that those ships were sailing close to us and the island of Capo-Passero. The ships were approaching us slowly because the wind was contrary; each ship had only two sails unfurled. And the Maltese galleys came to sea in order to come upon the Turks and to fight; but once they came out to the open sea they found it was impossible to fight these ships, because the Turks had many cannon on board. However, the galleys did not flee from them, but stayed, awaiting them close to the island;[1] likewise, I, having been placed on guard in my felucca, could not leave that place without the permission of the captain; and a guard from my felucca went on shore to observe the ships, in order to learn fully when those ships would reach us ready for battle.

And I myself stood on guard for many hours and saw that on the other side of the land was a porto, that is, a harbor, one verst or less from the place where we waited. I saw that if the Turkish ships entered that port where the Maltese galleys and I waited, Providence might favor us over them. But those [Turkish] ships did not enter the port, but instead sailed on the open sea; and at the first hour of night a cry reached us from the island that the Turks call the Capo-de-Oro, from the guardsman who said to come quickly /115/ in our felucca to the fortress, because the Turkish ships had sneaked up on us from behind the land and were only a verst away. The captain sent two masters on foot from the galley on shore to me, and they ordered me to come by felucca to the galley. And on the order of the captain I came by felucca to his galley, which waited on the sea; they expected small barques to come from the ships at night to plunder, and if those Turkish barques approached the shore, we would not allow them to go back to sea. And thus we stood all that night, with guards posted from the galleys as needed; and the captain sent one felucca with eight men from the galleys to secretly approach the ships to learn for certain where they had gone or where they stood, for the Turkish ships could not be seen for the darkness of night.

July 17. Early in the morning, even though there were no Turkish ships near us, we went in our felucca along the shore to meet the barque that the captain had sent from the galley to observe the Turkish ships. The people on this barque told me that the Turkish ships had gone south that night. And so again we went along the Sicilian coast in our felucca and came to a place called Liatora-Putsala (Pozzallo) on

[1]The Maltese captain's plan was apparently to stay close to shore, where manned galleys could maneuver freely and where the wind-driven Turkish warships would be at a disadvantage.

the island of Sicily. In this place of Pozzallo right on the seacoast, a well-fortified stone tower is built. Close to it is a small stone kaplica, that is, a small Western church. In this place live 12 soldiers with their wives and children to guard against the Turks. We did not approach this place; we encountered a tartan on the sea, which sent mariners to us in a barque, and they said to us that in the night the Turkish ships had passed close to the tartan and had gone south to the same area where our felucca had to go in order to cross from Sicily to Malta. And we stood in that place on guard the whole day, and toward the side where the tower stands we saw the Turkish ships; they stood in a port 10 versts from us. And we waited for night and decided to cross the sea to the island of Malta at night, so that we might pass by those Turkish ships secretly; but with evening a wind arose that was contrary to our desired course. That wind did not stop the whole night, and because of it we could not cross over to Malta, but stayed at that guard-post that night. /116/

July 18. Early in the morning, seeing that the Turkish ships had left the port, we also departed the place we had spent the night and went along the shore of Sicily and came to a place called Sankt-petro (Sant Pietro), that is, St. Peter, also on Sicily. At this place is a harbor for small vessels, but it is a very small village, six Italian miles from Pozzalo. In this harbor of St. Peter we came upon a felucca, which also wanted to go to the island of Malta; mariners in this felucca told us that in their felucca that evening they had gone to sea toward Malta, but having gotten 30 Italian miles from St. Peter, they turned back because the same Turkish ships had blocked their path, and they could not get to Malta in their felucca. And we stayed in the harbor of St. Peter until 12 o'clock of that day, watching for those Turkish ships that could appear, but we did not see them anywhere. Then, four hours before night, placing our hope in God, we left the harbor of St. Peter and went from Sicily across the sea to the island of Malta by oars, because there was no wind; and the felucca, which had returned 30 miles from the Turkish ships to the harbor of St. Peter, also left the harbor for Malta with us, but along the course it separated from us because it was heavily laden with people, and could not keep up with us. And so this day until night and for three hours of night we went on oars, and in the 4th hour of night arose a slight wind, but favorable to Malta, and on our felucca we unfurled two sails and sped on. This night was very cloudy, and it was impossible to see the stars, and the star we had to see [to navigate] was covered by a storm cloud and could not be seen; but the *patron* (It. *padrone*), that is, the chief of our felucca, strayed from our correct course through the dark of night only a little; I understood this well when I talked with him, and I protested when he playfully said he would take me to Barbary, that is, to Arabia. Then this padrone acknowledged he was not going there, and that he was really going to Malta, and he asked me if I would steer the felucca. And with the help of God I steered our course to Malta well, and all night we ran on two sails until sunup.

In the first hour of July 19, we saw before us the island of Malta, and the padrone was grateful that we had made the course directly to Malta. At that hour, being ten or more Italian miles from Malta, we encountered a large Turkish /117/ ship, and we saw it was a great distance from us, and at first we did not recognize it; we thought it was a Christian tartan coming from Malta. And the Turks on that ship spotted our felucca and turned its sails toward us and quickly pursued us; and we, realizing that ship was not a tartan but an unfriendly vessel, tried to get to Malta. But that ship steered behind us and drove us away, and pursued us for over three hours, so we had to alter our course for Malta. And seeing that the ship was driving us away from our course and that we could not reach Malta, we lowered the sails on our felucca and the mariners began to row with oars. We came opposite that ship but judged that it would sail by us on the wind. And so, with the help of God the encounter with that ship passed, but we had come in great proximity to it. And when the Turks saw that our felucca had come opposite their ship within cannon range, they began to fire from cannon, and then as we came even more directly across from their ship they fired at us with small arms; however, the Lord God had mercy on us: no one was killed or wounded. And when the Turks saw that the wind had driven their ship past us and that they could do nothing to us, they again pursued us to Turino (Comino), very close to Malta itself, and realizing that they could not keep us from Malta, they soon turned away from us and raced out to sea. And we, by the invisible power of God, having been freed from the pursuit of the Busurman, arrived in Malta in good health.

July 19. In the fifth hour of day I arrived in Malta and entered beneath the city of Malta into the Maltese porto, that is, the harbor where, holding our felucca some 50 sazhens off-shore, a man met us in a barque and took my *pashporta* (It. *passaporto*), that is, my passage papers, which I had brought from Naples; and that men went with my passage papers to the shore, and we were ordered not to land on the shore, and for an hour we stood off shore. Then the man who had taken my passage papers from me returned and told me that we were free to land on the shore and could go about the city at will; and I left the felucca and entered the city of Malta and stayed in an inn, which was called Delorsa (the Orso?). In this inn the *padrone,* that is, the proprietor, a born Frenchman and a good man, bargained with me for a room in which I could stay; and for the bed on which I slept and for meals (for dinner and supper) I paid him half a golden chervonets; but the soldier who was with me ate separately and paid separately for his meals and lodgings. And this proprietor assigned me /118/ a fine room in which to sleep, and in it was a bed with curtains and clean covers; also in the room were a table, armchairs, and several chairs, and the other room assigned to me where I ate was large, and I was well fed. And this day I did not leave the inn because I had not yet inquired after or found my acquaintances in Malta.

July 20. In the morning I sent notes to two knights of Malta; these notes were written by a knight of Malta in Naples, and they asked if they would deign to receive me and to show me kindness. One of these two Maltese knights, named Joseph Manoel Poliavichina (?), immediately came to me and for some time sat with me and told me that he had this day informed the *granmeistera* (It. *granmaestro*), that is, the chief of the knights of Malta, of my arrival; he said that he would order that everything that had been promised would be done. And the other knight of Malta, for whom I also had a letter from the knight in Naples, did not come to me this day for he was very old and ill; but he is a great knight, one of those who are called *grankrutsy* (It. *grancroci*); they wear large white crosses sewn on dark cloaks on their shoulders, and are the first people under the Maltese granmaestro.

And this morning I did not leave the inn where I stayed; but after dinner the Maltese granmaestro sent his carriage for me and for the knight Joseph Manoel, and in the name of the granmaestro this knight asked that I go in the carriage to the granmaestro's home, and I went there in that carriage. And his home is large with many rooms and is well built of stone; and one enters it by a circular staircase, which was made with the most marvelous workmanship and which is very wide and spacious; at the top a guard of 20 soldiers stands. Then I entered very large passageways made of fine workmanship; in these passages stand the granmaestro's cavaliers, that is, his courtiers. Then I entered a very long and large hall; this room is 15 sazhens 3 arshins or more in length, well decorated, all covered with fine silk fabrics, and on the wallpaper below the level of door frames very fine Italian paintings are hung. In this room at the front wall is the seat of the granmaestro, and over it hangs a fine canopy. From this room I entered another; this hall is smaller than the first, but still large. All the walls are of the same size, and they are also covered with silks, and in this room the seat /119/ of the granmaestro is also under a fine canopy. From this hall I entered yet another small room, also covered in silks. In this room Maltese knights met me and greeted me warmly.

Then I entered a room in which the granmaestro himself stood in the middle of the room; this room was all decorated in silks. And when I entered this room the granmaestro approached me, and having taken off his cap, bowed to me and said: "I greet you with great happiness because you, great lord, have come graciously from a great distance to see my possession, this island of Malta." I also bowed to him and thanked him for his gracious reception: and I asked him if he would allow me to look at everything on the island of Malta that was appropriate for a forestiero, that is, a foreigner, to see; and he graciously granted my request and ordered the abovementioned knight to guide me in his carriage to see whatever I wished, and for this he gave me his own carriage. During this conversation the granmaestro asked me to put on my cap, and he also donned his cap, and thus we spoke standing; and in the room in which we stood there was a knight near him, one in addition to Joseph Manoel, who had come with me. Those knights who met me in the other room did not enter the granmaestro's room, as is their custom. After the conversation I left the room, and he bowed to me, dismissed me graciously; and the above-mentioned knight Joseph Manoel who had come with me, was sent out with me and ordered to see to all of my needs. And when I left this room and entered the other one, the knights again greeted me, and I bowed down to them and went to the carriage with the knight Joseph Manoel; and this knight was born of Torino, and his home is still in Torino, which is under the power of the duke of Savoy.[2]

Then I entered the Roman-faith church of John the Forerunner.[3] This cathedral church on Malta is very large and done of the most miraculous workmanship of great wealth, and in this church is much silver and all sorts of things; and there are two fine organs; the columns in this church are of green marble, and around them are carvings of gilded alabaster. The vaults and walls in this church are carved of marvelous workmanship of the same alabaster, and there are many gilded places with carved alabaster. The painting of this church is of very intricate Italian workmanship, and there are also many other decorations /120/ in this church, which from a Maltese knight in Naples had been written. This knight was very old and ill, but he seemed gracious to me, and asked that I visit him in his home when I was free.

Then I left this church for the inn in which I stayed, and the knight Joseph Manoel came with me, because it was hot at this hour; and in the inn the Maltese knight and I enjoyed ourselves with lemonades. Then, as the hour of torridness waned, again the granmaestro's carriage came to me, and the granmaestro sent me his *camerera* (It. *cameriere*), that is, his chamberlain, to inquire about my health, and to tell me that if I needed anything I should tell him, and he would see to my requests. I thanked him for the attention he paid to me, but I had no requests whatsoever. And

[2]Tolstoi here begins his visit to the Order of St. John of Jerusalem, now the Sovereign Military Order of Malta, which has extraterritorial sovereignty in Rome.

> The Order was founded during the Crusades as a benevolent fraternity of knights devoted to the protection of pilgrims to the Holy Land. During the rise of Turkish power in the eastern Mediterranean, the knights fought valiantly as the rearguard of Christian Europe. The order's citadel for holding back the Turks was the beautiful Greek island of Rhodes. The knights, however, were dislodged from Rhodes by the Turks and were given a refuge by Emperor Charles V in 1530 on the smaller and less attractive island of Malta. From Malta the order continued its war against the Moslems through territorial units called langues and their subdivisions, the priories located on the continent. The main bases of these langues were in Catholic southern Europe—in Spain, France, and Italy—but priories existed farther north, in the British Isles, Bavaria, Bohemia, and Poland. The order's revenue consisted of annual taxes collected from the priories, which were in turn supported by gifts from wealthy nobles and monarchs, and of proceeds from trade, privateering, and miscellaneous services. (Saul, *Russia and the Mediterranean*, p. 33)

[3]This is the Church of San Giovanni, 1576.

in his carriage the knight Joseph Manoel and I went to see the fortress, that is, the city of Malta. I arrived at the gate called Portaderealo (Porta Reale) and entered the fortress [Fort St. Elmo], and saw with what kind of *kyshtaltom*[4] it was made, and with what kind of ramparts. And it is impossible to describe briefly the workmanship of the fort and fortifications, because the human mind just cannot grasp the details well enough to write them down, so wondrously is this fortress constructed. About it I can only write that nowhere in the whole world does such a marvelous thing exist, and a hostile attack by a multitude of troops could only conquer this fortress if God so willed. I had a good look at this fortress and departed to arrive at the inn where I was staying, for the hour of night had come.

July 21. In the morning the knight Joseph Manoel came to the inn in which I stayed, and asked if I would like to see the Maltese armory with him, and at his request I went to the armory court with him, where I saw the masters of arms who sat making weapons. Then they conducted me to an upper chamber, which is very large, and in it is a multitude of all kinds of well-decorated weapons. There are also many iron helmets, fine suits of armor, *barterets* (It. *bardatura,* horse-armor), spiked helmets, shields, and other military attire, among which I saw three fine bardatura that the Maltese had taken the previous summer from Turkish pashas on a Turkish ship. In this same room I saw a large cannon made of calfskin; its brass parts are /121/ thinner than the thickness of a single finger, but it is all covered with this calfskin; and they told me that this cannon was strong enough to be fired.

In this same room I saw ten intricate iron arquebuses, the primers of which were fine pieces, and they told me that there was enough military attire and weaponry here to equip 60,000 men. In this same chamber I saw many banners and *pul'varanov* (It. *polverino,* pulverain, powder horn), and in this room are especially many *mushkatonov* (It. *moschettone,* blunderbuss), which are very useful on ships and on galleys.

Leaving this room I also saw at the armory two Barbary sheep, that is, Arabic rams, which are very large, much larger than the great Ordin (Kirghiz) sheep, and their wool is red and very long, and their tails are long and thick, and on their heads are four great horns.

From this armory I went to the inn where I stayed, and the knight Joseph Manoel went to the magistrate where he had some business, but he promised to come for dinner at my inn. At dinnertime this knight arrived, and having dined with me he sat that day with me until evening, and in the evening I went with him in a barque from the city of Malta to the other side of the Maltese port to look at a certain fortress called Derigazoli (Fort Ricasoli). This fortress is built on the other side of the Maltese port, opposite from the fortress of Malta; it is built on a stone hill, is of fine workmanship, and is unspeakably well fortified; all of it is done in the most mar-

[4]This word may be *kshtalt,* form or shape, from the Polish *kształt;* cf. German, *Gestalt.*

velously crafted hard white stone. In this fortress the keep, the bastions, the belvederes, and the other things are so built that it is impossible to describe the likes of them; likewise, the powder cellars are so miraculously done and all the stores are so miraculously devised, and it is so fortified against unfriendly bombs, that I cannot describe it accurately. Thus they say that this fortress is the most marvelous in the whole world, and even now it is slightly incomplete, and at present 250 laborers are working continuously in order to finish it quickly. Inside the fortress is one small Roman church named for Nicholas the Wonder Worker. In this fortress are also seven wells of fine clean water; here, too, they have built fine rooms beneath the walls for the soldiers to live with their wives and children; in the same fortress many fine large and small cannon stand over the gates; and in this fortress they have built large chambers of fine craftsmanship for the governor. When I entered this fortress its governor and his comrades met me at the gate, where a guard of 30 soldiers stood. This governor, a knight of Malta and a fine young man, greeted me graciously and /122/ requested that I sit a while with him in [the shade of] the gates, where many fine chairs had been placed, because it was hot from the scorching of the sun; and that is where I sat with him, and where he treated me to lemonades; and when the burning of the sun had passed I strolled about the fortress with the governor and saw all the fortifications. Then the governor invited me to his chambers; there I saw his fine decorations, and we sat a while in his rooms and amused ourselves with lemonades. And I left the fortress for the barque in which I had arrived, and the governor guided me out of the gate with great civility, and I thanked him for his affection and went back to my inn. And when I arrived on the shore beneath the city of Malta the granmaestro's carriage stood there awaiting me; and I left the barque and went to the inn where I was staying, and the knight Joseph Manoel conducted me to the inn's gate, and then he went to his home. And as I departed the fortress in my barque, I had come opposite an English ship, on which was a good acquaintance, an English captain; this captain, spotting me from his ship, greeted me with a great bow, and he would have been glad if I could have boarded his ship, but I could not, because the ship stood in *kontomatsiia* (It. Campo Marzio, quarantine), because it had arrived from the Levant, that is, the East. It is the custom of the Maltese that no one may visit this ship or quit it for the city for a fixed period of time for fear of disease; in the East infectious plagues often happen. And so, after I greeted this English captain from afar, we separated. At night this English captain sent to me a Maltese mercante, that is, a merchant, who was his friend, and he asked me this: if I should like to go to Spanish or French cities, I could go on his ship, and need have no fear of the Turks, and if I should deign to go on his ship, he promised to wait in Malta as long as necesary. I thanked him for his kindness to me, but I did not want to leave Malta on his ship, because I intended to go from Malta back to Naples, and from Naples to Rome.

July 22. Early in the morning the knight Joseph Manoel came to my inn; soon the granmaestro's carriage arrived and the knight Joseph Manoel and I went in it to see a *shpital* (Ger. *Spital;* It. *ospedale,* hospital). This hospital was built by the general treasury of Malta for the care of the sick, and it is very large. /123/ In this hospital are long rooms, over fifty sazhens long and some six sazhens wide. In these rooms are placed bedsteads with good covers and curtains, and the sick lie on them, and each sick person has his own cover and curtain. In the midst of these rooms is a small church, and all day there are Roman services for the sick. All day long doctors and druggists come to the sick and cure them gratis. These sick people are served daily by a knight who is changed every day. These knights are from various states—Frenchmen, those of the Empire, Italians, Poles, Spanish, and those of other lands. The ill are always fed from silver; the plates, spoons, dishes, cups, tureens, and the salt cellars are all silver, and every comfort is provided for the sick from the general treasury for the love of Christ. Beneath these rooms in which the sick people lie sit Turkish and Barbary slaves, and above the chambers of the sick are more fine rooms where the sick can rest. In the midst of the buildings a fine garden is built, and in it are fountains for the pleasure of the sick. Around the building are chambers in which the menials who serve the sick live, and there are some 1,000 sick in this hospital; but when I was there there were only 200 sick. This hospital accepts sick of every rank so long as they are Christian; but they have a special place for the Busurman sick people in this same hospital.

From this hospital I went with the knight Joseph Manoel in the granmaestro's carriage to see the other knight, the one who wears the *grancroce,* that is, the great cross. He too had been sent a letter about me from the Maltese knight back in Naples, so that he would be friendly to me. This knight is called Karavita (Caravita) and is of honorable birth, and he is very old and sick, but he received me into his home with great affection, meeting me on the porch. And having entered his chambers he sat with me for some time and conversed in the Italian language. Then I departed, and although he could hardly walk he conducted me to the carriage, and from there I went to the inn where I was staying. This knight Caravita has a well-built home with many rooms, all well decorated and hung with silk, and with many fine mirrors and pictures; he also has many fine young men serving him. And this day I did not leave the inn again until dinnertime.

This day after dinner the knight Joseph Manoel came to my inn, and then another knight arrived and sat with me some time, and two hours before nightfall the granmaestro's carriage arrived for me. With the knight Joseph Manoel /124/ we went in that carriage to take a walk; but the other knight who had visited me went home. And we came to a house where seven Maltese knights stayed; one of these asked me if I would go to the chambers of an acquaintance who had visited me at the inn the previous evening. And I went to his chambers, and saw naval and geographical maps, and they treated me with lemonades, and having amused ourselves for a while, I went out to walk. He walked with me, and we came to a fortress called Sal'talina (Sliema).

The governor of this fortress met me at the gate and received me affectionately, and I saw everything in this fortress there was to see. This fortress is not very large; it is built on a corner of the city on the very seashore and has large fine fortifications; on the fortress are many fine large cannon; a very large round tower is also built here, and on the top of this tower is a large lantern, in which from the first day of December until Easter they burn all night some 40 lamps filled with lamp oil, so that those Christians who go to sea at night can see the Maltese island from afar. Atop the same fortress they place small canvas flags on poles so that the sentry who stands on the fortress can see with certainty, which way the wind blows at sea; and when he sees a ship at sea off in the distance, he knows on which wind that ship sails. This fortress in Malta was built in ancient times, and many years ago the Turks entered Malta and seized this fortress; at that time there were 100 Knights of Malta in this fortress who did not want to surrender alive to the Busurmans, and all in the fortress were killed and were chopped into small bits by the Busurmans.[5] In this same fortress at that time was the granmaestro of Malta himself, and at the time of the assault the granmaestro's legs had been severed by a cannon; however even without his legs he sat in an armchair in this fortress, and taking up two pistols he did not allow the Turks to approach the place until he was killed.

Now this fortress is even stronger than before. It is circled with a new wall with three belvederes, strongly fortified, and now no ship can come close to this fortress from the sea. In this fortress live soldiers with their wives and children. In times of siege they bring into the fortress much clean water through a trough; deep down in this fortress is the chamber where they confine knights judged guilty [of a crime]. And having looked over this fortress, we left it for the carriage; and the governor of this fortress conducted me to the gate, and having bowed, he dismissed me with affection. /125/ From this fortress I arrived at the inn where I stayed, and the two knights, Joseph Manoel and the other whose chambers I visited, conducted me to the inn.

July 23. In the morning the knight Joseph Manoel again came to me, and then the carriage of the granmaestro arrived, and we went to look at the fortifications of the Maltese city, and we arrived at a belvedere called Posta-de-Italia. This belvedere is large, on a high stone hill, and very well fortified both from sea and from land; and around it is a moat of very marvelous craftsmanship and it is unspeakably well fortified. On this belvedere in the upper and lower magazines are 38 very large and fine cannon; among them is one immeasurably large one that was taken from the Turks when they came previously beneath Malta; and another equally large cannon was taken at the same time from the Turks, but it dropped into the sea close to the shore where it still lies visible; it is impossible in any way to raise that cannon from the sea; many various instruments have been used to raise that cannon

[5]This is a reference to the Great Siege of 1565 by troops of Sultan Soliman II, led by Mustapha and Piale. Fort St. Elmo, manned by one hundred knights and five hundred soldiers, was ordered by de Valette to fight to the last man; the siege, planned for three days, took five weeks.

from the sea, but they could not raise it. This belvedere is called the Posta-de-Italia because during hostile attacks on Malta, Maltese knights born as Italians occupy this tower, and they defend it.[6] And this belvedere was built by the treasury of those Knights of Malta who were born Italians.

From this belvedere I went with the knight Joseph Manoel to another belvedere, which is called the Posta-di-Castille. On this belvedere on the upper and the lower magazines are 15 very large cannon, of which one is immeasurably large, very long, and done of such marvelous workmanship that it is just amazing. This belvedere is built on a corner by the sea on a high place, and clears the entry to the porto of Malta, that is, the harbor, so that no enemy ship can enter the harbor. On this belvedere are fine garden plots where they grow many various fruits, and in the belvedere is a fine fountain, from which flows stored clean water for every purpose. And on both of the belvederes described above the cannon are all brass and of fine proportions, and over them are built fine strong roofs on tall stone pillars, so that during a rain the cannon do not get wet. The cannon rest on carriages that are very strong and of fine proportions.

Then I went to my inn because it became hot from the burning of the sun. /126/

This same day after dinner the same knight, Joseph Manoel, came to my inn, and after he visited with me we went in a barque to the other side of the Maltese port to look at a fortress called Santo-Anelo (Fort. St. Angelo). This fortress is not large; it is built on a high stone mountain of fine craftsmanship, and it is all made of white stone and marvelously fortified, and it has many large and small cannon. On this fortress toward the sea are four magazines, one larger than the other, and on all are placed many cannon; fine roofs on stone columns are placed over them. In this fortress is a fine Roman church; in this same fortress are the soldiers' homes where the soldiers live with their wives and children. A governor lives in this fortress and his home is not large, but well built, and the ascent from the sea into this fortress is very extensive and of course barren, for up the ascent to the fortress one could otherwise bring cannon and all manner of supplies. This fortress is set opposite the entrance to the porto of Malta, that is, the harbor, so that entry into the harbor by hostile vessels is prohibited. From this fortress I went in the same barque, and having cruised along the sea for a while, I went back to the shore where the granmaestro's carriage awaited me. In this carriage I went to the inn in which I was staying; the knight Joseph Manoel having conducted me to the inn and went home.

July 24. Early the granmaestro sent the knight Joseph Manoel to me and with him were 5 other knights and 5 carriages, and the Maltese knights asked me on

[6]Each of the eight nationalities in the Maltese Order (Aragon, Auvergne, Provence, Italy, France, Castile with Portugal, England, and Germany) had its own "House" or *auberge;* they were later regrouped as the Portuguese, Spanish, Provençals, Austrians, Italians, French, and Bavarians.

behalf of the granmaestro if I would go with them in the carriages to walk in a place called Bushketno (Buskett/Boschetto; west Malta). I could not refuse this request so I went with them in the carriages. Soon we came to a place called Groto-di-san-Pavlo [in the Baia di San Paolo],[7] that is, the cave of St. Paul the Apostle; and the holy apostle Paul visited this cave when he was on the island of Malta with the evangelist Luke. On this spot a great Roman church is built of fine craftsmanship. Beside this great church is a smaller church, and in it I saw a part of the arm of the holy apostle Paul. Near this church are two small churches, one named for the holy apostle Paul; in this church on the altar is an image of the apostle Paul carved of alabaster of fine work; and the other small church is named for the evangelist Luke, and both are Roman; and in this church is an image of the evangelist Luke carved of alabaster of marvelous workmanship, and it is placed on the altar on the right side. When one enters this small church /127/ there is in the earth a small cave carved out of the rock where Paul and the evangelist Luke dwelled. Images of St. Paul and St. Luke, finely crafted of alabaster, are placed in this cave and a lamp burns continuously in front of them. In this cave Christians in their faith revere the earth and stone because they are holy. In the same cave one finds something resembling white stones and other things, which they call the serpents' eyes and tongues, and they say that they heal through the prayers of the apostle Paul; and this is because on the island of Malta a viper bit the apostle Paul. This place is 15 Italian miles from the cave, and at the time that the viper bit St. Paul, he shook it off his arm into the fire, and damned all the vipers who were on the island of Malta, and to the present none of the vipers on the island are harmful to man. A man who holds the soil or a stone from the cave of the apostle Paul in his hand can pick up a snake in his hand, and it cannot harm him. In the same places one finds white stones shaped like vipers; about them they say that they are the vipers who were here when St. Paul damned them, and all were turned to stone, and now they can be found in the mountains and fields, and in the earth.

Not far from this cave is a *kurgan* (burial mound), which is not very high or large. Around it is built a stone fence that is not tall, and on the top of the kurgan is one short column, and on it is placed the image of the apostle Paul, finely carved of alabaster in the size of a man. This image was made because when St. Paul was on Malta he always came to this kurgan and preached that Christ was the true God, and truly a man; he preached to the people who were in confusion and brought them to the Christian faith. Through his preaching at that time those living on the Maltese island came to recognize the true God.

The above-mentioned Maltese knights, whom the granmaestro had sent to me, asked if I would go with them a short distance from the church of the apostle Paul to

[7] Tolstoi visits the Citta Vecchia, or La Notabile, the ancient capital of Malta. He describes the cathedral, the parish church San Publio, and the famous Church of San Paolo, situated over the grotto occupied by the apostle Paul for three months.

see a home of the granmaestro, which he keeps for amusement on Malta, some distance from the city of Malta; and around this home are fine gardens. This request was carried out, and I arrived at the granmaestro's home. This home is built on a rather large stone mountain; it does not have many rooms but is built of fine proportions. Inside, some of the rooms have the paintings of artists and others are covered with silks; and fine bedsteads are placed in them /128/ and all the beds' curtains and spreads are of silk taffeta, and in another room the bed's curtains and spread are of silk. The granmaestro sleeps on this bed when he comes to stay in this house, and on the other beds sleep the knights who accompany him for amusement. In the great central chamber along the wall is the granmaestro's throne with a canopy over it. And the above-mentioned knights, who came to this house to entertain me, played cards among themselves. When dinnertime neared, the knights asked me to dine in the granmaestro's house; to this end the granmaestro sent to this house from the city of Malta his majordomo and his cooks, and they prepared dinner for me in that house. And this day I ate in his home, sitting at a round table with those knights. On the table was a fine tablecloth and napkins that were nicely decorated in the French manner, and the dinner was luxurious and consisted of many courses, and the viands were marvelously done in various forms. We also drank various wines of Wallachia,[8] Florence, and Naples, which we drank mixed with clear water. After dinner they placed on the table many confections, including marvelous sweets and all kinds of things cooked in sugar, and fine fresh fruits. At this dinner the dishes, plates, spoons, salt cellars, and all other vessels were of silver, and the confections and fruits were finely arranged on silver dishes and plates. And after dinner I walked with those knights simply and without ceremony, and those who wished slept, and those who wanted walked; others played cards.

And when the midday heat subsided, those knights and I strolled in the granmaestro's garden which was built by the house. His garden is very large, built among hills, and in it are many trees—lemon, pomegranate, olive, fig, walnut, almond, pear, plum, apple, peach and other kinds, chestnut, *tsukat, shtot* (?), and dates, and also many kinds of grapes, white and red, and other fruits that grow on bushes. In this garden are fine fence rows made of fine fragrant bushes and flowers. In his garden I saw many marvelous fountains from which fine fresh clean water flows in streams, and among these fountains I saw one of very fine craftsmanship, from which water flows in many various ways: in one the water flows like a sun with long rays around it, and then it flows like the stars, also with rays, and then in many other forms, which I refrain from describing in detail because I lack the time. /129/ But the rest of this fountain's parts are most marvelous. When they block up the water so that none flows forth, they place a pomegranate on the top of the fountain, and they release the water, and the water raises the pomegranate high above the fountain and holds it for a long time on the water, and it cannot fall; and again it falls to the place

[8] *Voloskii;* here the meaning could be "Italian."

where it was before and again it rises. And they do this as many times as they wish, and when that pomegranate is held aloft by the water, they can keep it there atop the water all day and it will not fall; and it is raised to a height of a sazhen and a half or two or more from the fountain and is held as if in the air. This is a very fine fountain and is most miraculously crafted.

Then we went to an enclosure built on a hill, and it is filled with many wild deer and goats. Then I left that garden in the carriage with the knights and returned to the city of Malta, and those knights conducted me to the inn in which I stayed, and having bowed to me, they went home.

July 25. In the morning the knight Joseph Manoel came to me, and then they sent the granmaestro's carriage in which I and the knight went to the Church of John the Baptist, which has a bishop of the Roman faith. This church is large and marvelously built. At this church live 120 priests who serve in this church and in the chapels of the church. These priests wear on their black habits a white linen cross sewn on the left shoulder, and others of them wear a gold knightly cross by permission of the granmaestro. This church has a very fine and large chapel, and in it is an altar of the Roman faith, and on it are two angels of cast silver, and one finely crafted cast figure also of silver but gilded in places. It is very large. This figure holds a large vessel of silver more than an arshin in height, and three quarters of an arshin in width. This vessel rotates and on it is another vessel, also of gold, which bears the right forearm of St. John the Prophet and Forerunner, the baptizer of the Lord. When they want to remove this holy forearm from the silver vessel, a priest ascends the altar from behind and rotates this silver vessel toward himself with a key; he can then remove the holy arm. Or he opens the case so that the golden vessel with the holy arm can be seen by turning the silver vessel so its door faces the people. And when I entered this chapel that holy arm was /130/ in the golden vessel, having been taken from the silver vessel; one Roman priest placed the golden vessel with the Baptist's arm on the altar. This vessel of gold is of fine work and is more than half an arshin high, and wide enough to contain a human forearm. It is four-sided and on all four sides crystals are set, so that the arm of the Blessed Forerunner is visible in it. On the top of this vessel is a four-pointed cross similar to the crosses worn by Maltese knights, all of gold and diamonds. In it there are more than five hundred large and small diamonds and in the middle is one very large and immeasurably pure four-faceted diamond. And when I approached the altar wishing to see that holy arm, a Roman priest took note of my desire and deigned to show that holy arm to me; he took the golden vessel from the altar. The holy right arm of the Baptist from the elbow to the fingers is all covered with gold, and on the fingers openings are made in the gold. The Roman priest opened them for me, and showed me the naked holy hand of the Forerunner; this holy hand has on it skin and flesh and veins and nails, all undecayed and scarcely withered, just like a living man's and not dark, but only a little bit darkened. And thus I was able to kiss that holy arm; and the Roman priest again concealed it with the gold vessel and placed it in the silver vessel on the altar where the arm of John the Forerunner always rests.

Then I went from this chapel to a vessel repository that is attached to the great church of the Forerunner. In this repository they showed me many things:

An image of the Savior drawn by Luke the Evangelist and printed on some kind of thin skin or other such material, so long ago one cannot tell, and it is pasted on a board; and in this image the Savior is painted in a crown of thorns and in crimson robes, as at the time of His blessed passion. The size of this image is three-fourths of an arshin high and a half arshin in width; and on the other side of the board on which the holy image is pasted is an image of the Blessed Mother of God inscribed on paper; it was also done by Luke the Evangelist.

Then they showed me a cross in which there is wood from the holy cross of Christ. In this cross is a spike of the crown of thorns of Christ, and also in that cross is the most pure blood of Christ our Divine Savior in a small crystal vessel.

The foot of St. Lazarus, whom Christ raised from the dead, the whole metatarsus and toes undecayed. /131/

A small part of the Blessed Baptist's nose.

A part of the relic of the hand of the great teacher of the Eastern Church, the Blessed St. John Chrysostom, patriarch of Constantinople.

A part of the relics of the holy chiefs of the apostles Peter and Paul.

Part of the relics of the apostle St. James.

Part of the relics of the apostle St. Bartholomew.

Part of the arm of St. Anne, the mother of the Blessed Mother of God.

Part of the skull of the martyr St. Panteleimon (Pantaleon).[9]

A finger of the Holy Mary Magdalene uncorrupted, having flesh and skin, and a nail, all whole.

The hand of St. Cyriacus, likewise all undecayed.

Part of the relics of the great martyr St. Ephim (Euphemia), the most praised.[10]

A bone from the hand of the great martyr St. George the Victorious.

Part of the relics of the martyr St. Clement.

[9] St. Panteleimon, or Pantaleon, was a martyr, d. 305. Known as the Great Martyr and Wonder Worker and one of the Holy Moneyless Ones, he practiced medicine gratis. He survived six assassination attempts before he was beheaded; his relics liquefy, as do those of St. Januarius in Naples.

[10] Euphemia the Far-Renowned was a martyr at Chalcedon, d. 303, for refusing to attend a pagan festival.

Part of the relics of the hand of St. Augustine, teacher of the Western church.

Part of the relics of the pennyless Sts. Cosmas and Damian.[11]

A small cross on a pedestal, before which the Maltese granmaestro swears when he is consecrated as granmaestro. In it is a small piece of wood from Christ's cross.

A cross in which there is also a piece of wood from the cross of Christ, and also a spike from the crown of thorns of Christ, stained with the most pure and precious divine blood. In it are also two small pieces of a certain ancient material. The Maltese say that this is a part of the chasuble of the Savior, but it resembles lapis lazuli and glass—colored, thick, uncommon, and unpolished.

In one great silver casket are many various blessed things of martyrs and other such people, all visible behind glass.

Then they showed me two gold crosses that they carry in processions; they are four-pointed, of a size a little less than an arshin, and in them are many marvelous stones: sapphires, rubies, large emeralds, and diamonds, one of which is valued at 20,000 gold chervontsy, and another is even more costly. These crosses are of marvelous enamel work.

Then they showed me a golden monstrance in the manner of the Roman Church of turned work, in which there is half a pud of gold.

Then they showed me many golden vessels of marvelous work, and in these vessels and monstrances and in the crosses described above there are more than five puds of gold. Then they showed many silver vessels of fine work; also many bishops' vestments and /132/ sewn caps of bishops with stones; and rings that bishops of the Western church wear customarily during the service; and also many panageia (breast-icons) and crosses that Roman bishops wear at the time of the service. Then I saw a standing image of the Blessed Mother of God in this vessel repository, and she holds in her arms the Eternal Child-Christ, our Savior, cast of silver and more than an arshin in height. They also have an image of the twelve apostles, also cast of silver of the same size, in which there are 20 or more puds of silver. In this same repository they showed me the relics of the Roman saints, who lived after the schism of the Faith: Sts. Baldeshki (?) and Tafshkana (?) and St. Kiary the Franciscan (?).[12]

Then from this church I went to the inn where I was staying, and the knight Joseph Manoel with me. Arriving at the inn, I dismissed the granmaestro's carriage and gave a present to his servant who had served me with the carriage, because this day I

[11] Cosmos and Damien are venerated in the East as Moneyless Ones for practicing medicine free of charge; with St. Luke, they are the patron saints of doctors. The Orthodox Church honors three pairs of saints of these same names.

[12] Tolstoi's syntax is precise; he lists three Roman saints since the schism of the Churches. *Baldeshki* may be Balthasar Ravaschieri, d. 1492, Friar Minor of the Observance, who had a vision of Our Lady. Saints *Tafshkana* and *Kiary* the Franciscan are more of a problem. I suspect he means Blessed Claritus, or *Chiarito*, d. 1348; *Tafshkana* may be "The Tuscan."

would depart from Malta. Then I gave a present to the knight Joseph Manoel and thanked him for the affection he had shown me on Malta; and through this same knight Joseph Manoel I conveyed a deep bow and my thanks to the granmaestro of Malta for the many kindnesses that he had ordered be shown to me throughout his realm.

Then knight Joseph Manoel gave me a passaporto, that is, a travel certificate, with which I could enter all of Sicily and Calabria, even as far as Naples.

Then this knight Joseph gave me from the granmaestro a certificate in which the granmaestro of Malta greeted me and gave me presents for my coming to Malta; and I accepted this certificate as a great gift, and I thanked the Maltese granmaestro very much for it. In the certificate it says:

> Brother and Lord Raimund Perellos Rokaful [Ramon Perellos y Roccaful, Grand Master, 1697–1720], by the grace of God humble and miserable Master of the hospital of St. John of Jerusalem and of the *zhelnerskoi* (protecting?) order of the Holy Tomb of the Lord, and of the Passion of Jesus Christ.
>
> When to our island of Malta and to our monastery came the honorable and honorably born gentleman Peter Andreevich [Tolstoi], a noble of the most glorious tsarist throne of Muscovy, in possession of a certificate of his tsarist majesty, by which he delivers to all the sovereigns of Europe a greeting, we ordered him to be received and did ourself receive this same honorable and honorably born Peter Andreevich and his effects, with the civility and favor appropriate to him, as his glorious civility and manifest deeds entitled him, /133/ and commended him to the right forearm of St. John of the Holy Cross, Our Patron, endowed for our respect, in order that he might see all that he wished. And we showed him the fortresses and stores of our island; and he could not see all of the galleys of our armada because we had sent most to aid the Venetian armada; however, he did see two of our galleys when they came to us from Sicily, and on them he sped from the ships of the heathen Turks and would have been overtaken, but that a strong and contrary wind for their insolence made this impossible. The hostile ship did chase the felucca that carried this honorably born Peter Andreevich, but through the grace and care of God he came happily to our port, and then after turning toward that port the two galleys could again be seen in good time. And we, having respected his arrival among us, upon his departure gave him this, our certificate, with which we sincerely request from our heart that all, especially the most glorious sovereigns and princes wherever he happens to go, deign to receive the gentleman Peter Andreevich with esteemed *gonor* (It. *onore*) and *favor* (*favore*), and with every courtesy, and to this end this certificate testifies, impressed in wax with the seal of our chancellor, on Malta, on our monastery, on the 21st of July, 1698.

On the certificate is written: "Written in the chancellery."

On this same certificate the chancellery governor signed it: "Gerat Ferdinand Kontreraz (Contreras), Governor of the Chancellery."

On this same certificate is the seal of the Maltese island impressed in black wax.

And I lingered on this island until the 12th hour, and in the 12th hour, having paid the innkeeper for everything, I went to the felucca, where the knight Joseph Manoel conducted me, and in the felucca on this 25th day of July at four hours before night I left the island of Malta for the island of Sicily.

The island of Malta is not large, in all 60 It. miles around it, and from the island of Sicily it stands on a southern wind, which in Italian is called *ostro* (It. *austro*). The whole island of Malta is stone, and there are few places on it where grain and grapes and other fruit grow.

There are many dwellings on the island of Malta, and many people, cities, towns, and villages on the island, and all are under the Maltese granmaestro. Horses on the Maltese /134/ island are few, and none of them are good, and they work and haul all things on mules and on hinnies. The base people on the island of Malta live with their wives and children, they are permitted to marry, and they are all Catholics of the Roman faith.

The chief city on the island is called Malta; it is not small and it is populous. In this city live the granmaestro and all the knights as if in a monastery, and they do not have wives.

In this city are two stone Greek churches, one named for the Blessed Mother of God and the other for Nicholas the Wonder Worker. Greek priests serve at these churches, and there are a few wretched Greeks; there are also some people of the Greek faith who have fled, and have been rescued from Turkish slavery; they are from Constantinople and from other Turkish cities.

Of Roman churches in Malta there are 24 parish churches; besides the chapels, there are 7 monasteries of various orders of the Roman faith and 4 convents of the Roman faith. These Roman monasteries and churches are well built and very rich.

The homes of the knights and of all inhabitants of Malta are built of stone and are very fine.

The streets of Malta are all paved with cut, four-cornered stones with slopes, so that water never stands, and they are never dirty.

The city of Malta stands on an uneven place by the sea on the slope of a hill, and those streets and lanes in Malta that are on the slope have fine stone stairways so that one can climb them without difficulty.

In Malta there are many shops and wares of all kinds, and also bread and foodstuffs of all kinds, and many fruits, too, and food is not expensive. The Maltese mercante, that is, the merchants of Malta, have fine homes and live with their wives and children.

They employ in slave labor very many Turks, both men and women, who were captured at sea and enslaved, and there are also Arabs, only not so many, and there are more Berbers from Barbary.

The island of Malta is very close to Barbary; the Berber cities of the Turkish Sultan are 100 versts from Malta or closer.[13]

On the island of Malta in the summer it is very hot from the sun, for this island is

[13] Tolstoi underestimates the distance; it is 335 kilometers from Malta to Tripoli.

in Africa and has a latitude of 39 degrees, close to the equator, and therefore on Malta /135/ it is immeasurably hot, and there is no cold season and never any snow.[14]

The city of Malta is fortified with strongholds from the sea and the land such as the human mind cannot comprehend. Around it are 8 forts so constructed as strongholds that one can scarcely describe them.

On both sides of the city of Malta are great sea inlets, into which ships and galleys enter, and they call these inlets porto in Italian, and ships' harbors in Slavonic. Of the two, in one is a small island on which there is a building called a lazzaretto, or Campo Marzio. When a slaver or any other vessel arrives from the East, it comes to this island, and the people from such ships stay on that island in that house; and they cannot leave that little island, and no one can go to them for 40 days, for fear of pestilent plague and all the other infectious illnesses; in the Levant, that is in the East, on the island of Morea and other such places, and even in Constantinople there is often pestilent plague, and other illnesses in people. And so on this island arriving people stay for 40 days and if no illnesses show in them, they and their ships are given freedom to leave the island and to go where they wish and to sail unhindered. On Malta 60,000 soldiers are collected, and more when needed.

The Maltese granmaestro has 7 large galleys in Malta, one of which has a general and six have captains. Of these seven galleys the general's and four of the captain's are obliged to go all year to the Levant, that is, to the East, to Morea to aid the Venetian armada and to fight the Turks; and two captain's galleys are obliged all year to stay in Malta and go constantly from Malta to the island of Sicily and from Sicily to Malta, clearing this route of the Turks, so that from Sicily to Malta and also from the Maltese island to Sicily there is a route for travelers. The cursed dogs,[15] watching the Maltese galleys go to the East and knowing that only two galleys remain at Malta, roam incessantly in large and small vessels on the Maltese canal, and prey on those Christians whom they can catch, and this often happens.

[14] Malta's capital is at latitude 35°54′; the mean temperature in January is 61°F, and in August, 95°.

[15] Here and throughout the Diary, Tolstoi expresses strong anti-Turkish feelings, but they are not too surprising. The Eastern Church had reasons to hate Islam, and at the moment Russia and the European nations were at war with the Ottomans; in addition, the language of contemporary diplomacy was hardly conducive to fence mending. For example, one can cite the hostile words of the Sultan's Declaration of War on the emperor in 1683:

> I declare unto you, I will make my self your Master, pursue you to the end of the Earth; . . . [I will] trample under feet with my Horses all that is acceptable and pleasant in your Eyes. . . . It will be a pleasure to me, to give a publick establishment of my Religion, and to pursue your Crucified God, whose Wrath I fear not, nor his coming to your Assistance, to deliver you out of my hands. I will according to my pleasure put your Sacred Priests to the Plough, and expose the Brests of your Matrons to be Suckt by Dogs and other Beasts. [From Macartney, ed., *The Habsburg and Hohenzollern Dynasties*, p. 58.]

In Malta the knights are all travelers from various states—from Germany, Spain, France, Poland, Italy, and from other places, and all are Catholics. The custom of the Maltese /136/ knights is this: when someone arrives in Malta, wishing to join the knighthood and to be wedded to the knight's cross, he must previously have been a true Catholic of the Roman faith, and no one of another faith can be a knight. Then he must bring to Malta from his fatherland a testimonial that he is of noble birth through his father and his mother and to four generations, and that he is unmarried; in addition, he must swear that to his death he will not marry, but will keep himself pure even to his death. Then he must give to the Maltese treasury one hundred and twenty five Spanish rupees, that is, 250 golden chervontsy. Then he must go for two years on the Maltese galleys to the Levant, that is, to the East, to Morea to fight against the Turks in the aid of the Venetian armada. For two additional years he must be on those Maltese galleys that remain in Malta to guard the Sicilian routes. And in these four years on the galleys he gets food from the captain on whose ship he serves; the Maltese treasury pays the captain for the feeding of the knights who are on his galley. And only when he has been on galleys at sea and in the Maltese canal for the appointed time is he given the knight's cross for swearing three causes: first, piety; second, obedience; third, poverty; and this is done by the Maltese knight. For his sustenance he receives 80 scudos a year from the Maltese treasury while he lives in Malta, and if a knight does not wish to take this pay he may eat each day with the other knights who are not supported by pay. And to house the knights they built 7 houses in Malta. In the first dine the Germans, that is, those of the Empire; in another, the Spanish; in a third, Italians; in a fourth, French; in a fifth, Poles; and in a sixth, Hungarians. In the seventh live the knights of various other states.[16]

In Malta there are various knights: the first are called *grancroci,* that is, the elder and honorable people, who wear large crosses of white calico sewn on the upper part of their black habits. The granmaestro is selected from among these.

Then there are the knights who wear the knight's cross, having gone on two armadas, as I have written in this book above.

Then there are the knights who are granted the cross "of piety" by petition or on the basis of some recognized honorable reason. They are free to wear these crosses on themselves and on their coat of arms wherever they wish. /137/

Then they grant the cross *grazie,* that is, "of grace," to anyone whom the granmaestro wishes, and these crosses too may be worn however they wish.

The Maltese knights are free to live wherever they wish. Those who do not wish to live on Malta are free to go to their native land or wherever they wish to serve; but when needed, when enemies come to Malta in great force, and when the Maltese granmaestro sends a notice to the Maltese knights that all knights of Malta should speed to Malta, then every knight is obliged to quit his affairs and to go to Malta; even if an enemy is in his own native land, he cannot be barred from his journey to Malta.

[16] These are the *auberges* of the nationalities.

The people in Malta are very civil and respectful toward forestiere, that is, to foreigners, who come there because on Malta are honorable people who have all come from other lands.

A good number of craftsmen of all sorts are on Malta.

Among the Knights of Malta, as well as among the inhabitants, there are no coaches, and the knights and people do not go about the city of Malta in coaches or on horseback; if one wishes to go outside the city, one goes in a carriage or on horseback. But in the city of Malta only the Maltese granmaestro goes about in a coach with six coachmen, and he has two or three coaches, in which there are two or four coachmen, and grancroci sit in them when they go somewhere instead of the granmaestro. And the granmaestro of Malta goes about all day, and he walks and looks at the fortifications of his city, and then he goes to a garden that is built in the city of Malta on the seacoast, and there he is refreshed with fruits, and he looks at the fountain, the fine one built in this garden. But the Knights of Malta, who because of old age or sickness are unable to stroll about on foot, are carried in sedan chairs, and they have their own fine gilded chairs covered with velvet and with other fine work.

The city of Malta has three passage gates, which are strongly fortified against unfriendly entry, and all three gates are locked all night. At the entrance, where all kinds of vessels enter Malta, is a fine wharf. The whole shore is paved with cut white stones, and from the shore to the sea they have made passages like fine stone staircases. And on the shore opposite the city gates is a stone column; on it is placed a half-length image of John the Forerunner, cast of brass, to show that he is the protector of Malta. /138/

To go from the city of Malta to other places, one is carried over the sea in barques, and the Maltese knights and all the people go in barques, and these barques have a linen cover and are made in a distinctive fashion. As naval vessels on Malta they use galleys, tartans, feluccas, brigantines, and other such vessels, but they do not have cargo ships, frigates, *marciliane*, and the like.[17]

The Maltese galleys, when they are in Malta, stand away from the city's port on the other side near their captains' homes; this is also close to the mariners' homes. And beneath the captains' homes they situate four galleys, and beneath the mariners' three, so that should an enemy accidentally approach, the galleys can depart the Maltese port with great speed to pursue the enemy's vessels, and to seek out the enemy.

When the Maltese granmaestro deals with weighty affairs and the urgent business of Malta, 40 elderly and honorable Maltese knights sit with him in chamber.

The Maltese granmaestro receives great respect from the knights and all the people, as is befitting a *gospodar* (Lord), and they harken to him in all things; but he is solely concerned with the affairs of the knights of Malta, and does not rule the people.

[17]The list suggests that the Knights of Malta have warships and coastal craft, but not large cargo vessels.

And this 25th of July upon my departure, the granmaestro sent a Knight of Malta to me, and he greeted me in the name of the granmaestro. He wished me good health and sent me on my way with great affection.

The Maltese granmaestro always wears black attire; a large white cross is sewn on the top of his habit over the left shoulder. The grancroci, that is, the elderly and the best of the Maltese knights who are selected by the granmaestro, wear similar attire.

The Maltese knights wear habits of various fashions, but most use French dress of various colors. On Malta no Maltese knight can wear a golden kaftan or other outer or under garment, and no Knight of Malta can wear on his dress any spun gold or silver, and no buttons of spun gold or silver. The present granmaestro issued this command three years ago, so that the Knights of Malta would not expend the treasury on such attire, but instead the money could go for war and for service attire.

The women folk in Malta wear a dress of the same fashion as the Turkish, and on top they are covered with long black taffeta that goes from head to foot; /139/ and they cover their heads in the same way as do the nuns of Kiev.

The city of Malta has 700 large and small cannon, all of bronze, along the walls and on the bastions.

Around the city in Malta are many stone windmills, which grind all kinds of grain with sails, and the sails are woolen.

On the island of Malta there are no forests anywhere, and they transport coal and wood from the island of Sicily. There are no horned cattle or cows on the island of Malta, and they bring cheeses and butter from Sicily and other places. Likewise, there is never any snow or ice on the island of Malta, and it too is brought from Sicily. And they bring all the wares on the island of Malta from France, England, Italy, and other places.

The money in Malta is all brass, and they have no silver coins; they change gold chervontsy to bronze money, which they call tara, and in each tara are 20 grana, and in a scudo are 12 tara, and for each gold chervonets they give 3 scudo, that is, 36 tara.

I left the port of the island of Malta in a felucca by oars, and having gone a little way, we raised the sail, the wind being unfavorable and slight, and we ran on this wind along the sea of the Maltese gulf for an hour. And then it became bonaccia, that is, windless, and we went on oars until the third hour of night. In the fourth hour of night a favorable and strong wind arose, and we raised two sails and raced on that wind all night, and in the first hour of ***July 26*** we neared the island of Sicily. And then the wind ceased, so we furled our sails and proceeded by rowing. In the 3rd hour of the 26th of July we neared a place called Capo Passero; and in that place we stood until the 12th hour of that day, and we also went by rowing. Then a favorable and strong wind arose, and we raised two sails and sailed in our felucca on that wind all day, and in the 3rd hour before night we neared a place called Bonachi,[18] 130 Italian miles from Malta. We stayed the night in the harbor beneath this place; a few people live here, and they are all fishermen, but few in number.

[18] This is possibly Fontane Bianche, between Avola and Siracusa on Sicily.

July 27. We went by rowing because it was calm; and then a slight wind arose and we hoisted two sails; we also rowed with oars for it again became bonaccia, that is, windless, and again there was a wind, and all day we went sometimes on oars and sometimes on sail. Six hours before night we stopped at a place called Liadretsa (Trezza), and we stayed there six hours /140/ of day and one hour of night, and we rowed out of this place and wanted to go the whole night so as to enter Messina in the morning. And as we left the port, at that time the wind was strong and contrary to our course, and also the influx and outflow of sea water in its natural course were contrary to our desired course. Therefore we could go no further this night, but stayed close to one of the guardia, that is, a watchtower, which stands on the seacoast on the island of Sicily to prevent hostile raids, as I have written in detail above in this book. Those soldiers who stand on guard there did not let us draw near to them, and did not believe us and feared we were the enemy, and so they fired at us from muskets; however, with the help of God all of us were preserved intact from this shooting. We stayed away from this watchtower in a place, one Italian mile or less from Trezza, waiting for the time when the contrary wind would lessen and the sea water, in accord with its nature, would return to a course agreeable to our route. And at midnight we left this place because the sea water in its natural movement in this hour was not contrary to our course. It drew us favorably along our desired route, but the wind was contrary and very strong after midnight. And until daybreak and the five hours of daylight we rowed along the shore with great difficulty.

July 28. In the 5th hour of day we stopped beneath the city of Santa-Lizina because the wind was contrary to us and very strong, and we could not go either on sail or on oars. We stayed in this place 10 hours, waiting for the contrary wind to stop, or for the blowing to change, so that we could go either by sail or by oars. And all day the wind did not cease or change, and we stayed there four hours of night. In the fifth hour we left that city by rowing, for there was a wind, but it was contrary; only it was not so strong, and we rowed all night, and in the first hour of the day of July 29th, being still 12 Italian miles from Messina, we hired a horse and fastened our felucca with a rope to that horse, and thus that horse drew us along the shore to Messina, because the mariners were exhausted from rowing against contrary and strong winds.

July 29. In the third hour of day we arrived in Messina at the time of the Messina fair; having landed I showed them my pratica, that is, my travel document, which had been given to me in Malta; and having looked at my travel document they allowed me to enter the city. And I left the felucca and went to an inn where I stayed before I went to Malta, and in this inn I dined. /141/ I stayed this day until the 12th hour, and at four hours of night I left the inn for the felucca, and we left on our course to Naples along the shore of the Sicilian island.

The above-mentioned Messina fair is held every year in July for 15 days; mercante, that is, merchants from various places with various wares, from France, England, Italy, and other states, all come here to trade in Messina outside the city on the seashore; for this fair they make stalls of boards, and in these stalls the itinerant merchants and the inhabitants of Messina are all gathered together with all kinds of wares; and if a traveling merchant is unable to sell all his goods at the time of the fair, he will afterwards exchange his wares for those of another merchant, and thus he will return to his former region.

On the sea at Messina are many feluccas and fishing barques in which they catch large fish; these fish the Spanish call *shpad* (It. *pesce spada,* swordfish), which resemble the sevruga fish, only they are large like a beluga [sturgeon], and have a long nose, as much as half a sazhen in length. The fish does not have a *viziga* (spinal cord) but has spinal bones like a ling. They also catch other large and small fish that one finds in the sea; it is not expensive to buy any kind of fish in Messina, and the *rak* (lobster, crab) are large, an arshin in length, and very thick.

This day at two hours before night we went to a place called Tortodefar (Torre di Faro), 12 Italian miles from Messina, which stands on the corner of the Sicilian island opposite Calabria. And we stayed at this place until nightfall, and in the first hour of night we went across the narrow sea to Calabria, because we could not spend the night beneath Torre di Faro. In this place the island of Sicily and the Calabrian island [*sic*] are close together, and the sea passage between Calabria and Sicily is very narrow. When the sea water in its nature flows in and out, through this narrow place the sea very much resembles a fast-flowing river, and thus we were afraid to stay in this place, lest our felucca be broken up by the water, or by its sails at night. And in the fourth hour of night we neared the Calabrian shore, and we stopped under the city of Liabaniarom (Bagnara), 15 Italian miles from Tore di Faro. We stood beneath Bagnara all night because we could not go further at night; we were prevented [from moving] by a great cloud which produced heavy rain and hail all night, and lightning flashed immeasurably.

July 30. Early in the morning we left Bagnara on oars because there was no wind at all, and the island of Sicily /142/ remained behind us to the left, and Calabria was to our right. Then we came opposite a little island called Strongolo (Stromboli).[19] On this islet is a high mountain that has burned incessantly since the creation of the world; in the day one can see a great smoke coming from it, and at night great flames of fire arise from it. This mountain was to my left and Calabria to the right, and in this place we picked up a west wind, which the Italians call *potent* (It. *potente*), and we raised two sails and sped on that wind most of the day, and two hours before night we came to the city of Liabonteia (Tropea) in Calabria; we spent the night beneath this city.

[19] Stromboli, called Strongyle for its circular form, has a volcanic cone (3,040 feet high) in a constant state of activity.

July 31. A half hour before daybreak we left Tropea on oars because there was no wind at that time, and in the third hour of day we came to a place called Pavlo (Paola). Beneath this place we stopped because the padrone, that is, the master of the felucca that carried me, and the mariners wanted to hear Mass, because this was a feast day.[20] And having heard Mass, we again went in the fifth hour by rowing because we had a calm, and we came this day at five hours before night to a place called Porto-di-Santa-Maria in Calabria, and we spent the night in this place.

August 1. Three hours before daybreak, we rowed out of Porto-di-Santa-Maria, for there was no wind, and then a slight wind arose and we raised two sails for a short time; then the wind again ceased and we lowered our sails and again rowed past all of Calabria. Then we came opposite the coast of the Neapolitan kingdom; in this place a considerable wind arose, and we sailed on that wind, but not all day, for at six hours before night we sailed to a place in the Neapolitan kingdom called Palianudo (Palinuro). We stopped and spent the night beneath that place. In this place there is no city, only one inn, that is, a guest house at the port, where vessels can avoid the contrary winds.

August 2. In the first hour of day we left Palinuro on oars; but we could not leave the port for fear of the great agitation of the sea, and we turned back. Three other feluccas that wanted to go to Naples stood together with our felucca in the same port, and to prevent the great waves from breaking up the feluccas on the land, we drew all of them out of the water and onto the shore. In this same port stood three tartans that could not go to sea because of the rough weather at sea. In /143/ this port they catch many fish called *tundy* (tunny fish) in Spanish. These fish are the size of a small sturgeon, with a head like a salmon, and this fish has a peculiar *ipostas* (Gk., visage). The body of this fish is grey but reddish like beef flesh; but when this fish is boiled or baked it becomes white. The body of this fish is also flaky and very tasty. The Spanish make great use of this fish. In this port fishermen took one hundred twenty of these fish in one night. And this 2nd day of August we stayed

[20] August 10 by the Roman calendar is the feast of St. Laurence, martyr, a feast on which every parish priest says Mass for the people of his parish.

In early-modern Europe the number of feast days had multiplied, and only in the 1740s under Benedict XIV was there a movement to reduce them. Modern logic would suggest that the reason was to benefit the capitalists, who were, with Sundays, denied as many as one hundred days of labor a year. In fact, the chief argument was the opposite: the large number of feasts "made it hard for the poor to earn bread." Eventually eighteen feasts were removed, but public objection was strong. When one pastor announced the new orders (1770) "the congregation stood up and shouted, crying 'Drive him from the pulpit, the seven sacraments are abolished.'" Benedict's abolition of feasts caused him to be suspected of Lutheranism, and police charged with enforcing the new workdays often refused to prosecute for fear of popular discontent. See Chadwick, *Popes and European Revolution*, pp. 28–32.

in this port, awaiting favorable times for sailing a whole day, and we could not leave the port obstructed by a great contrary wind, and we spent another night in that port. We had with us only scant bread and wine, and nothing could be found for sale in the port except the above-mentioned fish, for this place is empty and far from inhabited places, and we could not find fruits, that is, clusters of grapes, for sale, either, for around this port the hills are rocky and the forests small, and there is very little arable land where they sow wheat, and no fruit trees grow on these hills. The inhabitants of these hills are very poor, and one meets very few of them in this place, and all of them are engaged in fishing, and they sell fish to a cloister, that is, to a monastery close to this port in the hills. In this port I found three Frenchmen, who told me that the French prince is coming to Naples with 20 galleys, and he now was staying close to Rome in the city of Tsitaveche (Civitavecchia); and we had hoped to sail to Naples during these days.

August 3. In the first hour of day we left Palinuro rowing. Having left the port at sea we raised two sails, for the wind was from the side but favorable to our desired course, and on this wind we sailed three hours and came to a place called Liatseron (Ascea), and entered the port under it. Coming up to the shore, we drew our felucca from the water onto the shore, because this port is rocky, and we feared the great sea waves would break our felucca on the rocks; and we could not go on our desired course from this place because the wind blew from the side and was very strong; the sea's waves were also unnaturally high. And from Palinuro with great fear we had gone as far as the place called Ascea, and beneath Ascea we stayed until dinner that day, awaiting a change or a cessation of the foul weather. At dinnertime the wind changed, and a very great wind contrary to us arose, and then a very great rain began, /144/ and therefore we could not leave Ascea but stayed there until night. In the night, too, there was a contrary wind and a great rain, and we stayed the night because of this great fortuna.

August 4. A half hour before daylight we rowed from Ascea because the wind had stopped, and it was calm and the sea was not greatly agitated. And thus we went this day until the 3rd hour, and in the third hour we sailed into the city of Lalakosa (Licosa). A guard from Naples stands here for all traveling vessels on the sea that go from Naples to Calabria and from Calabria to Naples. In this place every vessel that sails from Calabria to Naples must stop and show all the things that are in the vessel, so that no wares are carried to Naples without paying a tax. And when our felucca stopped at the shore at this place, a Neapolitan came to me on the felucca; he stays here on guard for the authorities, and he examined all the things that I had with me on the felucca and looked into my trunk, which had my things in it. He also examined everything of the master's and of the mariners', and seeing that there were no merchants' wares of any kind on the felucca, he released us promptly.

Having gone a little way from this place, we raised two sails, for the wind arose favorable to us, but it was not strong, so even on this wind with two sails, we rowed as well. We went this day until the 5th hour and in the fifth hour the wind again stopped, and it was windless until the 7th hour, and we went by rowing, and in the 7th hour a large wind arose, but not favorable to us, and this wind the Italians call the *nepont* (It. *ponente*), that is, the west. And we raised two sails and sailed on this wind to the land, but we could no longer follow our route with this wind; and at three hours before nightfall we arrived beneath a place called Santo-Andrea (Sant'Andrea), and we stopped in the port where smaller vessels stand.

This city stands on the very shore beneath high hills; its buildings are all stone and it is built on a pleasant spot. In this city lives an archbishop of the Roman faith. In this same city in a chamber rest 100 human bodies, all undecayed; and who these people were and to what faith they belonged is uncertain, because their bodies have laid here undecayed since antiquity. Around this city are very high stone hills above the sea, and on these hills are built many fine stone dwellings, and among the structures on one hill is a monastery of the Roman faith in which live monks of the Franciscan order. In this monastery is a church named for the Blessed Mother of God and a miracle-working icon. This monastery stands on a very pleasant place, and its buildings are all of stone and quite fine. And we stayed in this port until night, and we spent the night in this same port.

August 5. 4 hours before daylight we left this place rowing, and we went 3 hours along the shore. One hour before daybreak we found over us a large cloud from which came thunder, lightning, and unnaturally heavy rain, and a wind contrary to our desired course, and we could not go further, but were thrown into a port in an empty place; and had we not been drawn into that little harbor we would have been at sea in great fear. And we stayed in that empty place for an hour, and three other feluccas stayed there with us. When daylight came, we left this port rowing, because the cloud passed, but there was still a little rain, and we were prevented from sailing. And thus we rowed two hours of day, and then a slight wind arose, favorable to us, which the Italians call the *siroka* (scirocco), that is, between east and south. We raised two sails and sped on this wind to Naples, and we ran one hour through the canal. In one place it smelled damply of the great amber oil as if a great deal of it had spilled where we were. The Neapolitans told me that in antiquity there was a great city in this place where they made a lot of oil of amber (*Iantarnoe maslo,* probably ambergris), and by the will of God in antiquity this city and the island on which it stood were flooded by the sea. From that time even to today one smells the amber oil in this place. When it is calm and the sea is still, and when there are not even small waves, they come in small barques to this place, and the amber oil comes to the surface of the water, and they can collect it in vessels and use it for the illnesses of animals. From this place our favorable wind diminished and we sailed both with sails and with oars for speed, so as to sail quickly into Naples. We were still afraid of the cloud that had so troubled our route this day, about which I have written above. And thus we sailed another hour and the city of Naples came into view and we went on oars into Naples, and the sails we did not furl; and in the fifth hour of day we sailed into Naples, and landing on the shore in the Neapolitan port, and showing my pratica, that is, my travel document that was given to me in Malta, I left the felucca and went to an inn in Naples where I had previously stayed, which was called the Gelimbadeoro (Alla Colomba d'Oro).

This same day, having heard of my arrival in Naples, the Knight /146/ of Malta, Niccolo, and his brother, the Neapolitan Gaetano, surnamed Ricco, came to me at the inn and greeted me joyfully; likewise, in gratitude I thanked them for their affection for me and for the letters to Malta that had gained me all manner of affection from the Knights of Malta. And having sat with me for a while, these Neapolitans went home, and this day I went nowhere from the inn.

August 6. After dinner the Neapolitan Maltese Niccolo Ricco sent his servant to me at the inn, and he sent with him a gift of a small holy icon painted on ivory of fine artistic craftsmanship; it is the image of the Crucifixion of Christ. This same day the same Neapolitan Knight of Malta, Niccolo Ricco, and his brother Gaetano came to me in the inn and asked if I would go in the coach with them to walk around. At their request I went with them in their coach, and having strolled about Naples, we came to a pharmacy in which they sell all kinds of pharmacist's drinks. In this shop the Neapolitans Niccolo and Gaetano treated me to various sherbets and lemonades, and having drunk them by the cup,[21] we went to walk along the shore where it is the custom for the honorable Neapolitans and their wives and daughters to walk; others ride in coaches all day. And along that seashore we walked until night and saw there many honorable Neapolitans riding in coaches, and also girls walking along the same seacoast. And when night approached the Neapolitans and I went to the inn in which I stayed, and the Maltese knight Niccolo Ricco and his brother Gaetano, having been at the inn with me, went home.

August 7. I hired myself a coachman from Naples to Venice.[22] He was to drive me in a carriage with all my things from Naples to Venice, and along the whole

[21] Here, earlier in Naples, and on Malta, Tolstoi has enjoyed the cooling relief of iced drinks and sherbets during the August heat. In fact, already in the sixteenth century one could get iced drinks throughout the Middle East, in Egypt, in Spain and Portugal, on Malta, and throughout southern Italy. Eastern pashas made huge fortunes on the ice trade; the Maltese knights regarded snow as both a "sovereign remedy" for illnesses and as a great luxury they could not do without.

In the passage here, Tolstoi, to paraphrase loosely, visits the soda fountain of a Neapolitan drugstore; the pharmacists controlled the exotic flavorings used in these concoctions. On the ice and snow trade, see Braudel, *Mediterranean,* I, 27–29.

[22] Here, and to the end of his travels, Tolstoi makes use of the *vetturino* system, "commonly the most economical, and assuming reasonable honesty on the part of the conductor,

route he would provide food and drink and a chamber and a bedstead, and I would pay him. I would be guided along the way and receive travel documents, and all of this would be done by the coachman, and I would have to do nothing for myself; and I gave him for this transportation and for food and drink and for all described here 23 golden chervontsy. And for this amount the coachman would stop in Rome five days, and in Florence one day, so that in Rome and in Florence I could see all the things that a forestiero should see. And should I stay in Rome or Florence or in some other place longer than the agreed days, for these extra days I would pay the coachman for my food and lodging. I gave this coachman /147/ one half of the fare, 11 and a half golden chervontsy, and the other half I would give to the coachman when he brought me close to Venice to the city of Mestre. And I took from this coachman a letter with a guarantee, and the master of the inn in which I stayed, by birth a man of the empire named Martin, guaranteed all of this. He signed this letter, which I took to the coachman, and Martin did so in his own hand to insure that this coachman would do all according to this agreement and would serve me well in my every desire.

This day after dinner I squared accounts with Martin the master of this inn, and I had to pay him 20 ducats for food and drink and for the room and the bedstead and for everything that he provided both before the Maltese trip and for the stay after returning from Malta. I did not have the means to pay him, but left a pledge with him to be redeemed later, because I had no more money and lived in great poverty; and the pledge left with him was this letter: when another Muscovite happened to come to Naples, he would redeem my pledge and I would pay what I owed.

This same day the felucca on which I had gone to Malta came to me, and its padrone and the mariners greeted me; and in addition to our agreed price I could only give them six efimki for saving me from the hands of the Busurman Turks because I had grown impoverished; and having divided it among them, I dismissed them, having paid what I could.

This same day a French ship arrived in Naples and announced that the 20 French galleys, about which I had heard on the route from Malta, were 60 versts away from Naples, and were waiting for a favorable time, when they could enter Naples; but they said the French prince was not on these galleys, but only a general and knights and noblemen of France who had come to walk about and to see the world. However this statement is disputable, for this French *caravan* did not go to sea and did not arrive in Naples merely to see the city; there are other hidden reasons, because the king of France is a wise man and has a great dream about expanding his realm; and this is why they dispute the notion [of sightseeing], because the French expedition

---

by far the most satisfactory" way to travel in Italy. Mead, *Grand Tour*, p. 181. The vetturino, a kind of courier and travel agent, organized the itinerary, hired the horses and vehicles, and paid hotel expenses exclusive of wine and extras. In the south of Italy, known for its bandits, the vetturini were reputed to be familiar with them, and their services guaranteed protection from attack. See Sells, *Paradise*, p. 143.

has so many galleys; it seems they are merely making some kind of *shkud* (It. *scusa*, excuse), and must have some other reason to be in Naples or in other places in the Spanish kingdom.[23] And I wanted to see this French caravan so I did not leave on my journey /148/ from Naples this day, but delayed my departure until the 9th of this month.

This day the Neapolitan Gaetano came to me in my inn and asked me to go with him in his carriage to go along the seashore, where the Neapolitan viceroy and the inhabitants of Naples customarily ply the sea in feluccas, as I have written above in this book. The wife of the Neapolitan viceroy and the wives and daughters of honorable husbands of Naples ride along the seacoast in coaches. And I went with Gaetano in a coach, and having arrived at the seashore, we strolled and saw many inhabitants of Naples and their wives and maiden daughters along that shore; also on the sea we saw the feluccas in which the honorable people of Naples sail; and drawing up to the shore, they bow and greet the wives and girls who sit in coaches on the shore. And approaching me where I sat in a coach, some Neapolitan inhabitants in a felucca—dukes, marquises, and knights—asked me to join them in their felucca and to cruise about the sea; and I did not wish to refuse their request, so I sat with them in the felucca, and we went out to sea until nighttime and even into the second hour of night. Then, in the third hour of night, we came to a certain place in Naples called Santaliotsiia (Santa Lucia). This is where those dukes, marquises, and knights had left their coaches. We left the felucca and sat in the coaches, and they put me in their coach, too, and two of them sat with me, and the others bowed to me, got into their coaches, and went home; and the knights and I in our one coach went to the inn in which I stayed, and they too bowed to me and went home; but I stayed at the inn at which I was staying.

August 8. Early in the morning five Spanish galleys called enovskiia (Genoan) sailed into Naples, and these galleys of the Spanish king are from a city called Vartseloniia (Barcelona). This city is 1,000 Italian miles from Naples. These galleys came to Naples because French galleys, those I have written about above, were wait-

[23] Tolstoi's and the Neapolitans' suspicions were well founded. The French expedition of 1698 was indeed the expression of French interest in the area, and Tolstoi gives an accurate portrait of Louis XIV who was seeking to cause trouble and to further French interests in the area.

There was a tense political situation in southern Europe between the Treaty of Ryswick, September 30, 1697, and the death of Charles II, November 1, 1700; his death would spark the long War of Spanish Succession (1701–15). Two marriages, first to Marie Louise of Orleans in 1680 and then to Marie Anne, daughter of the Elector Palatine, in 1689, had failed to produce an heir for the Spanish throne. All knew of Charles II's ill health, and all sensed the imminent extinction of the Spanish Hapsburgs, and therefore French Bourbon and Austrian Hapsburg interests in Naples were keen indeed. Eventually the Austrians would occupy Naples (1707); it would be ceded to them by the Treaty of Utrecht in 1713 and returned to Spanish rule in 1735.

ing near Naples; and because of the Spanish king's fear, these Genoan galleys had come to Naples. When these Spanish galleys entered Naples, the French galleys that were 60 Italian miles away turned toward Naples; altogether /149/ there were 20 galleys and four ships. And [out at sea] the French galleys and ships, by way of greeting the Genoan galleys, had fired a *sal'vo,* that is, the sign of respect by firing from cannon. But the Spanish galleys had not given a similar honor and greeting to the French galleys and ships. The Spanish did not fire their cannon because they had promised that a similar honor, and in Italian, a salvo, would be given in Naples by the order of the viceroy-pospolito of Naples from Neapolitan galleys and from the other vessels, which one finds in the Neapolitan port. And when these five Spanish galleys entered the port of Naples, they fired their cannon to honor the Neapolitan viceroy and all the Neapolitans; and these five (Spanish) galleys stood together in the port of Naples with the Neapolitan galleys, and the Neapolitans had 10 galleys in addition to other vessels in their two ports. In these same ports are very many ships, frigates, tartans, feluccas, and other naval vessels.

This same day before dinner a Neapolitan duke and two knights came to me in the inn, and they sat an hour or so with me and showed me printed pages that were sent to Naples from Venice concerning recent events.[24] These pages contained written news about the Venetian *armada,* that is, its naval caravan, which is at sea against the Turks, and about its activities. Next, news was written concerning the arrival of a Muscovite envoy into the imperial state in Vienna, and how he was received, honored, and entertained by the [Holy] Roman emperor, and news of which places the Muscovite envoy wanted to go—about all of this much was written on these pages. And then these dukes and knights left me for home.

This same day after dinner, three Neapolitan knights came to me and asked if I would stroll with them; and at their request I went to the upper city, which is called Castello, and in Italian is called Kashtel'novo (Castel Nuovo).[25] This city is well built, and consists of a great fortress, and in it are large fine cannon, and it is very large, with four thousand inhabitants of all sorts in it. In this castle are 300 soldiers who are always there on guard. In it lives a *kastelian* (It. *castellano*), and his home is very large. It has many rooms and is three stories high, and I walked through those rooms and looked at everything, and the rooms are built of fine proportions. In the castle is also a fine, rather large Roman church,[26] and inside it is decorated with carved alabaster and fine paintings, and the choir in this church is of fine gilded work, and in it stand large, fine organs. From this church up to the castellano's chambers a circular stairway of the most miraculous work is built, and it is very

[24] This is a newspaper, possibly the informative Gazzetta di Venezia, one of several in existence. Peter the Great would found the first Russian newspaper only after his own trip to western Europe, but Tolstoi would have been aware of the *kuranty,* the digests of foreign news used at the Russian court since the 1630s.

[25] Built by the Angevins, 1277–83, this is a massive turreted fortress; it would be enlarged by Charles, brother of Philip V, when the Spanish regained Naples in 1734–35.

[26] This is Santa Barbara (1470), with ceiling paintings by Luca Giordano.

/150/ tall. In this same church I saw on one altar the image of the archstrategist carved out of a single, pure alabaster stone. It gives off a sound just like gold when it is struck with a rod, and this image is made of the most marvelous work. At the entrance to this castle is a gate of white marble, carved marvelously, and it is very tall. The doors at this gate are made of sheets of brass of the most glorious workmanship.[27] Over these gates hangs a serpent called a *korkodil* (It. *coccodrillo*), very large and thick; and this coccodrillo was killed in the moat that surrounds this castle; this coccodrillo lived in this moat.

From this castle I went to the naval port where the Neapolitan and Genoan galleys, about which I wrote above, stood. I went to a general's galley but at this moment the general was not on it; the general's chief was there, and he received me onto this galley with great affection, and I looked around this galley and sat with the general's chief for an hour or so and then left the galley for the coach. He sent his son to conduct me to the coach, for he himself could not conduct me, for his legs were sore and he could not stand up from his armchair. This son of his conducted me to the coach, where I bowed to him and went to the inn where I was staying. The Neapolitan knights who had come with me conducted me to the inn, and, having bowed to me, went home.

This general's chief told me that he had seen the French galleys that are approaching Naples, about which I have written above. On these galleys the authorities keep very great wealth—gold and silver in vessels and all sorts of fine decorations. The French galleys and those of the Maltese knights are very rich and well appointed, and he said that the king of France gives the general of this galley annually for its maintenance 20,000 scudos, and a captain gets 200 scudos per month, and for food each captain gets 500 scudos per month. After visiting Naples, these French galleys would go to the island of Sicily, to the city of Palermo; they wished to see it because that city is very large and well constructed. When these French galleys go to Palermo from Naples, these Genoan galleys and all those belonging to Naples would go with them, and in all there will be 17 Genoan and Neapolitan galleys. They go both to honor the French caravan and also out of fear, to prevent the French from making any kind of *konfuziia* (It. *confusione*), that is, trouble on Sicily. There are always six Spanish galleys in complete readiness in Palermo. The Spanish /151/ are apprehensive about the French, even though there is peace between them, because they do not trust each other completely.

August 9. I wanted to depart Naples for Rome early, and they said to me that this very day the above-mentioned French galleys and ships would sail into Naples; and I, wishing to see this French caravan, awaited it in Naples until the 12th hour, to see what honor the Neapolitans would give the French caravan. The Neapolitan viceroy had prepared many marvelous things, as did all the inhabitants of

[27] Tolstoi is describing the Renaissance Triumphal Arch, elaborately carved and incongruously placed between the two medieval towers.

Naples to honor this French caravan. However, I saw nothing because the French caravan did not enter Naples this day, and I could not wait for it in Naples any longer; I had hired a coachman, and in the letter of agreement with him it said that I was to go from Naples to Rome on this 9th of August, and I did not want to linger in Naples; because of this I did not await the French caravan in Naples. This day, two hours before evening, the coachman came to me at the inn with a carriage, and having placed my belongings on this carriage, and having set things right with the master of that inn where I stayed, I departed from Naples to go to Rome.

At the time of my departure from Naples, Neapolitan noblemen came to me in the inn and greeted me with affection upon my departure and discussed my journey to Rome with great diligence. They told me how to preserve my health from the evil air along the route; for every year in these days [of summer] from Naples to Rome the air is dangerous, and whoever goes from Naples to Rome or from Rome to Naples during this time of year should eat and drink little, and sleep during the day. One should sleep little at night but rather travel all night and stop over during the day; and along the way one should use smoking tobacco and snuff, because smoking tobacco dispels the painful air, and the snuff does not allow one to smell the evil air, and thus with these two things along the route one can preserve his human health and arrive in Rome from Naples, or in Naples from Rome, in good health. This day the following occurred: There is beyond the city of Naples a building in which they make a powder; it is not far from that mountain that has burned since the creation of the world [Vesuvius], about which I have written in this book above. Somehow from this mountain a fire broke out in this building of powder making, and the powder caught fire, and it was enormous, and this building and the 60 Neapolitans who were in it at the time all burned up, and /152/ these 60 men were all killed. And the Neapolitan viceroy and all the Neapolitans mourned this occurence and the fact that such an unfortunate event could have happened.

As I left Naples we passed the three gates in Naples where Neapolitan soldiers stand to examine all travelers and to examine all ranks of people who go to or from Naples, so they do not transport hidden wares; and at these gates I showed the soldiers my travel documents and gave them a gift, as is the custom, and was able to pass all three gates without inspection; and in the next hour of the night I came to the city of Avertsa (Aversa). This is a city of the Spanish king of the Neapolitan province, 8 Italian miles from Naples; its buildings are all of fine stone, and it is a rather large city. From Naples to this city along the road are many fine stone dwellings and many grapes in the fields, which grow alongside high trees, and the trees alongside them grow very high. I did not stop in the city of Aversa, but passed close to it, and in the fourth hour of night I came to the city of Kapua (Capua), 8 Italian miles from Aversa. In this city I stayed in an inn. This city is very fortified and large, and it stands on a river called the Capua.[28] Beneath this river in the earth a most

[28]The river is now known as the Volturno. "Here we saw the slender ruines of the once mighty Capua contending at once both with Rome and Carthage for Splendor and Empire; now nothing but an heape of rubbish, with some goodly Vestigias of its pristine magnificence.

miraculously contrived road has been dug, through which one can pass easily on horseback. The Neapolitans call this city the Neapolitan key because it is a great fortress. This city was the ancient Neapolitan capital, and to this day in this city are the thrones of the Neapolitan kings. And when the French king fought the Neapolitan king and took all his cities and even took Naples itself, he was unable to take Capua by any means because it is so immensely fortified.[29] I stayed in this city in the inn until the third and a half hour, and at the fourth hour I left this city and traveled all night and until the second hour of day. And along the road from the city of Capua are many grapes and fields where they sow wheat on the level places and on the smaller hills; there are also small forests but few dwellings along this road.

August 10. In the third hour I came to an inn called Santagata (Sant'Agatha), and in this inn I stopped to dine, 18 Italian miles from Capua. I stayed in this inn until the 12th hour, and at that hour I left, because along this road these days one does not travel because of the great heat of the evil air in July [sic], but one goes at night. And I came to a river called Garliane (Garigliano); along this river I went an Italian mile or two and came to a ferry called Trasta.[30] This river is rather large, steep-banked, /153/ and deep, and except for the ferry it is impossible to get over it, for it has no bridges, and they cross it on a small ferry. At the ferry on both sides of the river are rather large stone towers, and in the towers are built chambers for the sentry; in these chambers at all times are a captain and soldiers on guard against bandits, so that any traveler can pass without fear of bandits. The pay of this captain and the soldiers comes from the Spanish king, and the captain and the soldiers accept nothing from travelers.

From this place, having crossed the river, I proceeded in the hours after daybreak and came to an inn called Simunel (Simonelli), two Italian miles from the ferry. In this inn I stayed until the second hour of night and had supper there. From the inn to Sant'Agatha it is 8 Italian miles as far as the ferry. Along this road I saw no grapes, but I passed fine fields in which there were many plots under wheat and much fine hay. In these fields are many herds of cows and groups of bulls, and from the ferry in which I crossed I went to the inn Simonelli. In this place I noted many stone structures of antiquity, all in ruins, and it was clear they had been built of fine workmanship. Among these structures from the great mountains had been built stone columns with arches, and atop these columns were built stone troughs, through

. . . There is yet a new Citty, neerer to the road by two miles, fairely raysed out of these heapes." Evelyn, *Diary,* II, 324.

[29] This is a reference to Charles VIII's expedition to claim the Valois inheritance of Naples, 1495–96. At first victorious, Charles was obliged to withdraw in the face of the Holy League. The town did fall to the French under D'Aubigny and their ally, Caesar Borgia, in 1501.

[30] Tolstoi crosses the Garigliano near its mouth, at Minturno.

which fine spring water flowed from the mountains, and these columns even now stretch more than 1,500 sazhens. Even in this place these ancient structures appear more than 2,000 sazhens; but they say that in antiquity in this place there was a very great pagan city, and this spring water from the mountains was conducted along stone columns to that pagan city, because the river Garigliano was not in this place, but flowed a far distance from this spot, and then they re-dug and made it pass in the place where now it flows.[31] And in antiquity one proprietor of Naples, who was called Sibion Afrikan (Scipio Africanus?), drove the pagans from this city, destroyed their city and brought Christianity to this place, because he was a Christian.[32] And today there are no houses on this spot, and it is all fields and hayfields. But now there is built a city very high on the mountain, and from that mountain spring water is conducted, and they call this city Trasta. From the above-mentioned ferry the road is so /154/ wide that three coaches can pass, and it is paved with fine cut slabs of grey stone. In antiquity this road reached from Rome to Naples, but today it has decayed and there remains only the 30 miles or so from the ferry. And I stayed in the inn Simonelli until the 2nd hour of night, and in the second hour of night I departed and traveled all night. Along the road are many mountains on which small forests grow, and in other places there are fields in which they sow wheat, and there are also hay fields and fine herds of cattle. After the passing of the night, at the rising of the sun, I came to the city of Portelia (Portella), 25 Italian miles from Simonelli. In this place there are no dwellings but only one stone gate. This place divides Spain from the papal region. And having entered the papal domain, I went along the sea for five versts; the sea was on my left side, and on the right side were high mountains.

August 11. I arrived at the inn Terezin (Terracina)[33] in the Roman region, five Italian miles from the Spanish border. This inn stands on the very shore under high stone mountains, and on these mountains are nests carved of rock, and they place cannon there. Also in these places are towers on which cannon stand to guard against the coming of Turkish and Barbary peoples by sea, so that the Busurmans cannot enter the papal domain by sea undetected; and I stayed in this inn until the 12th hour, and in the 12th hour I left and came to the city of Trasta, one Italian mile from the inn Terracina. This city stands on the side of a mountain; its buildings are

[31] Evelyn noted "the ruines of the vast Ampitheatre and Aqueduct yet standing." *Diary,* II, 323.

[32] Sibion Afrikan is apparently Publius Scipio, entitled Africanus after his defeat of Hannibal in the battle of Zama in 202 B.C. Earlier, in 216 B.C., Hannibal had wintered at Capua, and in 211 B.C. he had marched to within a mile of Rome itself. Tolstoi thus alludes to the Roman campaign against Hannibal in southern Italy during the Second Punic War, but gives the episode a Christian-versus-pagan tone.

[33] Terracina is on the coast, at the end of the Via Appia.

all stone, and it is a small city. Then in the fourth hour of night I came to the city of Piperma (Piperno) [now known as Priverno]. This is a city of the pope of Rome. From Trasta to Piperno it is 14 Italian miles; and in this city of Piperno I stayed in an inn and had supper, and I left this city. This city stands on a high stone mountain, and on this mountain I could not ride in the carriage and so I went by foot. I also descended from this city by foot, because it was difficult to ride in the carriage, for the mountain is very large and all of stone, and I passed this city four hours before sunrise, and rode the whole night. Along this road are level places; on the left side of this road from Naples to Rome are fine fields and pastures that stretch to the sea, and in them I saw large herds of bison, and on the right side are very large high mountains. Along the road on the mountains are many stone dwellings and along the road are many forests, even a great oak forest. /155/ Among these forests are gardens in which there are all kinds of fruit trees.

August 12. Early in the morning I came to a city of the pope of Rome called Sermaneta (Sermoneta), 15 Italian miles from Piperno. This city stands on a very high mountain, its buildings are all of stone, it is fairly large, and it is built in a very pleasant place. In this city I did not stop, but I passed by it and came to another city of the pope of Rome, Valestra (Velletri). In this city I stayed in an inn called Dabost (d'Abbozzo), 13 Italian miles from Sermoneta. This city stands on a hill; its buildings are all of stone, and the city is extensive and populous. Around it are very large fields, fine plots and hay fields and pastures, in which I saw many bison, bulls, cows, and all sorts of cattle, and also much grain and wheat around this city. From Sermoneta to this city along the road are few forests, the place is all in foliage, and the mountains are stone and not so high. In this city I stayed all day and two hours of night, and in the third hour of night I departed for Rome. And the coachman who conducted me talked with me constantly so that I would not sleep or doze off, because in this place the air is very painful; if someone here should sleep or slumber all night, that person would contract an illness. Those people who sleep or slumber in this place for a night do so dangerously, get sick, and may even die; and in daytime one never passes through these places, for it is immeasurably hot, and from the heat travelers also get a dangerous illness, which few survive. One crosses this area only at night and takes great care not to sleep or doze off between the city of Velletri and Rome itself; this is the only way to pass through this evil air without illness and without great danger; it is 20 Italian miles from this city to Rome. I departed this city of Velletri, and in 2 Italian miles I came to a high mountain. On this mountain I could not ride in the carriage, for it is very high and the road on it is rocky; I walked on this mountain for 3 Italian miles.

Then I came to Marin (Marino), a city of the Roman pope. This city stands between the mountains on a level place, is very large, and its buildings are all of fine stone; around it are many fine gardens with all sorts of fruit trees. Along this road from Velletri to Marino are many grapes and forests, and the road is quite rocky. I did not stay in the town of Marino but passed it and went straight to Rome. Along the road from Marino to Rome are many fine gardens on both sides of the road with all kinds of /156/ fruit trees, and in these gardens are many fine cypress trees. Around these gardens are fine stone fences, with fine gates of good proportions. In these places from Marino to Rome one notes ancient structures, stone columns with troughs through which in antiquity clean spring water was brought from the mountains to Rome over tens of measured versts, and at present one still sees many of these columns. Alongside these ancient columns are newly built columns, and through them water now flows to Rome, and in Italian this is called the *kanal-de-lia-akva* (*canale del'acqua*).[34] Along this road from the city of Marino to Rome itself are many fine fields where they sow wheat and mow hay. Along the same fields are many homes of Roman senators similar to the Muscovite custom of country homes, only these Roman senatorial homes are all built of fine stone and are well proportioned. Also among these fields one notes many stone structures of antiquity that have fallen down with the passing of many years. Along these fields I saw many herds of bison, bulls, cows, and other such cattle.

[34] "In the right hand we saw the (Aquaeduct) of Ancq Martius, and those of Claudius, and the new ones of Sixtus Vth, being a stately piece of Arch work for near 20 miles." Evelyn, *Diary,* II, 317.

VI

August 13, 1698–August 17, 1698

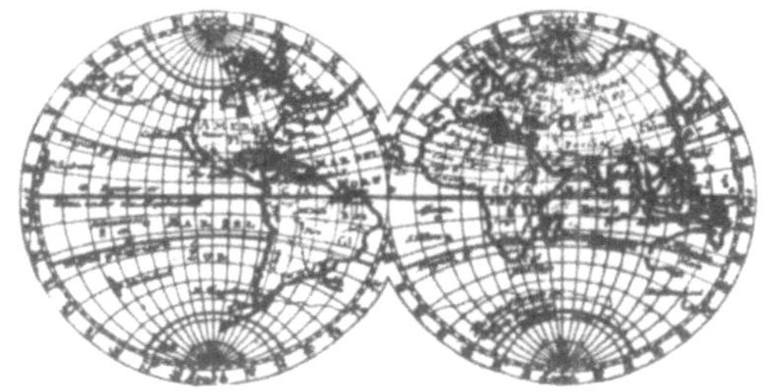

Rome

/225/ ***August 13.*** Early in the morning I arrived in Rome and stayed in an inn called Shkudo-de-Frantsa (Scudo de Francia).[1] This same day the master of the inn made my presence known to a person close to the pope, one who handles such things, and this same day a Lithuanian who lives in Rome in a Uniate monastery for study and who is named Ivan Shperkovich came to me at the inn. He wrote down my name in a letter so that he could talk about me in detail to the senator who is in command of such matters. And this day until dinnertime I did not go anywhere.

When I arrived in Rome, they stopped me at the Roman gates and looked for merchants' wares in my chest, according to their custom, as it is their custom to examine all travelers; even a great senator cannot enter Rome without an inspection. And having examined my things they immediately gave me a *litsentsiiu* (It. *licenza*), that is, a permit, to enter Rome.

In the inn where I stayed my coachman settled things with the master, so that he would feed me well and provide a room with a bedstead to stay in for seven pavlov (pauls) per day, and these pauls are the Roman money, and they change a golden chervonets for eighteen pauls. And the master gave me a fine room upholstered in golden leathers, and the bedstead and the coverings were fine, as were the tables, chairs, and armchairs—all were fine and everything that one could expect.

This day after dinner the Lithuanian Ivan Shperkovich came to me at the inn, and he told me that he had told the governor of Rome of my arrival and that the governor had /226/ ordered a certain papal gentleman to come to me, one who is called Urban, but it was impossible for him to come to me because he was sick with fever (*febroiu*, It. *febbre*). When the Roman governor learned that this Urban lay ill he ordered that another papal gentleman should be in my service; he promised to send

[1] Rome had many hotels and many guest houses. As likely as not, the traveler stayed in the region of the Piazza di Spagna, as did Tolstoi. See Sells, *Paradise*, p. 145. Tolstoi's choice was not among the more popular of the era.

him early in the morning on the 14th, and today this gentleman did not come to me. Therefore, I did not go anywhere this day. Awaiting specific instructions from the Roman governor, I did not want to hire a coach, and going about on foot in Rome is dishonorable for a person of good birth. No one else from the pope came to me this day.

August 14. Early in the morning the Lithuanian Ivan Shperkovich came to me, and learning that the assigned gentleman had not come to my service and no one else had been sent, this Lithuanian and I immediately went to the Roman governor so that the governor would order someone to be released from papal authority in Rome to walk about with me so I could see the sacred and other things that a forestiero should see; and he had to consent to giving me such a gentleman in service, because the permission of the papal authority is needed to hire a coach to see the holy churches and other things in Rome. This Lithuanian Ivan Shperkovich went to the Roman governor and returned to me and said that the Roman governor would immediately send to me a gentleman with a coach at my service, and indeed quickly this gentleman came with the coach in which they drove me around Rome.

This same day before dinner I walked to the Uniate church which is very close to the inn where I stayed;[2] and in this Uniate church that gentleman assigned to my service by the Roman governor came to me and asked that I not be angry with him, because today he could go nowhere with me until dinnertime, as he had certain important business, and he promised to be with me for dinner four hours before nightfall.

The Uniate church is not large but it is a good structure.[3] In this church the main Uniate altar is named for St. Athanasius of Alexandria and is built like a Greek altar; it has neither imperial gates nor southern and northern doorways, but only a set of curtains [in the middle]. The platform under the altar is like a Roman platform, but the altar is made like a Greek sacrificial altar. The image of St. Athanasius is painted

[2]Tolstoi confirms that he stayed in the area between the Piazza di Spagna and the Spanish Steps (to be built 1723–26), and the Piazza Popolo, the great tourist center of the age. Here over time Rubens, Tennyson, Liszt, Wagner, Byron, Keats, and a host of fashionable milords on the Grand Tour found lodgings. Among recent guidebooks to Rome, I found Masson, *Companion Guide to Rome,* pp. 189–93, especially valuable in its discussions of Rome before the reconstructions of the nineteenth and twentieth centuries.

[3]The Church of St. Athanasius is a typically Greek cross-in-square floor plan, with a single apse. There is a simple iconostasis, but as Tolstoi notes, no imperial gates and only a curtain in the archway. The side altars have been removed, as has the holy-water font at the front door, which Tolstoi notes below. At the sides, where the altars stood, are four frescoes of the sixteenth century by Cavalier D'Arpeno. The church was restored in 1760, and a new, taller iconostasis was constructed some six feet forward to accommodate a true, square Greek altar; its height now obscures the fresco of St. Athanasius on the wall of the apse. Being wider, the new iconostasis does have north and south doors on either side of the Door of Paradise.

St. Athanasius (nineteenth century).

at the altar behind the platform up on the wall; it can be seen /227/ through the iconostasis when standing in the church because the iconostasis is not high. In the iconostasis on the right side is placed the image of the Blessed Mother of God, and on the left side is the image of John the Forerunner.[4] In this same church along the sides are four Roman altars on which Catholics serve Mass.

And when I entered this church a Roman priest was serving Mass on a Roman altar, and the Uniates all heard that Roman Mass on their knees. And when the Roman Mass ended, a Uniate archbishop, who had come to Rome from Albania and was born a Greek, entered the church, and he had a *mantiia* (It. *matilla,* cloak) and cowl similar to a Greek hierarch's, and he does not cut his beard or moustache, and he is named Onufrii. And he entered this church and stood close to the imperial gates on the right side at one of the stalls that is placed alongside the altar; so he stood in the Roman custom beside the altar, and a Uniate priest began the Liturgy in the Greek language, just like the Liturgy is said in the Greek rite, and the Uniates also sang in Greek from the stalls. When the word "Christ" was said, the Uniate hierarch and all the Uniates went down on their knees, and four men holding four candles knelt before the imperial gates; and when they sang "Take and eat," this archbishop and all the Uniates stood, and they took the four candles from the imperial gates. Then when the priest said "Holy, Holy, Holy," again the hierarch and all the Uniates knelt down, and the four men with candles again knelt before the imperial gates. This was also done when the priest said, "Go forth in the fear of God and in faith," and the whole Liturgy was done in the Greek manner, with leavened bread, having a single communion bread, on which there are five imprints. At the conclusion of the Liturgy this Uniate hierarch held the antidor (host), which a Uniate took from him. And thus every day these Uniates must first serve the Roman Mass, and then their Uniate Liturgy, and at their own Liturgy they pray to God for the Roman pope. Two Uniate priests serve at this church, and all Uniates philosophize about the procession of the Holy Spirit, just like the Catholics.[5]

In this Uniate church holy water is placed in cups according to the Roman custom.

At this Uniate church is a house where three Jesuits live, and they teach the Uniates to philosophy and to theology and the other high sciences, and they keep 24 Uniate pupils at papal expense. The pope gives the Uniate archbishop annually 500

[4] Tolstoi notes the transposition of these two dedication icons. The new post-1760 iconostasis has Hogridritria (left) and Pantocrator (right), but the old icons are preserved in the refectory of the College of St. Athanasius (see below), arranged as Tolstoi describes them.

[5] Tolstoi alludes to the filioque clause and to the schism of the Eastern and Western churches that it helped to cause.

Tolstoi failed to mention the manner of making the sign of the cross in this church, since the number of fingers had been a central issue in the Great Schism in Russia in his lifetime. "I observ'd in the *Greeke-Church* they made the signe of the + from the right hand to the left, contrary to the *Latines,* & the *Schismatic Greekes* gave the benediction with the first, second & little finger stretch out, retaining the third bent down, expressing a distance of the 3d person of the H: Trinity from the first two." Evelyn, *Diary,* II, 399.

/228/ Roman scudos from his treasury.[6] And when the Uniates had sung the Liturgy they asked me to come see the chambers in which they live and study, and in their chambers I saw two libraries. And then their Jesuit master came to them, and he greeted me affectionately and showed me his rooms. Then I went with him from his rooms to the garden, in which there are many fruit trees and flowers and fine shrubs. In this same garden is built a fine fountain, in which there are living fish, just as in a pond. From this Uniate house I went back to my inn, for the hour for dinner had come.

After dinner the Roman governor sent his man to me and had him say to me that his coach would be sent to me four hours before nightfall.

And without waiting for his coach, I went by myself in a coach to the place where there is a cell in which, in the days of the persecutor Nero, the holy chief apostles Peter and Paul sat and suffered for Christ for preaching the Holy Gospel. In this place is a Roman church built in the name of the holy apostles Peter and Paul.[7] Beneath this church in the ground is a dark chamber; at the top of this chamber is a circular window built so a person can go into it. And in the ancient times of the persecutions there was no door to this cell; they cast prisoners into it through that round window at the top. And now in that cell there is a Roman church named for saints-apostles Peter and Paul, and a lamp always burns there, for there is no other light in this cell.

Beneath this cell, low in the earth, is another cell; between this lower cell and the upper cell there is another round window of the same size, and through this window they cast prisoners in antiquity. From this upper cell to the lower is a stairway on the side that leads to the lower cell of the apostle St. Peter; where he was struck in the face by a persecutor, and from this blow the head of the apostle St. Peter struck the stone wall, and in this place into the hard stone his holy face is impressed, as if into soft wax. Even now it is clearly noticeable, so I was able to see it. Then I went to the lower cell; in this lower cell there is a stone column, an arshin and a half high from the earth, and in thickness that which three finger-spans encircle. To this column were brought the holy apostles Peter and Paul at the time of their suffering for /229/ Christ. And now this column is enclosed with an iron grate; beside this column is a well in which there is fine pure water, and this well appeared by the will of God while the holy apostle Peter was in this cell; when in this cell he desired to

[6]Tolstoi here visits the College of St. Athanasius, a papal institution for Greek and Slav Uniates and the training center for the clergy that conducted the Counter-Reformation's offensive in eastern Europe. Feofan Prokopovich, the future spiritual advisor to Peter the Great and the first head of his Holy Synod, was a student here in 1698–1701. It still exists as the Pontoficio Collegio Greco di S. Atanasio. See Cracraft, *Church Reform of Peter the Great,* p. 50.

[7]Tolstoi provides a detailed and accurate description of the Chapel of St. Pietro in Carcere, on the site where Nero had St. Peter imprisoned in the dread Mamartine. Tolstoi apparently entered the lower chapel through the seventeenth-century doorway rather than through the old entry, the infamous manhole from the upper church to the dark chapel below. The site is preserved just as Tolstoi describes it.

drink, and had nothing to drink, he placed his finger to a stone, and from that stone from the pressing of his holy finger, by the will of God, fine water flowed forth; and even now it has not run dry, so I was able to drink it. Close to this well in this same lower cell is a small column, on which St. Sylvester the pope of Rome conducted the Sacred Liturgy.

Then I came up from this dungeon and went to a monastery that is built in the home of Flavian, the father of St. Aleksei, the man of God,[8] and passed a gate, which anciently was built in Rome in honor of the ancient caesar of Rome for his victory over his enemies. This gate is built of white marble of fine carved work.[9] There are many such gates in Rome along the streets, and these gates were built in *triumf* (It. *trionfo*), that is, to the honor, of the ancient Roman caesars and governors for victories over enemies. Then we passed that gate and saw many great and tall stone columns of an ancient building of fine work, on which was built the home of the cursed persecutor Nero.[10] This home of his was very large—6 Italian miles [*sic*]. Then I saw the baths, also an ancient building constructed at the time of the persecutor Nero.

Then I went to the monastery that is built in the home of the above-mentioned Flavian. In this monastery live canons of the Roman faith of the order of St. Geronim (St. Jerome). In this monastery is a rather large Roman church that has 22 stone columns, and the decorations are mediocre. In this church rest the relics of St. Alexis, the man of God, and the martyr St. Vonifatii (Boniface), bricked up in stone and invisible to all.[11] Along the right side of this altar is a small chapel of the Roman faith. Over the altar is an icon of the Blessed Virgin, Mother of God, of Greek painting, an arshin in height, and three-quarters of an arshin in width. In this monastery they gave me a printed image of it on paper, just as it is painted. And on the left side of the altar is a small chapel, also of the Roman faith. In a niche in this chapel is a carved image of Carlo, archbishop of Milan, in alabaster of the most miraculous craftsmanship. The arch in this chamber is made of small stones of various colors of the most miraculous workmanship. Then I went in this church in front of the altar. Down under the altar is a Roman church, and under /230/ the place where the relics of St. Alexis and the martyr Boniface rest is a Roman altar, in which are many parts of the relics of many holy martyrs, bricked up in columns. Then, coming from beneath the altar into the upper church we came to a well that is

[8]The Church of Sant'Alessio, until 1217 San Bonifacio, once was a Crescenti convent of the tenth century, then was occupied by the Basilians, Benedictines, and Premonstratensians.

[9]This is the arch of Septimium Severus dominating the Forum.

[10]The Domus Aurea of Nero, devastated by fire in A.D. 104, was partially leveled by Trajan; it was discovered and partially excavated in the late fifteenth century.

[11]St. Alexis, d. 417, lived incognito under his father's stairs after returning from a seventeen-year pilgrimage. In Sant'Alessio, the Chapel of San Bartolomeo, c. 1000, was modernized by Martino Lunghi the Younger in 1645; it contains fourteen ancient columns and the remains of an early mosaic. In 1426 the monastery came into the possession of the Order of St. Jerome.

in the church, from which St. Alexis, the man of God, drank at the time of his poverty, when he lived in poverty for the sake of Christ in the home of his father Flavian. From this well I was able to drink the water. In this same church close to the well stands a stairway, the one under which St. Alexis lived and labored for the sake of Christ in the home of his father. This stairway is made of wood and stands now on the place where it was formerly, and in this place under this ladder St. Alexis passed away. The canons of this monastery cut off a small part of the wood from this ladder and gave it to me as a holy object. Close to this ladder in the wall of this church stands an image of St. Alexis, the man of God, carved of wood and very similar to his holy face. Then, from this monastery I went to the church[12] where St. Gregory the Roman pope prayed to God for the soul of his dead relative, and through his prayers and by the making of a sacrifice the soul was delivered from torment. This church of the Roman order is not large but it is well built.

Then I came to a place where, in the age of the ancient Roman caesars, they persecuted people for the Christian faith and made martyrs in the name of Christ; here holy martyrs were given as food for beasts. This place is an anciently built circular structure, and its walls are of very high stone; here the ancient persecutors walked and watched as the beasts tore apart the holy martyrs. At these walls in the earth are the stone caves in which the beasts lived. In this place St. Ignatius, the Bearer of God,[13] was food for the beasts. The earth in this place is all stained with the blood of the holy martyrs.

Then I went to the building where all kinds of people who come to Rome study—not only Christians but also Busurmans, who wish to be enlightened by holy baptism. And the pupils in this building are supported by the pope.

Then I saw the houses of the Spanish and Venetian ambassadors. These homes are very large and are fine structures. Close to the home of the Venetian ambassador is a church of the Roman order named for the holy evangelist Mark.[14]

Then I went to my inn, and at this time the governor of Rome sent his coach to me and asked if /231/ I would go in that coach to walk and see whatever I wished, and I went in that coach to the home in which the children of Roman princes and all ranks of people study military affairs: to fight with *shpada* (It. *spada*, swords), to play

[12] The church between Sant'Alessio and the Colosseum is San Gregorio Magno.

[13] St. Ignatius, second successor of St. Peter in Antioch, was brought to Rome and thrown to the beasts, c. 107. These few lines are the extent of Tolstoi's comments on the Colosseum.

[14] Tolstoi mentions the Palazzo di Venezia, c. 1455, built of stones from the Colosseum for the Venetian cardinal Pietro Barbo, given by Pius IV (1559–65) to the Venetian republic for its embassy. He then mentions the Basilica of San Marco, 336, restored in 833, 1468, and again in the seventeenth century. It is one of the ancient titular churches of Rome and the national church of Venetians in Rome. Tolstoi's expedition this day has been to sites within walking distance of the Piazza Venezia, an area much different today because of the efforts of nineteenth- and twentieth-century town planners, and because of the construction of the Vittorio Emanuele Monument.

with pikes and with *bandiera*, that is, with banners and with other such weapons; but I was unable to see these things, for they had finished their studies at that hour and had gone home.

Then I came to a fortress, that is, a castle, which is built on the bank of the river Tiver (Tiber) in the middle of Rome, and across the river Tiber is a great and wide stone bridge of marvelous craftsmanship. Along both sides of this bridge are stone railings with iron grates of the most marvelous work; along these railings are 12 stone columns, six columns to a side. On all of these columns are angels carved of alabaster of fine work, and each angel has in his hand an instrument of the Passion of Christ.[15]

The river Tiber is not small and flows swiftly; the water appears muddy, as if mixed with sand. And having crossed the river Tiber on that bridge, I came to the castle.[16] This castle is a fine fortification of ancient work; its moat is fine, and indeed all the fortifications around it are fine.

Then I went to the great church of the apostle St. Peter, and on the approach to this church is a *piazza*, that is, a fine square, level and large; around this square are 576 stone columns in a circle, very tall, large, and round; on these columns around

[15] On his way from the area of the Spanish Steps to the Vatican, Tolstoi crosses the Ponte Sant'Angelo; the ten angels had just been added (1688) to complement the statues of Sts. Peter and Paul (1530) on the bridge.

[16] Tolstoi passes the Castel Sant'Angelo, now called Hadrian's Tomb. Most recently the defensive ditch and outer works had been rebuilt by Pius IV (1559–65).

The Ponte and Castel S. Angelo, Piranesi.

St. Peter's with Forecourt and Colonnades, Piranesi.

that square to the church of the apostle are built fine arcades for walking, carved of stone with railings. Along the railings are placed various images, carved of alabaster, of seventy holy apostles, all done of fine craftsmanship, and each has in his hand the weapon by which he was struck for preaching the Word of God.[17] In the middle of this square is placed a four-cornered stone column, hewn from a single stone, very thick at the bottom and thin at the top, of fine workmanship and very tall. On the top of this column is placed a rather small four-pointed cross. On either side of this column on this square is a large, fine fountain, and from them pure water spurts high aloft in many streams.[18]

The church of the holy apostle Peter is very large, of a size that one encounters nowhere else in the whole world, and it is of the most marvelous workmanship. In front of this church is a very large dais, and this dais is built of such marvelous

[17] Tolstoi describes the exterior of St. Peter's. The great colonnade consists of 284 columns and 88 pilasters, with 96 statues above. On Bernini and the colonnade of St. Peter's, see the useful and appreciative guide to Rome by Krautheimer, *The Rome of Alexander VII, 1655–1667,* the successor to his *Rome: Profile of a City, 312–1308.* Both are lavishly illustrated.

[18] Concerning the fountains, the Victorian guidebooks by Muirhead and Baedeker both date the first, by Carlo Maderno, to the pontificate of Sixtus V (1585–90). Muirhead dates the second to the time of Clement XI (1700–21), after Tolstoi's visit, and Baedeker to Innocent XI (1676–89), a decade before.

craftsmanship and proportions /232/ that it is difficult to describe the likes of it. From this dais is the entrance to the portico, which is made on the front of this church and is very large and built of the most marvelous work. At this portico are a series of five large doors to the church, on which are locks of cast brass of the most marvelous work. Inside the church are very large columns on which the church's vaults are set.

Between these columns are altars built according to the Roman custom, of most marvelous work, and the decoration in this church is really fine. In the middle of this great church is a Roman altar, over which is a canopy on four very tall columns. This canopy and these columns are built of the most marvelous carved craftsmanship, and on the corners of the columns are placed carved angels of marvelous work, and this canopy and the columns and the angels are all well gilded.[19] Beneath this altar rest the bodies of the saints-apostles Peter and Paul low in the earth, and leading to these holy bodies of the chief apostles are fine passage-stairwells from both sides, and they are protected by marvelous brass grates. Around these passages and beneath them around the most holy relics hang two hundred large and small silver lamps, in which wood oil always burns. And in front of the very holy apostolic relics are fine doors, and no one enters there except the pope himself, and he only once a year, on the feast of the holy apostles Peter and Paul[20] or some emperor or king, when he comes to Rome; only then are the doors unlocked and the holy apostolic relics shown.

Behind the high altar at the wall of the church up high is the throne on which the holy apostle Peter sat when he preached the holy faith in Christ and taught the people. This apostolic throne is built of fine craftsmanship, carved and gilded. Beneath the throne are the cast bronze images of saints Basil the Great, Gregory the Theologian, Athanasius the Great, and the Blessed Augustine, done of fine workmanship.[21] There are many other carved images of alabaster in this great church, done of very fine work. On the right side by a column is a carved alabaster image of the holy apostle Peter of really fine work, and he sits on a throne, and Christians who enter the church are allowed to kiss the foot of this holy apostolic image.[22]

In this same church behind the altar on the left side stand large organs, covered with carpets, and there is no structure around these organs. /233/

[19] Evelyn, describing the high altar, knew its origins and the date of its recent reconstruction. He described it in detail, knew its decorative bees were from the "Armes of the Barberini," and could ascribe the whole to "Cavaliero Bernini A Florentine Sculptor, Architect, Painter & Poet." *Diary,* II, 260–62.

[20] June 29 is the feast day.

[21] In 1676 Bernini had just completed the "ambitious and theatrical" Chair of St. Peter, which encloses the ancient wood chair. Tolstoi was mistaken; St. Ambrose, not St. Basil, is in the group, and likewise St. John Chrysostom, not Gregory the Theologian.

[22] The old statue of St. Peter, formerly believed to be fifth century and now ascribed to di Cambio, thirteenth century, stands at the last pillar on the right before the nave.

The inside of this great church is all done of white marble of fine workmanship, and in many places it is built of marvelous carved alabaster work.

The vault in this church is all marble, and the various marbles are worked marvelously.

The paintings in this church on the walls and the vaults are of the most marvelous glorious Italian artistic work.

While I was in this church I did not see any of the holy objects, and I did not examine all of this great church because I did not have permission from the pope to see the holy things found in this great church.[23] And I went from this church to see the papal home, which is built right near the apostolic cathedral. However, at this time I could not see this home at all because in the summer the pope never lives in this home, but he lives in a special home. Because the great apostolic cathedral is all covered with pure tin, and because there is a great heat from the rays of the sun on that roofing, there is a great heat in the papal chambers, therefore, in the summertime the pope goes from this home and lives in another home, and in winter he comes to live in this home. Because of this I did not see the papal chambers at this time, for they did not take the keys of this home from the pope. I only saw in this papal home the fine kitchen garden, in which grow many fine fruit trees and flowers of various kinds, which are planted in marvelous proportions. In this same garden are many glorious fountains from which marvelous pure waters flow. Among these fountains I saw one miraculous fountain, which was most marvelously done like a great mountain and very high.[24] From this mountain flow many waters into one garden spot of white stone, and the waters stand in a rather large pond. In the middle of this pond is a brass ship a sazhen and a half in length and 3 arshins in width. On this ship are mastheads and yardarms and cannon. When they allow water into this ship, the water causes the oars and sails and all the instruments that are needed on a ship to work; and waters rush out and give off a noise from the cannon on the ship as if they had been fired. Also in this garden are many other fine fountains made of the most marvelous craftsmanship.

Then I went to the papal library. On either side of the entrance I saw carved images in alabaster of the holy apostles Peter and Paul, seated and of marvelous /234/ workmanship. In this library I saw one stone column of smooth spiral work, with a thickness in the upper end of less than half an arshin, and in the lower end three-quarters of an arshin. This column is made of such a pure stone that if a lighted candle is placed on one side of the column, the fire of the candle can be seen through the column on the other side. And they say that this column is of a very high price and costs many thousands of golden chervontsy.

[23] The present pope was Innocent XII, Ant. Pignatelli, of Spinazzola (Bari), elected at age seventy-six; he was pope from July 12, 1691, to September 27, 1700.

[24] Evelyn too noted the cascade and the bronze ship by Carlo Maderno, at the foot of Bramante's spiral staircase. See *Diary,* II, 305.

In this same library I saw very large globes, earthly and heavenly, done of fine mathematical craftsmanship.[25] In this library I also saw a multitude of ancient books in various languages, among them I saw a Busurman al-Koran written by the hand of the false Busurman prophet Mohammed; and I saw other old writings, which were written in various languages on bark and on wood, very old and wondrous things. In this library in all there are some 40,000 books. This library is very large, and on three sides are long chambers, each side more than 30 sazhens long. In these chambers, along the walls and around the columns on which the vaults of these chambers are set, are fine cases that are filled with various books. From this library I went to my inn, and in the inn this evening there came to me a gentleman from the Roman governor, and he said to me that on August 15 I should go early in the morning to a place called Frashkato (Frascati), 12 It. miles from Rome, to see the marvelous fountains. The same Roman governor received from the pope both permission and the keys, so they could show me all the sacred things to be found in Rome. When I returned from this place [Frascati] to Rome, we would see all the sacred things that are in Rome. And for his affection I gave this gentleman my thanks and did as he wished.

August 15. Early in the morning I went to the above-mentioned place, Frascati, which is a distance of 12 It. miles. Arriving at that place I stopped at an inn and dined. I left the inn and went to the home of a Roman prince called Burgezo (Borghese), and his home is called Mondragon (Villa Mondragone).[26] From Frascati I walked to the Borghese home Mondragone through fine gardens that are built of the most marvelous proportions of cypress and other marvelous trees. I entered this home and saw very fine and large rooms, in which I saw many marvelous pictures, painted in glorious Italian artistic work, and there are many other fine decorations /235/ in these rooms. There are many furnishings of golden leather, beds with fine

[25] Tolstoi's tour of the museums and galleries of Vatican City seems abrupt by the standards of today. Part of this is explicable: some of the collections are later, notably those founded by Gregory XVI in the nineteenth century. However, Tolstoi did not visit much that was there, including the Sistine Chapel.

The globes he mentions are two famous spheres, a *globo celeste* and a *globo terrestre* by Blaeu (1640), among others. A similar pair had reached Moscow in the reign of Aleksei Mikhailovich.

Tolstoi mentions that the pope preserved a copy of the Koran; Evelyn was more forthcoming: "Nor are the most precious mix'd amongst the more ordinary, which are shew'd to the curious onely; Such as are those two Virgils written in Parchment, of more than a thousand yeares old; the like a Terence: The Acts of the Apostles in Golden Capital Letters: Petrarchs Epigrammes written with his owne hand (etc.)." Evelyn, *Diary,* II, 301.

[26] The villa was erected 1573–75 by Cardinal Altemps under Gregory XIII (1572–85), east along the Via di Villa Borghese, one mile from Frascati. The tour to Frascati was routine for travelers in the seventeenth century; see the notes from Evelyn below.

Villa Pamphili, Piranesi.

curtains, mirrors, and cases. In this home I saw a fine fountain built of marvelous work, and indeed many fountains. In the chambers in this home are built fine surrounding terraces set with small stones of various colors in the most marvelous patterns.[27] Also in all the chambers are fine flower and food gardens. The fountains are very skillfully and marvelously made in these chambers, and from them flow many great and pure streams of water.

Then I went to the other home of the same Roman prince, who is called Panfilii (Pamphili) and this home of his is called the Belvedere, not far from the Borghese home.[28] And around this home of Pamphili's are very large gardens in which cypress trees grow with their branches intertwined so that there are fine walkways under them. This large home of Pamphili's is also built very finely in these gardens. At this home in front of the chambers are large squares, with one square higher than the other; and around these squares are stone railings of fine work, and along the railings are placed great and fine urns. In these urns grow trees: lemons, pomegranates, and other fruit trees, and fine flowers of various kinds, and these urns are placed

[27] Tolstoi is describing the Loggia, the covered galleries by Vignola (1507–73), and the fountains by Giovanni Fontana (1540–1614).

[28] The lower palace at the site is known as the Pamphili. Evelyn had been in Rome for the "Ceremony of Pamfilio the Popes Newphew's receiving a Cardinals hatt." *Diary*, II, 254. This was Camillo Pamphili, who was made a cardinal on November 14, 1644, renounced the purple in 1647 to marry, and died 1667.

along the railings in fine proportions. On these squares in many places they have built fine fountains from which wondrously fine pure waters spurt very high upwards.

Then I entered the chambers of this Pamphili's. This home of his is built of fine architecture and is very large and it has many apartments. In these chambers are many fine wallpapers and pictures of marvelous painting, also bedsteads with fine curtains; all the furnishings are many and fine. In front of these chambers is a platform that ascends to the chambers; and if one wishes to squirt water, there are a multitude of sources from which water spurts very high, and those entering by this platform get soaked.

Also in the courtyard in front of these chambers are marvelous fountains. The first fountain is a lion carved of stone, and opposite it is a dog, also carved of stone, and when they squirt the water, the lion and the dog begin to fight with water, and the water from them splashes very high, and around them from many sources water spurts very high aloft. Then, opposite these chambers is a high mountain from which much water streams some three arshins wide, and it has a pattern just like that of a staircase. On /236/ top of this mountain are two tall spiral columns of fine work; from the tops of these columns water spurts upward and the water falls down onto those columns and flows from the tops of these columns to the bottom. The columns are spiral, and therefore the water twists itself around the columns and falls to the lower pool, which then flows down the mountain as a stairway. And all this water that flows as a stairway falls down upon one great brass globe, which is set beneath this mountain at the wall. The heavenly planets and the stars are depicted on this globe. And the water from this globe flows out of each star very quickly; and a man, carved well out of stone, is carrying this globe.[29] In front of this stone man who bears this globe on his head is a great stone basin, into which the water from the globe falls, and in the middle of this stone basin is a fine fountain from which water spurts very high aloft. On the right side of this globe is a man made of stone holding flutes; and when they let the water into him he plays fine dances on those flutes, quite loudly.[30] And on the left side of this globe is a similar man, waist-deep. Also waist-deep is a stone horse of marvelous work, and he holds a great horn in his hand, and the same water moves this horn, and it sounds like a horn for the hunt, and is so loud that it can be heard a distance of five versts away. There is also a man made of stone holding a bagpipe, and by the movement of water this bagpipe also plays. And when all the waters are going in all the fountains, they thunder just like a

[29] "In one of these Theaters of Water, is an Atlas spouting up the streame to an incredible height, & another monster which makes a terrible roaring with an horn; but above all the representation of a storme is most naturall, with such fury of raine, wind and Thunder as one would imagine ones self in some extreame Tempest." Evelyn, *Diary* II, 392–93.

[30] "Under this is made an artificall Grott, where in are curious rocks, hydraulic Organs & all sorts of singing birds moving, & chirping by force of the water, with severall other pageants and surprizing inventions." Evelyn, *Diary*, II, 392.

drum being beaten. Around these fountains are many other fountains, but it is difficult to describe them all.

Then I went into a small stone passage formed by these fountains. In these passages from the vaults and from the platform and from all the passages flowed a large volume of water so that a person in these passages cannot be sheltered by any means, so he must get wet. Then I went to a chamber in which I saw the most miraculous things: first, the inside of this chamber is built of marvelous carving and painted with the most intricate artistry. The length of this chamber is five sazhens, and the width is three sazhens. In this chamber opposite the door at the wall is a high hill made of the most glorious workmanship. Upon this hill sit ten maidens, carved of stone of the most wondrous craftsmanship, and painted with colors and with gold as if alive, and each maiden has /237/ a silver flute in her hand. And behind this hill stands a fine large organ. In front of this hill in the same chamber is a winged horse made of alabaster of the most intricate work and when the water falls the organ plays and fine bells chime. Then the organ stops and those above-described ten maidens all play on their flutes so finely that the mind of man cannot comprehend it. In this chamber in the middle on the floor is a stone circle; the center of this circle has been drilled out. The wind from the water blows out through this hole and they place an apple over this drilled hole; and because of the wind blowing up from the floor it is held a half-arshin aloft, and if the wind is not stopped, that apple will stay suspended, as long as one wants.[31] At the doors of this chamber on both sides in the lintels are pipes, from which the wind also blows. Likewise, there are so many other things in this building that it is impossible to describe the likes of them; and in other places in this building are a multitude of fine fountains, from which flows water in marvelous ways.

From this house I went to the home of a Roman prince. There I saw many marvelous fountains, among which there was one from which a lot of water shoots to a height of 30 sazhens. There are also other fountains made from the mountain and like the above-described fountains; they are built of the most marvelous workmanship, and there are a multitude of fine gardens that grow in glorious proportions. In this same house one fountain is built at the gates through which Roman maidens pass into the gardens to stroll about, and for fun they get wet to amuse themselves. In this same home in one garden is a rather large marble table, and opposite this table at the wall is a fountain of fine work, some five sazhens from the table. When the Romans, or their wives, or girls walk in this garden, they sit around this table to

[31] "In the center of one of these roomes rises a coper ball that continualy daunces about 3 foot above the pavement, by virtue of a Wind conveyed seacretly to a hole beneath it, with many other devices to wett the unwary spectators, so as one can hardly step without wetting to the skin." Evelyn, *Diary*, II, 392.

I have commented on Tolstoi's discovery of the fountains of Rome in my "Peter Tolstoi in Rome," pp. 35–41.

dine, have supper or in some other way to amuse themselves. This is when they squirt the fountain, and the water from that fountain splashes on that table from above, and all those sitting around the table get wet; they do this good-naturedly, and are much amused in this. And having looked at this home, I left Frascati for Rome.

Having arrived in Rome, I went to a place called *Santa-skala* (Scala Santa) in Italian and the Sacred Stairway in Slavonic. In this place is a rather small Roman church, and in this church are parts of the relics of many saints; the Romans say that here are parts of the relics of all the saints. This church is locked /238/ securely, and no one is ever admitted, and Romans say that this church was built in antiquity.[32] Formerly, certain popes tried to enter this church and were prevented by the invisible power of God by a blinding eye, and since that time and even to now no one can ever go into that church, but a glass window looks into the church, and whoever wants to pray by the holy relics placed within comes to that window and looks into the church through the glass and prays. There I looked into that window and prayed near the holy relics reposed there. Among the Romans there is a proverb concerning this church: if this church were opened, the prophets Elias and Enoch would come to earth.

Leading up to this church is the stairway that was in Jerusalem at the palace of Pilate; and up Pilate's staircase Christ Our Savior was led at the time of His redeeming Passion. In three places on this staircase is His divine blood that flowed from His most pure body; and on the places where His most pure divine blood flowed, they have placed bronze crosses. This staircase is made of white marble, 5 arshins wide and 28 steps high, and the steps are low and very wide. He who wishes to ascend by this staircase must do so on his knees, and no one is allowed to step with his feet on these steps on which Our Savior walked with His most pure divine feet. Kneeling on the first step, one must say the prayer, "Our Father," and, kissing the step, also on the knees, one climbs to the second step. Kneeling on the second step, he also says the prayer and kisses the third step, also kneeling on the third step. He does this all the way to the very top, and in this manner I was able to climb this holy staircase. And he who does not wish to climb this staircase thus, or he who is unable to do it, may go up by another staircase, for they have built a stairway on either side of this holy staircase; and they descend from this church of holy relics by these other staircases.

Then I went from this holy staircase to the church of the saint-martyr Evpraksiia

[32] Although the Scala Santa from Pontius Pilate's palace in Jerusalem is housed in a sixteenth century structure now, they lead to the pope's private chapel, the Sancta Sanctorum or chapel of San Lorenzo, dating back to the old Lateran palace. The legend, *Non est in toto sanctior orbe locus,* "there is no more sacred place in the world than this," refers to the many relics in the chapel, and to the image of Christ, "not painted by human hands," which came to Rome at the time of the iconoclastic persecutions of eighth-century Byzantium.

(St. Praxedes).[33] This church is built on the site where in the age of the persecutor Nero they martyred holy martyrs in Rome; here the cursed Nero martyred some in the name of Christ and spilled their blood, and he buried them in a place in the earth. Now this place is in the middle of this church; and built over /239/ the spot is a stone well in which there is an image carved of alabaster of the martyr Praxedes, done of the most marvelous work; the relics of the martyr Praxedes are buried in the same spot.

In this same church on the right side in the vestibule is the column at which Christ our Savior was taken from the Hebrews and flagellated at the time of His holy redeeming Passion according to His will.[34] This column is one and a half arshins high, and at the bottom a half arshin wide, and at the top thinner. On the top is a *kapital* (It. *capitello*) made of smooth work but worn since antiquity. And this column was made of a marble stone in the color of white mixed with black, as is usual with porphiry. This column is set over the altar, and around it are set four rather small silver lamps in which wood oil always burns; opposite it, beneath the altar, is the window, through which that column is completely visible. This church of the holy martyr Praxedes is large and finely decorated. And having been at that column, I went to the inn where I was staying.

And this same day a papal gentleman came to me from the Roman governor and said that I should go in that coach to see certain sacred things. So I went in that coach to a girls' monastery where nuns called Franciscans live. In this monastery is a large church named for John the Baptist, and the interior vaults are walls of the most marvelous carved and gilded work in alabaster and marble. In this church I was able to see an icon of the Christ our Savior not-made-by-hands, and Jesus Christ our Blessed Creator sent this icon to Avgar (Abgar).[35] This holy icon is a half-arshin high and a little less wide, and now it is all overlaid with gold, so that only the image of His most holy and divine face, which resembles ancient Greek paintings, is visible. On what kind of material the Savior's face is portrayed is impossible to know because of its many years.

Then I saw in this same church the head of John the Baptist, which has on it flesh

[33]This is Santa Prassede, dedicated to Praxedes, most recently restored in 1582 but dating to St. Pascal I (817–24). Santa Prassede sheltered persecuted Christians, but twenty-three of them were discovered and killed before her eyes. She collected their blood with a sponge and placed it in a well, where she herself was later buried.

[34]This is a fragment of a column of oriental jasper brought back during the crusades by Cardinal Giovanni Colonna, and it was part of the column to which Christ was bound when he was scourged. Tolstoi fails to mention the exquisite and famous mosaics of the chapel, known already in medieval times as the "garden of paradise."

[35]This is an icon of the Vernicle, "Christ not-made-by-hands," an image of the face of Christ on a towel. There are two types, the first being the towel of Veronica. This one, like the one kept in the Sancta Sanctorum mentioned above, was sent miraculously to Prince Abgar of Edessa (179–214) to cure him of a disease.

Isola Tiberina, Piranesi.

and skin and hair, and eyes that are open. His holy head is placed on a golden board kept in a crystal, through which all is clearly visible. From this girls' monastery, having thanked the Mother Superior, I went to a Jesuit monastery in which there is a great academy, and in that academy a large number of students always study. In this /240/ monastery is a large church in the name of the apostle St. Bartholomew, and it is very marvelously decorated inside with marvelous carved, gilded alabaster, and with glorious marble. Under the altar in this church are part of the relics of the holy apostle Bartholomew.[36] From this Jesuit monastery I went to another Jesuit monastery in which I saw a most marvelously decorated church, also with various gilded alabasters done of the most glorious work and of marvelous marbles in various colors. In this church on the left side in a chapel is an altar all made of various marvelous marbles of the most wondrous work; such glorious workmanship is impossible to describe.

[36]Tolstoi here visits two churches on the Tiber island, San Giovanni Colavita and San Bartolomeo, both now in considerable disrepair. Tolstoi does not mention the island. I "visited the Isola Tybertina (now St. Bartholomews) formerly cut in the shape of a ship, and wharfed with Marble, in which a lofty Obelisque represented the Mast: Here are the ruines of Æsculapius's Temple, converted now to a stately Hospital, & a pretty Convent: In the Church of St. Barthol: is the body of that Apostle: Opposite to it is the Convent & Church of St. Jo: Colavita, where I saw nothing remarkable save an old broken Altar." Evelyn, *Diary,* II, 358.

Then I went to a church that is done in the name of the Blessed Mother of God, and in Italian it is called the church *Kezalia Madona* (Santa Maria Maggiore on the Esquiline). The inside of this church is all done of various colored marbles of marvelous workmanship. When one enters this church a shine is given off from this marble, just like from a mirror. The ceiling of this church is all of carved alabaster and it is gilded.

Then I was at the home of a cardinal called Otoboni (Ottoboni).[37] This cardinal is of Venetian birth, and his house is a marvelous large structure, and the decorations in the rooms are most intricate. Then I was in the home of a Roman prince[38] whose house had been prepared for the arrival of the Muscovite ambassador who was expected in Rome. In this home I saw a bull of marvelous work, hewn from a single massive stone. I also saw hewn from stone the likenesses in wood of Hercules, Mercury, Achilles, and others, all done of fine work, and they say that the wooden likenesses were found in the earth in antiquity.

Then I went to the inn, in which I was staying, and the papal gentleman who traveled with me conducted me to the inn and then went home.

August 16. Early in the morning the papal gentleman came to my inn with a coach. I went with him to the great apostolic cathedral, and arriving at that church, I entered the room that is the vessel repository. This room is large, and around the walls in it are cases in which stand the vessels and in which are placed chasubles and other church things. In the middle of this room is a very large cabinet with removable drawers, placed on a platform. On this cabinet stands a cross with a miraculously carved body of the Lord Jesus on it. /241/ Popes put on their robes at this cabinet when they are about to say Mass. In the drawers of this cabinet rest the chasubles they use every day, and the every-day vessels as well. In this vessel repository I saw a rather large iron chain, which in antiquity a Roman caesar took from a Turkish port, that is, from a naval harbor, and the Turks prevented the entrance of unfriendly people to the port with that chain.

In this vessel repository three Roman priests called canons dressed, and, taking lighted candles, they went to that place in the great church where the image of the Lord Jesus Christ made-without-hands and many other holy things stand. This place in the great church is behind the great altar at the wall, high on a church platform, where there is a side chapel; from this chapel doors lead to the great church, and in front of the doors is a platform with a railing around it. Those three canons left the place where they dressed, came to the platform, and lit the eight large white wax candles along the railing. Then bells rang in this upper church, and all the people who were in the great church fell on their knees; and one of those three canons took

[37] Pieto Ottoboni of Venice had been Pope Alexander VIII, 1689–91.

[38] This is possibly the Barberini Palace.

from behind the doors of that elevated chapel a holy cross made of the wood of the very cross of Christ. It is overlaid with gold of fine work and with stones. This cross is in size a half an arshin and is four-pointed. And he showed it to me, holding this holy cross upon that platform for quite a long time; then he took it back into that chapel, and again the bells rang, and he brought out to the platform an icon of the Savior made-without-hands, the image of the Creator, which at the time of his redeeming Passion He gave to a believing woman named Veronica. This holy icon is a half-arshin in height and just a little less in width, the same size as the Greek icon made-without-hands, about which I wrote in this book above. This holy icon is overlaid with gold and with stones of the most marvelous work.[39] And this canon held it on that platform long enough for me to see it completely; however, I could not see on what kind of material this holy image is portrayed, for it was too high above me. And returning that holy image to that chapel, they rang the bells again. And the same canon brought out onto the same platform a lance, with which at the time of the Passion of our Lord Jesus Christ on the cross they pierced His divine side. And he held /242/ that lance on that platform also for quite a long time so I could see it well; however, I could not examine it completely because it was high above me. And that lance is in the middle of a pure crystal, and it can be seen through that crystal. That holy lance is a quarter of an arshin in length or a little more, and I could not see it long enough to tell how it was made. However, I saw that the lance was made like a boar spear, not long but flat. The crystal in which the lance is placed is covered with gold, diamonds, and other stones of fine craftsmanship. Having showed it to me, he took it back to that chapel and came down to me and said that I should go with him to a special room attached to the vessel repository. In this room a multitude of holy relics and all sorts of holy objects are placed, all of which they showed me.[40]

From this chamber I went to lower rooms under the great church. Here there are many rooms, among them kaplicas, that is, Roman churches. In these lower churches I saw an icon of the holy apostles Peter and Paul of ancient Greek painting. The holy apostles are painted on a single board, three-quarters of an arshin high and a little less in width. This image appeared to Tsar Constantine in Rome, and through this apparition he was compelled to accept holy baptism. Of these and other holy ancient things there are so many that it is impossible to describe them all. In these same

[39] Tolstoi refers to the other icon of this type, which he saw in San Giovanni Colavita on August 15.

[40] Tolstoi has just viewed some of the greatest treasures of St. Peter's. Today, four colossal statues by Bernini stand at the base of the four great piers that support the cupola of St. Peter's; they represent Longinus, Veronica, St. Andrew, and St. Helena. On the balcony above, formed by spiral marble columns from the Old St. Peter's, were formerly displayed Longinus's lance, which had pierced Christ's side at the Crucifixion, Veronica's veil with its image of Christ's face, the head of St. Andrew, and a fragment of the true cross discovered by St. Helena. Evelyn devoted much space to the altar of Santa Veronica, the Conservatory of Longinus's "Iron Launce," the statue of "our Country-Woman St. Helena," and the head of St. Andrew. *Diary*, II, 261–64.

lower chapels I saw in the walls holy images done in small stones without paint, made of the most miraculous craftsmanship. There in the lower chambers I saw many tombs of the ancient Roman caesars, popes, and others. I also saw there carved images of alabaster and of other kinds of stone, of fine marvelous work of antiquity, among them an image of the apostle St. Peter that formerly stood in the great church on the right side; people entering the church kissed it on the foot, and now in that place they have placed an image of the holy apostle Peter cast of bronze.[41] This holy image of the apostle Peter, which is in the lower chambers, is hewn of alabaster and is of fine ancient work; he is sitting, and now those who come into these lower chambers kiss its foot, and I was able to kiss it. Here, too, in the lower chambers is one small Roman church, where the holy apostolic bodies of Peter and Paul rest. On this altar stands the icon of the holy apostles Peter and Paul, painted /243/ from the icon that appeared to Tsar Constantine.[42]

Then having come up from the lower chambers into the great church, I asked the above-mentioned canons if I could go to the top of this great church. These canons immediately unlocked the doors for me, and I went to the top of that great church by a fine, extensive, round and straight stairway, which is of the finest craftsmanship and very extensive. And so I came to the top of that great church, and on that church are many fine large rooms for all church uses. The roofing on this church is all of tin, and in other places it is covered with white iron and tile. Then I went to the top of the outlook, which on this church is very large and immeasurably high and all covered with tin. From this outlook one can see all of Rome, which lies close by, and places twenty versts away and more—many cities and villages and towns. From this outlook one can see the sea 25 Italian miles from Rome. From this outlook I went still higher to the neck, which is large and high up on the dome. From this neck along a very narrow stone and iron ladder I climbed to the apple at the very summit, which is made of brass and is gilded.[43] This apple is large enough to hold 20 people in it, but from the ground it appears very small, as if it could be embraced by two handspans, because the church is immeasurably high to the dome, and the dome is very large and very high, and on the dome the neck is immeasurably high, and on the neck is the apple, and on the apple is placed a large cross that appears very small from the ground.

The inside of this church is decorated with marvelous Italian paintings and with glorious carved alabaster and with intricate stone marbles, and one cannot describe the likes of the decorations of this church. In this great church /244/ are very many

[41] In the crypt, this is the statue of St. Peter that stood in the old cathedral; the figure is a classical one of the third century, to which someone, possibly Arnolfo di Cambio, added a head in the Middle Ages. For a contemporary description, see Masson, *Rome*, pp. 462–63, 472.

[42] Tolstoi notes the ancient pictures in the Confessio.

[43] Tolstoi ascends the dome of St. Peter's, stopping first at the Lantern (the outlook), and then climbing farther to the bronze ball at the very summit.

Roman altars, in many of which are holy relics. Among them, on the left side of this great church in one chapel under the altar, one finds the holy relics of the firm pillar of the church and the universal teacher, the preacher of the confession, the most holy patriarch of Cyprus, of Constantinople, John Chrysostom, and they say that his holy relics were brought to Rome from Constantinople in antiquity. There are also many other holy relics in the chapels. The size of this church in length from the altar is _______ sazhens, and the width _______ sazhens.[44] There are more than a hundred canons and priests at this great church. The riches in this great church consist of intricate stones, diamonds, rubies, and emeralds in the whole church structure; also the pearls, gold, and silver, and other expensive decorative things of all kinds are of untold multitudes, collected in antiquity by the popes and the Roman caesars of old. There are many marvelous holy icons of ancient Greek painting, and also along the walls there are in many places ancient holy Greek icons. In front of the platform, which is made in this church and about which I have written above, along the sides are two short stone columns; on one is St. Peter and on the other is the image of St. Paul the Apostle, hewn of alabaster of marvelous workmanship. St. Peter has the keys in his hand, and St. Paul holds a sword in his hand, showing that the cursed Nero cut off his most honored head with a sword for professing Christ. There under the great church I saw a *retrata* (It. *ritratto*), that is, a *persona*, carved of white stone, of the cursed persecutor Nero, which not only looks real but seems like the devil himself.

Leading into this great church from the portico are fine doors; among them the middle doors are always locked with a cast brass lock of fine work. No one ever enters this door, and it is never opened for anyone, and even the pope himself never enters the church through these doors; and the pope himself only enters this church through these doors when he wants to give thanks to God *pubblico*, that is, collectively, for some great mercy from God to the people. Then the pope approaches these doors holding an iron hammer in his hand, and with that iron hammer he strikes these doors three times, and standing in front of these doors, he says a certain prayer of thanks to God. Then, after the third blow of the /245/ hammer these doors are opened, and the pope with the whole council enters, and there is a remission of sins for all the Catholic people, for as many years as he chooses to designate.[45]

From this church I went to the papal hospital and entered the lower rooms, in the middle of which is a kaplica, that is, a Roman church for the ill. In front of this church is a large fine organ. In these rooms I saw many sick people resting on beds with featherbeds and white sheets, and everything in the rooms of those ill in the way of food and medicine and everything else is paid by the papal treasury. Then, from these lower chambers I went to the upper chambers in this hospital, where I saw sick people of noble birth who, because of poverty, could not have a doctor of

[44] The dimensions of St. Peter's are left blank in the manuscript.

[45] This is, in the age of the Counter-Reformation, Tolstoi's only reference to the issue of Indulgences in the Catholic Church.

their own. They come to this hospital and lie in these rooms. Their beds are well made with curtains, and the rooms are finely built. On the other side of these upper chambers are marvelous rooms that are finely decorated inside. In these rooms are fine gilded bedsteads with silk curtains and fine beds with fine clean sheets. And when a man of high birth or a Roman prince, or one of a noble senatorial family, falls ill and cannot hire a doctor himself because of his own lack of means, he comes to this papal hospital and lies in these well-decorated chambers.

Then I came to a pharmacy, which is built at this hospital for the use of the sick. In this pharmacy I saw many instruments with which they cut off people's hands and feet and fingers. There I also saw an instrument they use on a man when they wish to remove a stone from inside him. Also I saw in this pharmacy many drugs stored in various vessels and placed in marvelous order. In this pharmacy for the service of the sick are four doctors, and also druggists, pharmacists, and medical men—all kept at papal expense. Then I saw the kitchen in which they prepare food for those sick people. This kitchen is well made and has many brass and tin vessels, and they are very clean. Then I went to a room where those people who serve the sick in this hospital—the doctors and other ranks—dine. In the hour when I entered that room, the servants of the sick were dining in that room. A monk, by birth a Pole, whom the pope had made chief over all in this hospital, entered that room with me. This monk asked all those who were dining to drink wine to my health; they took up wine glasses and they all drank /246/ together to salute me, and they drank the entire glass in our honor. There are 18 such hospitals in Rome in various places. Then I went from this hospital to my inn, for the hour of dinner had come.

This same day after dinner the same papal gentleman who had driven with me before came to me again and brought me a coach in which I went to a church called Santa-Mariia Maior (Santa Maria Maggiore), that is, St. Maria the Great. In this church I saw many riches in the vessel repository, of gold with diamonds and various stones and a multitude of silver church things. I saw here on the Roman altar instead of the altar cover a great cast silver panel done of marvelous workmanship, in which the weight of silver was great. Then I saw an image of Christ and the images of the twelve apostles cast in silver, each of which weighed some 30 funts (pounds); and also in the candleholders and lamps and crosses and other church things there was very much silver.

In this same church I saw a small lecturn well made of a single tree of Chinese work. This lecturn was recently sent to Rome by the Chinese tsar to this church, for he now believes in the icon of the Blessed Mother of God, the icon of her painted by Luke the Evangelist that is in this church.[46] The Chinese emperor did this because of the preaching of the Jesuits, and these Jesuits are even now in Khinakh, that is, in China, to preach the Word of God, and they bring the idolators to a faith in Christ.[47]

[46] In the Borghese chapel (1611) is a blackened, ancient picture of the Virgin that tradition ascribes to St. Luke. It was carried in procession by Gregory I as early as 590.

[47] Tolstoi refers to the contemporary mission to Emperor K'ang-Hsi.

S. Maria Maggiore, Piranesi.

I could not see the other sacred things in this church this day because the holy objects one finds in this church are locked up, and this day the priests, who have the keys, were not in that church. This church is very large; it was formerly a Greek church, and now it is Roman. The decorations in this church are marvelous, carved alabaster, gilded in places, and fine marbles of various colors.

From this church I went to a church called San-Ian-Liuteran (San Giovanni in Laterano).[48] This church was Greek, built by the tsar of Constantinople near his home, and it was the Roman cathedral in the time of Tsar Constantine; it is very large and contains many columns. Along its length this church is constructed on columns set in four rows, and there are slightly fewer than a hundred columns. At these columns now are Roman chapel altars of marvelous work of various marbles, and every altar costs some five thousand Roman scudos. All the adornments in this church are also really fine. /247/

In the middle of this church, opposite the main altar, is placed the altar on which

[48] Tolstoi here and below writes "Lutheran" rather than "Lateran." This was one of the five patriarchal churches in the early period, the principal church after the time of Constantine; the first church was installed in the palace of the Laterani family; it was toppled by an earthquake in 896, and was re-erected by Sergius III (904–11); most recently it had been altered by F. Borromini, 1650.

the apostle St. Peter conducted the Holy Liturgy.[49] This altar is made of cypress boards of simple carpenter's work, and it is put together with iron nails. This altar is three arshins in length and an arshin wide, and three-quarters of an arshin high. This altar is covered with fine shrouds, and when someone wishes to see it bare they remove these shrouds and show it. Around this altar at the corners are four high gilded columns made of wood of fine carver's art. The heads of the holy Apostles Peter and Paul are placed on this spot. Over their holy heads the roof[50] is of fine carved work and also all gilded. I was unable to see these holy apostolic heads this day because there was no one to show them, there being no priests there at this time; but on this day I saw a board of the table, on which the Glorious Tsar Jesus Christ said the secret vespers in the home of Zebedea with his holy disciples.[51] This board is made of simple carpenter's work of cypress, and now from the passing of many years it is black, but there is almost no rottenness in it. Beaten into this board in many places are iron nails, and in other places small iron nails are beaten into [pieces of] white iron, that is, tin. This board is an arshin and an eighth in length

[49] This is the *altare papale* at which the pope or his substitute reads the Mass; it is an ancient table from the catacombs.

[50] Tolstoi's "roof" is the canopy over the altar.

[51] By the "secret vespers" Tolstoi means the Last Supper.

S. Giovanni in Laterano, Piranesi.

and an arshin and a little more in width, and now it is cut in half, and both halves are put together and placed in the church wall behind a glass window and encased tightly with an iron grate.

In this same church this day I saw the ark of the Old Testament in which the Jews kept their manna. This ark is made of boards of simple carpenter's work; it is not large, an arshin in length, and in width and height less than an arshin, and it is placed in a cabinet in the church wall behind an iron grate. Beneath this ark I saw the staff of Aaron, broken in half, and it is made of white and black bone in a pattern on an iron rod, and it resembles the crozier of a Roman bishop.[52]

Then I left this church for the home of a Roman prince, in which I saw a fine garden plot. In these gardens are fine fruit trees and flowers and fine bushes of various kinds, all set out in fine proportions. In this same garden are many /248/ marvelous fountains, which accidentally splash those in the garden walking along the path that is built in this garden. In front of the gates that enter this garden are fountains; from this garden to the chambers in many places are also marvelous fountains. In this garden at the wall is built a small cage covered with netting, and in it are many fine birds. In front of this cage near the doors rests a stone, and he who wants to go into this cage or to look into it, must strike that stone with his foot; then this stone turns a little bit, and water spurts upward from the ground around that stone, so the person who struck that stone gets completely soaked. And in other places stones are also placed so that water will accidentally splash and soak those who strike those stones. Also, in many places when someone opens a certain door [he causes] a fountain to squirt, from which he gets all wet from the water. Then I went into a chamber that is built in that garden and entered an underground passage; here I saw crocodiles and very large serpents suspended for display under the vaults in these passages. Then I went up to the central chambers, where the glass doors have locks like those they use on windows; and many chairs are placed alongside these doors, and among them is one chair made with some kind of figures; and on this figured chair are armrests that look like apples turned of wood, and they revolve. When people wish to look through the glass doors while sitting in the above-described chairs, the person who sits in the figured chair turns that apple, and from the glass doors water spurts out from lead pipes through places in the glass, and those who are looking into these doors accidentally get all wet.

Then I went to an upper chamber, in which I saw many weapons and pistols of Turkish, Muscovite, and German work, and among these arms I saw two marvelous *karabina* (It. *carabina*) in silver boxes; the entire boxes were lined with silk, and there were many rubies placed in a pattern in gold. I also saw many other things in the upper chambers of this house, and among them I saw reclining in the middle of a

[52] Visiting the Church of St. John Lateran and adjacent courts, Evelyn too saw these relics. "A robe of the B: Virgins which she gave to Christ, and the towell with which he dried the Disciples feete; the reede, sponge, some of the blood & water of his precious side: some of the Virgins haire, the Table on which the Passover was celebrated, the rods of Aron & Moses, and many such bagatells." *Diary*, II, 275.

room on a fine bedstead a *mumiia* (It. *mummia*), that is, a person from antiquity, which they found in a sandy sea. In a sandy sea when a man becomes covered with sand, this man and his clothes cannot rot, even to the end of the world. Doctors make great efforts to acquire such people because they use them in their pharmaceuticals; /249/ and this whole man lies in these chambers on that bedstead as a mummy in the same clothes in which he was covered by the sandy sea; and he is dressed in these same clothes on that bed, and the clothing is made of very fine birds' feathers. In this same chamber I saw a detached human skin that was taken whole from a Turchanin (Turk), and it was detached just like one removes a deer's skin. This skin is thick, thicker than a deer's, similar in thickness to Morocco [leather], and its color is like paper, and it has a luster on one side like paper, and on the other side it is like deerskin.

In this chamber I saw many birds, beasts, and serpents of various kinds dried for show, and also whole bones of monkeys and Indian mice, and these bones have not fallen apart, only the skin and flesh and sinews have been taken away. There I also saw four birds called *gamaiany* (?), whole and in their feathers, and also other kinds of birds placed in glass vases in double-wine and with feathers, because no creature will decay in double-wine. In this same chamber I saw the skin of a ram with two heads. There I saw the skin of a calf with two heads, eight legs, and two tails; so that they can be examined both of these skins, the ram's and the calf's, are stuffed with hay and stand just as if they were alive. There I also saw ancient people who are called *giganty* (It. *gigante*); their teeth are very large, and the bone from the neck is as large as a small stool. There I also saw other marvelous things of antiquity, which are difficult to describe quickly. Among these things I saw one *peniaz*, the coin that Judas, the cursed servant of Satan, took from the cursed Jews for our Savior Jesus Christ.[53]

[53] Evelyn identifies this site. He was also interested in the mummy, mentioning it twice. This was "Prince Ludovisio's Villa, where was formerly the Viridarium of the Poet Sallust: The house is very magnificent, and the extent of the Ground exceedingly Large, considering it is in a Citty." It had been laid out by Cardinal Ludovico Ludovisi in 1621–23, and little survives. Evelyn was more interested in its statuary, but he did describe the mummy: "There is likewise in the Villa-house a mans body flesh & all Petrified, and even converted to marble, as it was found in the Alps, and sent by the Emp: to the Pope; it lay in a Chest or Cofin lined with black velvet, where one of the armes being broken; you may see the perfect bone from the rest of the flesh, which remains intire." It was one of the great attractions of the villa, but now it has disappeared. As to the other natural wonders that so intrigued Tolstoi, Evelyn mentions only "divers other exotique curiosities." *Diary*, II, 234–36, 391.

One recalls that Peter the Great was equally astonished by European collections of natural curiosities; he purchased several of them, which became the basis of the holdings of the future Russian Academy of Sciences on St. Basil's Island in St. Petersburg. It was, of course, an age of science, amateur and professional, and down to the twentieth century one could see shelves of deformed babies in their pickling jars. What Tolstoi calls "double-wine" we would call distilled spirits, brandy, or fortified wine.

Then I walked from this house to the coach that stood at the gates of this garden; and the Roman who was conducting me from the garden caused me to be squirted with water, and they opened the fountains, which squirted up around my coach. In the evening I went from this house to the inn in which I stayed. At this hour the pope sent his equerry to me, the Knight of Malta-*commendatore* called Shpreto (?). This equerry gave me greetings from the pope and told me that His Papal Majesty deigned to ask me which things I still wanted to see in Rome, so that this equerry could go with me to show me all I wished to see. For this papal favor I thanked him and told him what I wished to see, and this equerry left me this evening and promised to be back early in the morning. /250/

This same evening the pope sent me 20 bottles of various wines and five fine cheeses, as it is the custom for the pope to dispatch such from his household to notable arriving foreigners, and for these things the pope sent I sent him my thanks and contributed what was appropriate.

August 17. Early in the morning the above-mentioned Knight of Malta and papal equerry came with two coaches in which I went with them to walk about. We came first to a very large hospital in which there are 500 sick of the male sex, and on the other side of this hospital in special rooms are 300 souls of the female sex. This hospital is built like the one I saw previously in Rome, about which I have written above in the book; only this hospital differs from the one described above in that to this hospital come Roman princes and senators and all sorts of honorable people and their children of the male sex to serve the sick voluntarily for the sake of Christ; they don the base clothing that the hospital workers wear and bring from their own homes fine foodstuffs to the sick in this hospital, as well as sugars and confections and fruits on fine silver dishes finely adorned. With these foodstuffs and sugars and confections and fruits they treat the sick and serve them with great zeal. Likewise, the wives of honorable people and their maiden daughters do the same thing in this hospital for the sick wives and girls, and they do these favors for those who have nothing, wishing for themselves the grace of God.[54]

From this hospital I went to a church called St. John Lutheran [*sic*], about which I have written in this book above, and this day in this church they showed me the heads of the holy apostles Peter and Paul. These holy heads are done in silver, and also done in silver are their images from the waist up. On these images are placed their most revered heads, and these holy images with the most revered heads are placed in a spot that is made in the middle of this church high over the altar of the apostle St. Peter, about which I have written in this book above.

Having looked at these heads of the chiefs of the apostles, I left this church on

[54] The Ospedale del Gelio stands across the piazza from the Church of St. John Lateran. Tolstoi seems especially impressed by the nobles' charitable work in this hospital.

foot for the home of Tsar Constantine,[55] because this home is very close to this church. This building is large, built four-cornered, and along the walls are large chambers four stories high. There are many of them, built finely architecturally, and it is known that these walls were painted with Greek paintings /251/ of fine work in antiquity, and these paintings are still now visible. There are no vaults in these chambers; all of them have flat ceilings, and from the floors to these ceilings in all of the rooms it is very high, a sazhen and three arshins. Also, the doors in these rooms and the windows are very high and wide. Around these rooms on the inside of the building are fine, wide passages with railings, and along the railings are columns carved of white marble stones of fine marvelous work in the shape of men and women. Likewise, the stairways in these rooms are built fine and very wide and very towering; and also in these rooms are descents that are wide, and the platforms to the kitchens are marvelously towering. Entering these rooms I first entered one high and great passage, and from this passage are great doors to the court of Tsar Constantine on a square, and in front of these doors beyond the chamber are small balusters with railings, but there is no stairway to these doors from the square. And when there is a new pope in Rome, he has to come to this house of Constantine; there these doors are opened and the pope sits at these doors and gives his blessing to the people, who kneel on the square in front of the court of Tsar Constantine.

At present, orphans live in this house of Constantine, those who have no fathers or mothers, or girls who are maintained by the pope. In this house they care for little girls from age seven; younger than seven they do not accept. In this home there are old wives to teach these girls all sorts of trades—to spin, to weave, to sew, to knit stockings, and to make lace. There are more than 500 of these girls in this house, and they work constantly, making what they can and selling what they make; of the price one third is given to the girl for her needs, another third goes for her food, and with the third third they buy flax and wool from which they make other kinds of things for sale. And the pope adds from his treasury to the total when it does not satisfy their needs. And when an under-age girl from this house grows up, they teach her to read and write at first, and then a trade; and they do not send them away from this home to any other place, and when a girl grows up she is free to go from this home to a monastery, or to an order, or to marry, whichever she wishes.

In these same chambers of Tsar Constantine there is a Roman church in which they conduct every day Mass for the wives and girls who are there, so that each day all /252/ of them hear Mass, for among the Romans on a single altar there may be many Masses; but various priests serve them, and a single priest cannot say two masses on any one day, except for the feast of the birth of Christ.[56]

[55] This is the Palazzo Laterano, built as the summer residence for Sixtus V by Domenica Fontana, on the site of the old "patriarchate," the residence of the popes since the days of Constantine.

[56] The "house of tsar Constantine" in the above passages is the temple of Fausta, the wife of Constantine. The hospital was the center of the Arte de' Speziali, the druggists. "We visited

From the house of Tsar Constantine I went to a church called Santa Maria Maggiore, about which I have written above in this book. In this church they showed me in a marvelous repository the sacred cradle in which the Creator of the whole world, our Lord Jesus Christ, did not disdain to rest with His most pure flesh at His birth in infancy.[57] This cradle is made of simple wood of the same simple carpenter's work such as one now encounters in small wood cradles among the impoverished simple people. One can tell that this cradle was hung on four straps, because on the sides of it places are cut through, and in those places straps or braids were pushed through it. And in those places where the cradle is split, one can see that it was bound together with iron of simple blacksmith's work, and in other places it is bound with thin cords (*snurkami*, Ger. *Schnur*), with scraps of some common material, and also with thin cords, sky-blue in color, as if dyed. In this holy cradle is the hay that was under our Lord Jesus Christ, and there is a certain small shroud in this cradle in which the most pure divine body of Christ lay. This cradle is placed in a silver case; above it is an image of the eternal Christ-Child made in silver of marvelous work. The silver case containing the holy cradle is in a wooden case that is covered with sky-blue velvet, and the wooden case is placed on an altar aloft on four columns, and this altar of fine work is at the left aisle.

Opposite this altar in this same church at the right aisle is another altar that is exactly identical to the one on which stands the holy cradle of Christ; and on this altar at the right aisle are the holy relics of many saints, all of which they showed to me. Anyone who wishes to know in detail which saints they are can read a printed history of Rome; because of the passing of time I do not describe them in detail here. In this church on the right side in a chapel under the altar is a manger, the one that was in the cave at the birth of Christ; in this manger our Lord Jesus Christ did not disdain to lay His flesh, but now /253/ no one can see this manger because it is tightly sealed under the altar, and around this altar oil burns in silver lamps.[58] In this same church in a chapel on the left side over an altar is an icon of the most Holy Mother of God, and in her arms is the eternal Christ-Child, our Lord Jesus Christ, and this image of the Most Pure Virgin was painted by Luke the Evangelist in Rome.[59] I was able to examine this holy image closely, and having taken a printed image on paper resembling this image of the Blessed Mother of God from this church, I left at dinnertime and went to my inn.

---

the Temple of Faustina; It is now made a faire Church, with an Hospital, which joynes to it." Evelyn, *Diary*, II, 219.

[57] Beneath the high altar in the church is the richly decorated Confessione di San Matteo, in which are preserved five boards from the Santa Culla, the cradle of the infant Christ. In the Chapel of Sixtus V "was shown us part of the Crib, wherein Christ was swadl'd at Bethlem." Evelyn, *Diary*, II, 244.

[58] Tolstoi describes the chapel, which contains the fine Bethlehem stable by Arnolfo di Cambio. Although stripped of many of its riches during the sack of Rome in 1527, it was here that the pope celebrated the first of his three Masses on Christmas.

[59] Tolstoi has previously described this ancient and miraculous icon.

This same day after dinner the pope sent a coach and four horses to me and directed that I go in that coach to see the place where the head of the holy apostle Peter was cut off; and we went in that coach to that place. Leaving Rome I saw the place where the holy apostles Peter and Paul said good-bye when they were ordered to their death.[60] And today a chapel is built on that spot, and over the doors of this church is the image of the holy apostles Peter and Paul carved of alabaster in such a way that these holy apostles are taking leave of one another, embracing one another, kissing, and they are happy, [knowing] they will die for preaching the word of God.

Then I came to a church of a Roman order that was formerly a Greek church.[61] This church is very large; in it are 90 large stone columns, and many chapels are built in this church. The altar in this church is rather large and all painted as in a museum (*musieiu;* It. *museo*), of ancient Greek painting. Opposite the altar is a throne of fine workmanship, and around this throne is a fine railing, along which stand silver lamps in which oil always burns. Beneath this throne are placed parts of the holy relics of the great chief of the apostles, Paul, and this throne is built on this spot because when the apostle Paul was in Rome before, he stood on this spot and taught the people to believe in the Christ God.

In this same church I saw the cross on which in antiquity the body of Christ was carved of wood of fine work, and now it appears decayed, and the Romans say that a voice came from this holy cross to a certain wife after the schism of the Greek and Roman faiths, and this woman was of the Roman faith and was called Bridzida (Bridget), and she was of the Benedictine order. This woman is now a Roman saint, and her body rests in the ground under this church. /254/

Then I left this church and came to a place where they cut off the revered head of the great luminary and universal teacher, the chief of the apostles, Paul, and I entered a very large Roman church in which there were no decorations.[62] In this church is an image of St. Anastasia that was cast into the fire at the time of the iconoclast heresy at the council; and it was unharmed after a long time in the fire, so it was drawn out. And now this image appears decayed. In this church too are many sacred relics, which I fail to describe in detail in order to continue this history.

From this church I entered the chamber that is built upon the spot where the head of the apostle Paul was cut off. This chamber is quite large and very wide, and on

[60] This is the little Church of SS. Pietro e Paolo. It now stands in the modern E.U.R. development.

[61] This is San Paolo fuori le Mura, the largest church in Rome after St. Peter's. It was one of the four great patriarchal basilicas. The building Tolstoi saw was destroyed by fire in 1823. In the Chapel of the Crucifix, the only one saved from that fire, is the Crucifix by Pietro Cavallini, which is said to have spoken to St. Brigit in 1370.

[62] Here and below Tolstoi visited the site of St. Paul's martyrdom, the Abbazia delle Tre Fontane, 2 miles from San Paolo; St. Paul's severed head rebounded three times, causing three fountains to spring up, and three churches were built on the sites. He visited first the largest, Santi Vincenzo e Anastasio. Then he saw San Paolo alle Tre Fontane, rebuilt in 1599, which contains the fountain and the pillar of St. Paul between the altars.

the right side is a Roman altar named for the apostle St. Paul, and on the left side opposite that altar is another Roman altar named for the apostle St. Peter, and over these altars are placed images of the apostles Peter and Paul that resemble the apostles' suffering for Christ; they are painted on linen of such marvelous artistic mastery that there could be no better mastery in the whole world. Beneath the altar of the apostle St. Paul is the column on which his head was severed. This column is marble, not very tall or thick, and now around it is wood of fine joiner's work, and on one side in this wood is a window, through which the column can be seen; in addition, around this column above the wood is an iron grate.

A sazhen away from this column is a spring in which there is fine water that one can drink, and that water tastes like milk. Three sazhens away from this spring is another spring in which there is always warm water. Three sazhens from this warm-water spring is a third spring in which there is cold water. These three springs are in a row, and the water never grows scarce, even though they take many barrels of water from there. And these springs began at the time when, by the order of the cursed Nero, the Roman caesar, the revered head of the apostle St. Paul was severed, and it dropped to the ground and said, "Jesus." And on that place at that moment the first spring's water bubbled up, and it tastes like milk. Then this severed apostolic head jumped to the other place and again it said "Jesus," and on this spot bubbled up the spring of warm water. Again from this place the holy apostolic head skipped to a third place, and again it said, "Jesus," and on that spot bubbled up the spring of cool water. And now /255/ over these three springs are built fine *ankery* (It. *ancora,* anchors) of various marbles of marvelous workmanship, and at each spring they have placed a brass bucket on an iron chain, with which those who come to these springs drink water, and the Italians call these springs Tre Fontane.

Having left these springs, I went to a circular church that was built in the name of the Roman saint, Bernard, and the Romans say that St. Bernard prayed in this place and served Mass, and by his prayer drew a certain soul from the fire of purgatory, which the Catholics profess.[63] Beneath this church rest the relics of 10,000 holy martyrs who were martyred by Zeno [*sic*], and there are passages down to these

[63] The third church at Tre Fontane is the octagonal Santa Maria Scala Coeli, rebuilt in 1582, which owes its name to the legend that St. Bernard, while celebrating Mass, saw in a vision the soul for which he was praying ascend by a ladder from purgatory to heaven. The Orthodox Church does not accept the existence of purgatory.

Evelyn's description of Tre Fontana is full of skepticism: "We went without the Walls of the Citty to visite St. Paules; to which place *'tis sayd,* the Apostle bore his owne head after Nero had caus'd it to be cut off." "Here they shew'd us that Miraculous Crucifix which *they say* spake to St. Brigit" [italics mine]. And finally, "In this they shew the Pillar in which s: Paule was bound when his head was cut off, & from whence it made three prodigious leaps where there immediately brake out the 3 remaining fountaines which gives denomination to this Church; The Waters are reported to Medicinable, and indeede seeme a little sharp; . . . Over each of the Fountains is erected an Altar, and a chayned ladle, for the better tasting of the waters." *Diary,* II, 306–308.

The Pyramid of Caius Cestius, Piranesi.

martyrs' relics from this church. Beneath this church is a small chapel; at the side of this chapel the martyrs' relics are locked up and sealed with the papal seal in a chapel, and these holy relics are not shown to anyone.

Then from this church I went to Rome, and arriving at the gates of the city of Rome I saw at the gates built into the city wall a rather large chamber, on which very high up was a four-cornered, tentlike roof covered with lead. In this chamber is interred one very wealthy Roman merchant who, when he died, ordered himself buried in this place, so that half of his body would be in Rome, and the other half outside Rome; and he was interred as he willed, and this chamber was built over his body.[64]

Then entering Rome I came to an inn that is built close to the city walls of Rome beside a hill; and such hills were built in Rome of earthenware tiles; the people who built them in Rome would walk around all the homes in Rome and collect broken earthenware vessels; they would take them to this hill and dump the earthenware tiles on this very high hill; and soon these earthenware tiles would spill over into other places close to this hill; and already these earthenware tiles have spread over other hills. Beneath this tiled hill is a great stone cellar in which there is always a

[64] This is the pyramid of Gaius Cestius, a wealthy praetor who died in 12 B.C., built at the city walls at the Porta Ostiense.

Vue de Quirinal. (Giuseppe Vasi, *Delle magnificienze di Roma aticae e moderna* [1761].)

great coldness from the earthenware tiles. It is colder than from ice or from snow, and in these cellars are fine wines; there are none better in Rome.[65] The inhabitants of Rome, honorable people and merchants with their wives and children, come to this inn to stroll about all day. And close to this tiled hill are many chairs and benches where those who come can sit and cool off from the great heat, and they drink fine wines from the cellars. Whoever wishes can come to this /256/ inn and for those who come they keep fine foodstuffs in the inn. And I came to this inn, strolled, drank fine wine, and ate all kinds of fruit. Then I went to my inn and settled accounts with the master of that inn, and paid him for the room and the food, because I intended to leave Rome on ***August 18.***

[65] This is the green hump of Monte Testaccio, built up of fragments of broken amphorae, the containers in which wine, oil, and other commodities were shipped into Rome; formerly, as Tolstoi notes, it was an urban oasis in the heat of summer.

From Rome Tolstoi crossed to Tvastere to see San Pietro in Montorio, the site of Peter's execution *inter duas metas;* from there he went to the little Church of SS. Pietro e Paolo. Returning to Rome he would pass San Paolo fuori le Mura, and at the walls, the pyramid of Gaius Cestius, and Testaccio.

"Now were we got to Mons Testaeceus an heape of Potshards almost 200 foote high, thought to have ben amassed & thrown there by the subjects of the Common-Wealth bringing their Tribute in Earthen Vessels. . . . Walking hence to the Citty old Wall, We with much admiration view the Pyramid or Tomb of C. Cestius, of White Marble, & is one of Romes most antient Monuments, intire, & inserted in the Wall." Evelyn, *Diary,* II, 360–61.

This evening I was at the papal home, where he lives in the summer.[66] This home is very large and has many rooms four stories high, and around the papal home are separate horsemen's homes and others in which the soldiers for defense live; and in other chambers live the officers. In this building the cavaliers, that is, the papal knights, live in special rooms, and also many artisans live in his home.

And around his home are the very large papal gardens. The rooms in which the pope himself lives are marvelous, with fine decorations, and his house is built most lordly and is extraordinarily large. In this home is a chapel where they conduct Mass all day and where the pope serves, and there is a small chapel in his own rooms where the pope hears Mass. From the papal home I went to my inn and tidied up completely, so I could go on the road; and I ordered my coachman to come to me in the inn with the carriage early in the morning of the 18th of August.

The Description of Rome

The city of Rome is a large place, not very populous, and it stands close to the hills on a level place, and has in its middle small gentle hills on which there are settlements.

Through Rome flows the river Tiber, which is rather large and deep, steep-banked, and it always flows muddy as if it were mixed with clay. The inhabitants of Rome do not use water from the Tiber in their food or for drinking because it is muddy: instead they have a fountain in every home. This river flows from Rome 30 It. miles and falls into the *Andriatitskoe* sea.[67] Along this river from the sea come smallish vessels with all kinds of trading goods. Around Rome are stone city walls of ancient work, not very tall or thick, and broken in many places. The towers are not large, and have many parts, and the passage gates to Rome are few. The first is called Portopopuli (Porta del Popolo), and then there is a gate called San-Ian Liuteran [sic] /257/ close to the home of Tsar Constantine; and then the gate called Pinchana (Pinciana); and then the next gate called Saliure (Salaria); and the next gate called Di-San-Petro; and the next gate called Di-San-Paulo, and then there are two more gates.[68]

In Rome are two papal homes, which I described above in this book. His homes are very large; in the house close to the church of the holy apostles Peter and Paul

[66] This is not the papal residence at Castel Gondolfo, but the Quirinal Palace into which Clement VIII moved in 1592 and which remained the papal residence until 1870. A 1692 illustration of coaches and sedan chairs at the Quirinal Palace is in Krautheimer, *Rome of Alexander VII*, p. 26.

[67] The Tiber, of course, flows into the Tyrrhenian Sea, not the Adriatic.

[68] Tolstoi lists the following: The ancient Porta Flaminia, with inner face executed by Bernini in 1655, the outer face by Vignola after a design by Michelangelo; the Porta San Giovanni, 1574, by Giacomo Della Porta; the Pinciana, Byzantine, c. 537; the Salarian gate; and the Porta San Paolo, formerly the Porta Ostiensis, from the time of Aurelian.

The Piazza del Popolo, Piranesi.

are eleven thousand living rooms; in the other home the pope lives in summer and in it are six thousand living rooms.

In Rome are monasteries of various orders and some two thousand parish churches, and all are marvelously well built, and the decoration in them is marvelous. On the outside they are built of the most glorious workmanship, with marvelous carved alabaster and marble and decorated with colored patterns.

In Rome in many places and even at churches and on the squares are tall columns of fine workmanship of both ancient and new work, and among them is one fine column placed where three great streets meet; this column may be seen from the very ends of these three streets.[69]

Also, many of these squares are finely paved with stones. In Rome there is one great square that is very fine on a high place, toward which are built very high stone

[69] One thinks, in Rome, of the column of Marcus Aurelius in the Piazza Colona, or of Trajan's column, but almost certainly this is the obelisk erected by Sixtus V in 1589 in the Piazza del Popolo, just down the Via dei Babuino from the Church of St. Athanasius where Tolstoi lodged. It forms the point where the Babuino, Via del Corso, and Via Ripetta meet at the old Porta del Popolo in the Aurelian wall. Tolstoi apparently did not visit Santa Maria del Popolo to see its famous Madonna, an ancient icon, Hodigritria, attributed to St. Luke. On the Piazza del Popolo and its trident of streets, see Krautheimer, *Rome of Alexander VII*, p. 117 and passim.

entries that can be called stairways, and at the entry from these stairs to the square are placed two horses, made of whitestone of fine ancient work. In the middle of this *pliatsa* (piazza) or square is also on a column a horse of brass made anciently under the tsar Constantine in the most marvelous work. Close by on this square are marvelous palaces, in which the Roman princes and senators sit to advise in governmental affairs.[70]

In Rome are *iustitsiia* (It. *giustizia*), that is, great offices, which the governor of

[70] This "fine square on a high place" is the capitol; its steps are flanked by equestrian statues, and in the center of the Piazza dei Campidoglio stands the bronze Marcus Aurelius on his horse in front of the Palazzo del Senatore.

Compare Evelyn: "The Capitol, to which we climed, by a very broad ascent of degrees, is built about a square court. . . . The front of this Court is crown'd with an imcomparable fabrique, containing the Courts of Justice, and where the Criminal Notary sitts, and others. . . . To this joynes an handsome towre, the whole faciata adorn's with noble Statues both on the out side, & battlements, ascended by a double payre of staires and a stately posario. In the center of the court stands that incomparable Horse bearing the Emp: Marcus Aurelius of Corinthian mettal, as big as the life, placed on a Pedistal of marble, . . . and esteemed one of the noblest pieces of worke now extant in the world, antique, & very rare." There follow four pages of descriptions of "incomparable statues &c. . . . We now left the Capitol, certainely one of the most renowned placed in the World; even as now built by the designe of the famous M:Angelo." Evelyn, *Diary*, II, 220–26.

The Capitol and the Steps of S. Maria in Aracoeli, Piranesi.

Rome directs. These offices are well built, and in them are many judges and scribes, and they report in all matters to the governor of Rome, and the governor can handle most matters himself, and for important affairs he reports to the pope.

At the papal home there are always 500 soldiers for a guard, and with the soldiers are also knights, and all are from the Empire, and they live at papal expense. The leaders of these soldiers and of the knights are all from the Empire, and they are also kept at papal expense.

The senators and princes of Rome and the cardinals ride very lordly in fine coaches; and on holidays they have six horses but otherwise /258/ two horses. Their coaches are very marvelous and rich, and their horses are adorned with glorious blinders; and behind them ride servants in coaches, and a great number of other people walk behind them. Likewise, the princely and senatorial wives and maiden daughters ride in fine coaches, and a few people walk behind them. Also the merchants and their wives and children ride in coaches. Honorable people and wealthy merchants and their wives and children do not go on foot, or they are dishonored. The men's dress has its own fashion; it is mostly black, but some love French dress and many use it, and the female sex in Rome dresses well in a particular fashion, and the people in Rome, both the men and the women, are very handsome and very politic. In Rome in all there are always 5,000 soldiers at papal expense for a guard.

In Rome in one monastery live those of the Jesuit order of various peoples: Italians, Spanish, French, of the Empire, English, Hollanders, Swedes, and Turks who have been caught by the Catholics; and Hungarians, Uniate Greeks, Poles, and Slavs; and also Turks, Tatars, Arabs, Armenians, Persians, Chinese, Bukharans, and Kalmyks, who also have become Catholics.[71] And the pope keeps these Jesuits at his expense for this reason: when a person of a people that is not of the Catholic faith, or a Calvinist, or a Lutheran, or a Busurman, or an idolater, when any of these becomes a Catholic and wants to be instructed, and knows no Italian or Latin or anything except his native tongue, then they take from this monastery a Jesuit who speaks the language of the person who desires instruction; and that Jesuit is ordered to instruct that person in his native language, so that he can completely repent for his sins and so that the preacher can completely know his confession and can truly judge him about his sins.

In Rome are two great academies in which are a multitude of students of various peoples, and the teachers in these academies are Jesuits.[72]

[71] Also in Tolstoi's Roman neighborhood at the far end of the Piazza di Spagna stands the vast Palace of the Congregation of the Propaganda Fide, founded by Gregory XV in 1622. Like the Uniate College of St. Athanasius down the street at the other end of the piazza, it still functions.

[72] There were many colleges in Rome, San Pantaleone, the Clementino, the Nazareno, the Bandinelli, and others. But Tolstoi here probably refers to the Jesuit Collegio Romano, founded by Pope Gregory XIII (1572–85), and to the older Sapienza, which dated from the thirteenth century.

Bread in Rome is fine white wheat bread, and foodstuffs are cheap, and there is much fruit of all kinds and very cheap. The people of Rome are very kind and friendly to foreigners who come here, and they are especially friendly to Muscovite people.

Even now one can see in the environs of Rome those places where Rome formerly extended, and one can see that old Rome was of unspeakable size. There are ancient Roman palaces in all directions /259/ that in antiquity were inside Rome itself, but now they are 12 or 15 miles outside the city of Rome. In places that in antiquity were in the middle of Rome there are now great fields, where they sow much wheat and plant grapes, and today everywhere one can see an old stone building or a fallen-down palace or columns in many places. And outside the Rome of today are the many homes of the Roman inhabitants built for strolling. There they have fine large gardens in which there are many fruit trees: lemons, *tsukat,* almonds, pomegranates, figs, *shkot,* citrons, chestnuts, peaches, walnuts, paradise apples, cherries, sour cherries, various pears, apples, olives of various kinds, black olives, and all sorts of other fruit trees, among which they plant great cypress trees to decorate these gardens. There are also many grapes of the white and red kinds, and these gardens are decorated with marvelous shrubs that grow in marvelous figures and in all kinds of designs, and among these shrubs they plant fine flowers of all kinds. They also set out very large marvelous pots in which they plant large fruit trees and glorious flowers. They set these pots in the gardens among the trees and bushes in marvelous arrangements. Also in these gardens are glorious fountains from which clear and cold waters constantly flow; and concerning the intricate forms in which these fountains are made, this cannot be described for the sheer number of them; if someone wanted to see all the fountains in Rome, he would have to live there two months and look at nothing else, but at fountains only, and even then it would be difficult to see them all.[73]

[73]Tolstoi was impressed with the Romans' ability to have the exact tree they want on the spot where they want it; and he has been most impressed with the many fountains of Rome.

Behind these simple observations rests an important lesson for Tolstoi. A relatively new historical literature indicates that, from medieval times to the present, Western Europe had a unique attitude toward nature as a cosmos of energies to be tapped and used according to human intentions. Western man was power conscious to the point of fantasy. Western man alone took technologies discovered elsewhere and turned them to the transformation of old ways of doing things; from the stirrup to movable type, Western man alone developed technologies to their full potential. Unlike other civilizations, the West, almost constantly since the Middle Ages, has regarded nature as something to be used, controlled, exploited, refashioned, understood scientifically, and ultimately harnessed to the will of man. All of this was new to Tolstoi, but in the Diary we can sense his growing awareness of these values, so necessary to Russia in the age of Peter the Great's transformation on the horizon.

The story of these Western attitudes can be traced in the works of Fernand Braudel and Jean Gimpel, already cited; in the classic by White, *Medieval Technology and Social Change;* and in the recent retelling of Renaissance science, Goldstein, *Dawn of Modern Science.*

The air in Rome is difficult for human habitation, especially in the summer; and therefore in the middle of summer, when the sun is in Leone, that is, in the Lion, which the Italians call *Kanikula* (It. Canicola), that is, "dog days" in the Slavic language, many inhabitants leave Rome for distant places, and they do not come back to Rome until the time when the sun is in Virginy, that is, the Virgin, and enters into *Libry,* that is, in the Scales; then the air in Rome has cooled and is healthy for people.[74]

The present pope has ordered that there should not be secular operas and comedies in Rome but only spiritual ones, and those not large.[75]

The present pope hears Mass each day in his chapels, that is, in the churches in his own home. Indeed, in all of Rome he has ordered that there be no part-singing with organs or other kinds of music; and he has ordered them to sing only simple songs, /260/ and he has even ordered that in girls' monasteries the nuns do not sing at all, but the priests who serve in monasteries may sing, but in comedies and operas girls are never to sing anymore.

However, both vocal and instrumental music in Rome is finely performed by the male sex on holidays in parish churches and in *komventakh* (It. *conventi*), that is, monasteries; they can solicit the pope for a *litsentsiia* (It. *licenza*), that is, an approbation, to sing in part-singing, but this does not happen often.

When the pope wants to go somewhere in Rome, to some church on a feast day, or to a hospital, or to the house of Constantine where the orphans live, they carry him there in a sedan chair. This sedan is made of fine work, like a carriage without the wheels and without the [equestrian] mountings; and when he so wishes, he goes by a coach. Every week on Saturday the present pope rides to the home of Tsar Constantine, in which he keeps maiden orphans at his expense for the sake of Christ. The present pope has made another home beyond the river Tiber of fine architecture, and in it are many fine rooms; in these rooms also at papal expense live orphans of the male sex. First of all they teach them to read, and this is done until the age of 9, and then they teach them various trades—the tailor's, the bootmaker's, the joiner's, the goldsmith's, and those of all sorts of craftsmen's, and their wares are sold and divided into three parts, just as among the girls who live in the home of Tsar Constantine.[76]

Beyond the river Tiber they have recently built a large building with many large rooms. This house was built so that when bastimenty (It. *bastimenti*), that is, river vessels, from ships or galleys laden with goods sail to Rome up that river Tiber from

[74] Dog days: July and August, when the Sun and Sirius rise and set together.

[75] There is a good introduction to the theater in Rome in Andrieux, *Daily Life in Papal Rome,* pp. 156–66 and passim. Living where he did, Tolstoi may have seen the Alberti, or Teatro delle Dame, which was near the Piazza di Spagna. The present pope was Innocent XII.

[76] On orphanages, hospitals, and charitable institutions in Rome, see Andrieux, *Daily Life in Papal Rome,* pp. 60–68. Andrieux stresses both the charity and the civic pride that Tolstoi noted, and which is caught in the old formula, "Civis sum Romanus."

the sea, these wares can be placed in this house and then sold, so the ships that carried the goods to Rome need not be detained.

The womenfolk of Rome have a sense of shame and are not brazen, and the sin of fornication is held to be a great mortal sin, and shameful, and especially damning. Drunkenness is also greatly shameful in Rome; drunkenness is avoided not only among honorable people but among the base people. They sell brandy in Rome early each morning, and again at the beginning of the night hours they carry it along the streets. Every day, very early before daybreak or at dawn, every Roman drinks down a small wine glass of brandy, and even those people who go from Rome to work the fields drink some brandy early in the morning. The Romans do this because of the bad air: the spirit of the brandy /261/ protects against the infectious air; but during daytime there is never anywhere any brandy for sale in the streets, and no one drinks it during these hours.

At all times the ambassadors of the Empire, of Spain, France, Venice, and the other Christian states live in Rome, and they have great and wondrous homes that have many marvelously decorated rooms. These ambassadors also have their own coaches and drivers and saddlery all liveried, and they drive gloriously and with a large retinue in fine attire. Among these ambassadors the Spanish one has a coach that is supernaturally good and luxurious, and it cost 8,000 Roman scudos, and in Muscovite money over 5,000 rubles. This coach is very large, and ten people can sit in it without difficulty. It is done of such workmanship and richness that it is difficult to describe it in detail. That Spanish ambassador died during my stay in Rome.

In Rome there are fine libraries in many places, in which there are multitudes of books in various languages. In these libraries, too, are many land-water and celestial globes, *shver armiliaris* (armillary spheres), and mathematical instruments of all kinds.

In many places in Rome they print books in Latin and Greek and in the Italian language, and they also imprint heavenly and earthly spheres and cosmographical maps and other such sheets, and fine books of domestic architecture and of fountain design, and among other such marvelous things they print *kunshty* (Ger. *Kunst*), that is, all kinds of pictures.

In Rome the pope keeps military galleys that go all year to Morea in the East and stay in Morea all summer with the Maltese and Venetian galleys to fight the Turks. The Roman pope takes from the Spanish king much treasure because Naples and all of Sicily should be papal regions, and he ceded them to the Spanish king, and he takes a great treasure for them every year.

The honorably born people of Rome do not use smoking tobacco, and they disdain it, but they use snuff constantly; they bring it from Malta, Spain, Bologna, and from other places, and they pay very dearly for good snuff—a golden chervonets per pound. And all of the clergy in Rome use snuff constantly, and the cardinals, archbishops, /262/ and monks could not be without it. Roman princes and all the honorable people as well as the very rich merchants have large estates with grapes and gardens, from which they receive large treasures.

In Rome the carnival lasts only 15 days, and in that carnival they walk in mascarade only three hours a day; and custom has it that the wives and maiden daughters of honorable people ride in fine coaches, and get all dressed up, and take many small sweets with them in the coaches. When they meet with acquaintances or even with those they do not know, they throw the sweets at each other and amuse themselves this way, and so many sweets are poured on the streets of Rome that it is as if they were covered with snow. These sweets are picked up by the needy, and no one prevents them from doing so. At carnival time they perform small operas and comedies, but they are spiritual, for the present pope has ordered it thus.[77]

The Romans wear their hair cut short and light because of the great heat of summertime, to unencumber themselves. In winter there is no heavy frost in Rome, and because of this there are no stoves in Rome anywhere, and they do not make them, and in many places in Rome there are not even fireplaces. It is expensive to buy firewood in Rome, because firewood is brought to Rome from distant places, and firewood cannot be cut down anywhere close to Rome for there are no forests at all, and where there are a few they are small.[78]

In Rome there is one Greek church, which is scarcely allowed because they are banished by the Romans; this is because the Romans wish that all Greeks would be with them in a single faith.

Close to this Greek church in Rome is an Armenian church, which is united in all things with the Western church.[79] In Rome there are 15,000 Jews, who are very

[77] This is the second reference to the sumptuary regulations of the current pope, the very proper Innocent XII, Antonio Pignatelli, 1691–1700. A half-century earlier, during Evelyn's visit, Carnival, celebrated in Rome eleven days before Ash Wednesday, had been much gayer: "We were taken up the next morning in seing the impertinences of the Carnoval when all the world are as mad at Rome, as at other places, but the most remarkable were the 3 Races of the Barbarie horses, that run in the strada del *Corso* without riders, onely having spurrs so placed on their backs, & hanging downe by their sides, as with their motion to stimulate them; Then of Mares: Then of Asses, of Bufalos, of Naked Men [old men, young, & boys:] and abboundance of idle & ridiculous Passetime: One thing yet is remarkable, their acting Comedies upon a Stage placed on a Cart, or *plaustrum* where the Scene or tiring place is made of bowghs, in a Pastoral & rural manner, this they drive from streete to streete with a yoake or two of Oxen, after the antient guise; The streetes swarming with whores, buffoones & all manner of rabble." Evelyn, *Diary* II, 381–82, entry for February 28, 1645.

[78] These comments on the scarcity of firewood in the vicinity of Rome could be expanded to include much of Europe. In early-modern Europe usable wood was everywhere becoming scarce, the whole continent being increasingly deforested. In the short-run it meant considerable profit for Petrine Russia, which exported much timber, especially long straight trees for masts for the English fleet, among others. In the long-run, these casual remarks portend the coal revolution of the eighteenth century, necessity being the mother of new technological inventions. Perhaps the best account of the phenomenon is to be found in Braudel, *Structures,* pp. 362ff.

[79] The Greek Orthodox Church of St. Andrea on the Via Sardegna is fairly close to the Armenian Catholic Church of Santa Nicola da Tolentino in the street of that name.

poor, because the pope has ordered that not a single Jew may trade in any new wares, and the Jews all trade in old clothing, and cheaply; in all things the Jews who live in Rome are crowded together, and are injured by the Romans. And during Passion Week every day a pensioner comes to the place where the Jews live and climbs upon a throne and speaks a sermon to which the Jews all must listen involuntarily; and anyone who does not want to listen to that sermon will be beaten by the Roman soldiers and forced to hear the sermon; and in this manner two or three Jews every year repent their wickedness, enter into Christianity, and become Catholics.[80] /263/

Many trading people of every faith, Christians and Busurmans, arrive in Rome, and they come from very distant parts with their goods, from China, India, and Persia.

The pope does not keep wild beasts, lions, elephants, bears, leopards, and other such animals.

In Rome over the gates of the houses of the princes and senators and cardinals and archbishops and all other honorable people are two emblems: on the right side are the papal arms, and on the left the arms of the master of the house. Also, over the gates of the homes of the ambassadors of the various states who live in Rome, they place also two coats of arms, on the right side the papal arms, and on the left the arms of the state of which they are the ambassador.

There are many fine coachman's horses in Rome but there are no Turkish *argamaks* or Nogai horses,[81] because the honorable and the base people of Rome do not keep riding horses; instead, they have German coach horses, but ride in coaches and in carriages; and he who happens to ride a horse does so on a German horse.

In and around Rome are also many marvelous hinnies and mules and bison on which the base people ride, those who do all the work, and they also ride them on the road.

In and around Rome are many horned cattle, bulls, and large cows, all covered with fur; also many rams and great sheep, which have long wool and very long tails, and they are all white, and there are no black ones. Likewise, there are many large and heavy swine, and all are black, and none with other [color of] fur. There are

[80] It is not clear that Tolstoi actually visited the ghetto. Evelyn did: "I went to the Ghetto, where the Jewes dwell, as in a suburbs by themselves; being invited by a Jew of my acquaintance to see a Circumcision: here I passed by the Piazza Judea (where their Serraglio begins) for being invirond with wales, they are lock'd up every night: in this place remains yet part of a stately fabric; which my Jew told me had been a Palace of theirs, for the Ambassador of ther Nation in former times, when their Country was Subject to the Romans. There was a large Inscription on it, that I could not stay to reade." Evelyn then includes a page-long, detailed, description of the ritual of Circumcision. He concludes, "The Jewes do all in Rome weare yellow hatts, and live onely upon brokage & Usury, very poore and despicable beyond what they are in other territories of Princes where they are permitted." *Diary*, II, 292–94.

[81] The *argamak* is the durable Asiatic riding horse of the Kabardin and Turkhmen peoples. The Nogai Horde, long located east of the Volga, supplied Muscovy with mounts in early-modern times.

also many great goats, and also many Indian chickens, which in Rome they herd in great flocks, with some five hundred or a thousand or more in one flock of these Indian chickens; but there are not many geese or ducks, but many Russian chickens. In the inns they roast mostly pigeons for foreigners, and in soups they use pigeon more than chicken. In Rome among the honorable people in their homes and inns for foreigners they keep fine foodstuffs—roasts and soups and French pastries, and all the foods are marvelous. Foreigners in Rome of notable and honorable birth do not walk much but hire coaches and carriages. They ride in coaches and carriages wherever they wish, but others walk in Rome, those who do not know very much. And he who wishes to hire in Rome a fine coach with two good drivers for a whole day /264/ must pay for that coach one golden chervonets, and one rides the whole day wherever one wishes. When there are many foreigners in Rome in the winter, and especially at the time of carnival, then one pays two Spanish *dopia* for a good coach for the day, and in Muscovite money this is more than 4 rubles. And this is why at this time one pays dearly for a coach, because there are many foreigners in Rome, and everyone wants to ride decorously and to observe the customs of the Roman inhabitants at carnival time.

In Rome they speak the Italian language finely, purely, better than in many [other] Italian places.

The inns in Rome in which foreigners stay are very rich and decorous; the rooms in them are upholstered in golden leathers and decorated with fine pictures; the bedsteads are finely gilded, the curtains are of good satin and silk, the beds are also good, and the sheets are always white with fine lace. When the master of the inn feeds foreigners, there are fine white tablecloths on the table and also white hand towels every day, and the dishes and plates are of fine tin and clean, and the knives have silver handles, and the forks, spoons, and salt cellars are silver, and all are fine and always clean. The vessels from which they drink are of fine glass and are clean, and the washstands and washtubs are always of clean pottery. When a foreigner stays at a given inn, he pays seven pauls of Roman money each day for each person, and in Muscovite money this is a half-ruble. For this half-ruble in this inn they give him a fine dinner and supper, and also for that price they give him a fine sitting room with a table, armchairs, chairs, and a fine bed with curtains, and a bed with clean sheets. For that same price, early each morning the *cameriere,* that is, that man who will serve him in the inn, puts on his boots and washes him; and the soap and towels—all this is provided by the master of the inn. In the evening, in every room in which a foreigner stays, the lord of the inn places tallow candles in good clean candlesticks; and when one goes to sleep the cameriere places a lamp with wood oil in each room, so that there will be light in each room all night, and they do all of this for the same price.

VII

August 18, 1698–January 27, 1699

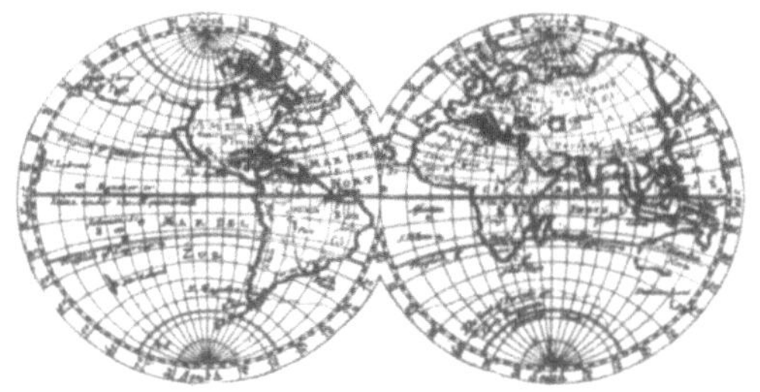

Rome · Venice · Vienna
Warsaw · Moscow

/369/ ***August 18.*** Early in the morning the coachman who had brought me from Naples to Rome in a carriage came to me at the inn, and having collected everything into the carriage, I left Rome in the first hour of day. After departing Rome I came to the river Tiber, where they have built a large stone bridge on large stone columns across the river. On this Roman bridge in antiquity the Roman caesar Constantine saw the holy cross composed of stars in the sky, and also certain letters also composed of stars, as history narrates; and tsar Constantine triumphed over Maksentiia (Maxentius) on that bridge.[1] And having crossed that bridge, I came to the gates that are built on the end of the bridge; and soldiers stand at the gates to inspect all travelers for any merchant's wares. At the gates I gave according to the Roman custom what was appropriate from my carriage, and went along the Florentine road toward Florence. From Rome to this place is 2 Italian miles. This day at noon I came to an inn called Bakana (Baccano), 17 It. miles from Rome. Along this road from Rome to the inn are small hills, and in other places there are level fields, among them fields of wheat, and there are also small forests in many places. In the inn called Baccano I ate dinner and after noon I left the inn and at an hour before night I came to a city in the papal region called Ridzhelion (Ronciglione); I stayed the night in this city, 15 Italian miles from the inn. From the inn to this city along the road are also small hills and level fields, in which /370/ they sow wheat; there are also small forests. In this city I stayed in an inn called Fortuna.

August 19. An hour before daybreak I left that inn and came to a city in the papal region called Tiverbo (Viterbo), 10 It. miles from the inn Fortuna. This city is

[1] At Grotto Rossa, on the Via Flamina, about 4 miles from the Ponte Milvio, is the site of the Saxa Rubra; here Constantine saw the flaming cross and the Greek words, "Conquer by this," and so armed, defeated Maxentius in 312.

large, and its buildings are all stone, but few are good. In this city is a fine fountain.[2] The hills are large and rocky along the road from the inn Fortuna to the city of Viterbo. I passed this city without stopping in it, and this same day came to the city Monto-Fiashkona (Montefiascone), 8 It. miles from Viterbo. Along this road are high stone hills. Close to this city I stayed in an inn called Liashkala (La Scala), and I stayed there this day until the 9th hour, and in the ninth hour I left to come to the city of Bonzene (Bolsena).[3] I passed this city without stopping in it. This city is not large, and its buildings are all stone. Then I came this day, in the second hour of night, to the city Akva-Pinent (Acquapendente),[4] and in this city I stayed in an inn, which is called by the same name, Acquapendente, and I spent the night in that inn. Along this road are many hills on which small forests grow. From the inn La Scala to this inn of Acquapendente it is 15 Italian miles.

August 20. Early in the morning I left Acquapendente and came to the city of Redegofona (Radiconfani). This city stands on a high hill and is not large. I passed it this day around noon and arrived at an inn called Liamadzhina-de-Redogofona (La Macina? di Radicofani) outside of the city, where I spent the night, 19 Italian miles.[5] Along this road are very high stone hills, on which I could not ride in the carriage, so I walked these hills on foot. And I stopped in this inn for three hours, and four hours before night I arrived in the city of Akvariko (San Quirico d'Orcia). Close to this city I stayed in an inn called Fonte-Aliavina (Montalcino), 14 Italian miles from the inn where I dined. Along this road are large hills, and the road is immeasurably rocky; there I spent the night.

August 21. From this inn I came to a place called Liutsian (Lucignano), and I stopped at an inn called by the same name, Lucignano, 16 Italian miles from the inn where I spent the night. Along this road are high rocky hills, and in other places are fine level fields; and I stayed in that inn until the 9th hour of day, and in the 9th hour I left and arrived in the city of Sana (Siena). This is a city of the grand prince of Florence and is very large, standing on a high hill; in this city are tall stone structures done of fine craftsmanship, and the buildings are all stone. /371/ This city

[2]This is the fountain in the Piazza della Fontana Grande. It was begun in 1206 by Bertoldo and Pietro di Giovanni, finished in 1279, and restored in 1424.

[3]Tolstoi does not mention the Lago di Bolsena, visible from Montefiascone and of course from Bolsena itself.

[4]The site is now a resort famous for its cascades. There was formerly a single inn, where most travelers to and from Rome stopped. "We were told that the man who kept the hostry [at Acquapendente] where we inn'd was the most wealthy person in the place. He had only two or three ragged servants, and waited at table himself." Cited in Mead, *Grand Tour,* p. 89.

[5]The inn at Radicofani on the frontier between Tuscany and the Papal States was a well-known state-sponsored hostelry, and everyone stopped there. See Sells, *Paradise,* pp. 144–45.

is very populous, and the people in it live a fine politics and are honorable personages who ride in fine coaches and have fine drivers and saddles. Likewise, the wives and girls of this city also ride in coaches. There are many trading people in this city and sufficient shops and wares. The monasteries and churches in this city are well built. From the inn to this city it is 8 It. miles. I did not stay in this city but passed by it, and this day, in the evening, I came to an inn named Kashtel-de-Liatselia (Castellina in Chianti), 8 It. miles from the city of Siena; in this inn I spent the night.

August 22. I left this inn and arrived at an inn named Tavernile (Tavernelle Val di Pesa), 15 It. miles from the inn where I spent the night. This inn is in the very small place of Tavernelle. Along this road are a few hills, but they are not large; here is a level place and many grapes,[6] and along the fields are many olive trees that grow on knolls and in the level places. Along this road are many villages and towns and inns, all built of stone. Along this road fine waters flow in many places, and there are stone bridges. And I stayed in the inn called Tavernelle, this 22nd day of August until the 9th hour, because in the above-mentioned inn Castellina I forgot some of my things when I departed. I sent my coachman on the road for those things, and my coachman returned but did not bring my forgotten things to me, and he said that he did not find those things of mine; and without finding those things I did not want to continue my journey, and I spent the night in this same inn.

August 23. Early in the morning, having found my forgotten things, I left the inn Tavernelle for Florentsiia (Florence, Firenze, formerly Fiorenza); from this inn to Florence it is 15 It. miles. All along this road are stone hills, and on and between them are many fields under wheat, and there are also trees: oaks, birch, and aspens on the hills and between them. Among the trees are placed white and red grapes, which they grow twisted around those trees, and they bear a great quantity of fruit. 6 miles before Florence there is a very broken dwelling, a stone structure, in the midst of which are great *conventi,* that is, monasteries, in which there are fine large stone buildings and great homes with large rooms.[7] In these same spots among /372/ the homes are groves of great cypress trees. And when I came to the Florentine gates, at the gates stood soldiers on guard who wanted to look at my trunk for merchants' wares, as is the custom. When they heard that I was a man of the Muscovite state, they did not look at anything of mine but immediately let me pass into Florence; having entered Florence, I stayed at an inn named San-liantsi (San Lancia).[8] In this

[6] Leaving Sienna Tolstoi skirts at least the edge of the Chianti region.

[7] Here, south of Florence, Tolstoi perhaps saw the Carthusian monastery at Galluzzo, "la Certosa," founded in 1338, with fortresslike buildings. See Moryson, *Itinerary,* pp. 331–32, for a visit a century earlier.

[8] In Florence the inns were all on the same street, but I have not found another traveler who stayed at this particular *albergo.* See Sells, *Paradise,* p. 145.

inn the master assigned me a fine room in which there was a gilded bedstead with fine curtains, also a good bed with clean white sheets and a fine blanket, and a table and chairs and fine armchairs and all kinds of decorations—mirrors, pictures, as the Italians usually decorate their rooms. For food and the room and every convenience I paid the master for myself seven Roman pauls a day, and in Muscovite money this is half a ruble.

This same day after dinner I went for a walk and came first to the Church of John the Forerunner.[9] This church is large, made eight-sided of fine architecture and marvelous craftsmanship, and its decor is also good. On this church are four great doors,[10] and on them the locks are made of brass of marvelous carved workmanship, and on these doors there are figures of brass exactly as if they had been carved most marvelously of wood.

Then I came to the cathedral that is named in the Italian language Santa-Mariia-Fiore (Il Duomo, or La Cattedrale di Santa Maria del Fiore), that is, St. Maria of the Flowers. This church is very large,[11] and the outside is all done in white marble. Fitted into the white marble are black stones in fine patterns, and in proportions this church is marvelously done. But there are no decorations at all on the inside of this church; only the altar is done of fine carved alabaster work, and its platform of various marbles is also of fine work.

Then I walked to another building in which the Florentine grand prince keeps beasts and birds.[12] In this building are extensive places for the beasts, and the rooms in which the beasts live are fine. In this place they have built a large window with heavy iron grates attached to it, and through the grates people can see the beasts. In the middle of this building among the rooms is an extensive place in the middle of which stands a great wooden column; and this enclosure was made so that when the Florentine grand prince wishes to amuse himself with these beasts, the beasts can be released into this place and they fight one another, and the grand /373/ prince can look at this from above, where fine stone arcades surround this enclosure. And if

[9] This is Battistero, the octagonal Church of San Giovanni Battista, seventh–eighth century, remodeled about 1200, with its celebrated bronze doors, added in the fourteenth–fifteenth centuries.

[10] There are three sets of brass doors on the famous baptistry. See Evelyn, *Diary,* II, 197.

[11] It is the third largest church in the world. Its name, "of the flowers," comes from the lily in the coat of arms of Florence.

[12] Tolstoi here visits the *serraglio delle fiere,* one of the principal sights of Florence, and probably the best zoo in Europe in the period, mentioned by virtually all visitors. "Nere this is the Place where are kept several Wildbeasts, as Wolves, Catts, Bares, Tygers, & Lions. I tooke greate pleasure to see what an incredible height one of the Lyons would leape, for which I caused to be hung downe a joynt of mutton: They are loose in a deepe, Walld-Court, & therefore to be seene with much more delight than at the Tower of Lond, in their grates." Evelyn, *Diary,* II, 195. A century earlier Moryson had described the machine used to enter the tiger pit, although he did not call it a "toad." Moryson, *Itinerary,* pp. 325–26. The zoo disappeared in 1777 after five centuries of existence.

one beast fails to overcome the other and they cannot be separated because of their ferocity, they can separate them with this *instrument* (It. *strumento*): they made a large clay image, immeasurably frightening, like a very horrifying toad, and people go inside this representation and set fire in it, so that the smoke and flames of the fire issue from the mouth and eyes and ears and the sides of this representation, and the people in this frightening thing ride into that place where the beasts fight, and when the beasts catch sight of this representation, they become frightened, thinking that some live beast is approaching them, and they separate and cease their fighting. Then the animal keepers are able to put them in the cages where they live. And this frightening representation is made on wheels so the people within can go wherever they wish. In this house I saw one great lion, which they say is 9 years old. Then I saw a large lioness, and they tell a surprising thing about her; apparently she was sick with a fever, and I saw her lying there, and she roared very loudly, as if she were suffering. Then I saw a young lion, which did not yet have a mane or tassel on its tail; and they say that this lion is already three years old. Then I saw two small lions, and they sit in one place and play together, and in size these little lions are like a medium-sized wolf; and they say that these lions are 7 months from birth. They were brought from Spain.

In this same building I saw a great and very fine leopard. In the same building I saw three large bears, among which is one that is great and straw-colored; and they say that this straw-colored bear has sat in this building 30 years already. In this building, too, I saw several large wolves. In this building, too, I saw one black vixen; and they say that this vixen was brought to Florence from Moscow a long time ago.

There I saw many large grey eagles.

Then from this house I walked to the church of the archdeacon St. Lavrentii (San Lorenzo), which was conceived 94 years ago, and they have constantly worked from the time of its conception to the present, and still it is incomplete, and they expect that it will not be finished for more than ten more years.[13] This church is large, eight-cornered, with all the sides equal and a face made of grey stone of marvelous workmanship. In many places around the windows is placed alabaster of fine smooth work, and the inside of this church is all made of /374/ various marbles of such glorious work that one could not encounter better in the whole world. And into this marble are set colored Indian and Persian stones and shells and corals and ambers and topazes and crystals of such miraculous work that it would be impossible to describe such craftsmanship in detail. Around these various marbles are placed cast brass statues, gilded with heated gold. These colored marbles are placed to re-

[13] The dates and descriptions make it clear that Tolstoi is writing not about the ancient San Lorenzo proper, but the Capella dei Principi, the octagonal burial place of the Medici family, constructed after 1604 by Matteo Nigetti from designs of Giovanni dei Medici. Tolstoi notes its exquisite mosaics and, below, the gilded statues of Cosimo II (d. 1621) and Ferdinand I (d. 1609).

semble fine mirrors, and looking into these stones one can see the church and the people in it, just as in mirrors. In this church a Roman altar is made up, done all of pure gold of the most marvelous workmanship, which cost one million golden chervontsy.

In this same church along the walls are tombs, also of various marbles, in which lie the bodies of the ancient grand princes of Florence; among them is the tomb where the body of the present *granduka,* that is, the Florentine grand prince, will rest after his death. This tomb is done of such intricate work that it is incomprehensible to the human mind. Over these tombs are the portraits of these Florentine grand princes,[14] and the present grand prince of Florence stands over his tomb, and all these portraits are carved in fine alabaster of fine craftsmanship and with figures whose likes are impossible to describe.

From this church I went down to where a Roman church is built.[15] On the altar stands an image of the Crucifixion of Christ and an image of the Blessed Mother of God and an image of John the Theologian, carved of alabaster of such marvelous craftsmanship as one seldom encounters in the whole world. Columns under this church are executed to support the upper church, and the walls of this lower church are of a thickness of fourteen Italian *lokots,* and an Italian lokot is less than a Muscovite arshin by two vershok.[16] Having gone out from this church, I walked to a church that is called in the Italian language the *Nuntsiata* (Santissima Annunziata), that is, the Annunciation of the Blessed Mother of God. At this church is a monastery in which monks of the order of St. Benedict live. In front of this church is a four-cornered square instead of a church porch, each wall being seven sazhens and three arshins long.[17] On this square up high along the wall are carved statues of many Roman popes, done of fine workmanship and painted with colors /375/ exactly as if alive. On this same square along the walls are many statues of various ancient people who received favors from the icon of the Blessed Mother of God that stands in this church; and in her memory they place their statues in this church, and they do this for this reason—[to recall] an illness, injury, or some misfortune; thus have they placed these statues, and they stand to the present.[18]

[14]These are the six Medici sarcophaga, beginning with Cosimo I (d. 1575); the present grand prince was Cosimo III (1670–1723). The house of Medici would become extinct after Giovanni Gaston (d. 1737). Tolstoi describes the portraits, *persony,* the gilded bronze statues.

[15]Having descended, Tolstoi is now in San Lorenzo itself.

[16]That is, the wall is very thick, fourteen times a measure of about 24 inches.

[17]This is not, as the language suggests, the arcade on three sides of Piazza del SS. Annunziata, but the Renaissance courtyard at the entrance to the church, now enclosed by a glass roof. Tolstoi is about to visit the miraculous picture of the Virgin and Gabriel, a thirteenth-century fresco, in the Capella della Vergine Annunziata, 1448–52.

[18]A century earlier Moryson had noted the extraordinary faith of Italians in the Virgin; *Itinerary,* p. 324. Evelyn was a nonbeliever: he went to the Annunciata, "being a place of extraordinary repute for Sanctity; for here is a shrine that dos greate Miracles, as they pretend, by innumerable Votive Tables & other trinkets, which almost quite cover the Wales of

Then I entered that church in which I saw a fine structure; this church is decorated inside with fine colored marble and also with fine alabaster carvings. There are no vaults in this church, but they have made flat ceilings of marvelous carved work, all gilded; the other fine decorations in this church are also marvelously built. In this same church is the kaplica, that is, the small chapel done in the name of the Blessed Mother of God, and it is marvelously built. Its altar is all of cast silver, as are the rather small silver candlesticks, and on the altar are large images of the holy angels cast of silver. Also around the altar up high are the images of the cherubim and the seraphim and of angels, all cast of silver. There are many large silver lamps in this chapel; among them in the middle hangs one very large lamp, silver and all gilded and done of fine workmanship. This small chapel is partitioned off from the great church by a fine brass railing, and along this railing are placed very large silver chandeliers, made to resemble great pitchers, in which they place candles and flowers to decorate the church; these chandeliers are 25 in number. Likewise, there are many other silver figures, and all the decor is marvelous and very rich.

I left this church and went to my inn, because it was hot from the scorching of the sun, and I could not stroll about more because of that heat.

Then when the heat of the sun had lessened, I again went walking and again came to the great cathedral, and on the forward wall are three entrance doors, and over two of the doors is writing in Latin letters, and specifically over the first door: "They labored for a long time on the ecumenical cathedral in Florence when Victor the Second was pope and beyond, and Hendrick was the August Caesar, in the year of the Lord 1055. Amen."

On the other doors of this same church is written: "The holy ecumenical seventeenth council was held in this Florentine church, in which both the Greeks and the Latins came to a single true faith before Eugene the Fourth, pope of the Ecumenical church /376/ and before Johann Augustus, the Greek tsar, in the year of our Lord 1439."[19]

At this cathedral is built a very tall four-sided bell tower of marvelous work, with fine carvings of white and black stone, and the work is all very subtle and fine.[20]

---

the whole Church." *Diary,* II, 194. The references are to the *ex votos* representing ailments that had been cured.

[19] The cathedral is famous as the site of the Council of Florence (1439), which met under the Patronage of Cosimo the Elder and which reconciled the Greek and Latin churches. It is therefore of considerable interest to Tolstoi. The old doors with the inscriptions seen by Tolstoi were replaced at the end of the nineteenth century in Emilio de Fabris's reconstruction of the façade, with new doors by Pasaglia and Cassioli.

Mentioned in the inscriptions are Victor II, pope, 1055–57; Henry III the Black, Holy Roman emperor, 1039–56, crowned 1046; Eugene IV, pope, 1431–47; John VII Paleologus, Byzantine emperor, 1425–48.

[20] This is the Campanile, 1334–36, completed in 1387; Tolstoi introduces a new art term, *subtel'naia,* subtle, Latin, *subtilis;* Polish has *subtelna* as well as *delikatna.*

Then I walked to a place where there is a broad street, and on the sides of this street are large homes of fine architecture. Here are built marvelous palaces, with justices,[21] that is, offices *(prikazy)* above. Below these palaces are two stories, also fine palaces, which are called in Florentine *galliariia* (It. *galleria*). In these palaces lie all sorts of marvelous things of the old Florentine principality. At the end of these palaces, across the street, are broad passages from palace to palace, built of fine workmanship and decorated with fine alabaster carvings.

Then I came to a large bridge, which is built across the river on very tall and broad columns.[22] On this bridge along both sides are shops, in which sit mercante, that is, merchants, and they trade in silver; in these shops there is not much silver, and I did not see very good work in silver in these shops.

Then having crossed the bridge, I walked to the court of the Florentine prince.[23] This court stands on a knoll, and it is a large palace built in the old fashion. At his gates stands a guard with a halberd, and I saw no one at his court. I did not enter his court because I wanted to walk as a private person, and not as someone special, because it was my intention not to stay in Florence more than one day. If I gave my identity in Florence and the grand prince of Florence detained me warmly for the sake of my Sovereign, and would want to pay *gonor* (It. *onore,* honor) to me, it would be an obstacle to my journey. And having looked at the house of the grand prince, I went to my inn.

This same day I ordered my coachman to come to my inn early in the morning of the 24th of August, so that I could leave Florence early in the morning of that day; and having settled everything in the evening, I myself paid the innkeeper, so that nothing would detain me. /377/

A Description of Florence

Florence is a large place between great hills on a level place, and in it dwells a *granduka,* that is, a grand prince, who has a *corona,* that is, a crown; he has beneath him other large cities, and his domain is quite large and populous.

Around Florence itself is a stone fortress of ancient construction, with stone towers and passage gates in the ancient fashion, but of fine craftsmanship.

In Florence are very fine homes, of which a few are of the most fine proportions; all the Florentine homes are old structures. The whole city of Florence is paved with stone, and the palaces are tall, three or four stories high, but simply built, and not according to one architectural [principle].

[21] This is the Palazzo degli Uffizi, 1560–74, by Vasari, built for the municipal government; above, Tolstoi noted the Galleria degli Uffizi.

[22] This is the Ponte Vecchio, which has been the seat of goldsmithing since the fourteenth century.

[23] This is the Palazzo Pitti, begun c. 1440, colonnade court, 1558–70, wings added after 1620; in 1550 it replaced the Palazzo Vecchio as the residence of the reigning sovereign of Florence.

Through Florence flows a rather large river, which is called the Arno. Across this river four large stone bridges are built on stone columns. Among them is one very large bridge, about which I have written above in this book, and on which is built the silversmith's row.

There are more than 200 monasteries and churches in Florence, which have fine decorations in them and are rich in silver and in every sort of church utensil.

In Florence the people are clean and very warm to foreigners. The honorable people wear French attire, and the others something like the Roman, and the merchants dress in black like the Venetians, and the female sex in Florence dresses in the Roman fashion.

The honorable people in Florence and the wealthy merchants ride in coaches and in fine carriages, and there are many fine coach horses and saddles in Florence; also the wives and girls ride finely attired in carriages with good horses. There are in Florence many shop-rows in which the merchants and artisans sit, with a good supply of all kinds of wares. There are also many master craftsmen; Florence especially boasts of its master craftsmen, who make all things great and small most marvelously of various marbles, in color and lifelikeness, just as if painted.

In Florence bread and meat and poultry are not expensive, and there is plenty of it. There is also much fish, which is not expensive, and a great deal of fruit, very cheap, and especially many fine grapes, of which they make fine wines, which /378/ in the whole world are the glorious Florentine wines. There are many white and red, which are immeasurably delicious and not intoxicating, and one buys them cheaply, and they are bought and carried to distant places for their glory, for the Florentine wines are glorious.

There are many inns in Florence, in which the rooms are quite fine and the beds and tables and chairs and armchairs and bedding are also fine. The tablecloths and sheets and towels are white, and the food and drink for the foreigner is really fine and sufficient. The base people in Florence are godly, politic, and very courteous and righteous.

Around Florence are great mountains, and on and among them are many dwellings, all large stone buildings; they stand in many places and are good. There are also good gardens with all sorts of fruit trees and with cypresses and various flowers.

In Florence are many columns on which they place, in memory of glorious people of ancient times past, statues carved of alabaster and of white stone, and on others are brass [statues] on horses done of the most glorious work. In Florence in many places are fountains, some of which are deteriorated; however, they are of good craftsmanship, but none as in Rome, and water does not flow from all the fountains in Florence. In Florence are many fine craftsmen, including fine painters of the Italian art, who paint finely, and for one rather small image they get 50 golden chervontsy or more.

August 24. Early in the morning I left Florence and arrived to dine at an inn called Ponta (Petrona, or S. Piero a Sieve, on the river crossing), 12 It. miles from Florence. This road is through stone mountains, and there are many dwellings in these mountains, and among the mountains they are close together and populous. There are small forests in a few places, and many grapes in fields, and there are fields of wheat. Between the mountains are clear waters, and from the mountains are springs of fine cold water. And I stayed in that inn until the 10th hour of day, and in the 10th hour I left and came to a city of the Roman papal region called Florentsano (Firenzuola), 12 It. miles from the inn where I dined. Along this road are great and very rocky mountains, and I descended from the mountains on foot. Along these mountains and between them are rather large forests, and many fruit trees on which chestnuts grow. On these same mountains are a few fields on which they sow wheat and other grains, which they call *tsaregradskiia* (It. *monachella*); there are also hay fields and some dwellings in the mountains. And in this city of Firenzuola I stayed in an inn /379/ called La Scala, and I spent the night there. This city of Firenzuola is not large; the stone walls around it were made anciently, and the buildings are all of stone. I spent the night in this city.

August 25. From this inn in the morning I left and came to an inn called Liuiana (Loiano), 17 It. miles from the inn La Scala. Along the road from the inn La Scala to the inn Loiano are very great stone mountains on which it was impossible to ride in the carriage, and my vetturino, that is, my coachman, hired a saddle horse for me on which I rode in these mountains. On and between these mountains are many forests; in these forests are fruit trees on which chestnuts grow. In these mountains are many fine waters, clear, spring-fed, which flow from these mountains. In many places they have built stone bridges. Along this road are a few dwellings; also on and along the mountains are fields where they sow wheat and millet; there are also hay fields. In this inn this day I dined and stayed until the 9th hour of day, and in the ninth hour I left and I came this same day an hour before night to the city of Boloniia (Bologna), and I stayed in an inn called Sanmarko, that is, St. Mark. In this inn the master ordered me an expensive and fine room, covered with golden leather and decorated with fine pictures and large mirrors. In this room is a fine bedstead, a table and chairs, and armchairs covered with velvet. This inn in Bologna was the best, and it has many fine large rooms with marvelous decor, because many foreigners stay in it. From the inn Loiano to Bologna it is 16 It. miles. I rode from Loiano 10 It. miles through great stone mountains, through which I could not ride in the carriage but descended on foot. On these mountains are a few dwellings, and many forests of all sorts of trees, and small fields and hay fields. Then, 6 Italian miles from Bologna, I descended from the mountains and rode along a level place between the mountains; through these narrow places were many dwellings close by, houses built of stone, with fine food gardens around them; also in these places are many fine channeled waters, over which they have built stone bridges. Then, coming closer to Bologna, the dwellings become closer [together], and within three miles of Bologna the dwellings are very close together, and here live the artisans, tailors, bootmakers, carriage makers, blacksmiths, joiners, and other sorts; and the buildings are all stone, and among them are many kaplici, that is, small churches of the Roman faith.

Then I arrived at the city gates of Bologna. At the gates that stand at the gateway, they wrote down my name and /380/ the state from which I came. They asked me whether I had any merchant's wares and immediately permitted me into Bologna; and I stayed the night there, and in the morning I left Bologna in the 2d hour of day.

A Description of Bologna

Bologna in Italy is a large city and a glorious possession of the Roman pope, and it stands on a level place. The city walls and stone towers are of old construction. The homes in Bologna are large; the structures are all of stone, and the palaces are fine. The streets and lanes in Bologna are wide, and along both sides of the streets and lanes high stone columns are built with parts of the dwelling on top of them; and in all of Bologna, no matter how great is the rain, people on foot can walk in all of Bologna in their good clothes without a cloak, and the rain never soaks them, and there never is any dirt in these places under the columns. Even if someone walks in fine shoes through all of Bologna, he will never get them dirty.[24] And thus in Bologna they always walk on foot on these built-up streets, and these built-up streets are paved with fine stones, and in other places with bricks. In the middle of the streets in Bologna, between rows of the columns, they ride in coaches and in carts and on horseback, and all traveling people ride in carriages. Through Bologna flows a river that they call a canal. This river is not small, and on it from Venice to Bologna and from Bologna to Venice go barques and other small vessels.

There are sufficient shops in Bologna, with all sorts of wares, and also wealthy merchants and many artisans of all kinds. They say there are more than two hundred monasteries and Roman churches in Bologna with chapels, and all the monasteries and churches are fine stone buildings.

In Bologna a cardinal sent by the pope in Rome lives as the governor, and he directs all worldly and spiritual affairs in Bologna.

The Bolognese inhabitants are good people and very friendly; they dress in the Roman fashion, and the merchants go about like the Venetian merchants, and all in Bologna speak in Italian, but closer to the Florentine language. The female folks in Bologna are fine, well formed, and they dress just like the Romans.

In Bologna the honorable and wealthy people and their wives and girls ride in fine

[24] These are the arcades, the covered walkways for which Bologna was and is famous. Evelyn was equally impressed: "The whole Towne is so cloystered, that one may passe from house to house through the Streetes without being exposed either to raine or Sun." *Diary*, II, 422.

coaches and in carriages on good horses, and the decor in their coaches is quite fine, and the honorable people and their wives and daughters do not go on foot, and it is a disgrace to do so. /381/

Bread and all viands—fish and meat and all poultry—in Bologna are not costly, and cheaper than in Venice.

In Bologna there is much fruit of all kinds and it is very cheap, and especially there are many large onions that are very cheap. They send onions from Bologna to many Italian places.[25] There are many fine inns in Bologna; but the best, where I stayed, is St. Mark's.

There are always many foreigners in Bologna: those from the empire, Frenchmen, Englishmen, Spaniards, Dutch, Genoese, Turinese, and those of other states.

In Bologna, at the homes of honorable people, are fine and large gardens in which there are many various fruit trees, and also many flowers and all sorts of bushes and cypress trees.

I saw neither good nor bad fountains in Bologna.

In the Jesuit monasteries in Bologna are academies and fine schools in which they study to the high sciences, as far as philosophy and to theology.[26]

In Bologna is a great building in which they print all kinds of books in the Latin and the Italian languages in all the various high sciences; they also print geographical and naval maps and various other figures of fine craftsmanship.

In Bologna are many marvelous lap dogs,[27] which are famous in the whole world, and they are very small and immeasurably good, but to buy one is very expensive, and for one good dog one must pay 20 or 30 golden chervontsy.

August 26. In the second hour of day I left Bologna in my carriage and came to an inn, 20 Italian miles from Bologna. This inn is called Padzha (Poggio Renatico). Along this road are fine dwellings, stone buildings, and many fine gardens with all sorts of fruits and flowers; in these gardens are many fine trees that

[25] Evelyn too was impressed by the food of the Bolognese, but he did not mention onions. "This Citty is famous also for *Salsicci,* & sell a World of Parmegiano Cheeze, with Botargo, Caviare &c: which makes some of their shops perfume the streetes with no agreable smell." *Diary,* II, 426.

[26] This is the Archiginnasio for which Bologna was famous, the institution that gave old Bolognese coins the inscription "Bononia docet." Evelyn wrote: "This Towne belongs to the Pope, & is a famous University, situate in one of the fattest spots of Europe, for all sorts of Provisions." *Diary,* II, 420.

[27] In Tolstoi's terms, literally bed-dogs, *postel'naia sobaka.* "Many of the Religious men here nourish those Lap-dogs had so in delicius by the Ladies, which they sell, they are a pigmie sort of Spaniels, whose noses they breake when puppies, which in my opinion deformes them." Evelyn, *Diary,* II, 425.

grow in the most miraculous shapes:[28] on one tree it grows just like a boat, on another like a man, on another a beast or a bird, and another tree stands tall; and on it grow branches and leaves from below in a circle with fine shapes, and from this circle there grow upwards branches and leaves just like a circular stairwell around the tree, and on the top of that tree it grows just like a fine garret with a roof, and there are many such trees along this road. Also along this road are many fine white and red grapes. From Bologna to the inn Poggio is a level place of fields, and along these fields is much wheat and hay. This road is very fine, level and rocky; /382/ but along the sides of the road are bad standing waters, from which at times there is a severe stench. In this inn I dined and stayed until the 10th hour of day, and in the 10th hour I left and came to a river, which is called the Reno, 6 It. miles from the inn Poggio. This river Reno is rather large, and it flows all muddy from the sand and the clay, and it is just like a clay sludge itself. It is impossible for anyone to drink, eat, or wash with the water of this river: useless to man, it is not usable by cattle, either. The road along this river is smooth; there are no hills of stone, and along the sides of this river are great bogs, in which grow very large and tall marsh grasses and reeds, and along this road are log paths like those of Muscovy, made of brushwood and logs [corduroy roads].

And having crossed that river I came to the city of Ferara (Ferrara); it is 4 Italian miles from the river to Ferrara. Along this road on both sides are many trees, aspens, willows, and birch, among which grow many red and white grapes that grow entwined around those trees and bear much fruit. Also in these places are fields where they sow wheat, and a few hay fields; there are also many dwelling places where the buildings are all stone. Then this same day at the middle hour of the day I arrived in the city of Ferrara, and when I arrived at the city gates, the guard wrote down my name and took from me all my arquebuses and pistols that I had with me because in Ferrara it is the custom that no traveling foreigner is allowed in Ferrara with arms, and during the time someone wishes to stay in Ferrara, his arms remain with the guard. And having unscrewed one screw from the arquebuses, they return them to those who own them, and thus when the foreigner departs from Ferrara and passes the city gates, he must show the screw at those gates, and soldiers take his arquebuses and pistols outside the city and return them to him outside the city, and into the city no traveler ever takes an arquebus. Thus, entering Ferrara, every traveler at the city gates must take a *boletina* (It. *bollettino*), that is, a travel certificate, and with this certificate any traveler can leave Ferrara, and without this certificate no one may leave Ferrara. And all that is written above about entering and leaving Ferrara I did, and having entered Ferrara, I stayed at a large inn called the Holy

[28] In the lush farmlands and orchards around Poggio many hedgerows are still carved geometrically, if not in full topiary, and many fruit trees are espaliered. Tolstoi appears to believe still that boxwood and other trees grow in these shapes.

Angel. In this inn they gave me a large fine room, in which were tables and chairs and armchairs and a fine bedstead, and a bed with clean sheets and with a fine blanket. In this inn I had supper and spent the night.[29] /383/

The city of Ferrara is a possession of the Roman pope and is very large; around it is built a stone city (wall) in the new fashion, with fine belvederes and with every fortification. The passage gates to this city are also fine, built with great fortifications, and at the gates stand soldiers on guard.[30] In Ferrara are many churches and monasteries all of stone, and all the domestic structures are also fine and of stone. There are great and very tall palaces in Ferrara; in this city is one great square, and around this square are placed low stone columns, three sazhens from column to column, and on the tops of these columns are thick iron brackets in holes, and into these are inserted thick iron chains, and the whole square is hung with these chains from column to column, so that it is impossible for anyone to ride into this square in a coach or in a cart or on horseback. And large shrubs grow on this square, and in the middle of this square is a large white stone column, very tall and thick and carved of a single stone and made of fine carved work. On the top of this column is a fine armchair, also made of the same stone, and in this chair is seated a statue of a Roman pope carved of stone of marvelous work; and around this column also are stone columns through which are inserted iron chains through holes, so that no one can come close to this column. All of this is done to honor the statue of the pope.[31]

In Ferrara are many shops with all sorts of wares, but especially much fine soap, which is praised throughout the whole world. Also there are famous vodkas, and it is not expensive to buy them; also there is a fine red grape wine, which the Italians call *vindol'ts* (*vino dolce?*); also there is bread and all foodstuffs and all kinds of poultry, and much fish, and all are cheap.

In Ferrara lives a cardinal who is sent from the pope in Rome in the place of a governor, and this cardinal directs all affairs, secular and spiritual.

In Ferrara the people are naturally clean, the male and the female sex, and men and women wear clothing resembling the Roman.

In Ferrara there are many fine coaches and carriages and coach horses, and all the decor of the coaches is fine, and the honorable people in Ferrara and their wives and

[29] Tolstoi's introduction to Ferrara was not unusual. On the matter of disarming of travelers, Evelyn noted the same experience: "Got to *Ferrara,* where before we were admitted entrance, our Gunns & Armes were taken from us, of Costome." *Diary,* II, 427. He stayed in the same inn: "The inn where we lodg'd was a very noble Palace bearing an *Angel* for its signe." Ibid., p. 428.

[30] The Castello, fourteenth century, was rebuilt after a fire in 1554 and again after an earthquake in 1570.

[31] The statue of Pope Alexander VII stood in the square between the Palazzi Strozzi-Bevilacqua and Rochegalli-Rondinelli; it was pulled down in 1796, replaced by a statute of Liberty, then a statue of Napoleon I, demolished in 1814, and finally by a statue of Ludovico Aristo (1833), for whom the square is now named.

maidens do not walk on foot but ride in coaches and in carriages; and anyone who walks about in Ferrara, any honorable man or wife or honorable girl, is disgraced.

The money in Ferrara is the Roman silver and brass. /384/

It is the custom in Ferrara that at night no one is allowed to walk with a sword or with a saber or with any kind of weapon, and anyone who is caught with a weapon is punished according to the custom of Ferrara, but those who have permission from the cardinal of Ferrara may walk at night with a sword.

There are many merchants and all sorts of artisans in Ferrara.

August 27. In the morning I left Ferrara, and at the city gates they returned my arms to me, having carried them outside the city, according to the custom about which I wrote above. Then I came to a river whose name is Po. This is a very large river and it flows all muddy, all mixed with sand. I crossed this river on a ferry that goes on oars. From Ferrara to this river it is 5 It. miles. Along this road in the fields grow many towering willow trees, finely set in proportion, and among them grow many white and red grapes, but more of the red. Along this road too are many fields, and also hay fields, and in other places are bogs in which very high marsh grasses grow two sazhens in height. Along this road too are many stone buildings in which the Italian farmers live.

Having crossed this river and gone two Italian miles, I came to the Venetian border, and in this place the Venetian province is divided from the domain of the Roman pope. Having ridden 4 It. miles from this border, I came to a river called Kanale-Bianka (Canal Bianco). Along this road are many white and red grapes, and there are also fields and hay fields and marshes. On both of these rivers are built many mills on ponds, of which I saw 18 on the river Po. On the other river there are also many of these mills, and these mills are built quite finely and very artfully. And having crossed the river, I came to a city of the Venetian province, which is called Ruvigo (Rovigo),[32] and in this city I stayed at an inn called Corona. In this inn I dined and stayed until the 10th hour of day, and in the tenth hour I left this city. This city of Rovigo is a rather large place, its buildings are stone, and there are many churches and monasteries, and it stands on a level place. From Ferrara to Rovigo the road is fine and smooth with no hills, and there are level fields with many white and red grapes, but mostly red. In this city, bread and foodstuffs of all kinds, and all poultry and fish and fruits of all kinds, are cheap, and all are abundant in this city. And I left /385/ this city and came the same day at night to a city of the Venetian state called Molt-Selize (Monselice), and I stayed at an inn called Shetekeza (?),[33]

[32] Rovigno is the capital of a province that had belonged to Venice since 1484.

[33] Monselice, picturesquely situated at the base of Monti Euganei, is partially surrounded by old walls and a castle (*mons silicis*, silica mountain). I did not identify the inn, but possibly it is *la cheta casa*, quiet or tranquil house.

14 It. miles from Rovigo. Along this road from Rovigo, not having gone very far, I came to a river called Liadizhe (Adige), or Fime (It. *fiume*, river), and I crossed it on a ferry that is most artfully made: it goes across the river without the labor of people; only one man stands on the stern and steers it with a paddle. On this river are many mills, which are built most artfully on vessels. And having crossed this river I drove to the city of Monselice through level places without hills at all, and on both sides of the road were many willow trees, and among them many red grapes; also there are fields and hay fields and marshes. There are many stone dwellings, and marvelous and great homes, in which the fine rooms are built of fine architecture and of marvelous craftsmanship. Also, there are fine gardens built of fine proportions with fruit trees and with various flowers; here, too, are many flowing waters, over which I crossed on stone bridges; also on both sides of the road and around the grapes are dug wide and deep ditches that conduct water. The city of Monselice is Venetian, its buildings are all stone, and it stands on a high hill. The castle of this place is built on the top of that hill and is very fortified. This city is not large, and bread and all foodstuffs and poultry and fish and all fruits are not expensive and are abundant, and the red grape wine is fine and sweet. In this city in the above-mentioned inn I had supper this day and spent the night; a fine room was assigned to me, covered with golden leather, and in it were fine tables, chairs, and armchairs, and a fine gilded bedstead and a bed with clean sheets and a satin spread. In this room, too, were fine pictures and many large mirrors.

August 28. Early in the morning I left this city for the city of Padve (Padova, Padua). Along this road are many dwellings of the base sort of people, and all the buildings are stone; among these dwellings are also many large and marvelous homes, and in them the rooms are large and built very finely architecturally; there are also gardens with fine fruit trees and with cypresses and fine food gardens, in which they have made marvelous flower gardens, and they are filled with fine flowers of various kinds. Along this road are many stone chapels. From the city of Monselice to Padua flows a stream, dug to a width of 10 sazhens and deep, and along this stream from /386/ Padua to Monselice and back again to Padua go rather large barques with firewood and stone and all necessities.[34] Across this man-made stream they have built fine broad stone bridges in many places, and one can drive across it without difficulty. At these bridges on this man-made stream are fine mills, stone granaries, and at one granary there are four or five (grist) wheels. From the city of Monselice to Padua it is 10 It. miles. The road is all level without hills, and it is not rocky, and on both sides in the fields grow many towering trees: birch, aspen, willow, oak, and others, and they are situated in fine proportion. Among these trees grow many grapes, and they entwine around those trees and bear red and white

[34] This is the Canal Battaglia. Tolstoi has passed without comment Arqua Petrarca where Petrarch lived and died, 1304–74.

fruit, but mostly red. Also on both sides of the road are fields in which they sow wheat and millet; there are also fine hayfields, and in other places there are bogs.

This same day at the fourth hour of day I came to the city of Padua and stopped in an inn, and I stayed in it until the 8th hour of day, and in the 8th hour I left Padua.

Padua is a large place of the Venetian province, and I have written about it above in this book at length.

This day my coachman asked me if he might not transport me from Padua to Mestre in the carriage; instead he would hire for me from Padua to Venice a vessel called a peata; I would ride in it from Padua to Venice by water. And at his request I allowed him to do this, and he hired me a peata in which this day after dinner I rode from Padua to Venice by those streams, which are made for the passage from Venice to Padua and from Padua to Venice, about which I have written at length formerly in this book.

This same day in this peata I arrived from Padua in Venice at the 6th hour of night and stopped at an inn called Leonbanko (Leone Bianco). In this inn the master assigned me a room in which I stayed until the 30th day of August, and I paid for the room and food and for the bed and for all necessities for myself a ducat of Venetian money per day, and a ducat is 15 altyns of Muscovite money.

August 30. I rented for myself a furnished home, in which there were enough rooms for me, and I rode to that home from the inn Leone Bianco on the 30th day of August. For this home I paid 6 Venetian ducats per month. In this home were enough rooms /387/ for me and the soldier who was with me, and for my slave, and I bought food for myself, the soldier, and my slave separately for 6 ducats; I also bought the candles and other necessities separately. In this house were only tables, chairs, armchairs, cupboards, and prepared beds, and also the kitchen and all the utensils were the housekeeper's. And I stayed in this house one month. On ***September 30*** I went to another house, and I rented for myself a house near the Greek church of St. George, where the Greek metropolitan lives.

In this house my room was fine, and it was all covered with fine silks, and the mirrors and pictures in it were also fine, as were all of the necessities, and the bedstead, too, was finely gilded and the bedding was quite fine. The soldier's and my slave's comforts were fine, and the kitchen and all its utensils were the housekeeper's, and I paid for the food for myself and the soldier and my slave, and I stayed in this house until the 28th of October, and I paid for it 8 Venetian ducats.

October 25. The boyar Fedor Alekseevich Golovin[35] sent me a letter from Moscow, and in it is written:

[35] Golovin had negotiated the Treaty of Nerchinsk for Sophia, and in the 1690s had headed a number of state offices simultaneously. He was generally in charge of foreign affairs and

> My lord Peter Andreevich [Tolstoi], may the Lord preserve your health through the ages, this I truly wish; and about myself I inform you that with the help of God I live in Moscow this 29th day of September. Also your grace should know, that all of the chamberlains, who have learned science, are ordered to return to Moscow from Venice and from Amsterdam, and should it be your will, to deign to come without danger. Fed'ka Golovin. From Moscow, September the 29th day.

I spoke of this letter with my masters so that they could give me testimonial certificates, on which were the words of my masters, which pertained to me, and they gave me testimonial certificates.[36]

My teacher who taught me mathematical things gave me a testimonial certificate, and in it is written:

> In the name of Christ. Amen.
>
> The sciences are a marvelous shield for people, and especially for those honorably born; it is no wonder that they have a great inclination to apply themselves to such weighty matters, but the undersigned had a manifest experience of this matter, and I affirm with my oath that I gave him a comprehension of the mathematical sciences, both theoretical /388/ and practical, without which no one can acquire the whole of naval science; to whit, first I taught the *sfera armillare*,[37] the heavenly and earthly globes with all the *traktat* (It. *tratto*, extent) of naval science. Peter Andreevich [Tolstoi], a Muscovite gentleman to his majesty the most glorious tsarist majesty, was my pupil, who labored with every effort, and was accomplished in that science and now has grasped it; he is able, worthy, and deserving to be released to the ranks of those who know navigation, having turned his will and his disposition to mastering this science, and to confirm this I am impowered to sign this with my hand, and impowered to signify with the seal from my school of mathematics. The 27th day of October in the year of the Lord 1698.

On the letter itself is the signature in the hand of the teacher, the priest Petr Lutsianni Venet (Pietro Luciano of Venice), master and professor.

The true copy was proclaimed to the Venetian prince and signed by his counselor's hand, to whit:

---

was a constant companion of Peter after his assumption of power. He would raise new regiments for Peter in 1699–1700, and would be the head of the office of Foreign Affairs until his death in August 1705. Tolstoi tells nothing of his own activities for the previous two months, from his return to Venice until the arrival of Golovin's letter.

[36] Having been summoned home, Tolstoi solicited the documentation necessary to convince Peter the Great that he had done his duty.

[37] Previously Tolstoi had noted the existence of celestial and earthly globes in libraries and museums. Here his teacher of mathematics testifies that he had practical experience using the armillary sphere, the sphere with brass circles showing the relations of the solar system and used in celestial navigation.

Hall of Collegio. Doge and Signoria Giving Audience to Legate.

> I, the undersigned counselor, confirm this truth: that I saw in this place that the above-described letter from the great father Pietro Luciano, which was ordered to be brought through my chancellery for my oath, that it is signed by his hand and sealed with his seal, which is signified by the best assurance. It was written in Venice on the 27th day of October in the year of the Lord 1698, without any notations. I, Ian Peter Rossi, Venetian public counselor, assure this with my hand, sign it, and affix [my seal] to it."

This above-described certificate was read before the prince of Venice himself and noted in a book, and to my teacher, the mentioned Pietro Luciano. To his certificate on science was added a certification, that of the prince of Venice, written on parchment, the seal affixed with lead, and in this certificate the prince of Venice himself wrote a confirmation, to whit:

> Silvester Valerio, by the grace of God the Prince of Venice, to all and to friends in particular, and to those of other faiths who should see our certificate, we give to know that counselor Pietro Rossi, who on the 27th day of this month, witnessed the signature of our great father Pietro Luciano, who is of good morals and of good repute, and his letter here is fully confirmed by this [seal]. Entered in our princely

palace on this 27th day of October, under the *index six* in the year of our Lord 1698. Dominico Balli.[38]

Then my master the sea captain gave me his own testimonial certificate concerning naval science, and in it is written:

There is no argument that the greatness of a good and noble heart inclines one to the higher studies and to the finer sciences, by which the brilliance of high families and the well-born is multiplied;[39] therefore I give to be known that his grace, Lord Peter Andreevich [Tolstoi], Muscovite gentleman, who, being under my captainly direction and wishing to understand naval science, /389/ not only wished to apply himself to the theoretical sciences, but also wanted the practical; thus he and a [Muscovite] soldier boarded a ship the *St. Elizabeth* under my command, and sailing the sea for months and in hours not without fright, he showed the strength of his courage during hostile attacks, applying himself to every labor and to the science of the *bussola* (It. compass) and to naval maps, and to the observation of places where the water is shallow and full of rocks and to other places that are not without their dangers at sea; also applying himself to the disposition of the *timone* (It. rudder) and to the use of woods and sails and *sortiiamov* (It. sartiame), that is, ropes, the names of which he learned very well; and in every instance how and when it is used, and what purpose it has for the steering of naval ships and galleys. He also applied himself completely to the use of cannon and of all things needed for that science, and for the use of sails and ropes and other things that pertain both to ships and to galleys. Also, he fully took notice of the winds and of every practice useful to ships and galleys; and al-

[38] Tolstoi's certificate from his mathematics teacher is thus twice affirmed as accurate and genuine, first by a Venetian notary and second by the *principe* himself, who witnessed the notarization.

Silvester Valerio, or Silvestro Valier, son of Bertucci Valier, who had been briefly grand prince some forty years earlier, was a caretaker prince. After the death of the powerful Francesco Morosini, who had been both military commander and doge of Venice, it was decided that never again should there be such a dangerous concentration of military and civil power in the hands of one individual. Thus the supreme command of the armed forces was entrusted to Antonio Zen, who died in prison in 1697 while being investigated for his role in the loss of Chios. His successor, Alessandro Molin, was more successful in the struggle against the Turks during Tolstoi's stay in Venice, gaining effective control of the Aegean by defeating the Turks at the entry of the Dardanelles in September 1698. There is no suggestion in the Diary that the news had yet reached Venice. For the above, see Norwich, *History of Venice*, pp. 569–72.

[39] This simple phrase contains an echo of contemporary natural law theory. By the late seventeenth century, most political theorists were willing to concede that noble birth alone did not guarantee superior strength, courage, or intelligence. On the other hand, they did argue that such virtues were more likely to be found in individuals nurtured in the homes of parents whose ancestors had won nobility by their exploits in military or civil service, and who thus cultivated these traits for the edification of their children. One can find such sentiments in the writings of Locke, Grotius, and other contemporaries of Tolstoi.

> though there was no *occasione* (It. occasion) to be in battle, still, with practice, he took sufficient notice and understanding and is sufficiently able [to do so]. For this purpose I, in order that it be known that he is able and worthy of this station, pledge my faith and fully give testimonial at any place and at any time, that all of this should be known, and in good faith I now sign with my own hand and seal with my customary seal this certificate. Given this 27th day of October, 1698, in Venice.

On the detailed certificate at the bottom it is signed by the captain's hand, to whit: "I captain Georgio Radzhi (Raggio), mentioned above, confirm that which is above." On the same certificate is the seal of the captain.

Then at my departure from Venice I was with the Venetian prince; I bowed to him at my departure and thanked him for the affection he had shown to me during my stay in Venice, and the prince of Venice affectionately dismissed me from his realm, and at my departure sent to me his secretary, who is called Savoni, and ordered him again to conduct me with affection to him, and personally sent me a certificate, written on parchment beneath the golden coat-of-arms of the Venetian principality under the picture of the lion, which is the image of the evangelist St. Mark. In this certificate he wrote, to whit:

> Silvester Valerio, leader, Prince of Venice. To the most honorable lord, Peter Andreevich [Tolstoi], gentleman of the throne of the tsar of Moscow and to all friends, and to those of other faiths who see our certificate, I wish you health. The humility of your heart among your other comrades of your people has been made manifest to us, that having been in this our Venetian locale and now returning from our state to the threshold of your fatherland, we deigned to give you upon your departure a certificate that attested to your diligent pursuit of the sciences /390/ and especially those of naval warfare, and thus to all and to everyone and also to yourself (should it be needed by you for your most powerful monarch), I hand over this certificate, so that on the strength of this our certificate we give it to be known that this honorable Peter Andreevich, gentleman of the throne of the tsar of Moscow, did apply himself to the sciences, having diligence in both the theory and the mathematics pertaining to the naval sciences, and to a practice of the best understanding of naval problems. He did apply his labor and diligence, when, according to the testimony before us of various captains, but especially of our naval captain on the ship *St. Maria Elizabeth,* Ivan Lazarevič, who manifestly gave us to know that the above-mentioned Peter Andreevich in the fall of 1697 went on a naval journey and crossed our gulf, on which for two months he was fearless in the turbulence of the sea and in the halyard of a naval fortuna, and was not afraid, but in all this he smartly struggled with the inconstant winds, and he very much wished that he might encounter the enemies of the cross of Christ at sea, and might fight with them, but God did not then provide such an opportunity to him. But he did not spend this time in vain, but again this year he returned to sea, and having crossed our gulf on a frigate, he went by land, so that in the shortest time he could arrive at the Mediterranean Sea, where, boarding another bastimento, he rode past Calabria and Sicily, where he encountered Turkish ships, which drove after him even to Malta itself, where, having arrived, for the Christian

Francesco Morosini, 1618–1694, who as Doge and Commander reestablished Venetian power in the late seventeenth century.

The Galley of Doge Francesco Morosini.

faith and for the honor of his people, he wished to set out on a Maltese galley against the enemy, but the enemy had departed and did not provide such an opportunity to him. For his courage in the pursuit of his sciences and for his good demeanor during his stay in our realm, we have given him this certificate, so that at any place where he might be, that he has given complete faith as a glorious pupil, and so that from all he might be received as a brave man, wise and able. Given in Venice, in our princely palace, on the 30th day of October 1698, at the command of the prince. Ermii Balli (Ermio Balli), chancellery-governor, I confirm that which is above.

On the certificate itself is the imprint of a lion on red wax in an iron frame. Then I left Venice, having cleared up everything on the shore on the ***30th day of October*** in the city of Mestre, 5 It. miles from Venice by sea, and I gave thanks to God, that in good health I had left the sea for land and was going to my own country.

November 1. I hired a Fuhrmann to conduct me and the soldier who was with me and my slave from Mestre to Vienna in a carriage with all the things I had with me. For the transport of myself and the soldier and my slave from Venice to Vienna I gave 7 golden chervontsy, and in the same contract for him to take with each man his things up to one and one-half puds, and should there be a weight above that, for this I would pay separately at /391/ a golden chervonets per pud from Venice to Vienna. And having settled everything, I left Mestre this day and arrived to spend the night in the city of Treviso, 10 Italian miles from Mestre.

November 2. From Treviso I rode 10 It. miles, crossed the river Piava on a ferry, and for the crossing paid a lira per person, and that is 7 Muscovite kopecks. From this river I went a German mile and arrived at the city Keneman (Conegliano) of the Venetian domain, 15 It. miles from Treviso. I spent the night in this city. This city is large, and there are many cypress trees in it.

November 3. I arrived in the city of Shadalei (Sacile) of the Venetian possessions, 15 It. miles from Conegliano, and this is a stone city, and I arrived this day to spend the night in an inn called Fatom-Dadrizo (Ponte de Delizia), and spent the night there, three Italian miles from the city of Sacile.

November 4. I arrived to dine at an inn called Kardinala (Cordelons), 8 It. miles from the above-mentioned inn. This same day I arrived to spend the night at the inn Provezak (Provesano), 10 Italian miles from the inn.

November 5. I crossed the river Tialiamento (Tagliamento) in two places on ferries; this river is not large but it is very swift, and having crossed it I dined in an inn called Taiamen (Tagliamen, at Dignano), 5 It. miles from the inn. From there I arrived to spend the night in an inn called Santomasei (S. Tomaso), 10 It. miles from the inn. Before reaching that inn I passed the city of Sandanal (S. Daniele del Friuli), a possession of Venice, which stands on a hill, and its buildings are stone.

November 6. I arrived at the mountains at the city of Vendon (Venzone). I spent the night in this city, stayed at an inn called Kavaliabianka (Cavalla Bianca), 14 It. miles from the inn. In this city I stayed until the 8th hour because all night and day there was rain, and the river in front of me was overflowing from the rain, and it was impossible to cross it. A certain necessity called me to go quickly to Vienna,[40] but I could not go quickly with the carts because the mountain road was deplorable and very muddy; so I abandoned my carts, the soldier, and my slave in the city of Venzone, and by myself, hiring a riding horse, went forward alone, and on the 8th of November I came to the Italian gate where I paid a duty for the horse, and arrived at the empire's border in the city of Paltava (Pontebba), 8 It. miles from Venzone. In

[40] Tolstoi nowhere explains why he suddenly left his baggage and sped onward alone.

this /392/ city I stayed in an imperial inn called Akvilianegro (Aquila Negra). This same day I arrived to spend the night in the village of Mol'berget (Malborghetto) and spent the night in the inn at the Golden Sun, 5 It. miles from the city of Pontafel.

November 9. I arrived to dine in the village of Orlshtan (Arnoldstein) and stopped at an inn called Malt (Fürnitz?), 3 German miles from Malborghetto. This same day I arrived to spend the night in the city of Filok (Villach), 2 Ger. miles from Arnoldstein.

November 10. I arrived to dine in the village of Feltkirkha (Feldkirchen), 3 German miles from Villach. This same day I arrived to spend the night in the city of Senfant (Sankt-Veit), 3 Ger. miles from Feldkirchen.

November 11. I arrived to dine in an inn called Giert (Gurk), 3 German miles from St. Veit. This same day I arrived to spend the night in an inn called Pot (?), 2 German miles from the mentioned inn.

November 12. I arrived to dine in the city of Guntsmork (Unzmarkt), 4 German miles from the mentioned inn, and I stopped at an inn called Upainresil (Perchauer Sattel). This same day I arrived to spend the night at the city of Iudinburka (Judenburg), 3 German miles from Unzmarkt, and I spent the night in an inn called the Pain Gershin (?).

November 13. I arrived to dine in the inn Kubenits (Kobenz), 2 German miles from Judenburg. This same day I arrived to spend the night at the city of Liuim (Leoben), 4 German miles from the inn.

November 14. I arrived to dine in the city of Prukht (Bruck an der Mur), 2 German miles from Leoben, and I stopped at the inn Shcharts-Kok (Schwartzkopf?). This same day I arrived to spend the night in the village of Kinberkh (Kindberg), and stayed at the inn at the Black Eagle, 3 German miles from Bruck.

November 15. I arrived to dine in the village of Mertsiulshlykh (Mürzzuschlar Stuhleck), 3 German miles from Kindberg. This same day I arrived to spend the night in the village of Shotvein (Schottwein), 2 Ger. miles from the mentioned village.

November 16. I arrived to dine in Pratnaurt (Pottschach), 10 German miles from Schottwein. This same day I arrived to spend the night in the city of Nalshtat (Wiener-Neustadt), 2 German miles from the mentioned village. In this city I stayed at the inn at the Black Eagle, and I abandoned there the horse I had ridden, and I hired myself a carriage to Vienna, and gave four Romans, that is, a golden chervonets, and I rode early in the morning of the ***17th day of November,*** and I arrived this day to dine in the village /393/ Traskirk (Traiskirchen), 14 German miles from Neustadt. I stayed at an inn at the White Bear, and I could go no farther this day because of immeasurably snowy weather and high winds, and the whole road was snowbound; because of this I spent the night in this village.

November 18. In the morning I left Traiskirchen and arrived in the carriage in Vienna and stayed in the inn at the Black Eagle beyond the city on the bank of the river Danube. In this inn they gave me a fine room with every necessity and with bedding on a fine bedstead; and I paid an efimok per day in this inn for the room and for the bed and food and every need, and I stayed in this inn until the 30th of November.

November 28. I was in the church of St. Stephen. This day among the Catholics is the feast of the conception of St. Anne,[41] and on this day in the church of St. Stephen was the emperor's son Joseph, the king of Hungary, who stood at his place in the choir where the emperor stands. At this place where he stood was a silk velvet carpet trimmed with lace and another woven gold carpet. His retinue stood by him, and below in the church opposite this place stood a large guard, that is, soldiers with halbards; and they played on various instruments, on pipes, and on kettledrums. King Joseph wore black French attire.

November 30. In the 5th hour of day I left Vienna and crossed the river Danube in four places by bridges, and arrived to spend the night in an inn called Shtarushtaver (Stamersdorf),[42] fully 2 German miles from Vienna.

[41] The feast of the Immaculate Conception is on December 8.

[42] After his long stay in Italy, Tolstoi's renderings of German place names here and of Polish towns and inns below are almost undecipherable. Some have been found on maps, old and new, and others have been reconstructed by sound, and these are listed as questionable (?). Others, however, occur in Korb's *Diary,* used above to illustrate Tolstoi's route from Moscow two years earlier. Since they traveled the same route within a year of each other, I use Korb's spellings consistently, indicating modern German or Polish forms where available.

December 1. I arrived to dine in the hamlet of Kaunashtor (Gannersdorff?), 3 German miles from Stamersdorf. This same day I arrived to spend the night in the hamlet of Beshkel (Shrick?), 2 German miles from the mentioned hamlet.

December 2. I arrived to dine in the inn Denk (?), fully 3 German miles from the mentioned hamlet. This same day I arrived to spend the night at a mill, 2 German miles from the inn, and a mile before this mill I passed the city of Nikolshpurk (Nikolsburg/Mikulov), about which I wrote at length above in this book. And at Nikolsburg the Moravian border is crossed.

December 3. I left there and arrived to dine in the village of Iatsino (?), 2 German miles. This same day I arrived to spend the night in the city of Vitsa (Wistriz), 1 mile from Iatsino. /394/

December 4. I arrived to dine at the city of Vyshkov (Wishau/Vyškov), fully 4 German miles. This same day I arrived to spend the night in the village of Brodek (Brodek), one mile from Wishau.

December 5. I arrived to dine in the village of Kral'nets (Kralitz), 2 German miles from Brodek. This same day I arrived to spend the night in the imperial city of Olomouc, 2 German miles from Kralitz. About this city of Olomouc I have written at length above in this book.

December 6. I arrived to spend the night in the little place of Berok (Beroun/Berna), 3 German miles from Olomouc.

December 7. I left the little place of Beroun and arrived to dine at the river Morava (Moravice), 2 Ger. miles from Beroun. This river divides Moravia from the Silesian land. This same day I arrived to spend the night 2 German miles from the river Moravice at the tavern Gerlits (?).

December 8. I arrived to dine in the little spot of Kachitsa (Krzanowice?), 15 [*sic*] German miles from Gerlitz. This same day I arrived to spend the night in the imperial city of Racibórz, 2 German miles from Krzanowice. About this city I wrote in this book above at length.

December 9. I arrived to dine in the village of Enkovich (?), 3 full German miles from Racibórz. This same day I arrived to spend the night in the little place of Pulkhovets (Pyskowice), 3 full German miles from Enkovich.

December 10. I arrived to dine in the city of Glivitsa (Klawiz/Gliwice), 1 German mile from Pyskowice. This same day I arrived to spend the night in the imperial city of Ternowskie Gory, 3 Ger. miles from Gliwice. About this city I wrote above in this book.

December 11. I arrived to dine in the village of Sara (?), 3 German miles from Ternowskie Gory. This day I crossed the river Kamenitsa (Kamieniec), and this river separates the imperial land from Poland. From the village of Sara to the border it is 2 Ger. m. This same day I arrived to spend the night in the village of Zbov, 1 German m. and a half from the border.

December 12. I arrived to dine in Częstochowa in the Polish city, one Polish mile and a half from Zbov, and this day I was at the monastery of Częstochowa at the wonder-working icon of the Blessed Mother of God at the time of Mass. About this monastery I wrote in detail above in this book. This same day I arrived to spend the night in the village of Radomok, 3 German miles from Częstochowa. /395/

December 13. I arrived to dine in the hamlet of Radomsko, 3 Polish miles from Radomok. This same day I arrived to spend the night in the village of Gorol'dok (Gorzkowice), 2 Polish m. and a half from Radomsko.

December 14. I arrived to dine in the village of Raspria (Rosprza), 2 full Polish m. from Gorzkowice. This same day I arrived to spend the night in the Polish city of Petrokov (Petrikow/Piotrkow Trybunalski), 2 Polish m. from Rosprza.

December 15. I stayed in Piotrkow until noon, because among the Catholics this was the feast of the birth of Christ, and my coachman did not want to drive but went to church. This same day I arrived to spend the night in the tavern Zaborov (Wolbórz?), 4 Polish miles from Piotrkow.

December 16. I arrived to dine in the hamlet Ravva (Rawa), 4 Polish miles from Wolbórz. This is a rather large hamlet, and there are two stone churches in it. This same day I arrived to spend the night in Bobsk (Babsk), 2 Polish miles from Rawa.

December 17. I arrived to dine in the hamlet of Mstianov (Mszczonow), 3 Polish miles from Babsk. This same day I arrived to spend the night at the tavern Borets (Bulow?), 3 Polish miles from Mszczonow.

December 18. I arrived to dine in the city of Warsaw, 4 Polish miles from Bulow. The city of Warsaw is the Polish capital, and I have written about it at length above in this book. These days the king of Poland was not in Warsaw, but in Grodno in Lithuania. And I lived in Warsaw until the 24th of December, and I hired a coachman.

December 24. I left Warsaw early in the morning and stayed at the river Wisła until the 6th hour of the day, because the rain and the wind were strong, and the ferry was on the other side. And this day I crossed the river Wisła and spent the night in Praga on the Wisła.

December 25, that is, on the day of the birth of Christ, I dined and spent the night in Praga.

December 26. I arrived to dine in the hamlet of Okunev (Okuniew), 3 Polish miles from Praga. This same day I arrived to spend the night in the village of Mikhaleva (Michalowa), 1 Polish mile from Okuniew.

December 27. I arrived to dine in the hamlet of Dobroe (Dobre), 3 Polish miles and a half from Michalowa. This same day I arrived to spend the night at the tavern Makovets (Makowiec?), a mile and a half from Dobre. /396/

December 28. I arrived to dine in the town of Livets (Liwiec), 3 Polish miles and a half from Makowiec. This same day I spent the night in this same town, because beneath this town the river Liwiec overflowed, and it was impossible to cross it.

December 29. I rode to the detour and arrived at the town of Fortetsa (Forteca),[43] of the voevoda of Kiev, one Polish mile from Liwiec. This same day I arrived to spend the night in the village of Starvoda (Starwoda?), 2 Polish miles from Forteca.

December 30. I arrived to dine in the town of Starovets (Starowiec?), 5 Polish miles from Starwoda, and I crossed the river Liwiec by bridge below the village, where I spent the night. This same day I arrived to spend the night in Vengrov (Węgrów), one Polish mile from Starowiec. The place Węgrów is on the river Liwiec, and the river Liwiec divides Mazovia (Mazowsze) from Podlasie.

December 31. I left Węgrów after dinner and arrived to spend the night in the village of Kremen (Krzemieniec) at the river Bug, 5 Polish miles from Węgrów.

The Year 1699

January 1. I left the village of Krzemieniec and crossed the river Bug on a ferry. The crossing was very difficult, because the banks were overflowing, and I crossed it with great difficulty; and having crossed it I dined in a tavern on the bank of that river, and this same day I arrived to spend the night in the village of Goroditsa (Grodzisk), 2 Polish miles from the river Bug.

January 2. I arrived to dine in the hamlet of Buts (Bocki), 3 Polish miles from Grodzisk. This same day I arrived to spend the night in the city of Bel'sk (Bielsk Podlaski), 2 Polish miles from Bocki. In this city is a church of the pious Wonder Worker Nicholas.

January 3. I arrived to dine at the tavern Gnil'shits (Klenick), 2 Polish miles from Bielsk. This same day I arrived to spend the night in the town of Narov (Narew), 2 Polish miles from the tavern. This town is on the river Narew, which divides Crown Poland from Lithuania.

January 4. I arrived to dine at a tavern in the forest, 2 Polish miles from Narew. Below the town of Narew the river Narew is crossed by bridge, and I crossed by that bridge; the crossing was difficult for me /397/ because the ice was not strong.

[43] In Polish, *forteca* is the word for fortress.

This same day I arrived to spend the night in the hamlet of Elouka (Jałowka), 2 Polish miles from the tavern.

January 5. I arrived to dine in the village of Studen (Stoteniki), 4 Polish miles from Jałowka. This same day I arrived to spend the night in the hamlet of Lyskov (Lyskovo), 3 Polish miles from Stoteniki.

January 6. I arrived to dine in the hamlet of Rozhanii (Rosana/Rużany), 3 Polish miles from Lyskovo. This is a hamlet of the great hetman of Lithuania, Sapieha, and living in it are all Uniates, and there is one stone Uniate church and another wooden Roman one. This same day I arrived to spend the night at the town of Deviatkovichi (Dewiatowieze?), 3 Polish miles from Rużany.

January 7. I arrived to dine in Zhuravichi (Žorowice), 2 Polish miles from Dewiatowieze. In Žorowice is a Uniate monastery, and in this monastery a great stone church, and in this church stands the wonder-working image of the Blessed Mother of God of Žorowice; it is a very small circular icon, hardly larger than an efimok, made of carved craftsmanship on stone that is like slate; this icon stands on the right side of the imperial gates; it is adorned with gold and with stones, and many diamonds, rubies, emeralds, and sapphires are around this icon for adornment. I was in this church at the time of the Liturgy, and a Uniate priest served Mass at the main altar with a deacon in the Slavonic language, and they sing there in the Kievan manner; and they sang while I was there for the Liturgy in part-singing in the choir in 8 voices. In this church are many Roman altars in front of the holy icons [on the walls]. There are 50 brothers in this monastery, all Uniates, and their habit is like that of monks of the Greek order, and they call these Uniates Basiliane, that is, of the order of Basil the Great. And I was in the cell of the chief of this monastery. In this monastery is another stone church; in this church is the stone on which the above-described image of the Blessed Mother of God appeared, and they say that the stone heals many ailments. This same day I arrived to spend the night in the town of Polonka, 2 Polish miles from Žorowice.

January 8. I arrived to dine in the hamlet of Storlovich (Stolowiz), 4 Polish miles from Polonka. This same day I arrived to spend the night in the tavern Vol'na (Wolna), 2 Polish miles from Stolowiz.

January 9. I arrived to dine in the city of Mir, 3 Polish miles from Wolna, and in Mir I stayed until the 11th day because this same day the Lithuanian chamberlain /398/ Sapieha arrived in Mir, and he came before me to cross the river Niemen, and there were many people with him, and I waited until he had crossed the river Niemen with all those with him.

January 11. I left Mir and crossed the river Niemen on a ferry, 2 full Polish m. from Mir, and I arrived to dine in the tavern Zasulia (Sasiulle), 3 full Polish m. from the Niemen, and 4 Polish m. from Mir. This same day I arrived to spend the night in the hamlet of Kaidanovo (Kajdanowo), 3 and a half Polish miles from Sasiulle.

January 12. I arrived to dine in the tavern Viazin (Viasen), 2 full Polish miles from Kajdanowo. This same day I arrived to spend the night in the city of Minsk, 4 full Polish miles from Viasen, and I stayed in Minsk 2 days because I transferred myself from a cart to a sleigh.

January 14. I arrived to spend the night at the tavern Gorodishche (Horodyszcze), 4 full Polish miles from Minsk.

January 15. I arrived to dine in the town of Smolevichii (Smolowice?), 4 full Polish miles from Horodyszcze. In this town is a church of the Greek faith. This same day I arrived to spend the night in the town of Borysów, 7 Polish miles from Smolowice, and in Borysów I was at the image of the Blessed Mother of God, about which I have written above in this book, and on that image there are more black places than before, when I saw this holy image when coming from Moscow.[44]

January 16. I arrived to dine in the town of Nacha (Naga), 6 Polish miles from Borysów. This same day I arrived to spend the night in the town of Krupets (Krupiec), 2 Polish miles from Naga.

January 17. I arrived to dine in the town of Sloveni, 5 Polish miles from Krupiec, and two miles before that town I passed the hamlet of Bobr. This same day I arrived to spend the night in the village of Perevolochna (Paulowicz?), 5 Polish miles from Sloveni, and 3 miles before that village I passed a large place called Tolochin (Toloczyn).

[44] See above, April 11, 1697.

January 18. I arrived to dine in the city of Orsha (Orsza), 6 Polish miles from Paulowicz. This city of Orsza was a rather large place, with a stone castle, but now it is fallen down, and in the fortress all stands empty. Orsza is on the river Dnepr. In it are 4 Roman cloisters—Jesuit, Bernardine, Dominican, Franciscan— /399/ and besides these there are no Roman churches, and most of the people are of the Greek faith. The churches are all Greek, and there are no Uniates or Uniate churches in Orsza. In Orsza on the other side of the Dnepr river is a monastery of the Greek faith, called Kuteishii, and there is another one as well. In one live monks, and in the other, nuns, and in it is a miracle-working icon of the Blessed Mother of God of Smolensk. I spent the night in Orsza, because they changed coachman's horses on which I rode.

January 19. Beneath Orsza I crossed the river Dnepr on the ice, and arrived to dine in the city of Dubrovna, 3 Polish miles from Orsza. The city of Dubrovna is not very large, and around it is an earthen rampart on the Dnepr river. In this city are three wooden Greek churches; one, named for Nicholas the Wonder Worker, is a fine structure. In Dubrovna live a few people who are not of the Greek faith, but the Uniates do not have a single church. In this city is one Roman church, in which the Bernardines live. In this same city live a few Jews who abide in [their own] homes. This same day I arrived to spend the night in the town of Baevo, 5 Polish miles from Dubrovna. Beneath Dubrovna I did not cross the Dnepr.

January 20. From the town of Baevo I went a Polish half-mile and arrived at the Muscovite border at the river Ivata. This little stream divides the Muscovite state from the principality of Lithuania; and I arrived to dine this day at the court's town of Zverovichi, 2 Polish miles from Baevo. This same day I arrived at the town of Krasnoe, 2 Polish miles from Zverovichi. This same day I arrived to spend the night in the town of Zharkovki, 3 Polish miles from Krasnoe.

January 21. I arrived to dine in Smolensk.

January 23. I left Smolensk and arrived to dine in the postriders' settlement near the town of Pnëvo, 40 versts from Smolensk. This same day I arrived to spend the night in the village of Bykovo, 25 versts from Pnëvo.

January 24. I arrived to dine in the city of Dorogobuzh, 15 versts from Bykovo. This same day I arrived to spend the night in the town of Chebotovo, 30 versts from Dorogobuzh.

January 25. I arrived to dine in Viaz'ma, 40 versts from Chebotovo. This same day I arrived to spend the night in the town of Tsarevo-Zaimishche, 40 versts from Viaz'ma. /400/

January 26. I arrived to dine in Ostrozhek, 40 versts from Tsarevo-Zaimishche. This same day I arrived to spend the night in Mozhaisk, 30 versts from Ostrozhek.

January 27. I arrived to dine at the hereditary estate of the boyar prince Boris Alekseevich Golitsyn, in the town of Viaz'ma, 60 versts from Mozhaisk. This same day I arrived in the 3rd hour of night in the tsarist city of Moscow, in my own home in good health, for which I thanked the Most Merciful Lord God and Most Blessed Mother of God and those [saints] pleasing to God, that I had, by the will of God, returned from my required travels from such distant regions to my fatherland in good health.

Bibliography

Alexander, John T. "Medical Developments in Petrine Russia." *Canadian-American Slavic Studies* 8, no. 2 (Summer 1974): 198–217.

Andrieux, Maurice. *Daily Life in Papal Rome in the Eighteenth Century*. London, 1968.

Ariès, Philippe. *Centuries of Childhood: A Social History of Family Life*. New York, 1962.

Artz, Frederick B. *The Development of Technical Education in France, 1500–1850*. Cambridge, Mass., 1966.

Baron, Samuel. "European Images of Muscovy." *History Today* (September 1986): 17–22.

Boss, Valentin. *Newton and Russia*. Cambridge, Mass., 1972.

Braudel, Fernand. *Capitalism and Material Life, 1400–1800* (orig. French ed., 1967). New York, 1973; revised ed., *The Structures of Everday Life: The Limits of the Possible*. New York, 1981.

———. *The Mediterranean and the Mediterranean World in the Age of Philip II* (orig. French ed., 1949). 2 vols. New York, 1972–73.

Bromley, J. S. *The Rise of Great Britain and Russia, 1688–1715/25*. Cambridge, 1971.

Burckhard, Jacob. *The Civilization of the Renaissance in Italy*. New York, 1971.

Burke, Peter. *Popular Culture in Early Modern Europe*. London, 1978.

Butler's Lives of the Saints. 4 vols., ed. Herbert Thurston, S.J., and Donald Attwater. New York, 1956.

Chadwick, Owen. *The Popes and European Revolution*. Oxford, 1981.

Cipolla, Carlo M. *Clocks and Culture, 1300–1700*. New York, 1978.

———. *Fighting the Plague in Seventeenth-Century Italy*. Madison, Wis., 1981.

Cracraft, James. *The Church Reform of Peter the Great*. Stanford, Calif., 1971.

Crummey, Robert O. *Aristocrats and Servitors: The Boyar Elite in Russia, 1613–1689*. Princeton, N.J., 1983.

Danilevskii, V. V. *History of Hydroengineering in Russia before the Nineteenth Century*. Jerusalem, 1968.

Davies, J. G., ed. *A Dictionary of Liturgy and Worship*. New York, 1972.

Davis, Natalie Zemon. *Society and Culture in Early Modern France: Eight Essays*. Stanford, Calif., 1975.

Drobinina, D. P. "Iz istorii ogogashcheniia russkoi leksiki (Terminy arkhitektury, skul'ptury, zhivopisi." In *Uchenie zapiski Arkhangel'skogo pedagogicheskogo instituta*. Vol. 13, 1963. (See Val'kova, D. P.)

———. "K voprosu o proiskhozhdenii sovremennoi muzykal'noi i teatral'noi terminologii." In *Uchenie zapiski Leningradskogo pedagogicheskogo instituta im. A. I. Gertsena*, Vol. 257, 1965.

Erlanger, Philippe. *The Age of Courts and Kings: Manners and Morals, 1558–1715*. New York, 1967.

Evelyn, John. *The Diary of John Evelyn*. 6 vols. Ed. E. S. De Beer. Oxford, 1955.

Faesen, Hubert, and Vladimir Ivanov. *Early Russian Architecture*. New York, 1975.

Fedotov, George P. *The Russian Religious Mind*. 2 vols. Belmont, Mass., 1975.

Florovsky, Georges. *Ways of Russian Theology*. Belmont, Mass., 1979.

Frantz, R. W. *The English Traveller and the Movement of Ideas, 1660–1732*. London, 1934.

Fuhrmann, Joseph T. *The Origins of Capitalism in Russia*. Chicago, 1972.

Gardner, Johann von. *Russian Church Singing*, vol. 1. *Orthodox Worship and Hymnography*. Crestwood, N.Y., 1980.

Gerhard, Dietrich. *Old Europe: A Study in Continuity, 1000–1800*. New York, 1981.

Gimpel, Jean. *The Medieval Machine*. New York, 1976.

Goldstein, Thomas. *Dawn of Modern Science*. Boston, 1980.

Hazard, Paul. *Books, Children and Men*. 3d ed. Boston, 1965.

———. *The European Mind, 1680–1715* (orig. French ed., 1935). New York, 1963.

Hellie, Richard. *Enserfment and Military Change in Muscovy*. Chicago, 1971.

———. *Slavery in Russia, 1450–1725*. Chicago, 1986.

Herberstein, Sigmund von. *Rerum Moscoviticarum Comentarii*. Vienna, 1549.

Honour, Hugh. *The Companion Guide to Venice*. London, 1981.

Hughes, Lindsey A. J. "The 17th-Century 'Renaissance' in Russia." *History Today* (February 1980): 41–45.

———. "Western European Graphic Material as a Source for Moscow Baroque Architecture." *The Slavonic and East European Review* 55, no. 4 (October 1977): 433–43.

Jones, Charles Williams. *Saint Nicholas of Myra, Bari, and Manhattan: Biography of a Legend*. Chicago, 1978.

Kaminski, Andrzej. "The *Szlachta* of the Polish-Lithuanian Commonwealth and Their Government." In *The Nobility in Russia and Eastern Europe*, ed. Ivo Banac and Paul Bushkovitch. New Haven, 1983.

Korb, Johan-Georg. *Diary of an Austrian Secretary of Legation* (orig. ed. 1863). Reprint, New York, 1968.

Krautheimer, Richard. *The Rome of Alexander VII, 1655–1667*. Princeton, N.J., 1985.

———. *Rome: Profile of a City, 312–1308*. Princeton, N.J., 1980.

Kucharek, Casimir, *The Byzantine-Slav Liturgy of St. John Chrysostom: Its Origin and Evolution*. Allendale, N.J., 1971.

Landes, David S. *Revolution in Time: Clocks and the Making of the Modern World*. Cambridge, Mass., 1983.

Lane, Frederic Chapin. *Venice: A Maritime Republic*. Baltimore, 1973.

———. *Venetian Ships and Shipbuilders of the Renaissance*. Baltimore, 1934.

Longworth, Philip. *Alexis: Tsar of All the Russias*. New York, 1984.

Lorenzetti, Giulio. *Venice and Its Lagoon*. Trieste, 1980.

Lupinin, Nickolas. *Religious Revolt in the XVIIth Century: The Schism of the Russian Church.* Princeton, N.J., 1984.

Macartney, C. A., ed. *The Habsburg and Hohenzollern Dynasties in the Seventeenth and Eighteenth Centuries.* New York, 1970.

Macey, Samuel L. *Clocks and the Cosmos: Time in Western Life and Thought.* Hamden, Conn., 1980.

Manoussacas, M. "Aperçu d'une histoire de la colonie greque orthodoxe de Venise." In *Anatupoapeta Theaurismata,* Vol. 19. Venice, 1982.

Manuel, Frank E. *Isaac Newton—Historian.* Cambridge, Mass., 1963.

Manzoni, Alessandro. *I Promessi Sposi.* Vol. 21 of The Harvard Classics. New York, 1909.

Masson, Georgina. *Companion Guide to Rome.* Englewood Cliffs, N.J., 1983.

Mead, William Edward. *The Grand Tour in the Eighteenth Century.* Boston, 1914.

Meehan-Waters, Brenda. *Autocracy and Aristocracy: The Russian Service Elite of 1730.* New Brunswick, N.J., 1982.

Molmenti, Pompeo. *Venice: Its Individual Growth from the Earliest Beginnings to the Fall of the Republic.* Trans. Horatio F. Brown. Part III, *The Decadence.* Vols. 1 and 2. Chicago, 1908.

Montesquieu, Charles de Secondat. *Persian Letters.* Trans. George Healy. New York, 1964.

Moryson, Fynes. *An Itinerary Containing His Ten Yeers Travell.* Glasgow, 1907.

Norwich, John Julius. *A History of Venice.* New York, 1982.

Okenfuss, Max J. "The Cultural Transformation of Peter Tolstoi." In *Russia and the West,* ed. A. G. Cross. Newtonville, 1983.

———. "The Jesuit Origins of Petrine Education." In *The Eighteenth Century in Russia,* ed. John Garrard. Oxford, 1973.

———. "On Crime and Punishment: The Moral Awakening of Russia in the Age of Peter the Great." *History Today* (September 1986): 23–27.

———. "Peter Tolstoi in Rome: The Hydraulics of Mystery and Delight," *Study Group on Eighteenth-Century Russia Newsletter,* no. 12 (1984): 35–41.

———. "Russian Students in Europe in the Age of Peter the Great." In *The Eighteenth Century in Russia,* ed. John Garrard. Oxford, 1973.

———. "Technical Training in Russia under Peter the Great." *History of Education Quarterly* 13, no. 4 (Winter 1973): 325–45.

Olearius. *The Travels of Olearius in 17th-Century Russia.* Trans. Samuel H. Baron. Stanford, Calif., 1967.

Onasch, Konrad. *Icons.* New York, 1963.

Otten, Fred. *Der Reisebericht eines anonymen Russen über seine Reise nach Westeuropa im Zeitraum 1697/1699.* Berlin/Wiesbaden, 1985.

Pavlenko, N. I. *Ptentsy gnezda Petrova.* Moscow, 1984.

Pavlov-Sil'vanskii, N. P. "Graf Petr Andreevich Tolstoi (Prashchur grafa L'va Tolstogo)." *Sochineniia,* vol. II. St. Petersburg, 1910.

Pocknee, Cyril E. *Liturgical Vesture: Its Origins and Development.* London, 1960.

Raeff, Marc. *Origins of the Russian Intelligentsia: The Eighteenth-Century Nobility.* New York, 1966.

Saul, Norman E. *Russia and the Mediterranean, 1797–1807.* Chicago, 1970.

Sells, A. Lytton. *The Paradise of Travellers: The Italian Influence on Englishmen in the 17th Century.* London, 1964.

Sinel, Allen. *The Classroom and the Chancellery: State Educational Reform in Russia under Count Dmitry Tolstoi*. Cambridge, Mass., 1971.
Smith, Preserved. *A History of Modern Culture: I, Origins of Modern Culture 1543–1687; II, The Enlightenment, 1687–1776*. New York, 1934 (rev. ed., Crane Brinton, ed., New York, 1962).
Smolitsch, Igor. *Russisches Mönchtum*. Wurzburg, 1953.
Solovey, ,Michael. *The Byzantine Divine Liturgy: History and Commentary*. Washington, D.C., 1970.
Szeftel, "The Title of the Muscovite Monarch." *Canadian-American Slavic Studies* 13, nos. 1–2 (1979): 59–81.
Tolstoi, P. "Putevoi Dnevnik P. A. Tolstago." *Russkii arkhiv*, 1888, Vol. 26. Pts. I and II.
Tolstoy, Nicholai. *The Tolstoys: Twenty-four generations of Russian History, 1353–1983*. New York, 1983.
Val'kova, D. P. *Leksika "Puteshestviia" P. A. Tolstogo (K istorii formirovaniia slovarnogo sostava russkogo natsional'nogo iazyka)*. Leningrad, 1965. (See Drobinina.)
Vico..*The Autobiography of Giambattista Vico*. Trans. Max Harold Fisch and Thomas Goddard Bergin. Ithaca, N.Y., 1944.
Ware, Timothy. *The Orthodox Church*. Baltimore, 1969.
White, Lynn, Jr. *Medieval Technology and Social Change*. Oxford, 1962.
Wittram, Reinhard. *Peter I: Czar und Kaiser*. 2 vols. Göttingen, 1964.
Wolf, John B. *The Emergence of the Great Powers, 1685–1715*. New York, 1962.

Index

www.ingramcontent.com/pod-product-compliance
Lightning Source LLC
Chambersburg PA
CBHW060816310726
48980CB00002B/307

9780875801308